FIFTH EDITION

SHORT ESSAYS

Gerald Levin

FIFTH EDITION

SHORT ESSAYS

Gerald Levin

Professor Emeritus of English
University of Akron

HARCOURT BRACE JOVANOVICH, PUBLISHERS

San Diego   New York   Chicago   Atlanta   Washington, D.C.
London   Sydney   Tokyo   Toronto

ISBN 0-15-580920-2
Library of Congress Catalog Card Number 88-81969
Printed in the United States of America

Preface

The Fifth Edition follows earlier editions in presenting concrete, contemporary essays of interest to students. The majority of essays in this edition are three to five pages long—about the length assigned in many composition courses. The book also contains longer essays by Wendell Berry, Arthur L. Campa, Robert Coles, Joan Didion, John Gregory Dunne, Noel Perrin, L. E. Sissman, and Lewis Yablonsky. Whereas the range of topics is wide, changing values in American life, problems of growing up, and stereotypes of people continue to be important themes. Among the 28 essays new to this edition are ones dealing with small town and city life, homelessness, the "right to die," and boxing as a dangerous sport. Most of the new essays complement those retained from the previous edition.

As in the previous editions, Part One discusses strategies for organizing and developing the essay. These strategies now include example, process, comparison and contrast, cause and effect, definition, and classification and division—methods usually associated with exposition and presented as methods of exposition in previous editions. Part One shows how these methods may be used to organize and develop essays of all kinds. Part Two discusses strategies for expressive writing, with a focus on narrative, descriptive, and reflective essays. Part Three discusses strategies for exposition—returning to example, process, and other methods discussed in Part One to show how they are combined in various essays—most of them expository.

Sentence style and diction were discussed separately in the previous edition. Part Four of this edition discusses effective sentences and diction together, focusing on differences between Formal, Informal, and General English. Six topics are discussed: emphasis, parallelism, sentence variety, concreteness, figurative language, tone, and usage. In another change from the previous edition, the book concludes with the discussion of argument and persuasion in Part Five.

Each section of the Fifth Edition again opens with a discussion of the general topic and an analysis of an essay in light of the specific topics that follow. Part Five contains separate introductory analyses of an argumentative essay and a persuasive essay. Throughout the book, each essay is followed by a comment on the rhetorical principles introduced at the beginning of the section. The Questions for Study and Discussion begin with the content and rhetoric of each essay, developing points in the comment and concluding with questions about the ideas of the essay. The Vocabulary Study supplements these questions by teaching the uses of the dictionary and by emphasizing the importance of context in reading and writing.

This textbook includes a thematic table of contents. Since each essay illustrates rhetorical topics other than the one specifically illustrated in the book, instructors may want to switch essay and topic to fit the needs of their classes. Many of the Suggestions for Teaching and Suggestions for Writing in the Instructor's Manual provide such alternatives.

I wish again to thank Andrea A. Lunsford, The Ohio State University, and Ann Raimes, Hunter College of the City University of New York, for their advice on the first edition. Eben W. Ludlow helped initially to plan the book and gave me his encouragement and support. I also owe thanks to William Francis, Bruce Holland, Robert Holland, and Alice MacDonald of the University of Akron, and to the many teachers who have made suggestions for this and earlier editions. I owe special thanks to my acquisitions editor, Marlane Agriesti Miriello, for her wise judgment and her contributions to this edition. Finally, I thank Eleanor Garner, the permissions editor, for arranging for use of the essays; Jane Carey, for her imaginative design of the book; and Melissa Rose, Dee Salisbury Welborn, and Robert Shelburne, who copyedited the manuscript. My debt to my wife, Lillian Levin, is as always a great one.

GERALD LEVIN

Contents

Preface   v
Thematic Table of Contents   xvii
Introduction   xxiii

PART 1
Strategies for Organizing and Developing the Essay

Introduction   3
Edward Hoagland / STUTTERING TIME   4
*A person who stutters makes a discovery about personal
and business life.*

Unity and Thesis   7
Susan Walton / THE CAUTIOUS AND   9
    OBEDIENT LIFE
*The author considers the reasons that she lives a "cau-
tious, obedient life."*

Topic Sentence   14
Francine Prose / GOSSIP   16
*Though gossip is often identified with spreading false ru-
mors or slander, it performs an important job for society.*

Order of Ideas   21
Harold Krents / DARKNESS AT NOON   23
*The world has not yet learned that blind people are not
necessarily deaf and dumb.*

Coherence   28

L. E. Sissman / THE OLD FARMER'S ALMANAC,   29
  1872
An issue of the 1872 Old Farmer's Almanac reveals surprising facts about the past and the present.

Narration   36

Edward Rivera / THE SOCIOLOGY FINAL   37
"Over forty students were bent over their examination booklets, most of them looking confused by the questions."

Description   42

Maya Angelou / PICKING COTTON   43
The early morning world of Southern black cotton pickers seems touched by the supernatural, but the late afternoon shows the real harshness of their life.

Example   48

Tom Wicker / "COURT DAY" IN MOORE   49
  COUNTY, NORTH CAROLINA
A journalist learns one difference between good and bad reporting.

Process   54

Maxine Kumin / BUILDING FENCE   55
Building a fence on rugged farm land is not a perfect science.

Comparison and Contrast   60

Noel Perrin / CLASS STRUGGLE IN THE WOODS   61
"Why cross-country skiing and snowmobiling reflect class lines so perfectly is not easy to figure out."

Cause and Effect   70

Appletree Rodden / WHY SMALLER   71
  REFRIGERATORS CAN PRESERVE THE
  HUMAN RACE
Smaller European refrigerators reveal different cultural values from American ones.

Definition   77

August Heckscher / DOING CHORES   78
Chores can be one of the minor pleasures of life if performed in a certain way.

Classification and Division 82

Michele Huzicka / ON WAITING IN LINE 83
(STUDENT ESSAY)

Waiting in line at the dormitory dining room is a different experience morning, noon, and evening.

PART 2
Strategies for Expressive Writing

Introduction 89

Gloria Emerson / TAKE THE PLUNGE 90

"Jumping from a plane, which required no talent or endurance, seemed perfect. I wanted to feel the big, puzzling lump on my back that they promised was a parachute. . . "

Autobiography 95

Mary E. Mebane / THE RHYTHM OF LIFE 96

The author describes the daily routine of her North Carolina girlhood.

William Flynn / THE LOVING WALLS OF 103
GRANDMA'S CASTLE

Visiting the home of grandparents was never an ordinary experience.

Perri Klass / THE FIRST TIME 106

A medical student makes an important discovery in observing a patient undergo a painful examination.

Leonard Kriegel / TAKING IT 112

A man stricken with polio in childhood discovers that "how one faced adversity was, like most of American life, in part a question of gender."

Reflection 117

Henry Beetle Hough / ON SMALL THINGS 117

The world is so much concerned with great things that it forgets that small things are the sum of life.

Phyllis Theroux / BICYCLING TOWARD 124
WISDOM

The author wonders whether problems can all be solved through thinking.

Andrew A. Rooney / ELEVATORS   129
"No one is ever completely comfortable in an elevator."
John Gregory Dunne / QUINTANA   133
The father of an adopted child learns through his special
relationship that children are not possessions.

PART 3
Strategies for Exposition

Introduction   **145**
Lewis Thomas / TO ERR IS HUMAN   147
Making mistakes, rather than getting things right all the
time, is the source of our humanity and our freedom.
Louis Inturrisi / ON NOT GETTING THERE   152
    FROM HERE
How Italians give directions tells us much about Italian
life and character.
Sue Hubbell / FELLING TREES   157
"My female Ozark friends envy me having my firewood
supply under my own control, and they are interested
when I tell them that they have had the hardest part of
the job anyway, carrying the wood to the trucks."
Jack Trueblood / FOR A LOVE OF FISHING   162
In learning how to fish, children learn important lessons
about living.
L. Rust Hills / HOW TO EAT AN ICE-CREAM   168
    CONE
The joys of eating an ice cream cone depend on careful
planning and skillful execution.
Richard Selzer / MY BROTHER SHAMAN   178
Though the surgeon and the shaman are different in their
techniques and outlook, they have many qualities in
common.
Don Richard Cox / BARBIE AND HER   184
    PLAYMATES
The Barbie doll has "reshaped our culture's way of look-
ing at dolls and the way children now define their rela-
tionship to these dolls. . . ."

Arthur L. Campa / ANGLO VS. CHICANO: 192
WHY?
*Present day conflicts between Hispanic-Americans and
Anglo-Americans are rooted in profound cultural differ-
ences.*

Sydney J. Harris / CLIMBING THE MOUNTAIN 200
OF SUCCESS
*"Climbing the ladder" is a misleading metaphor for
achieving success.*

John Garvey / THINKING IN PACKAGES 203
*"We have an investment in our ideas which has nothing
to do with the particular worth of our ideas. Our ideas
are like clan totems or old school ties."*

Michael Nelson / THE DESK 209
*The hostility and misunderstanding that exist between
citizens and government bureaucrats arise from causes
neither can control.*

K. C. Cole / WOMEN AND PHYSICS 214
*The author refers to her personal experience in discussing
whether women are less gifted than men in sicence and
mathematics.*

Lewis Yablonsky / THE VIOLENT GANG 220
Delinquent gangs reflect the values of their societies.

Robert Coles / SETTLING IN 233
*A young man discovers that life in a northern city is dif-
ferent from life in rural Kentucky.*

William Safire / DEMAGOGUE 247
The word demagogue *has an interesting history in American politics.*

Robert Ramirez / THE WOOLEN SARAPE 251
*The Chicano district of any Southwestern town has its
own personality and customs.*

Susan Allen Toth / CINEMATYPES 257
*The author makes discoveries about her male friends
through how they behave at the movies.*

Robert J. Samuelson / COMPUTER 262
COMMUNITIES
*"Americans exalt individuality, but our economic success
rests on a mass market that stresses commonality."*

Wendell Berry / THE RISE   266
*A canoe ride on a dangerous river is an illuminating but
also humbling experience.*

PART 4
Effective Sentences and Diction

Introduction   283

Joan Didion / BUREAUCRATS   287
*The Operations Center of the Los Angeles freeway sys-
tem proves to be a strange world.*

Emphasis   295

Richard P. Feynman / THE AMATEUR SCIENTIST   297
*A budding scientist learns to look at the world through
his own eyes rather than through books.*

William Zinsser / JURY DUTY   306
*Jury duty turns out to be the experience of "organized
solitude."*

Michael J. Arlen / "RING AROUND THE   312
    COLLAR!"
*The Cinderella princess of the detergent commercial dis-
covers her true place in life.*

Parallelism   317

Rachel Carson / SUMMER'S END   318
*Life on the Atlantic shore changes as summer comes to
an end.*

Sentence Variety   326

Russell Baker / THE BEER CULTURE   327
*The men and women of Beer World are a special breed
of people.*

Concreteness   332

William G. Wing / CHRISTMAS COMES FIRST   333
    ON THE BANKS
*Christmas comes in an unusual way to fishermen on
trawlers in the North Atlantic.*

Carol Bly / GREAT SNOWS   336
*Being out in a Minnesota blizzard is not fun, but great
snows have their special pleasures.*

Figurative Language   343

David R. Scott / WHAT IS IT LIKE TO WALK ON   344
THE MOON?
*An astronaut describes the experience of walking on the
moon.*

Annie Dillard / UNTYING THE KNOT   353
*"Yesterday I set out to catch the new season, and instead
I found an old snakeskin."*

Tone   359

William Aiken / HANGING OUT AND LOOKING   360
GOOD
*Turning fifteen is a special experience for a boy and for
his father.*

Hilary DeVries / REAL YUPPIES   364
The baby-boomers have come into their own, but becoming a yuppie proves a difficult job.

Frank Deford / BEAUTY AND EVERLASTING   368
FAITH—LOCAL LEVEL
*A sports writer makes discoveries about contestants and
judges at a local Miss America beauty contest.*

Usage   376

Art Buchwald / JOB HUNTING   377
*An out-of-work physicist shows how he found another
job.*

James Thurber / THE PRINCESS AND THE   381
TIN BOX
A princess considers which of three suitors to marry.

Sydney J. Harris / THE MAN IN THE MIDDLE   384
"I am the man in the middle; for where I stand determines where the middle is."

PART 5
Strategies for Arguing and Persuading

Introduction   389
Inductive Argument   390

Edward H. Peeples, Jr. / . . . MEANWHILE,   393
HUMANS EAT PET FOOD

A medical doctor asks whether we must wait for unchallengeable evidence of hunger in America before doing something about it.

James M. Dubik / AN OFFICER AND A   396
   FEMINIST
An infantry officer challenges common stereotypes of women.

Richard Moran / MORE CRIME AND LESS   401
   PUNISHMENT
A criminologist explains why we must start thinking about crime and punishment in a new way.

Page Smith / HUMAN TIME AND THE COLLEGE   405
   STUDENT
A university teacher criticizes the examination and grading system in American colleges and universities.

Ellen Goodman / WAVING GOOD-BYE TO THE   415
   COUNTRY
The migration from small towns to cities has changed how people think of themselves and their communities.

Kathy Seelinger / THE HAMLET HANDICAP   419
"Villagers may proudly praise the champion athlete, the all-state vocalist and the scholarship winner and advise them to sally forth and demonstrate their accomplishments for all who will attend. But in almost the same breath, they sing a different tune. . . ."

Deductive Argument   **424**

Introduction   **424**

Norman Cousins / CONFESSIONS OF A   427
   MISEDUCATED MAN
An education that deals only with the differences between cultures fails to meet human needs as the world grows smaller.

Timothy S. Healy / IN DEFENSE OF DISORDER   432
A college president argues that universities are disorderly because they are places of growth.

Margaret Mead and Rhoda Metraux /   437
   NEIGHBORS VS. NEIGHBORLINESS
The authors describe changing attitudes in America toward neighbors and neighborliness.

Ellen Goodman / WHOSE LIFE IS IT ANYWAY? 442
"Deep down, I'm afraid it is too easy for society to 'understand' the unhappiness of a quadriplegic instead of alleviating it. It's too easy for us to begin to regard suicides of the sick or the aged as 'thoughtful' solutions."

George F. Will / BEARBAITING AND BOXING 446
"Good government and the good life depend on good values and passions, and some entertainments are inimical to these."

Strategies of Persuasion 451

Introduction 451

George F. Will / ON HER OWN IN THE CITY 452
The human tragedy is sometimes beyond the control of those responsible for helping the needy.

The New Yorker / THE ADJECTIVE "UGLY" 455
Cities express their attitude toward homeless people in unusual ways.

E. B. White / THE DECLINE OF SPORT 459
"In the third decade of the supersonic age, sport gripped the nation in an ever-tightening grip."

Charles Osgood / "REAL" MEN AND WOMEN 465
In defining the "real" man and the "real" woman, we must be careful not to rob people of their humanity.

Harvey and Nancy Kincaid / A LETTER ON STRIP MINING 468
A West Virginian husband and wife describe the effect of strip mining on their lives.

Roger Rosenblatt / THE MAN IN THE WATER 473
In the crash of an airplane into the Potomac, a passenger performs a heroic act.

Glossary 478

Index 491

Thematic Table of Contents

Growing Up

William Aiken / HANGING OUT AND LOOKING GOOD   360

Robert Coles / SETTLING IN   233

John Gregory Dunne / QUINTANA   133

Richard P. Feynman / THE AMATEUR SCIENTIST   297

L. Rust Hills / HOW TO EAT AN ICE-CREAM CONE   168

Leonard Kriegel / TAKING IT   112

Education

K. C. Coles / WOMEN AND PHYSICS   214

Norman Cousins / CONFESSIONS OF A MISEDUCATED MAN   427

Richard P. Feynman / THE AMATEUR SCIENTIST   297

John Garvey / THINKING IN PACKAGES   203

Timothy S. Healy / IN DEFENSE OF DISORDER   432

Edward Rivera / THE SOCIOLOGY FINAL   37

Discovering People

Arthur L. Campa / ANGLO VS. CHICANO: WHY?   192

William Flynn / THE LOVING WALLS OF GRANDMA'S CASTLE   103

Michele Huzicka / ON WAITING IN LINE   83

Charles Osgood / "REAL" MEN AND WOMEN   465

James Thurber / THE PRINCESS AND THE TIN BOX   381

Susan Allen Toth / CINEMATYPES   257

Tom Wicker / "COURT DAY" IN MOORE COUNTY, NORTH CAROLINA   49

Human Values

Russell Baker / THE BEER CULTURE   327

Henry Beetle Hough / ON SMALL THINGS   117

Roger Rosenblatt / THE MAN IN THE WATER   473

Phyllis Theroux / BICYCLING TOWARD WISDOM   124

Susan Walton / THE CAUTIOUS AND OBEDIENT LIFE   9

Neighborhoods and Neighborliness

Robert Coles / SETTLING IN   233

Ellen Goodman / WAVING GOOD-BYE TO THE COUNTRY   415

Margaret Mead and Rhoda Metraux / NEIGHBORS VS. NEIGHBORLINESS   437

Francine Prose / GOSSIP   16

Robert Ramirez / THE WOOLEN SARAPE   251

Kathy Seelinger / THE HAMLET HANDICAP   419

Urban Life

Robert Coles / SETTLING IN   233

Joan Didion / BUREAUCRATS   287

Ellen Goodman / WAVING GOOD-BYE TO THE COUNTRY   415

Richard Moran / MORE CRIME AND LESS PUNISHMENT   401

Michael Nelson / THE DESK   209
William Zinsser / JURY DUTY   306

Stereotypes

Maya Angelou / PICKING COTTON   43
Michael J. Arlen / "RING AROUND THE COLLAR!"   312
K. C. Cole / WOMEN AND PHYSICS   214
Don Richard Cox / BARBIE AND HER PLAYMATES   184
Frank Deford / BEAUTY AND EVERLASTING   368
  FAITH—LOCAL LEVEL
Hilary DeVries / REAL YUPPIES   364
James M. Dubik / AN OFFICER AND A FEMINIST   396
Harold Krents / DARKNESS AT NOON   23

Discovering Nature

Wendell Berry / THE RISE   266
Carol Bly / GREAT SNOWS   336
Rachel Carson / SUMMER'S END   318
Annie Dillard / UNTYING THE KNOT   353
David R. Scott / WHAT IS IT LIKE TO WALK ON   344
  THE MOON?
William G. Wing / CHRISTMAS COMES FIRST ON   333
  THE BANKS

Work

Maya Angelou / PICKING COTTON   43
August Heckscher / DOING CHORES   78
Sue Hubbell / FELLING TREES   157
Perri Klass / THE FIRST TIME   106
Maxine Kumin / BUILDING FENCE   55
Mary E. Mebane / THE RHYTHM OF LIFE   96
Richard Selzer / MY BROTHER SHAMAN   178

L. E. Sissman / THE OLD FARMER'S ALMANAC,   29
1872

Sports

Gloria Emerson / TAKE THE PLUNGE . . .   90
Noel Perrin / CLASS STRUGGLE IN THE WOODS   61
Jack Trueblood / FOR A LOVE OF FISHING   162
E. B. White / THE DECLINE OF SPORT   459
George F. Will / BEARBAITING AND BOXING   446

Language and Thought

Art Buchwald / JOB HUNTING   377
John Garvey / THINKING IN PACKAGES   203
Sydney J. Harris / CLIMBING THE MOUNTAIN OF   200
SUCCESS
Sydney J. Harris / THE MAN IN THE MIDDLE   384
Louis Inturrisi / ON NOT GETTING THERE FROM   152
HERE
Francine Prose / GOSSIP   16
William Safire / DEMAGOGUE   247
Phyllis Theroux / BICYCLING TOWARD WISDOM   124
Lewis Thomas / TO ERR IS HUMAN   147

Contemporary Social Problems

Richard Moran / MORE CRIME AND LESS   401
PUNISHMENT
Michael Nelson / THE DESK   209
The New Yorker / THE ADJECTIVE "UGLY"   455
Edward H. Peeples, Jr. / . . . MEANWHILE,   393
HUMANS EAT PET FOOD
George F. Will / ON HER OWN IN THE CITY   452
Lewis Yablonsky / THE VIOLENT GANG   220

Technology and People

Joan Didion / BUREAUCRATS   287

Harvey and Nancy Kincaid / A LETTER ON STRIP   468
MINING

Appletree Rodden / WHY SMALLER   71
REFRIGERATORS CAN PRESERVE THE
HUMAN RACE

Andrew A. Rooney / ELEVATORS   129

Robert J. Samuelson / COMPUTER COMMUNITIES   262

Introduction

This book is concerned with essays of personal expression, information or exposition, and persuasion. It introduces various kinds of writing and shows how they each serve particular purposes. The purposes for which we write are so numerous that no one classification can account for all of them, but one recent classification distinguishes four purposes: personal expression, reference or giving information, creating literary effect, and persuasion. Thus, whereas an essay may express one's personal feelings or beliefs, it may also give information about a particular subject, as in a textbook, or generate laughter or pathos as in a play or novel, or seek to change opinion on an issue as in a political speech. These purposes are not exclusive of one another. A piece of writing may have several purposes. For example, a satirical novel may amuse and inform us about a contemporary issue while it seeks to persuade the audience to change their minds about the issue.

Part One of this book presents various strategies for organizing and developing essays. One strategy is to develop a central impression or central idea or thesis for the essay as a whole. The individual paragraphs of the essay would then contain a topic sentence or statement of the subject or guiding idea. In turn, the paragraphs would have some kind of organization or order of ideas, held together by transitional words and phrases. Other strategies or means of development include narration and description. In writing home about your first week at college, you might use narration to give a chronological account of the events of the week and description to give details about your room, new friends, or classes. Still other means of developing the essay include example, process, comparison and contrast, cause and effect, definition, and classification and division. In your letter you might use the registration of classes as an example of why college life can be frustrating, give details of the registration process, compare and contrast a college class with a high school class, give reasons for differences you find, define a new interest or activity you have taken up, or classify the various friends or teachers encountered during the week.

Part Two of the book describes two important kinds of expressive writing—autobiography and reflection. Part Three shows how various methods of development such as definition and comparison and contrast work together to give information. Part Four describes ways of making sentences and diction serve the various purposes of the essay. Part Five describes strategies for developing arguments and making them persuasive. Persuasive essays use narration, description, and other means of development such as definition, classification, and comparison and contrast, but they chiefly use argument. Argument is concerned with establishing the truth of statements; persuasion is concerned with getting readers to accept these statements and perhaps take action that the statements support.

The questions and suggestions for writing that follow each selection will give you practice in achieving various objectives through various means or strategies. Although an understanding of purposes and strategies alone will not make you a better writer, knowledge of how other writers develop their experiences and ideas will help you in drafting and revising your own essays. You will become a better writer only through constant writing and revision. The essays presented here are examples of proven ways of organizing and developing essays. They show how a wide range of writers who differ in background and interest, achieve their various purposes.

PART 1

Strategies for Developing and Organizing the Essay

The word *essay* has various meanings. To many writers the word describes a short, carefully organized composition that develops a single idea or impression. To other writers the word describes a beginning or trial attempt, in which the central idea or impression is explored rather than developed or analyzed completely. Thus, Samuel Johnson, the great eighteenth-century essayist and lexicographer, referred to the essay as "an irregular undigested piece."

Johnson's definition fits many essays that have the informality of a rough draft—those that contain loosely organized ideas and impressions. Informal letters sometimes are essays in this sense of the word. Like journal entries, trial essays help writers discover what they want to say. Much of your writing in your composition course may be trial essays of this kind.

Of course, upon revision the trial essay may become a carefully organized composition that focuses upon a single idea or impression. Although many essays in newspapers and magazines merely explore a topic, others contain a central idea or thesis and a careful organization or order of supporting ideas and details. A newspaper editorial that argues for energy conservation is one kind of essay; an extended magazine article describing methods of energy conservation is another; a newspaper column that describes personal experiences with energy-saving devices is yet another. The purpose of each essay is different and so may be the organization. The editorial is persuasive in intent, the magazine article informative. Both, however, organize the argument or exposition in ways that will best persuade or inform the readers of the essay. The personal column on energy-saving devices that expresses amusement or frustration about electrical devices may organize the description or narration to generate laughter or some other effect from the reader.

Edward Hoagland's essay on stuttering is neither persuasive nor informative, though Hoagland tells us something about changes in telephoning and banking that create discomfort in a person who stutters. Hoagland's purpose is to express his interest in the discomfort of his friend and the increasing problems these changes create in others without handicaps. He concludes the essay with the statement that he has "no solutions to offer."

Hoagland builds to the central idea or *thesis* of his short essay—stated at the end of paragraph 3:

> And inevitably, as we all become known more and more by account numbers, doing business will become still more impersonal, and any voice that doesn't speak as plainly as digits entering a computer will cause problems.

3

He restates his thesis in the concluding paragraph, in noting that an increasing number of people will be discomforted by the changes described in the essay. The word *thesis* is perhaps an inexact word to describe the central idea of this kind of essay because Hoagland is not arguing a proposition in a formal way. *Observation* is probably the better word. Nevertheless, the observation, like the central idea or thesis of a persuasive essay, organizes the details and gives direction. Hoagland might have presented only a series of details or observations from which readers could make inferences or draw conclusions. Had he done so, we might refer to this sense or impression as an *implied thesis*.

When writing your own essays, remember that few readers see the world exactly as you do. They may, indeed, see different things and have different ideas and feelings about them. Whether your purpose is chiefly to express your feelings or beliefs, to give information about the world, or to persuade readers to accept a belief of yours, you must help them see the world as you do. You must also help them follow the flow of your observations and thoughts. The sections that follow discuss ways of doing so.

Edward Hoagland

STUTTERING TIME

Edward Hoagland has taught at various universities, including Rutgers and Columbia, and has published numerous essays in *The New Yorker, The New York Times,* and other periodicals. His books include *The Courage of Turtles,* (1970), *Red Wolves and Black Bears* (1976), and *The Tugman's Passage* (1982). Hoagland writes on a wide range of subjects—from circuses to the changing seasons, animal life, and changes in American life. "Stuttering Time" discusses changes in our telephone system.

We have a friend who stutters; and while he notices no increase in rudeness or sarcasm from people in person, he does hear more impatience from telephone operators, secretaries, businessmen, switchboard personnel, and other strangers whom he must deal with over the phone. As he stands at a phone booth or holds on to the devilish device at home, the time allotted to him to spit out the words seems to have markedly shrunk; perhaps it has been halved in the past half-dozen years. This alarms him because at the same time the importance of the telephone in daily transactions has zoomed. Indeed, many people use answering machines to consolidate their calls, and soon voiceprinting may become a commonplace method of identification. Imagine, he suggests, stuttering into a voiceprinting machine.

Bell System operators, who used to be the most patient people he encountered, now often seem entirely unfamiliar with his handicap. They either hang up or switch him to their supervisors as a "problem call" after listening for only a few seconds, interrupting a couple of times to demand that he "speak clearly, please." They seem automated themselves, as if rigged to a stop clock that regulates how long they will listen to anything out of the ordinary, though twenty years ago, he says, they practiced their trade with a fine humanity.

But it is not just individuals in individual occupations who have changed. The division between personal life and business life has deepened, and the brusqueness of business gets worse all the time. At the bank, one can no longer choose one's teller but must stand in a single line. (The tellers seem to work more slowly, having less responsibility individually for the length of the line.) And inevitably, as we all become known more and more by account numbers, doing business will become still more impersonal, and any voice that doesn't speak as plainly as digits entering a computer will cause problems.

We have no solutions to offer. We have brought up the subject only because our friend sometimes feels like the canary that miners used to carry into a mine. He believes his increasing discomfort foretells a worsening shortness of breath in other people—even those who started out with no handicaps at all.

Questions for Study and Discussion

1. What is meant by the title of the essay "stuttering time"? How is the title related to the thesis of the essay?

2. How does Hoagland show that he is moving from a specific example—the experience of his friend who stutters—to general experiences and then to ideas?
3. Would Hoagland's thesis be clear without examples? Or could Hoagland have discussed the idea abstractly rather than concretely?
4. What example can you give of the problem discussed by Hoagland? Can you offer a solution to the problem?

Vocabulary Study

Explain the difference between the words in each pair. Then explain why Hoagland chose the first word and not the second.

a. *zoomed* (paragraph 1), *risen*
b. *consolidate* (paragraph 1), *combine*
c. *automated* (paragraph 2), *robotized*
d. *brusqueness* (paragraph 3), *rudeness*

Suggestions for Writing

1. Present your own example of the problem discussed by Hoagland or another similar problem created by modern invention. Discuss a solution to the problem if you have one to offer.
2. Hoagland suggests that occupations change individuals. Explain what he means and give examples from your own personal work experience. Draw a conclusion from your discussion.

Unity and Thesis

In a unified essay all ideas and details connect to the thesis or controlling idea. The reader sees their connection at every point and experiences them as a unit—much as one experiences unity in music in which different sounds heard together develop a single theme.

The central idea that organizes the many smaller ideas and details of an essay is called the *thesis*. Occasionally the thesis appears in the first sentence or close to the beginning, as in many newspaper articles and editorials. The effect is likely to be dramatic, as in these opening paragraphs of a newspaper article:

> "Don't you want to be one of the Now people?" asks an ad for a new soft drink, going on to urge, "Become one of the Now generation!"
>
> The only thing I can think of that is worse than being one of the Now people is being one of the Then people. As a member of civilization in good standing, I reject both the *nowness* and the *thenness* of the generations. I opt for the *alwaysness.*—Sydney J. Harris, "Now People and Then People"

In fact, the newspaper or magazine reader *expects* to find the main ideas or details of the editorial or column in the opening sentences.

Beginning an essay or article directly with the thesis can seem abrupt, however, and often the thesis may not be clear to the reader without background. So the essayist frequently builds to the thesis, sometimes through details of a controversy or issue, as in the following opening paragraphs:

> Over the past few weeks, the nation's colleges have taken a beating because of loudmouths who shouted down invited speakers. Eldridge Cleaver at Wisconsin, Ambassador Jeane Kirkpatrick at

Berkeley and Sheik Ahmad Zaki Yamani at Kansas were the speakers, and the noise raised in their defense is only slightly less deafening than the shouts that drowned their speeches. No one in the academy approved or condoned the shouting: the clearest defense of the university as an open forum has come from university people themselves through the national associations that represent presidents, faculty members and students.

Whether or not they are aware of it, our critics misread our vulnerability to disruption. They seem to think that universities are orderly places, and if they aren't, presidents and trustees ought to make them so, even by force. Force is, however, our last and least resource, and order in the universities has seldom been more than skin-deep [*thesis*]. We order our planning, our upkeep, our payroll, and the lawns. But where our most serious work is done, messiness, not to say a kind of anarchy, is part of our nature [*restatement of thesis*].—Rev. Timothy S. Healy, S.J., "In Defense of Disorder"

Such introductory comments and details before the statement of the thesis help to place the reader in the world of the writer.

Sometimes the thesis is stated toward the end of the essay rather than near the beginning. One reason for this delay is that the reader may not understand the thesis without examples and considerable explanation. Another reason is that the writer may want to make the reader receptive to a controversial thesis before stating it. Also, a thesis is highlighted when it appears toward the end, particularly if the writer builds to it gradually but steadily.

In some essays—especially those that are mainly narration (that recount a series of events) or description—the thesis is implied rather than explicitly stated. That is, a carefully planned accumulation of details, rather than any single statement in the essay, conveys the main idea or impression the writer wishes to share with the reader. In the absence of a stated thesis, it is especially important that the writer maintain a clear sense of purpose and a consistent point of view in presenting the details.

You will find that you can produce unified, well-developed essays of your own if you take time to formulate a clear preliminary thesis statement before you begin to write. The act of writing is often an act of discovery—of finding meanings and ideas you could not anticipate at the start. In the course of writing, you may discover that your details and discussion suggest another thesis. When you do state a thesis that you find completely satisfactory, you need to review what you have written to be certain that the details develop it and not another idea. This review is particularly necessary if you decide not to state the thesis explicitly in the essay.

Susan Walton

THE CAUTIOUS AND OBEDIENT LIFE

Susan Walton received her B.A. in anthropology from Carleton College and an M.A. in journalism from the University of Wisconsin—Madison. Walton has done scientific and technical writing for the National Academies of Science and Engineering and various federal agencies, and she has written on science and education for numerous periodicals including *BioScience, Education Week,* and *Psychology Today.* Her essay on living an obedient life originally appeared in *The New York Times.*

Little herds of people mill around intersections in the morning, waiting for the lights to change. Washington is full of traffic circles, so sometimes you have to wait through several lights, standing on narrow islands of concrete while traffic comes at you from unexpected directions.

Not everyone waits. Some people dash, even when they see the No. 42 bus bearing down on them or some squirrel of a driver running every red light for blocks. The particularly daring ones make the cars stop for them.

I seldom walk until the light turns green. It is part of being obedient, a manifestation of the misbegotten belief that you must do what people tell you to do, and if you do, you will be rewarded. This syndrome of behavior is characterized by a dedication to form at the expense of spontaneity and substance. It is turning papers in on time and expecting to receive better grades than those who turn them in late, even if theirs are superior. It is believing your mother—who probably didn't believe it herself—when she says that boys prefer nice girls. This toe-the-line mentality is not confined to women; men, too, lie awake wondering how things ended up so wrong when they so carefully did everything right. Which is exactly the problem.

Some people are born to follow instructions. They are quiet children who always finish their homework, are never caught being bad, never sneak off and do undetected wicked things. They never figure out that it is possible to ignore what others want you to do and do whatever you like. The consequences of deviation are usually minimal. Nobody really expects you to be that good. If you are born this way, you acquire a look of puzzlement. You are puzzled because you can't figure out how or why these other people are doing outrageous things when the rules have been so clearly stated. Nor do you understand why people are not impressed with your mastery of those rules.

Puzzlement may turn to smugness. At first, when people asked me whether I had completed an assignment, I was surprised: of course I had; didn't the teacher *tell* us to? After I realized that punctuality was not all that common, I became smug. Yes, of course I turned my paper in on time. I did not see that the people who got noticed were likely to be erratic and late, rushing in explaining that their thesis had not fallen into place until 4 A.M. of the third Monday after the paper was due. Us punctual types did not wait for theses to fall into place. Whatever could be knocked into shape in time was what got turned in. The thing was due, wasn't it?

The message did not sink in for years, during which I always showed up for work, double pneumonia and all. I wandered into a field—journalism—mined with deadlines and populated by more missed deadlines, per capita, than any other. I repeated the process—first the assumption that you had to make the deadline, or why did they call it a deadline? Then I realized that this behavior was not universal. By the time I began working for a weekly, I had deluded myself into thinking that reliability was the way to success.

And it was, sort of. At this job, however, I encountered one of those people apparently sent by life as an object lesson. For every deadline I made, he missed one. Stories that everyone was counting on failed to materialize for weeks, as he agonized, procrastinated and interviewed just one more person. Everyone was annoyed at the time, but when the work was completed, mass amnesia set in. Only the product mattered, and the product, however late it was, was generally acceptable.

We advanced together, but what I gained with promotion was the opportunity to meet more deadlines per week and to hang around waiting to edit the copy of those who were late. What he got was the opportunity to linger over ever more significant stories. In my case, virtue was its own punishment. The moral of this story is that you should stop to think whether being good is getting you anywhere you want to go.

The most common and forgivable reason for the cautious, obedient life is fear. It is true, something terrible could happen if you stray. Something terrible could also happen if you do not stray, which is that you might be bored to death. Some people are lucky; what they are supposed to do is also what they like to do. They do not need to muster their nerve. I do not consider myself a nervy person. Rather, I think of myself as a recovering coward. Cowardice, like alcoholism, is a lifelong condition.

The James boys, William and Henry, are instructive on the subject of following too narrow a path. William James wrote in a letter to Thomas Ward in 1868 that the great mistake of his past life was an "impatience of results," which, he thought, should not be "too voluntarily aimed at or too busily thought of." What you must do, he believed, is to go on "in your own interesting way." Then the results will float along under their own steam. Henry left the classic record of the unlived life in "The Beast in the Jungle." It is the story of a man convinced that fate has something momentous in store for him, and he sits around carefully waiting for it to arrive. Consequently, his fate turns out to be that of a man to whom nothing ever happens. Better for him had he not listened quite so earnestly to the inner voice murmuring about fate. Better had he been distracted from his mission.

Be bold, my graduate school adviser, Mr. Ragsdale, used   11
to say—his only advice. I see now that he was right. Think
again of your future self: the little old lady sitting on the
porch of the old folks' home. When she thinks back on opportunities, will she regret the ones that passed unused?

Or find some other device. Myself, I keep a dumb post-   12
card in my desk drawer. It is light purple, with a drawing
of a cowering person standing on the edge of a diving board.
Beneath the drawing it says, "If you don't do it, you won't
know what would have happened if you had done it." Think
about the possible headline: "Cautious Pedestrian Squashed
by Bus While Waiting on Traffic Island—Should Have Jay-
walked, Police Say." Then look both ways, and go.

Comment

Susan Walton echoes the advice given by Ralph Waldo Emerson
in "Self-Reliance": "Whoso would be a man must be a nonconformist. He who would gather immortal palms must not be hin-
dered by the name of goodness, but must explore if it be goodness." Emerson gives this advice in a sermon-like essay; the advice
is unqualified—Emerson does not suggest exceptions to being a
nonconformist. Although Walton's essay ranges widely over the subject, it is not a loosely organized series of ideas. Walton states a
thesis about the cautious and obedient life early in the essay and
supports it through her personal experience, observations of other
people, and the ideas of the American philosopher William James
and his brother Henry James, the novelist and short story writer.

Questions for Study and Discussion

1. What is Walton's thesis and how does she introduce it? How
   does she remind the reader of the thesis as the essay proceeds?
2. Is Walton one of the people "born to follow instructions" or
   is she describing other people?
3. What did Walton learn from her experiences as a journalist?
4. Walton states that the most common reason for the cautious
   and obedient life is fear. What other reasons does she give? In
   what order does she present these reasons?

5. Is Walton reflecting upon her character and that of others, or is she writing to persuade cautious and obedient readers to change their lives? How do you know?
6. Do you agree with Walton that the "most common and forgivable reason for the cautious, obedient life is fear"? If you disagree, what explanation seems a better one and why?

Vocabulary Study

1. In her opening paragraph, Walton states that "little herds of people mill around intersections in the morning, waiting for the lights to change." Would substitution of *groups* for *herds* change the meaning of the sentence?
2. What does Walton mean by "a dedication to form at the expense of spontaneity and substance" (paragraph 3)? What is a "syndrome of behavior"? Is it the same thing as a "pattern" of behavior?
3. What is the dictionary meaning of "erratic" (paragraph 5)? What images or feelings does the word connote or bring to mind? Is an erratic person necessarily eccentric or odd?
4. Walton states in paragraph 8: "In my case, virtue was its own punishment." What does she mean by *virtue*? What dictionary meanings of the words are inapplicable to the sentence?
5. Explain the word *distracted* in the closing sentence of paragraph 10.

Suggestions for Writing

1. Discuss the extent to which you live "the cautious, obedient life." Then discuss why you act as you do. State your agreement or disagreement with Walton on the issue of conduct discussed in the essay.
2. Describe how you meet deadlines at school or at work. Then discuss what your habits reveal about your character or draw another conclusion from your description.

Topic Sentence

The phrase *topic sentence* usually describes the main or central idea of the paragraph—the idea that organizes details and subordinate ideas:

> The competition between man and beast is keenest in an event called bulldogging [*topic sentence*]. Riding alongside a steer, a cowboy must jump upon him from his horse while all three creatures are in full motion. He must grab the steer by the horns, bring him to a halt, and wrestle him to the ground. Since the steer weighs three or four times as much as the man, this is no easy task. When one of the wrestlers gets hurt, it's usually not the steer. The cowboys in this event are always young and strong, as are those in the various bucking contests. Only in calf roping do the older cowboys get a chance to stay active in the rodeo.—Ray Raphael, *Edges*

Many paragraphs open with a statement of the topic idea, restrict the statement to an aspect of the subject, and then illustrate the restricted idea:

> Members of the barrio describe the entire area as their home [*topic*]. It is a home, but it is more than this. The barrio is a refuge from the harshness and the coldness of the Anglo world [*restriction*]. It is a forced refuge. The leprous people are isolated from the rest of the community and contained in their section of town. The stoical pariahs of the barrio accept their fate, and from the angry seeds of rejection grow the flowers of closeness between outcasts, not the thorns of bitterness and the mad desire to flee. There is no want to escape, for the feeling of the barrio is known only to its inhabitants, and the material needs of life can also be found here [*illustration*].—Robert Ramirez, "The Woolen Sarape"

Occasionally a paragraph opens with a descriptive statement that introduces a series of details, as in the following paragraph describing a journey through western Scotland:

> The train bucked and turned north at Arisaig. The bays were like crater crusts filled with water. And offshore islands: Rhum, Eigg, Muck, and Canna—names like items from a misspelled menu. The Scour of Eigg was a hatchet shape against the sky. And now beneath the train there was a basin of green fields for three miles to the Sound of Sleat—and above the train were mountains of cracked rock and swatches of purple heather. Suddenly a horse was silhouetted in the sun, cropping grass beside the sea.—Paul Theroux, *The Kingdom by the Sea*

Placed at the beginning of the paragraph, the topic sentence guides the reader's attention. However, the topic sentence may appear anywhere in the paragraph—at the beginning, the middle, or the end. The following paragraph is typical of those that open with a series of details and end with a generalization, which is the central idea of the paragraph:

> The first transcontinental New Year's excess occurred in 1894–95 when Amos Alonzo Stagg took his University of Chicago team to Los Angeles to play Stanford. The trip served as a multifaceted precedent for intercollegiate football. The distance travelled (6,200 miles), the duration (three weeks) and the trip's national publicity all served to demonstrate the possibilities of such intercollegiate games. When the teams from the two young universities met at the turn of the year far from either campus and for no discernible educational purpose, the modern bowl concept was established [*topic sentence*].—Robin Lester, "The Bowl as Cathedral"

When a paragraph ends with the central idea, the succeeding paragraph may open with a transitional sentence:

> Before coming to Bellevue, in the course of my medical school training, most of my meager experience had been with patients in private hospitals, well-to-do people who cooperated with us medical students at the request of their private doctor. It didn't take me long to see that there was an enormous sociological gap between Bellevue patients and private patients. Our Bellevue patients didn't think like private patients [*topic sentence*].
>
> Take their attitude toward hospitalization [*transition*]. Most private patients have absolutely no desire to be hospitalized. They'd

rather be in their nice, comfortable, warm homes, drinking mar-
tinis, eating steak, surrounded by their families. The most luxu-
rious of hospitals can't offer the comforts of home [*topic sentence*].

But what if you have no home? [*transition*] What if you sleep in
doorways in the warm weather and in a flophouse in the cold?
What if you never know where your next meal is coming from
and have no family to solace you? What, then, is your attitude
toward hospitalization? [*topic sentence*]—William A. Nolen, *The
Making of a Surgeon*

Beginning your paragraphs with the topic sentence will help
you organize the details and the many ideas coherently. In writing
or in revising the paragraph, you may decide to restate the topic
idea because new details and ideas may occur to you as you record
your experiences and think about their meaning.

Francine Prose

GOSSIP

A novelist and essayist, Francine Prose was born in Brooklyn, New
York, and attended Radcliffe College. She has taught writing at Harvard
University, University of Arizona, and Warren Wilson College. Her
novels include *Judah the Pious* (1973), *Hungry Hearts* (1983), and
Bigfoot Dreams (1986). Her essays have appeared in *The Atlantic
Monthly* and other periodicals. Her essay on gossip makes an interesting
and unusual point about a much criticized activity.

1   Once I met a woman who grew up in the small North
Carolina town to which Chang and Eng, the original Siamese twins, retired after their circus careers. When I asked
her how the town reacted to the twins marrying local girls
and setting up adjacent households, she laughed and said:
"Honey, that was *nothing* compared to what happened
before the twins got there. Get the good gossip on any
little mountain town, scratch the surface and you'll find a
snake pit!"

2   Surely she was exaggerating; one assumes the domestic
arrangements of a pair of Siamese twins and their families
would cause a few ripples anywhere. And yet the truth of

what she said seemed less important than the glee with which she said it, her pride in the snake pit she'd come from, in its history, its scandals, its legacy of "good gossip." Gossip, the juicier the better, was her heritage, her birthright; that town, with its social life freakish enough to make Chang and Eng's seem mundane, was part of who she was.

Gossip must be nearly as old as language itself. It was, 3 I imagine, the earliest recreational use of the spoken word. First the cave man learned to describe the location of the plumpest bison, then he began to report and speculate on the doings of his neighbors in the cave next door. And yet, for all its antiquity, gossip has rarely received its due; its very name connotes idleness, time-wasting, frivolity and worse. Gossip is the unacknowledged poor relative of civilized conversation: Almost everyone does it but hardly anyone will admit to or defend it; and of these only the smallest and most shameless fraction will own up to enjoying it.

My mother and her friends are eloquent on the subject 4 and on the distinction between gossiping and exchanging information: "John got a new job," is, they say, information. "Hey, did you hear John got fired?" is gossip; which is, they agree, predominantly scurrilous, mean-spirited. That's the conventional wisdom on gossip and why it's so tempting to disown. Not long ago I heard myself describe a friend, half-jokingly, as "a much better person than I am, that is, she doesn't gossip so much." I heard my voice distorted by that same false note that sometimes creeps into it when social strain and some misguided notion of amiability make me assent to opinions I don't really share. What in the world was I talking about?

I don't, of course, mean rumor-mongering, outright 5 slander, willful fabrication meant to damage and undermine. But rather, ordinary gossip, incidents from and analyses of the lives of our heroes and heroines, our relatives, acquaintances and friends. The fact is, I love gossip, and beyond that, I believe in it—in its purposes, its human uses.

I'm even fond of the word, its etymology, its origins in 6 the Anglo-Saxon term "godsibbe" for god-parent, relative, its meaning widening by the Renaissance to include friends, cronies and later what one *does* with one's cronies. One gossips. Paring away its less flattering modern connotations, we discover a kind of synonym for connection, for community, and this, it seems to me, is the primary function of gossip. It maps our ties, reminds us of what sort of people we know and what manner of lives they lead, confirms our sense of who we are, how we live and where we have come from. The roots of the grapevine are inextricably entwined with our own. Who knows how much of our sense of the world has reached us on its branches, how often, as babies, we dropped off to sleep to the rhythms of family gossip? I've often thought that gossip's bad name might be cleared by calling it "oral tradition"; for what, after all, is an oral tradition but the stories of other lives, other eras, legends from a time when human traffic with spirits and gods was considered fit material for gossipy speculation?

7   Older children gossip; adolescents certainly do. Except in the case of those rare toddler-fabulists, enchanting parents and siblings with fairy tales made upon the spot, gossip may be the way that most of us learn to tell stories. And though, as Gertrude Stein is supposed to have told Hemingway, gossip is not literature, some similar criteria may apply to both. Pacing, tone, clarity and authenticity are as essential for the reportage of neighborhood news as they are for well-made fiction.

8   Perhaps more important is gossip's analytical component. Most people—I'm leaving out writers, psychologists and probably some large proportion of the academic and service professions—are, at least in theory, free to go about their lives without feeling the compulsion to endlessly dissect the minutiae of human motivation. They can indulge in this at their leisure, for pleasure, in their gossip. And while there are those who clearly believe that the sole aim of gossip is to criticize, to condemn (or, frequently, to titillate, to bask in the aura of scandal as if it were one's own), I prefer to see gossip as a tool of understanding. It only takes a moment to tell what someone did. Far more mileage—and more enjoyment—can be extracted from debating why he did it. Such questions, impossible to discuss without touching on matters of choice and consequence, responsibility and will,

are, one might argue, the beginnings of moral inquiry, first steps toward a moral education. It has always seemed peculiar that a pastime so conducive to the moral life should be considered faintly immoral.

I don't mean to deny the role of plain nosiness in all this, of unadorned curiosity about our neighbors' secrets. And curiosity (where would we be without it?) has, like gossip, come in for some negative press. Still, it's understandable; everyone wants to gossip, hardly anyone wants to be gossiped about. What rankles is the fear that our secrets will be revealed, some essential privacy stripped away and, of course, the lack of control over what others say. Still, such talk is unavoidable; it's part of human nature, of the human community. When one asks, "What's the gossip?" it's that community that is being affirmed.

So I continue to ask, mostly without apology and especially when I'm talking to friends who still live in places I've moved away from. And when they answer—recalling the personalities, telling the stories, the news—I feel as close as I ever will to the lives we shared, to what we know and remember in common, to those much-missed, familiar and essentially beneficent snake pits I've lived in and left behind.

Comment

Francine Prose builds up to her topic sentences in her introductory paragraphs. She also builds the opening paragraphs up to the statement in paragraph 3 characterizing gossip. The topic sentences that follow fix our attention on this word.

Questions for Study and Discussion

1. Which are the topic sentences of paragraphs 1 through 10? If the topic sentence does not open the paragraph, what does the opening sentence do?
2. "Civilized" is the key word in Prose's statement in paragraph 3. How does her definition of gossip in paragraph 6 explain this word?
3. How is gossip different from "rumor-mongering" and slan-

der, discussed in paragraph 5? Why would Prose consider these kinds of talk uncivilized?

4. What is the thesis of the essay and where does it appear? Does Prose restate the thesis?

5. How does the discussion of children and adolescents develop the thesis? Why does Prose make the point that gossip has the qualities of good fiction?

6. How does paragraph 8 explain the "analytical component" of gossip?

7. How does Prose explain the fact that gossip is considered "faintly immoral" (paragraph 8)? And how does her discussion of this point in paragraph 9 further develop her thesis?

8. How is the concluding paragraph related to the opening ones? What reminder of her thesis does she give the reader?

Vocabulary Study

1. Examine the history of the word *gossip* in the *Oxford English Dictionary*. What support does this history give to the points Prose makes about gossip?

2. Use your standard dictionary to distinguish gossip, as Prose defines it, from the following:

   a. rumor
   b. hearsay
   c. libel
   d. slander

Suggestions for Writing

1. Illustrate Prose's definition of gossip through your talk with friends and family. Distinguish the kinds of talk you engage in, using the words you looked up in your dictionary.

2. Prose states: "Older children gossip; adolescents certainly do." Discuss similarities or differences in the talk you have observed in children and adolescents. Draw a conclusion from your analysis—a thesis that the various ideas and details of your discussion develop. You might build to a statement of this thesis at the end or in the opening paragraphs as Prose does.

Order of Ideas

Ideas in the paragraph as well as in the whole essay can be presented or ordered in various ways. We saw in the previous section that paragraphs commonly open with a general idea which is then developed through specific details. But, as in Robin Lester's paragraph on bowl games (p. 15), some paragraphs move from the *specific* to the *general*—building up to the central or topic idea.

Certain kinds of writing have their own order. Descriptions are *spatial*—perhaps moving from foreground to background or from earth to sky:

> Once we even saw a giraffe, but miles, miles away from us, alone under the clear sky among the thorn trees on the horizon, and we could see its silhouetted head and long neck turned to watch us; it seemed very lonely, very small, and very far away on the yellow flats; when the noise of our trucks reached it, it was frightened and began to run, heaving itself up and down. It ran away from us for a long time and got even smaller but never out of sight. At last it reached the horizon.—Elizabeth Marshall Thomas, *The Harmless People*

Narrative, in contrast, presents events chronologically—in the order of *time*. The paragraph just quoted combines spatial description with chronological narrative: the writer presents the sighting of the giraffe, the movement of the trucks, and the flight of the animal in their temporal order. In reporting an experience or explaining a process, the facts or steps are also presented as they occur. To a person learning to drive, you would not explain how to turn corners until you explained how to brake and steer.

In expository and persuasive writing ideas may be presented in numerous ways. The author considers the reader's knowledge of the subject, the purpose of the paragraph or essay, and the subject itself in organizing the paragraph. For example, in describing the care of an automobile you would probably describe simple procedures before complex ones, especially if your readers are owners of new models. In training mechanics to repair a new kind of engine, you might proceed from the most common to the most unusual problems mechanics are likely to encounter.

In the following definition of the potlach, a ceremony in which Indians of the Northwest dispose of property, the author clearly has his readers in mind in presenting details of the ceremony in the order of *importance:*

> A proper potlach involved prodigious displays of eating, since it was a point of honor with the host to provide much more food than his guests could consume. The eating would last for days, interspersed with singing, belching, speechmaking, dramatic performances and the ceremonial conferring of honorific names. But the vital part of the occasion was the bestowing of gifts—bowls, boxes, baskets, blankets, canoes, ornaments, sculptures—that the chief had collected among his people, from each according to his ability, and now distributed among his guests, to each according to his rank.—Frederic V. Grunfeld, "Indian Giving"

The greater the drama of the event, the greater our sense of *climax*—of increasing importance or intensity as the paragraph or essay moves to the end.

Some paragraphs (and essays) move from *question* to *answer:*

> How wide is the scope of physical law? Do life, thought, history fall within its orderly domain? Or does it describe only the inanimate, the remote and the very tiny? It is the claim of contemporary physics that its laws apply to all natural things, to atoms, stars and men. There are not two worlds: the cold, precise mechanical world of physics, and the surprising, disorderly and growing world of living things or of human existence. They are one.—Philip Morrison, "Cause, Chance and Creation"

A related order is the movement from *problem* to *solution.* The following paragraph states a problem in biology and then presents a tentative solution:

> How either whales or seals endure the tremendous pressure changes involved in dives of several hundred fathoms is not definitely known [*problem*]. They are warm-blooded mammals like ourselves. Caisson disease, which is caused by the rapid accumulation of nitrogen bubbles in the blood with sudden release of pressure, kills human divers if they are brought up rapidly

from depths of 200 feet or so. Yet, according to the testimony of whalers, a baleen whale, when harpooned, can dive straight down to the depth of half a mile, as measured by the amount of line carried out. From these depths, where it has sustained a pressure of half a ton on every inch of body, it returns almost immediately to the surface. The most plausible explanation is that, unlike the diver, who has air pumped to him while he is under water, the whale has in its body only the limited supply it carries down, and does not have enough nitrogen in its blood to do serious harm [*solution*]. The plain truth is, however, that we really do not know since it is obviously impossible to confine a living whale and experiment on it, and almost as difficult to dissect a dead one satisfactorily [*qualification*].—Rachel Carson, *The Sea Around Us*

As Elizabeth Marshall Thomas's paragraph on giraffes shows, paragraphs can combine various orderings of ideas and details— in this case, the spatial arrangement of details with the chronological presentation of events. A paragraph may, in addition, show that the events increase in importance or intensity. In writing your own paragraphs and essays, you may discover better ways of presenting your details and ideas as you see the paragraph or essay take shape.

Harold Krents

DARKNESS AT NOON

Harold Krents graduated from Harvard College and later studied law at Oxford University and Harvard Law School. He practiced law from 1971 until his death in 1986. Krents was the prototype for the blind boy in Leonard Gershe's play (and the later film) *Butterflies Are Free*. His experiences at Harvard are the basis of the film *Riding on the Wind*. Krents was long active in organizations and government agencies concerned with the employment of handicapped people.

Blind from birth, I have never had the opportunity to see myself and have been completely dependent on the image I create in the eye of the observer. To date it has not been narcissistic.

There are those who assume that since I can't see, I 2
obviously also cannot hear. Very often people will converse
with me at the top of their lungs, enunciating each word
very carefully. Conversely, people will also often whisper, assuming that since my eyes don't work, my ears don't
either.

For example, when I go to the airport and ask the ticket 3
agent for assistance to the plane, he or she will invariably
pick up the phone, call a ground hostess and whisper: "Hi,
Jane, we've got a 76 here." I have concluded that the word
"blind" is not used for one of two reasons: Either they fear
that if the dread word is spoken, the ticket agent's retina
will immediately detach, or they are reluctant to inform me
of my condition of which I may not have been previously
aware.

On the other hand, others know that of course I can 4
hear, but believe that I can't talk. Often, therefore, when my
wife and I go out to dinner, a waiter or waitress will ask Kit
if "*he* would like a drink" to which I respond that "indeed
he would."

This point was graphically driven home to me while we 5
were in England. I had been given a year's leave of absence
from my Washington law firm to study for a diploma in law
degree at Oxford University. During the year I became ill
and was hospitalized. Immediately after admission, I was
wheeled down to the X-ray room. Just at the door sat an
elderly woman—elderly I would judge from the sound of
her voice. "What is his name?" the woman asked the orderly who had been wheeling me.

"What's your name?" the orderly repeated to me. 6
"Harold Krents," I replied. 7
"Harold Krents," he repeated. 8
"When was he born?" 9
"When were you born?" 10
"November 5, 1944," I responded. 11
"November 5, 1944," the orderly intoned. 12
This procedure continued for approximately five min- 13
utes at which point even my saint-like disposition deserted
me. "Look," I finally blurted out, "this is absolutely ridicu-

lous. Okay, granted I can't see, but it's got to have become pretty clear to both of you that I don't need an interpreter."

"He says he doesn't need an interpreter," the orderly reported to the woman.   14

The toughest misconception of all is the view that be-   15
cause I can't see, I can't work. I was turned down by over forty law firms because of my blindness, even though my qualifications included a cum laude degree from Harvard College and a good ranking in my Harvard Law School class.

The attempt to find employment, the continuous frus-   16
tration of being told that it was impossible for a blind person to practice law, the rejection letters, not based on my lack of ability but rather on my disability, will always remain one of the most disillusioning experiences of my life.

Fortunately, this view of limitation and exclusion is be-   17
ginning to change. On April 16, the Department of Labor issued regulations that mandate equal-employment opportunities for the handicapped. By and large, the business community's response to offering employment to the disabled has been enthusiastic.

I therefore look forward to the day, with the expecta-   18
tion that it is certain to come, when employers will view their handicapped workers as a little child did me years ago when my family still lived in Scarsdale.

I was playing basketball with my father in our back-   19
yard according to procedures we had developed. My father would stand beneath the hoop, shout, and I would shoot over his head at the basket attached to our garage. Our next-door neighbor, aged five, wandered over into our yard with a playmate. "He's blind," our neighbor whispered to her friend in a voice that could be heard distinctly by Dad and me. Dad shot and missed; I did the same. Dad hit the rim: I missed entirely: Dad shot and missed the garage entirely. "Which one is blind?" whispered back the little friend.

I would hope that in the near future when a plant man-   20
ager is touring the factory with the foreman and comes upon a handicapped and nonhandicapped person working together, his comment after watching them work will be, "Which one is disabled?"

Comment

Krents states a problem and proceeds to a solution: this is the general organization of the essay. But Krents wishes to do more than state a solution; he wishes his readers to fully understand the difficulties of being blind and, through understanding and sympathy, provide the solution by changing the way they talk to and behave with blind people. Krents organizes the three misconceptions about blindness with this purpose in mind. He might have presented these misconceptions in a different order; the order he chooses helps us appreciate the bizarre situation he describes. A notable quality of the essay is the proportion of examples to discussion—just enough are provided to illustrate each of the ideas. Krents selects his details carefully. They must be striking enough to make his points vividly and clearly. Leonard Kriegel describes a different handicap and its effect on his life on p. 112.

Questions for Study and Discussion

1. In what paragraph does Krents state the basis for his ordering of the three misconceptions? How does this order help us to appreciate the bizarre situation created by blindness? How does the change in tone in paragraph 15 accord with the order of ideas?
2. What is his thesis? Does he state it directly, or is it implied?
3. What are the implied causes of the problems described? What is the solution? Does Krents state or imply this solution?
4. What attitudes and feelings does Krents express in the final anecdote?
5. Do you find the organization of ideas successful, or would you have organized them in a different way?

Vocabulary Study

Use your dictionary to distinguish the differences in meaning in the following series of words. Write a sentence using each of the words according to its dictionary meaning. The first word in each series is Krents's:

a. *narcissistic* (paragraph 1), *vain, conceited, proud*
b. *enunciating* (paragraph 2), *pronouncing*

c. *graphically* (paragraph 5), *sharply, starkly, vividly*
d. *disillusioning* (paragraph 16), *disappointing, frustrating*

Suggestions for Writing

1. Discuss the effect that a permanent or temporary handicap or disability has had on your life, or discuss problems you have observed in the life of a disabled, or handicapped, friend or relative. You may want to organize your essay as Krents does—working from a problem to a solution. Note that the solution need not be complete or permanent; you may want to discuss the extent to which the problems described can be solved.

2. Krents writes about his blindness with humor. Discuss how he achieves that humor and what it tells you about his view of himself and people in general.

3. Describe an embarrassing experience of your own—how it came about, the persons involved in it, its outcome. Then discuss its causes, focusing on the most important of them.

Coherence

In a unified essay all of the details and ideas connect to a central idea or thesis. To emphasize the unity, these details and ideas must obviously fit together into a whole: the reader must see how they cohere, or hold together. The ideas and details must seem to follow naturally.

Using pronoun reference and the repetition of key words and phrases are important ways to obtain coherence—ways that we depend upon with little if any thought. In the following paragraph, examples of key words have been italicized:

> In the 40's my parents and I moved from Hillside Homes to a neighborhood in the Bronx that is now dominated by what was then known as the Einstein–Jacoby medical center. *It* was bordered by hundreds of acres of undeveloped land. What I remember most distinctly abut *that land,* beyond a huge, flat-topped rock studded with a lifetime supply of mica chips, are the many hills that were covered by tiger lilies in the spring, poison sumac in the summer and perfect snow for sledding after any reasonable winter storm. Early on there were a few squatters farming land near *those hills;* later *they* disappeared. And early on I was content to stay in our beautiful new neighborhood, while later there wasn't enough there to hold me.—Judith Rossner, "The Dyre Avenue Shuttle"

Another important means of achieving coherence is through the use of parallel structure, the arrangement of similar words, phrases, and clauses to highlight similar ideas (again, examples have been italicized):

> Though perhaps Brooklyn is not quite a refuge anymore where sheep may safely graze, *there are places* there where you can listen in the dark of winter to the wind attacking from the Atlantic as moon-whitened waves break against the beach. *There*

are neighborhoods of nations so alien and incredible that crossing into them mobilizes beyond any expectation both distance and time. *There are streets* where, on January nights, fires burn on every floor of every house, sending fragrant smoke through the cold black trees. *There are meadows and fields, long rows of old oaks, bridges that sparkle from afar, ships about to leave for Asia, lakes, horses and islands in the marsh.*—Mark Helprin, "Brooklyn's Comforting Infinitude"

Where the natural course is clear through pronoun reference, repetition of key words and phrases, questions and parallel structure, no helping words or formal connectives are necessary. Sometimes, however, you will need transitional words and phrases when the connection of ideas or details is not immediately clear. If the steps of a process are presented chronologically and each step requires explanation, you may introduce the words *first, second,* and *third* to keep the steps distinct. You may also add the phrases *less important, just as important, more important* to show that you are presenting ideas in the order of importance. Connectives such as *thus, therefore, however, moreover,* and *nevertheless* show the logical relation of ideas. *Thus* and *therefore* show that one idea is the consequence of another or that certain conclusions can be drawn from the evidence presented. *However* and *nevertheless* show that one idea qualifies or contradicts another. *Moreover* shows addition.

L. E. Sissman

THE OLD FARMER'S ALMANAC, 1872

The poet and essayist L. E. Sissman was born in Detroit, Michigan, in 1928. After graduating from Harvard University he worked in advertising. His poems are collected in *Hello, Darkness* (1978); his personal essays for *The Atlantic Monthly* are collected in *Inner Bystander* (1975). Sissman died in 1976. In the essay reprinted here, Sissman compares our world today with the world described in an issue of a nineteenth-century farmer's almanac.

The homely publications of a hundred years ago have a   1
message for us. The *Official Railway Guide* of June, 1868,
for example, tells me the disheartening news that my regular
twenty-seven-mile commute took ten minutes less one hundred
and four years ago than it does today. And the 1872 *Old
Farmer's Almanac,* which I picked up in a New Hampshire
secondhand store some years ago, bears even odder tidings.

If you consult the *Almanac* today, you know that be-   2
hind its familiar yellow cover is a thick pack of oddments—
snippets of astrology, weather prognostications, old rhymes
and jokes, a spate of small-space ads for trusses, roach-killer,
and fish lures, and on pages that deal with the months of
the year ahead, a series of nostalgic, neatly written "Farmer's Calendars."

Things were different in 1872. The *Almanac* was thin—   3
a mere fifty-two pages—and the only ads inside its peach
covers (the original yellow was dropped for a time in the
middle of the nineteenth century) touted Hallet & Davis pi-
anos (endorsed by "F. Liszt, the First Pianist in the World"),
Webb & Twombly's Premium Chocolates (which "have taken
the highest award at every Fair in which they have been
exhibited"), Wheeler & Wilson's Sewing Machines, Worces-
ter's Quarto Dictionary (with a testimonal from Edward Ev-
erett), and the wares of Hency C. Sawyer, whose Waltham
Book Store also sold stationery, wallpaper, silverplate, lug-
gage, desks, Bibles, brushes, combs, perfumery, soap, pocket
knives and scissors, fans for ladies, umbrellas, picture frames,
and, of course, the *Almanac.*

But it is the editorial matter of the old *Almanac* that   4
startles the modern reader. Beginning soberly with a table
of Meetings of Friends in New England and a list of salaries
of executive officers of the United States ("Ulysses S. Grant,
Ill., Pres., $25,000; Hamilton Fish, N.Y., Sec. State, $8,000"),
it goes on through a page of astronomical data and rosters
of New England colleges and registers in bankruptcy to an
early crescendo: the spreads for the months of the year. Each
is laid out much as it is today: a table of astronomical calculations on the left, a rather sketchy forecast and the

"Farmer's Calendar" on the right. But these "Farmer's Calendars" are nothing like the rather bland, pleasant little essays of today. Each of them preaches and rails at the farmer to keep a better farm and live a better life; the Protestant ethic rears its minatory head in January and harangues the reader through the waxing and the waning year. The nameless scourge of slothful husbandmen begins the cycle, after a terse New Year's greeting, well into his evangelical stride: "Make up your mind therefore to be better and to do better, to aim higher and to have nobler ends in view. . . . Let us sit down by the crackling fire and lay out plans for the year. I suppose you have done the chores, of course, fed the cattle and the pigs, and cleaned up the barn. No use to sit down till the chores are done. . . ." In February, he has progressed a step further in his righteous indignation at his captive parishioners; now he begins by berating them: "Snug up about the barn this winter. Shut the door and the windows. Cold won't make cattle tough. . . . I wouldn't give a fig for a man who can't turn his mind to little things. All your luck in farming hangs on the chores at this season."

In March, he is quick to turn on the hapless, snow- ⁵ bound farmer who grouses about the weather. "No use to fret about the storm and the snow. Keep your temper is a good rule on the farm. This way of finding fault with heaven and earth won't do. . . . It's a pity you don't raise more roots. Hadn't you better look about for a spot to put in an acre of mangolds and another of swedes?"

The Old Farmer takes the offensive early and keeps the ⁶ pressure up; the shiftless reader won't get a breather, even in springtime: "All plant life is on the spring now, and animal life too, as to that matter. And so you'd better spring around, John, if you want to see your barn well filled in the fall. Yoke up and go at it with your fine and sprightly team. . . . The fact is, there is no end to the work this month, and no time to lose in standing around or leaning over the wall with a gossiping neighbor." And "It is of no use to find fault with work. We ought to thank our stars that we are able to work."

As the summer ends, the taskmaster's lips are thinner   7
than ever: "Now that the dog star rages, why don't you give
the dog a bullet [presumably a pill of dog-days medicine],
the boy a hoe, the girl the knitting needles. No work, no
eating, is the rule, you know. Can't afford to keep drones
on the farm." In September, to keep the enervated farmer
on the qui vive, the *Almanac* lays out an impressive list of
chores, including removing stones from fields to be tilled. "I
hope you got out those rocks. . . . It is a shiftless way to
lay down a lot with the bushes growing along the walls.
Why don't you dig them out, and clean up the lot?" In October, he notes, with relish, that "there is enough to do to
keep us on the jog all this month"; in November, after a
peremptory reference to Thanksgiving, he's off again about
stalling the cattle every night, fall sowing and plowing, and
trimming the grapevines. Even in December—notably, there's
no mention of Christmas—he's harping about the grapevines again, as well as pruning the fruit trees, making an
inventory of stock and tools on the farm ("the sooner you
set about it, the better you will be off"), and generally preparing for the worst: "Spruce up and get ready for a
hard winter."

The rest of the *Almanac* is similarly grim; it dispels a   8
number of common notions among farmers about cabbage,
kitchen gardens, grass for horses, and food for stock, calls
attention to the adulteration of commercial fertilizers, cau-
tions the reader about transplanting evergreens ("it is a mistake to suppose that the same rules apply to evergreens as
to deciduous trees"), and sagely discusses the pitfalls of stock-
breeding farms. Then a little light relief: three pages of poetry, anecdotes, and puzzles, most of them not so light, at
that. One poem, a tearjerker, was "found under the pillow
of a soldier who died in a hospital near Port Royal, South
Carolina." "Selections" includes Scott's "O, what a tangled
web we weave/When first we practise to deceive"; the jokes
include this epitaph: "I was well—wished to be better—read
medical books—took medicine—and died."

The 1872 *Almanac* ends there, with the exception of a   9
few population tables (according to the census of 1870, there

were 38,555,983 people in the United States, of whom
942,292 lived in New York City and 4,382,759 in New York
State; California could boast a mere 560,247), weather tables, tide tables, and post office regulations (first-class letters, 3 cents per half ounce). It ends with a sort of a whimper
and a curious feeling of oppression in the reader, as if he
had just been through that exhausting year with the poor,
bone-weary farmer. It ends, finally, with a question forming
in the modern reader's mind: Were the good old days that
bad? In an age when we are daily and sorely tried by all
sorts of mind-boggling disasters and injustices, when we daily
repair to the past for reassurance and refreshment, is it possible that we are really better off than our forebears, and
that our carefully cultivated nostalgia is founded on a mi-
rage? On the evidence of the 1872 *Almanac,* that could well
be. The stern preachments of the anonymous author of the
"Farmer's Calendar" are not mere mouthings; it seems clear
that the struggling farmer of a century ago really needed
these appeals to his pride and his sense of duty in order to
get on with the backbreaking, dawn-to-dusk job of cultivating his garden. It was a savage life of imponderables—blizzards, floods, crop failures, insect plagues, human and animal
diseases for which there were no known cures—and only the
most bitterly Calvinistic outlook could prepare one to compete in what had, eventually, to be a losing race. There was
no social security in those days, no government price supports, no anesthesia, and above all no leisure. The farmer
had literally nothing to look forward to except the fruits of
a job well done and another day, week, month, and year of
unremitting toil to keep ahead of a hostile nature.

　　To us, seated in our warm houses on our choreless days　10
off from work, knitted to all our friends by the telephone,
possessed of cars to take us across the county or across the
country as the whim strikes us, disposing of a hundred
diversions to beguile our leisure, protected by effective medical care (for those, at least, who can afford it), assured of a
cash competence in our retirement, this stark world of a
hundred years ago is hard indeed to believe in—which is one
of the reasons why we believe in a gilded age when all the

world was young, when cares were few, when love was true, when, over the river and through the woods, grandmother's house was filled with goodwill, provender, and jollity. What a shame the truth was otherwise.

Comment

The opening topic sentences of paragraphs 1 through 8 refer to the central idea; the details in these paragraphs illustrate this idea in various ways. Paragraph 9 is organized in a different way: details of the final pages of the almanac lead to the question "Were the good old days that bad?" The remaining sentences answer the question. In the concluding paragraph Sissman reflects upon that answer.

Sissman depends on a number of devices to hold together the various details and ideas. The opening sentences of some of the paragraphs make transitions to a new consideration or stage of the analysis of the almanac. For example, the opening sentence of paragraph 4 marks the turn from advertisements to the editorial matter; the opening sentence of paragraph 6 shifts the discussion to the attitude of the Old Farmer toward his readers. The long paragraphs require careful transitions to mark turns of ideas—for example, in the following transitional sentence in paragraph 4:

> But these "Farmer's Calendars" are nothing like the rather bland, pleasant little essays of today.

Sissman is describing a publication and a world unfamiliar to his readers, and he keeps his many details in focus through his much longer paragraphs, each devoted to one idea or feature of the almanac.

Questions for Study and Discussion

1. How late in the essay does Sissman state the thesis? What is gained by not stating it in the opening paragraph?
2. How are paragraphs 1 through 8 organized? Does Sissman describe the almanac cover to cover, or does he present the contents in a different order?
3. The "Protestant ethic" (paragraph 4) is the ideal of hard, unremitting work which exercises the virtues of the upright person. How is this ideal related to the "Calvinistic outlook,"

referred to in paragraph 9? How does the discussion of the farmer's life throughout the essay explain these phrases?

4. Do you agree with Sissman's explanation of our romantic view of the American past? What additional or different reasons for this romantic attitude would you cite?

Vocabulary Study

Give the dictionary meanings of the following words. Then write an explanation of how the word is used in the particular sentence:

a. paragraph 1: *homely, tidings*
b. paragraph 2: *snippets, prognostications, spate, nostalgic*
c. paragraph 3: *touted*
d. paragraph 4: *bland, harangues, minatory, scourge, evangelical*
e. paragraph 7: *enervated, qui vive, peremptory*
f. paragraph 9: *anesthesia, unremitting*
g. paragraph 10: *beguile, competence, provender*

Suggestions for Writing

1. Examine an issue of a magazine published in the 1940s or the 1950s, and describe some of its contents. Organize your description to develop a thesis—perhaps a conclusion about the world of your parents or grandparents based on the evidence of the magazine.

2. Discuss how closely a recent movie about teenagers or young adults is true to your own experiences and observations. Restrict your discussion to one or two characters or episodes; don't try to discuss the whole movie. Build your discussion to a general conclusion or thesis suggested by the similarities or differences you note.

❦
Narration

You are familiar with narration through works of fiction that present a series of events chronologically or weave past and present events into complex narratives or plots that explore the connection of events. Narratives are also basic in expository, persuasive, and expressive essays. An essay tracing historical events may do so through narrative. The following paragraph describing the first landfall of Christopher Columbus in the Bahamas shows how narration serves historical exposition:

> As the sun set under a clear horizon October 11, the northeast trade breezed up to gale force, and the three ships tore along at 9 knots. But Columbus refused to shorten sail, since his promised time was running out. He signaled everyone to keep a particularly sharp watch, and offered extra rewards for first landfall in addition to the year's pay promised by the Sovereigns. That night of destiny was clear and beautiful with a late rising moon, but the sea was the roughest of the entire passage. The men were tense and expectant, the officers testy and anxious, the Captain General serene in the confidence that presently God would reveal to him the promised Indies.—Samuel Eliot Morison, "First Crossing of the Atlantic"

Narration is also important in persuasive writing. In the legal brief it is essential in providing the background of the case—the events at issue. A simple argument may contain a supporting narrative of an event. A plea for a change in public policy may trace the consequences of present policy through a narrative illustrating them. We will consider examples in a later section.

Narration is important, too, in expressive writing. Gloria Emerson's account of her parachute jump in Part Two is a simple narrative. Here, Sue Hubbell begins her essay on woodcutting with a narrative of her experiences:

36

This morning I finished sawing up a tree from the place where I had been cutting for the past week. In the process I lost my screwrench, part screwdriver, part wrench, that I use to make adjustments on my chain saw. I shouldn't carry it in my pocket, but the chain had been loose; I had tightened it and had not walked back to the truck to put the wrench away. Scolding myself for being so careless, I began looking for another tree to cut and found a big one that had recently died.

In narration the amount of detail you present depends on the knowledge of your readers. Since you usually cannot know how much knowledge each reader possesses about a subject, you will do best to include essential facts and to introduce those nonessential facts that give the reader details about the world and the characters in your essay. It is important, however, not to give excessive detail that diverts the reader from the central event. In his paragraph on Columbus, Morison gives a necessary though brief description of the sailors and officers of the ship. To have described each of their reactions in detail would lessen the suspense and divert attention from Columbus himself, who is the actual focus of the narrative.

Edward Rivera

THE SOCIOLOGY FINAL

Edward Rivera teaches English at the City College of New York. Born in Orocovia, Puerto Rico, he grew up in New York City, attending school in Spanish Harlem and at nineteen entered evening school at City College. He returned to college after army service, graduating from City College in 1967 and later from Columbia University. Rivera describes the very different worlds of Puerto Rico and New York in his semi-autobiographical book *Family Installments: Memories of Growing Up Hispanic.* The experience described in this excerpt—taking a final exam in a college course—will be familiar to many students.

I took a cab up to school, but I was still late. On the way there, I reviewed the "material" in my head: almost total confusion, a jumble of jargon, ordinary things passed off as profundities with the aid of "abstractionitis." ("The home then is the specific zone of functional potency that grows about a live parenthood . . . an active interfacial membrane or surface furthering exchange . . . a mutualizing membrane between the family and the society in which it lives. . . .")

The classroom was packed for the first time since the opening day of classes, and filled with smoke. Over forty students were bent over their examination booklets, most of them looking confused by the questions. The professor, puffing an immense pipe, was at his desk (manufactured by Vulcan), reading Riesman on *The Lonely Crowd,* casually, as if it were a murder mystery whose ending he had figured out back on page one. He didn't look pleased when I stepped up to his desk: another pair of lungs in a roomful of carbon dioxide and cigarette smoke.

"Yes?"

I asked him for a question sheet and an examination booklet. They were on the desk, weighted down with the eighth edition of his anthology.

"Are you registered in this course?" he asked.

Yes, I was. He wanted to know my name. I told him. He looked me up in his roll book. Had I been coming to class regularly? Every time. How come I never spoke up in class? Because I sat in the back. It was hard to be heard from back there. I might try sitting up front, he said. I said I would. He said it was a little late for that. For a moment I'd forgotten what day it was. *Dies irae,* according to my paperback dictionary of foreign phrases. Do-or-die day.

There were no empty chairs, so I walked to the back of the room and squatted in a corner, keeping my coat and scarf on.

"Answer one from Part A, one from Part B, and one from Part C." I had no trouble understanding that much. But my mind blanked out on the choices in Parts A, B, and C. There was something about "group membership as the source of individual morality and social health" (Durkheim? I couldn't remember). I must have slept through that lecture, and I couldn't remember any mention of it in the eighth

edition. Another one asked for something or other on We-
ber's contention that "minorities in 19th-century Europe—
the Poles in Russia, the Huguenots in France, the Noncon-
formists in England, and the Jews in all countries—had
offset their socio-political exclusion by engaging in economic activity whereas the Catholics had not." This one had
to be explained in fifteen minutes. I got around it by drawing a blank.

The easiest choice in Part C asked for "a sociological   9
autobiography, demonstrating your command of certain relevant aspects in this course, as well as the terminology of
sociology."

"Terminology of sociology." That wasn't even a good   10
rhyme. It was also asking too much for fifteen minutes. It
wasn't even enough time for my nerves to calm down. Too
bad. I got up and left the room. No one noticed.

I went down to the student cafeteria for a cup of coffee,   11
and while I drank it, I read the opening chapter of Dr. A.
Alonso's *El Gibaro,* a Puerto Rican classic which I'd brought
with me to reread on the subway back home. "I am one of
those," it went, "and this can't matter much to my readers,
who are in the habit of not sleeping without first having
read something"—another one, I thought, nineteenth-
century version—"and this something must be of the sort
that requires more than usual seclusion, order and medita-
tion, since I think that at no time other than the night's
silence can one withdraw from the real world, to elevate
oneself into the imaginary; above all when the day has been
spent without affliction, something that a young man achieves
from time to time, before he becomes the head of a family,
or while he does not have to govern, on his own, the vessel
of his future."

In the examination blue book, which I hadn't bothered   12
returning, I translated some of these long, rhythmic sentences as best I could (no dictionary on me, for one thing),
just for practice, and then, when I'd finished a second cup
of coffee, I shoved the Alonso and the blue book back inside
my coat pocket and left for the subway.

Comment

"Let me tell you what the final was like," a friend says to you. The story she tells expresses various feelings—perhaps joy or anger or frustration. It may even develop a thesis—either an explicit or implicit point that your friend wants to make. You discover the implicit thesis largely through the tone of the narrative and the stress given particular details. Tone is an essential consideration, because it conveys the attitude of the narrator (see p. 359). These are matters to consider in Rivera's narrative of his sociology final.

The effectiveness of Rivera's narrative arises from the exactness of his detail. He does not tell us everything about the professor of the exam, but rather he selects the details that best convey the atmosphere of the classroom and that explain why he leaves without completing the exam. The episode is a small one, but it tells us much about the feelings of the outsider—of a Puerto Rican youth facing numerous barriers.

Questions for Study and Discussion

1. What are Rivera's feelings in arriving for the exam, in talking to the professor, in reading the questions, and in leaving the building? To what aspects of the experience does Rivera give the most attention in his narrative?
2. How do the details of the professor and the exam help you to understand Rivera's feelings? What may be the significance of the title of the book the professor is reading? What is the general tone of his description?
3. What does the quotation from Alonso's *El Gibaro* tell you about Rivera's attitude? What is the general tone of paragraph 11?
4. Is Rivera merely expressing his feelings about the sociology exam, or is he in addition making a point? If so, what is that point or thesis?

Vocabulary Study

1. How do Rivera's examples explain the word *abstractionitis?*
2. The *Dies irae* ("Day of Wrath") is a hymn describing Judgment Day, sometimes included in masses for the dead. What is the point of the reference?

3. Read the entry on *Vulcan* in a dictionary of classical mythology. Then explain the reference to Vulcan in paragraph 2.

Suggestions for Writing

1. Describe an exam you took, or a similar experience, and convey your feelings through your details and the tone of your description. Remember that your tone need not be the same throughout the essay.
2. Rivera shows how language, like the jargon or the directions quoted, sometimes creates barriers or difficulties in everyday situations. Discuss a barrier or difficulty that jargon or unclear directions created for you.

Description

Usually a narrative contains description of people and places—a drawing in words of what they look like. The narrator may pause to draw this picture, sometimes doing so in a few words and sometimes at greater length. Description is always spatial—the scene observed from a particular angle of vision. This angle may remain fixed or may change.

Robert Ramirez (p. 251) describes a barrio as most observers would see it, walking or driving through it at different times. Toward the beginning of his essay, he shows us the barrio as a whole—from a distant point of observation:

> Leaning from the expressway or jolting across the tracks, one enters a different physical world permeated by a different attitude. The physical dimensions are impressive. It is a large section of town which extends for fifteen blocks north and south along the tracks, and then advances eastward, thinning into nothingness beyond the city limits. Within the invisible (yet sensible) walls of the barrio, are many, many people living in too few houses. The homes, however, are much more numerous than on the outside.—"The Woolen Sarape"

This observation point changes in the course of the essay. In the following passage Ramirez shows us a neighborhood of the barrio at evening:

> In the evenings, the porches and front yards are occupied with men calmly talking over the noise of children playing base-ball in the unpaved extension of the living room, while the women cook supper or gossip with female neighbors as they water the *jardines*. The gardens mutely echo the expressive verses of the colorful houses. The denseness of multicolored plants and trees gives the house the appearance of an oasis or a tropical island hideaway, sheltered from the rest of the world.

42

The point of observation is closer to the scene than in the first passage. We are closer to the houses of the barrio—close enough to see what the people are doing. Ramirez is showing us the barrio as any observer would see it if sensitive to the special qualities of the barrio world.

Description is an essential part of every kind of writing. An expository essay on auto repair may include a description of some of the tools or the workplace. A persuasive essay may give us a picture of the people the writer wants us to help. The expressive essay centers on the writer primarily; a descriptive passage may therefore be colored by the writer's personal feelings. For example, not every student entering the classroom described by Edward Rivera would see it as Rivera does (see p. 37). The point of view in a descriptive passage may be an objective one, as in the Ramirez paragraphs, though no two observers will notice or stress the same details. Or, as in Rivera, the point of view may be a subjective one, shaped by and expressive of personal feelings.

Maya Angelou

PICKING COTTON

Maya Angelou was born Marguerite Johnson in 1928. When her parents separated, the three-year-old girl traveled with her brother from California to Stamps, Arkansas, to live with her grandmother. The woman Angelou called "Momma" owned the only black general store in town. Angelou and her brother later returned to California to live with their mother. During her long career, she has worked in the theater and television as a dancer, an actress, and a producer. She served as Northern Coordinator of the Southern Christian Leadership Conference, traveled in Africa, and taught school and wrote for newspapers in Egypt and Ghana. On her return to the United States, she wrote for television. Angelou has written several autobiographies and several volumes of poetry, collected in *Maya Angelou: Poetry.* Her description of black cotton pickers in Stamps is a self-contained section from her first autobiography, *I Know Why the Caged Bird Sings* (1969).

Each year I watched the field across from the Store turn 1 caterpillar green, then gradually frosty white. I knew exactly how long it would be before the big wagons would pull into the front yard and load on the cotton pickers at daybreak to carry them to the remains of slavery's plantations.

During the picking season my grandmother would get   2
out of bed at four o'clock (she never used an alarm clock)
and creak down to her knees and chant in a sleep-filled voice,
"Our Father, thank you for letting me see this New Day.
Thank you that you didn't allow the bed I lay on last night
to be my cooling board, nor my blanket my winding sheet.
Guide my feet this day along the straight and narrow, and
help me to put a bridle on my tongue. Bless this house, and
everybody in it. Thank you, in the name of your Son, Jesus
Christ, Amen."

Before she had quite arisen, she called our names and   3
issued orders, and pushed her large feet into homemade slippers and across the bare lye-washed wooden floor to light
the coal-oil lamp.

The lamplight in the Store gave a soft make-believe feel-   4
ing to our world which made me want to whisper and walk
about on tiptoe. The odors of onions and oranges and kerosene had been mixing all night and wouldn't be disturbed
until the wooded slat was removed from the door and the
early morning air forced its way in with the bodies of people
who had walked miles to reach the pickup place.

"Sister, I'll have two cans of sardines."   5

"I'm gonna work so fast today I'm gonna make you   6
look like you standing still."

"Lemme have a hunk uh cheese and some sody crack-   7
ers."

"Just gimme a coupla them fat peanut paddies." That   8
would be from a picker who was taking his lunch. The greasy
brown paper sack was stuck behind the bib of his overalls.
He'd use the candy as a snack before the noon sun called
the workers to rest.

In those tender mornings the Store was full of laughing,   9
joking, boasting and bragging. One man was going to pick
two hundred pounds of cotton, and another three hundred.
Even the children were promising to bring home fo' bits and
six bits. The champion picker of the day before was the hero
of the dawn. If he prophesied that the cotton in today's field
was going to be sparse and stick to the bolls like glue, every
listener would grunt a hearty agreement. The sound of the

empty cotton sacks dragging over the floor and the murmurs of waking people were sliced by the cash register as we rang up the five-cent sales.

If the morning sounds and smells were touched with the supernatural, the late afternoon had all the features of the normal Arkansas life. In the dying sunlight the people dragged, rather than their empty cotton sacks. Brought back to the Store, the pickers would step out of the backs of trucks and fold down, dirt-disappointed, to the ground. No matter how much they had picked, it wasn't enough. Their wages wouldn't even get them out of debt to my grandmother, not to mention the staggering bill that waited on them at the white commissary downtown.

The sounds of the new morning had been replaced with grumbles about cheating houses, weighted scales, snakes, skimpy cotton and dusty rows. In later years I was to confront the stereotyped picture of gay song-singing cotton pickers with such inordinate rage that I was told even by fellow Blacks that my paranoia was embarrassing. But I had seen the fingers cut by the mean little cotton bolls, and I had witnessed the backs and shoulders and arms and legs resisting any further demands.

Some of the workers would leave their sacks at the Store to be picked up the following morning, but a few had to take them home for repairs. I winced to picture them sewing the coarse material under a coal-oil lamp with fingers stiffening from the day's work. In too few hours they would have to walk back to Sister Henderson's Store, get vittles and load, again, onto the trucks. Then they would face another day of trying to earn enough for the whole year with the heavy knowledge that they were going to end the season as they started it. Without the money or credit necessary to sustain a family for three months. In cotton-picking time the late afternoons revealed the harshness of Black Southern life, which in the early morning had been softened by nature's blessing of grogginess, forgetfulness and the soft lamplight.

Comment

Angelou combines narration with description, beginning with her grandmother's rising at four o'clock in the morning and ending with a picture of workers mending their sacks under coal-oil lamps at night. Descriptive details at the beginning suggest the "soft make-believe feeling": "The odors of onions and oranges and kerosene had been mixing all night and wouldn't be disturbed until the wooded slat was removed from the door"; the sounds and smells of morning "were touched with the supernatural," she tells us in a later passage. In contrast to the morning, the late afternoon is harsh and ordinary, and she gives details of that world in the remaining paragraphs. The concluding sentence of the essay combines these impressions.

Questions for Study and Discussion

1. What details in the essay suggest "nature's blessing of grogginess, forgetfulness and the soft lamplight"? Why are these a blessing? What other details suggest the "features of the normal Arkansas life"?
2. How does Angelou suggest the influence of that world on her feelings about her race?
3. How do the details contradict a stereotype of the Southern black? How does Angelou remind us of that stereotype? What other stereotypes is she possibly criticizing?
4. Is her main purpose in writing to challenge this stereotype?
5. What personal qualities does Angelou stress in her description of her grandmother? What does this description contribute to the picture of Southern black life?
6. What mistaken picture or stereotype of a group—perhaps teenagers or high-school athletes—could you correct through a similar description?
7. What impression do you get of Angelou as a person, judging from the qualities of people she writes about and the things in her world that catch her eye?

Vocabulary Study

1. Which words in the essay are colloquial (words used conversationally and informally)?

2. What is *paranoia,* and how does Angelou use the word in paragraph 11?

Suggestions for Writing

1. Describe an aspect of your childhood or adolescence that tells the reader something important about your upbringing. Build your details to a statement of your controlling idea as Angelou does.
2. Describe one of your childhood or adolescent experiences from two points of view—that of the child and that of the young adult remembering the experience. Then comment on the differences between what the child or adolescent remembers and what the young adult understands. Use these differences to state a thesis.
3. Discuss a stereotype that shaped your view of other people or of yourself. Explain how you came to hold the stereotype, and how you discovered its falseness.

Example

An example is a picture or illustration of an idea. In explaining ideas, we fit our examples to the knowledge and experience of our readers or listeners. In explaining to a child that points of light in the night sky are really very large distant objects, we first have to explain why large objects can appear small. An example suited to the child's experience might be a ball that seems to get smaller as it flies through the air. In explaining to college physics students why the space of the universe is said to be "curved," a professor draws on mathematical formulas and scientific observations, but for the person who knows little or nothing about science, the professor would look for analogies in everyday experience.

The word *example* carries the meaning of typical: that is, the example represents the many occurrences or forms of the idea. Examples are essential in exposition, particularly to the explanation of complex ideas. For instance, it would be difficult to explain the following idea without an example:

> The attitude that produces the pseudo-technical tone is made up of a desire to dignify the subject and the writer, coupled with the belief that important matters require a special vocabulary.— Jacques Barzun, *Simple and Direct*

Barzun provides this example of pseudo-technical tone:

> I am sorry not to be able to accept the experience of more intensive interaction with your group and its constituency.

No amount of definition and descriptive detail can replace an effective example such as this. At the same time, many examples do require explanation or analysis, particularly when the idea is a complex one.

Tom Wicker

"COURT DAY" IN MOORE COUNTY, NORTH CAROLINA

Tom Wicker was born and raised in Hamlet, North Carolina, and studied journalism at the University of North Carolina, graduating in 1946. He worked as a sports editor, feature editor, and correspondent for several Southern newspapers, including the *Nashville Tennessean,* and in 1960 began working for *The New York Times.* From 1964 to 1968 he was the *Times* Washington bureau chief, and he has been associate editor of the newspaper since 1968. Wicker's novels include *The Judgment* (1961) and *Facing the Lions* (1973); his non-fictional books include *JFK and LBJ: The Influence of Personality Upon Politics* (1968), *A Time to Die* (1975), on the Attica prison uprising, and *On Press* (1978), from which this essay is reprinted.

Monday was "court day" in Moore County, North Carolina, in 1949, and I regularly spent it at the county seat, Carthage, as correspondent for the *Sandhill Citizen,* of Aberdeen, North Carolina (population 1603). I reserved most of the afternoon for peddling ads—another of my duties— to the Carthage merchants, in keen competition with the county seat weekly, the *Moore County News.* On first arrival at the courthouse in the morning, I checked with the register of deeds, the clerk of court, the sheriff, and other officials for suits newly filed, big property transfers, scandalous foreclosures, heinous crimes, and the like; then I laboriously copied down births, deaths, and marriages of note. Later I hastened to the courtroom, where County Judge Leland McKeithen dispensed evenhanded justice, or something as close to it as anything I've seen since.

That courtroom was rank with the enduring follies and foibles of mankind. It was segregated still, and in the summer months sweltering in the harsh dry heat of the North Carolina Sandhills in the days before universal air conditioning. But it provided a generous education in human nature, lawyers' tricks, oratory, and the law itself—in roughly that order. I witnessed court actions involving murders, manslaughters, crimes of property too numerous to define, vagrancies, seductions, desertions, auto offenses of every variety, bitterly disputed wills, breaches of promise and peace, recoveries of damage, alienations of affection, assaults, rapes, batteries, break-ins, reckless endangerments, ad infinitum. It seemed natural enough to me in the South of the 1940s that most defendants, and most victims, were black.

One divorce case—that of a white couple—had a particular impact on me, although I scarcely recall its details. They involved one party futilely chasing the other with an ax. The story plaintively related from the witness stand by the complainant, a worn-out woman with a ZaSu Pitts voice, haggard eyes, and hair just beginning to go gray, was the human comedy at its most ribald and perverse—Moore County transported to Chaucer's time and *The Canterbury Tales*. The spectators scattered around the courtroom, the press—another reporter and I—at its privileged table, even occasionally Judge McKeithen, rocked with laughter. The conclusion was foregone—divorce granted, with a fine crack of the gavel.

That was Monday. That afternoon, I hawked the *Citizen's* ad space, probably to no better effect than usual. The next day, armed with copious notes, I turned out a humorous account of the divorce case for my long lead over the agate type that summed up the other court cases ("Lonzo McNair, Star Route, Carthage, failure to observe stop sign, costs of court"; "A. C. Overby, Vermont Avenue, Southern Pines, aggravated assault, continued to Superior Court") and sent it back to the *Citizen's* ever-clacking Linotype machine (in a small shop in the days before offset printing, it was mandatory to keep "the machine" running, both to make the thing pay and to keep the lead pot from "freezing").

On Thursday, putting on my editor's hat, I wrote a two-column head for my court story and scheduled it for page one, above the fold—top play in the *Citizen* as in any other newspaper. We went to press routinely that night, got the mail copies to the post office in the nick of time, and went off for a few late beers.

Working late justified sleeping late; and when I dragged   6
myself into the *Citizen* office about noon the next day, I
had a visitor: a worn-out looking woman with a ZaSu Pitts
voice, but whose once-haggard eyes were blazing, whose
fluttering hands were clenched into fists, and whose graying
hair—I suddenly saw at range closer than that of the witness
stand—was that of a woman not too many years older than
I, who not too long before probably had been considered a
peach by the boys in her high school class.

"Mr. Wicker," she said without preamble, "why did   7
you think you had the right to make fun out of me in your
paper?"

I have never forgotten that question—and I still can't   8
answer it. In 1949 I doubt if I even tried. I remember thinking I had not bargained for such awful moments when I had
landed my first reporter's job a few months before. Accurate
though my story had been, and based on a public record, it
had nevertheless exploited human unhappiness for the
amusement or titillation of others. I had made the woman
in my office something less than what she was—a human
being possessed, despite her misfortunes, of real dignity.

Seeing that, I saw too that I had not only done her an   9
injury but missed the story I should have written. This is
one of the besetting sins of journalism—sensationalism at
the expense of the dignity and truth of the common human
experience. I have been fortunate to have worked mostly for
publishers and editors who sought to avoid that sin—not
always successfully. And reading some of the more lurid
journals, I've often thought that sensationalism and gossip
columns tend to be techniques employed mostly by big-
circulation publications for an anonymous audience. Not
many editors and reporters would be callous or unseeing
enough to engage in them if they had to face the victims the
next morning over a battered desk in an office not much
bigger than a closet.

Comment

Our understanding of the concluding paragraph depends on the example Wicker develops: without it the "sensationalism" that he refers to would be a vague term. In developing his example, Wicker gives us the setting as well as some of the important details—enough of them to make his point. Had he given all of them, the focus would have shifted from his own experience as a young reporter to the woman and the divorce hearing.

Questions for Study and Discussion

1. What information about the divorce does Wicker include, and what details show why he found it funny? What other aspects of the case might he have included had he wished to focus on its humor?
2. How does the episode reveal the "sensationalism" that Wicker refers to in the final paragraph?
3. What personal qualities does Wicker reveal in his account of the episode? Which of these qualities does he want to stress?
4. Is Wicker saying that the divorce was not newsworthy and should not have been reported?

Vocabulary Study

Use your dictionary to explain how Wicker uses the following words: paragraph 1: *heinous, dispensed;* paragraph 2: *foibles, sweltering, vagrancies;* paragraph 3: *ribald, perverse;* paragraph 4: *copious, linotype;* paragraph 8: *exploit, titillation;* paragraph 9: *lurid, callous.*

Suggestions for Writing

1. The character of a newspaper is often revealed by its front page—by what news, what pictures, what headlines the front page includes. Analyze the front page of a paper you read regularly to define its character. Do not try to describe everything on the page. Focus on key details.

2. We have all had experiences like Wicker's in which we made important discoveries about ourselves. Discuss one such experience of your own, giving enough details to let the reader discover what you did. Draw a conclusion from your example.

Process

Another important method of developing ideas is process analysis. A *process* is any activity or operation that contains steps which are usually performed in sequence. It may be a mechanical one, like changing a tire, or a natural one, like the circulation of the blood. The process referred to in the following statement is a natural one:

> Just as human individuals and populations undergo continual alteration in response to infectious disease, so also the various infectious organisms that provoke disease undergo a process of adaptation and adjustment to their environment.—William H. McNeill, *Plagues and Peoples*

These are two common types of process analysis.

A third type deals with a historical process—one that occurred in the past, and can occur again, according to identifiable causes and effects. In the following passage on bubonic plague, McNeill identifies both:

> First, the steamship network that arose in the 1870s was the vehicle that dispersed the infection around the globe, and did so, once the epidemic broke out in Canton and Hong Kong, with a speed that was limited only by the speed with which a ship could carry its colony of infected rats and fleas to a new port. Speed was obviously decisive in allowing a chain of infection to remain unbroken from port to port. Since it creates immunities among survivors, *Pasteurella pestis* was, after all, certain to run out of susceptible hosts among a ship's company of rats, fleas, and men within a few weeks.

Whether mechanical, natural, or historical, the steps of a process are usually described chronologically. In mechanical processes, you may have a choice of procedures or tools, and you may decide to describe more than one of these—for example, you may discuss several kinds of tire jacks and how they work. In the course of explanation, you may have to define and illustrate key terms, make comparisons, and comment on the uses of the process.

Many processes like the transmission of plague are complex: they contain several related processes, each of which must be carefully distinguished. For example, the instruction book that gives directions for wiring a stereo receiver and a tape deck to a turntable and speakers describes each process step by step. Assembling a receiver from a kit is even more complex a procedure.

Maxine Kumin

BUILDING FENCE

Born in Philadelphia, Maxine Kumin attended Radcliffe College and later taught at Brandeis and other universities. A novelist and poet, Kumin won the Pulitzer Prize for Poetry in 1973 for *Up Country.* In her collection of essays *In Deep,* she writes about her life in Warner, New Hampshire, where she and her husband live on a farm they cleared and fenced. The job of fencing is the subject of the essay reprinted here. Kumin describes her farm in another essay, "A Sense of Place":

> When I look left or right, I yearn for pastures with daisies and black-eyed Susans, hawkweed and Indian paintbrush visible at the far edges. Fields someone has paid attention to. The terrain is too hilly for mechanized equipment except for our ancient Gravely walk-behind rotary mower and the jackhammer-heavy weed whacker. It is the surprise of clearings come upon in the midst of tangled, second-growth forest. These New England upland pastures are like a secret garden, like the impulse toward a poem. Every dip and scarp is engraved now on my brainpan.

Making fences presupposes not only pastures but a storehouse of diligence. When you start from a tangle of sumac and blackberry, every reclaimed square yard seems more precious than an acre of riverbottom land. For a dozen years we've been pushing back the forest, clearing, seeding, and sustaining what now adds up to fourteen up-and-down acres of the once two hundred-odd that nurtured a dairy herd between the two world wars.

Building the fence itself is an imperfect science. Despite actual measurements, you have to yield to the contours of the land. Post holes are soul destroyers. Technology hasn't done much for the fence line on a hill farm. Even if you hire a neighbor's tractor with auger attachment, at least half the holes will have to be hand crafted as you ease them this side or that of expectation. Stones annoy, rocks impede, boulders break your heart as you tunnel down at a slant, hunting in vain for the earth bottom. If obdurate ledge or obstinate pudding stone does not require acts of faith and leaps of imagination, here and there you can count on a slope too steep for machinery to navigate. The gasoline-powered two-man auger is more adaptable, but even that ingenious tool will not maneuver between stump and bedrock with the same agility as the old manual clamshell tool.

Setting the posts exacts more faith from the dogged fence-pilgrim. Somehow there is never enough dirt in the pile you took out, even after you've placed a ring of stones in the bottom of the hole to brace the post. Even with a ring of stones stomped in nearly at the top for further support, your supply of loose dirt has vanished. You end up digging part of a second hole to make enough friable earth to hold the first pole solid. Clearly, you do not come out even. 3

You've set 225 posts, roughly ten feet apart. From an appropriate distance, if you squint, it's merely a toothpick stockade, inconclusive and raw-looking. You long to get on with it, to establish the feeling of fence, the ethos of enclosure. 4

The best part of building the fence is tacking up the string that denotes where the line of top boards means to be. You go around importantly to do this light work, trailing your ball of twine, wearing your apron of nails. You measure with your fold-up rule fifty-two inches from the ground—but where exactly *is* the ground? This mound, this declivity, this solitary flat patch? You tap in a nail, pull the string taut from the previous post, catch it with a few easy twists around, and so on. String stands in for wood, a notion, a suggestion of what's to come. Foreshadowing, you could call it. 5

Because this is New England, the fence travels uphill and down; only little bits of it are on the level. Although string lightheartedly imitates the contours of the land, boards 6 have to be held in place, the angle of cut defined by pencil. Invariably, both ends of the boards want cutting. The eye wants readjustments despite the ruler. Sometimes bottom boards catch on hummocks, outcroppings, or earth bulges which must be shoveled out or the board rearranged. But let's say you've tacked up your whole top line for the day, you've stepped back, eyeballed and readjusted it. Oh, the hammering home! The joy and vigor of sending nails through hemlock into the treated four-by-four uprights. Such satisfying whacks, such permanence, such vengeance against the mass bustications of horses and heifers through the puny electric wire of yore. Visions of acres and acres of fences, field after field tamed, groomed, boarded in; that is the meaning of gluttony.

Finishing the fence—painting, staining, or applying pre- 7
servative—requires the same constancy as the slow crafting of it. You put in your two hours a day, rejoice when rain interrupts the schedule and your Calvinist soul is permitted to tackle some other chore. Cleaning tack, for example, provides a pleasurable monotony compared to the servitude of the four-inch roller and the can of Noxious Mixture. In our case, it's composed of one-third diesel oil, one-third used crankcase oil, and one-third creosote. You are properly garbed to apply this Grade C syrup, wearing cast-off overalls, a battered felt hat, decayed boots, and thick neoprene gloves. You stand almost an arm's length away from the fence in order to get enough leverage so the mixture will penetrate wood grain—here tough, there smooth, here cracked and warty, there slick as a duck's feather. You invent methods for relieving the dreary sameness of the job. On one course you begin left to right, top to bottom, back to front. On the next you reverse the order. Sometimes you do all the undersides first, or all the backs. Sometimes you spring ahead, lavishly staining all the front-facing boards just to admire the dark wood lines dancing against the hummocky terrain of these young—yea, virginal—fields. The process gets you in the shoulder blades, later in the knees. You spatter freckles of the stuff on your protected body. Your protective eyeglasses are now freckled with iridescent dots. The stench of the mix

permeates your hair, your gloved hands, becomes a way of life. You can no longer gain a new day without putting in your two hours staining board fences. More compelling than tobacco or alcohol, that addictive odor of char, of disinfectant, of grease pits. The horses follow you along the fence line, curious, but even the fresh-faced filly keeps a respectful distance from you and your repellent mixture.

A year later you sit atop the remnants of a six-foot-wide stone wall unearthed along the perimeter of number two field and look across to the remarkable pear tree that stands alone in the third and newest field. Behind you, the first field; behind it, the barn. Between fields, hedgerow and hickory trees, red pine and hemlock. An intermittent brook further defines the boundary between number one and number two. A tributary meanders at the foot of number three. Beyond, a lifetime of second-growth woodland awaits. In your mind's eye, an infinity of fenced fields recedes but never vanishes. And all the livestock of a lifetime safely graze.

Comment

Maxine Kumin describes the process of fencing pastures in rocky soil. Since she is not writing a set of directions for people wanting to perform the same job, she omits details and steps the fence builder needs to know. Like Thoreau in his account of his experiences at Walden Pond, Kumin shows that a common job can be an extraordinary experience if one has the imagination to make it such. Her sentences convey information, but the construction of the sentence and phrasing frequently give us the feel of the experience by imitating the particular step or process Kumin is describing:

> Stones annoy, rocks impede, boulders break your heart as you tunnel down at a slant, hunting in vain for the earth bottom.

Kumin chooses words that are expressive as well as exact.

Questions for Study and Discussion

1. What is Kumin's purpose in writing, and how do you know?
2. If Kumin had been writing a set of directions on fencing pas-

tures, what additional details would she have provided about digging post holes?

3. What makes building fences "an imperfect science"? Are the tools for building fences inadequate for the job? Does the science of fence building depend on adequate tools?

4. Is Kumin writing for a special audience familiar with the process she describes, or for a general audience unfamiliar with it? How do you know?

5. Does Kumin give sufficient detail about how to fix the line for the top boards?

6. What one or more steps in fencing pastures does she omit from her account, and why does she?

7. On what step or procedure does Kumin give the most detail? Why do you think she does?

8. A year later, why does Kumin see "an infinity of fenced fields" receding but never vanishing? What is the meaning of the final statement, "And all the livestock of a lifetime safely graze"?

Vocabulary Study

1. How is an auger different from a clamshell tool?

2. Identify and explain the metaphors in the following statement: "Setting the posts exacts more faith from the dogged fence-pilgrim" (paragraph 3).

3. Kumin refers to "the mass bustications of horses and heifers" in paragraph 5. You will not find *bustication* in your college dictionary. What do you think the word means? On what in the paragraph do you base your answer?

4. What is a "Calvinist soul," and what is Kumin saying about it in paragraph 6?

Suggestions for Writing

1. Describe the pleasures and frustrations you have experienced in building or repairing something. Give enough details about the process to let your audience experience what you did.

2. Describe the same process in enough detail that someone who has never performed it can do so. Assume that this person is unfamiliar with the tools required.

Comparison and Contrast

Like definition and division, comparison and contrast is an important method of analysis in exposition. *Comparison* deals with similarities, *contrast* with differences. In comparing, you show what two or more people or objects or places have in common; in contrasting, how they are unlike. There are many ways of organizing paragraphs or essays of comparison or contrast. One way is the block listing of the qualities of the first person or place, then the block listing of the qualities of the second—in the same order:

> Chicago, at the southern tip of Lake Michigan, is a port city and an important commercial and industrial center of the Middle West. It is also an important educational, cultural, and recreational center, drawing thousands to its concert halls, art museum, and sports arenas. Cleveland, on the south shore of Lake Erie, is also a port city and a commercial and industrial center important to its area. Like Chicago, it has several important colleges and universities, a distinguished symphony orchestra, one of the fine art museums of the world, and many recreational centers. The location of the two cities undoubtedly contributed to their growth, but this similarity is not sufficient to explain their wide social diversity. (paragraph of comparison)

A second way is an alternating comparison or contrast, point by point:

> Chicago is on the southern tip of Lake Michigan; Cleveland, on the south shore of Lake Erie. Both are important commercial and industrial centers of the Middle West, and both offer a wide range of educational, cultural, and recreational activities. . . .

In developing such paragraphs or essays, transitions like *similarly, likewise, by comparison,* and *by contrast* may be needed to clarify the organization. The purpose of comparison and contrast is usually to provide a relative estimate: we discover the qualities of the first person or object or place through the qualities of the second (or third), and the qualities of the second through the first. If Cleveland and Chicago share these characteristics and have the same history of growth, we are better able to understand the causes that shape cities. A contrast with Atlanta or Omaha—large inland cities—would clarify these causes further through a similar relative estimate.

Noel Perrin

CLASS STRUGGLE IN THE WOODS

Noel Perrin graduated from Williams College in 1949 and later did graduate work at Duke and Cambridge universities. Since 1959, Perrin has taught English at Dartmouth College, in Hanover, New Hampshire, and has farmed in nearby Vermont. His numerous essays on Vermont life are collected in *First Person Rural: Essays of a Sometime Farmer* (1978) and later books. In the essay reprinted here from *Third Person Rural* (1983), Perrin compares two Vermont social classes and their diverse interests. Perrin reveals much about his own interests and background in the course of his discussion.

Americans are notoriously hard to divide along class 1
lines. With the exception of professors of sociology (who know exactly where in the upper middle class they fit) and a few billionaires—who hope they are upper-class, but have a horrible fear there may be a real aristocracy hiding somewhere in Boston or Philadelphia—most of us have only the vaguest idea what class we belong to.

American sports are notoriously even harder to classify 2
than most activities. I mean more than the obvious fact that rich and poor rub shoulders at baseball games, or that a carload of Cornell professors may turn up at a quite grubby boxing match, having driven four hours to get there. I mean that even where myth says there is a distinction, it won't stand up under examination. Myth says, for example, that people with yachts are upper-class and people with motorboats aren't. Myth is full of it. The board of directors of

any large corporation is likely to contain some old poop who owns a yacht and another old poop who is commodore of a power squadron. Sometimes it's even the same old poop at different stages of his career. Similarly, one and the same lower-income family on the Maine coast is likely enough to own both a little motorboat and a little sailboat.

There is one exception to all this camaraderie. At least   3
there is in New England. The two winter sports of snow-mobiling and cross-country skiing split along class lines so sharply that if I were a sociologist engaged in classifying some little town in Massachusetts or Vermont, I wouldn't even bother to study residence patterns or sexual habits. I'd just wait for winter. Then I'd hang around in the woods and see who came humping by on skis and who roared past on a snow machine. I could divide that town in one day, pro-vided snow conditions were good.

Why cross-country skiing and snowmobiling reflect class   4
lines so perfectly is not easy to figure out. Certainly it is not a conscious act of group loyalty. No one says, "Hm, I run the town dump, so I'd better get a snow machine," or "Well, I *was* a Wellesley drop-out; I need some knickers and a pair of Finnish touring skis."

It is tempting to think it must have something to do   5
with instant gratification versus patience and discipline. After all, what is supposed to characterize middle-class behavior is the ability to defer pleasure. Give a lower-class type a thousand dollars, and he blows it in three days, the theory goes; whereas if you give a middle-class person the thou-sand, he invests it at fourteen percent. Then six months later he blows the interest. (Unless he's *really* committed to bour-geois values, in which case he waits thirty-five years, and then spends the interest on the interest.)

But that won't wash. It's true enough that you can leap   6
on a snowmobile as a total novice and vroom right off, while the technique of cross-country takes some acquiring. But it's also true that the snowmobiler may be a devoted pool player as well, and he devoted plenty of time to learning *that*. Or he may have put in hundreds or even thousands of hours

practicing basketball shots, punting technique, you name it, all in hopes of future glory. Some other principle is at work.

Could it be the well-known theory of compensation? 7
This says that the poor, leading relatively powerless lives, make up for it as much as they can by owning powerful machines. The more menial your job, the greater your desire to spend your spare time scaring the wits out of people with your huge motorcycle. Or dominating the woods with your snowmobile.

That won't wash, either. *All* classes in America like 8
powerful machinery. People with very unmenial jobs still get excited about Mercedes-Benzes, and like to dominate the fast lanes. The really rich go in for private jets. We need a third principle.

I suspect, though I can't prove it, that the real reason is 9
that both snowmobiling and cross-country skiing started as rural sports. And to the rural mind the key difference is that one is a great deal more work than the other.

A countryman's life consists, basically, of an endless 10
amount of physical activity. You get up early in the morning in order to do the chores: feeding livestock, milking, cleaning the barn, etc. As soon as chores are finished, you go off to fix fence. As soon as that's done, you climb on the tractor and start mowing rowen. Since it's just one of the givens that you are going to be tired every night, you never waste a movement if you can help it. It is for this reason that summer people are sometimes amazed and even scornful to see a native who is cutting wood throw his chainsaw in a truck and drive three hundred yards back into the woods where he is working. *They* would have walked, carrying the saw, saving gas, observing the beauties of nature. They are environmentalists; he's a clod. Actually, he's just saving a little extra energy for splitting wood.

It is this Principle of Conservation of Energy, I think, 11
that originally determined who rode snowmobiles and who put on the cross-countries. In the old days, rural people simply didn't go out much in the winter—except to bring in wood and do chores. They could have; they had surplus time

and energy both. The work of a farm is lightest in the winter. But the principle is deeply ingrained, and their instinctive preference was to hang around the house, being bored if necessary, rather than go out and do a lot of hard slogging through the snow in pursuit of something as ephemeral as mere pleasure. It is for the same reason that Midwestern grain farmers, who are richer and don't have chores, tend to go to Florida in the winter. Florida is essentially the big house around which they hang, until it's time for spring planting.

Then snowmobiles came along. "Ski-doos" they were   12
first called in New England, after the original Canadian make. Every person in the country perked up his or her head. I stress "her" because ski-doos were especially appealing to rural wives. All spring, summer, and fall they were used to working as hard in the house (and sometimes the barn, too) as their husbands did out in the fields and woods. With so much cooking to do, lots of them became pretty hefty women.

Now suddenly here was a way to go effortlessly out in   13
the winter—and not only that, you're riding on the same machine with your husband. A second honeymoon! The two of you may revisit, traveling at high speed up the mountain-sides, places you once picnicked when you were carefree courting youngsters. I know one elderly farm couple in Vermont, avid snowmobilers, who particularly like to visit his old work sites. Fifty years ago, they were just married and didn't have a cent. It was in the depth of the great depression. He would be out chopping cordwood for two dollars a cord. She would walk all the way out to where he was, to bring him his dinner (which is what country people eat for lunch) in a pail. Now they whoosh out by snowmobile and recall old times.

But, of course, rural people are not the only ones who   14
live in the country. There are also large numbers of urbanites. There are the summer people, the young college graduates who have joined the counter-culture and moved here for good, the people with year-round second homes. Their working lives have been very different—mostly cooped up in offices. If they're tired at night, it's from too much mental

tension. Their bodies cry out for use. So their principle has been that when you have free time, you try to find a way to use up energy as rapidly as possible. (This is the true and original cause of jogging.)

Consequently, they tend to see the countryside as a sort 15 of enormous gymnasium, just as Midwestern farmers see Florida as an enormous living room. They naturally opt for skis. And their Principle of Hard Play, like the countryman's conservation of energy principle, applies even when the original conditions don't. The young back-to-the-landers aren't cooped up in offices; they're out logging with horses, or spading up a two-acre garden. But come the first big snow, they wouldn't dream of going out on a machine. Childhood conditioning is too strong. They snap on their skis, load a little backpack with gorp, and go out to spend even more energy.

I have been in an especially good position to observe all 16 this, because I happen to be right in the middle. I am one of perhaps ten people in my part of Vermont who is both a snowmobiler and a cross-country skier. I really like both sports. This reflects a deep division in my whole life. Half the time I am a middle-class teacher at Dartmouth, and the other half I am a working-class farmer. I mow fields on contract to summer people, sell wood and stack it for the customers, know what it's like to be one of the help. ("That's not where I told you to stack it," the lady informs me in a cool, regal voice; "move the pile behind the garage.") I am so deeply into rurality that my own childhood conditioning has almost been overcome.

There's just enough left, though, so that I understand 17 very well why cross-country skiers despise snowmobilers. Sometimes when I'm out on skis I do myself. Yes, snow machines are noisy. Smelly, too—fouling the crisp winter air with their exhausts. Yes, it's annoying to spend two hours skiing to some remote and peaceful ridge, alone or with a silent friend, and to think you are utterly away from everything—and suddenly a herd of nine snowmobilers roars up right behind you, and thunders on over the ridge, all but throwing beer cans at you as they pass. Maybe damaging the young forest growth without either knowing or caring. And, yes, it can just about wreck a weekend if some neighbor's nine-year-old child spends most of the daylight hours on daddy's machine, going monotonously round and round one field, wasting gas, forever gunning the engine, doing something very close to profaning the Sabbath. In such moods I reflect quite gleefully that as fuel prices continue to rise, snow machines may just up and vanish. At least in New England, they are already in decline. Ten years ago, there were 26,654 registered in Vermont. Five years ago, still building: there were 34,715. Now the number has shrunk to 22,107.

But when it's my own daughter out circling our own   18
back pasture, I feel quite differently. Then I admire the skill with which she takes sharp turns on a steep hillside, and the daring of her jumps. I love to see her shining eyes as she comes in from the kind of morning she wouldn't dream of spending on skis.

And when I go out myself, which is usually with a few   19
farmer friends and mechanics, there are two things I understand. One is the sheer pleasure of hurtling headlong across the landscape, and winding up in places one might otherwise never have reached in a lifetime. A clifftop two towns away, say, known to no one but the snowmobilers and an occasional hawk or owl. The damned skiers think we don't notice nature, because we're too busy steering our machines. What they don't realize is that we're usually going somewhere—a further place than *they're* likely to get—and when we reach it, we stop and dismount. Then we see everything. Especially the good views, since we go up a lot of hills. We know their landscape better than they do, as a rule. (A lot of skiers just shuffle around golf courses, anyway—jogging with flaps on their feet.)

The other thing I understand is just how infuriating the   20
middle class is, with its assumptions of moral superiority. They used to say we kept coal in our bathtubs. (If you have a stove right near the bathroom, it can be a handy place, too.) Then they criticized us for having big TV sets when we were poor, and buying expensive cars on time. They didn't

stop to reflect that if we didn't buy on time, they wouldn't be *getting* fourteen percent on their money. They need our installment payments to run their economy.

And now they scorn us for our snow machines. They're the ones who are aggressive, not us. If any of them are up here in the winter, they'll call the police in a minute if we go across a corner of "their" land. Even if, and perhaps especially if, it was land they bought from one of us about two years ago. They're the ones who pointedly avert their faces when we pass—do all but hold their noses. We're willing to share the outdoors with them, but they'd like to abolish us. (Though the ones that dare to venture off the golf courses and their little pre-arranged routes seem surprisingly often to take advantage of the trails we've packed down. Then they're outraged if one of us happens to come along our own trail that we made, while they're using it. They think they own that, too.) 21

I know what they say. They say we are perfectly welcome to be outdoors, but we should all learn to cross-country ski ourselves. Including Aunt Etty, who is sixty-eight, weighs 185, and has varicose veins. Maybe it would be better for Aunt Etty if she were only thirty-eight, weighed 125, and skied like an angel. But she's not an angel, she's a fat old lady who still works hard (she cleaned your house last week, skier), and this is the only way she'll ever be out here, and she loves it. 22

And you, you want to take her snow machine away, because it spoils your image of rural New England. It offends your eardrums. But you're smart, skier. You don't say that. You say in a sincere voice that she'd really be far happier, and in much better health, if she did high-energy sports like you. 23

One time one of you told us to eat cake, and that advice was just about as useful. 24

Comment

Noel Perrin writes about winter sports in Vermont from a double point of view. As a Dartmouth English professor and Vermont farmer, he belongs to both worlds—that of the middle-class skier and the working-class snowmobiler. He writes about the two groups with humor and insight, revealing American attitudes toward class. Although he discusses similarities between snowmobilers and cross-country skiers, his chief concern in the essay is with the differences. For these are central to his thesis. Perrin states his thesis early in the essay, but we do not understand it fully until he has completed his informal comparison.

Questions for Study and Discussion

1. Is Perrin writing a sociological analysis of Vermont winter sports? Or does he have another purpose in writing—perhaps to comment humorously on the character and life of Vermonters or Americans in general?
2. What is Perrin's thesis and where does it appear? Does Perrin restate the thesis in the course of the essay?
3. How does Perrin develop his thesis through his informal comparison between snowmobilers and cross-country skiers?
4. Is the comparison a block comparison or a point-by-point one? Or does Perrin employ both methods of organization?
5. Why are Americans "notoriously hard to divide along class lines"? What class lines does Perrin distinguish?
6. Does Perrin identify himself with middle-class cross-country skiers rather than with working-class snowmobilers? Or does he identify with both classes?
7. What does the analysis reveal about Vermont life? Does Perrin consider Vermonters typical of Americans? How do you know?
8. Can you think of other sports that reveal class differences? If so, are work habits the explanation for sport preferences, as in snowmobiling and cross-country skiing?

Vocabulary Study

Give the general dictionary meaning of the following words. Then explain the specific meaning of the word or phrase as used in the paragraph:

    a. *myth* (paragraph 2)
    b. *camaraderie* (paragraph 3)

c. *novice* (paragraph 6)
d. *compensation, menial* (paragraph 7)
e. *Principle of Conservation of Energy, ingrained, ephemeral* (paragraph 11)
f. *counter-culture* (paragraph 14)

Suggestions for Writing

1. Explain why you enjoy one sport more than another. If you enjoy two sports equally, describe the pleasures you derive from each. In the course of your discussion, compare and contrast the sports—noting similarities and differences.
2. Discuss another sport played by Americans that may reveal class differences. Explain why it does or does not.
3. Perrin describes the attitudes toward work in Vermont. Discuss whether these attitudes reflect your own or are the attitudes of people in your state or hometown.

Cause and Effect

Reasoning about *cause and effect* is often a simple matter of connecting two events. When I get wet during a thunderstorm, I know that rain is the cause. But making other connections is usually not this simple. If I catch a cold the same day, I may blame it on the rain. However, I might have caught a cold even if I had stayed indoors; and if I had been in the rain, the rain alone may not have been the single cause. A number of conditions together probably produced the cold: a run-down state arising from overwork or lack of sleep, poor eating habits, getting wet—these may have triggered a virus in the body.

The sum of these conditions is generally what we mean by *cause*. We ordinarily speak loosely of one of these conditions as the cause. Except where an immediate action (exposure to the storm) produces a direct consequence (getting wet), reasoning about cause and effect is probable rather than certain. Having identified conditions that produced colds in the past, I cannot be sure that they *must* produce one in the present. The identical conditions may be present, without producing a cold.

All discussions of cause and effect, formal and informal, include hidden or unstated assumptions or beliefs about people, society, the ways things happen in nature—human beings are naturally aggressive, adolescents are naturally rebellious, the Irish have hot tempers, the English are cold and reserved, opposites attract. Many who hold these beliefs unquestioningly seldom think about them, nor do they feel it necessary to test them through observation. In cause-and-effect reasoning such assumptions are hidden in the explanation and may be decisive.

Appletree Rodden

WHY SMALLER REFRIGERATORS CAN PRESERVE THE HUMAN RACE

Appletree Rodden did research in biochemistry at Stanford University and has been a member of the Staatstheater Ballet Company, in West Germany. His essay, first published in *Harper's* in 1974, is as timely today as it was when Americans were becoming aware of "the energy crisis."

1   Once, long ago, people had special little boxes called refrigerators in which milk, meat, and eggs could be kept cool. The grandchildren of these simple devices are large enough to store whole cows, and they reach temperatures comparable to those at the South Pole. Their operating costs increase each year, and they are so complicated that few home handymen attempt to repair them on their own.

2   Why has this change in size and complexity occurred in America? It has not taken place in many areas of the technologically advanced world (the average West German refrigerator is about a yard high and less than a yard wide, yet refrigeration technology in Germany is quite advanced). Do we really need (or even want) all that space and cold?

3   The benefits of a large refrigerator are apparent: a saving of time (one grocery-shopping trip a week instead of several), a saving of money (the ability to buy expensive, perishable items in larger, cheaper quantities), a feeling of security (if the car breaks down or if famine strikes, the refrigerator is well stocked). The costs are there, too, but they are not so obvious.

4   Cost number one is psychological. Ever since the refrigerator began to grow, food has increasingly become something we buy to store rather than to eat. Few families go to market daily for their daily bread. The manna in the wilderness could be gathered for only one day at a time. The ancient distaste for making food a storage item is echoed by many modern psychiatrists who suggest that such psychosomatic disorders as obesity are often due to the patient's

inability to come to terms with the basic transitoriness of life. Research into a relationship between excessive corpulence and the size of one's refrigerator has not been extensive, but we might suspect one to be there.

Another cost is aesthetic. In most of Europe, where grocery marketing is still a part of the daily rhythm, one can buy tomatoes, lettuce, and the like picked on the day of purchase. Many European families have modest refrigerators for storing small items (eggs, milk, butter) for a couple of days, but the concept of buying large quantities of food to store in the refrigerator is not widely accepted. Since fresh produce is easily available in Europe, most people buy it daily.

Which brings to mind another price the large refrigerator has cost us: the friendly neighborhood market. In America, time is money. A large refrigerator means fewer time-consuming trips to the grocery store. One member of a deep-freeze-owning family can do the grocery shopping once or twice a month rather than daily. Since shopping trips are infrequent, most people have been willing to forego the amenities of the little store around the corner in favor of the lower prices found in the supermarket.

If refrigerators weren't so large—that is, if grocery marketing were a daily affair—the "entertainment surcharge" of buying farm fresh food in a smaller, more intimate setting might carry some weight. But as it is, there is not really that much difference between eggs bought from Farmer Brown's wife and eggs bought from the supermarket which in turn bought them from Eggs Incorporated, a firm operated out of Los Angeles that produces 200,000 eggs a day from chickens that are kept in gigantic warehouses lighted artificially on an eighteen-hour light-and-dark cycle and produce one-and-a-half times as many eggs—a special breed of chickens who die young and insane. Not much difference if you don't mind eating eggs from crazy chickens.

Chalk up Farmer and Mrs. Brown as cost number four of the big refrigerator. The small farmer can't make it in a society dominated by supermarkets and big refrigerators; make way for superfarmers, super yields, and pesticides (cost number five).

Cost number six of the big refrigerator has been the   9
diminution of regional food differences. Of course the homogenization of American fare cannot be blamed solely on
the availability of frozen food. Nonetheless, were it not for
the trend toward turning regional specialties into frozen din-
ners, it might still be possible to experience novelty closer to
home.

So much for the disadvantages of the big refrigerator.   10
What about the advantages of the small one? First of all, it
would help us to "think small," which is what we must learn
anyway if the scary predictions of the Club of Rome (*The
Limits of Growth*) are true. The advent of smaller refrigerators would set the stage for reversing the "big-thinking"
trends brought on with the big refrigerator, and would eventually change our lives.

Ivan Illich makes the point in *Tools for Conviviality*   11
that any tool we use (the automobile, standardized public
education, public-health care, the refrigerator) influences the
individual, his society, and the relationship between the two.
A person's automobile is a part of his identity. The average
Volkswagen owner has a variety of characteristics (income,
age, occupation) significantly different from those of the average Cadillac owner. American society, with more parking
lots than parks, and with gridded streets rather than winding lanes, would be vastly different without the private automobile. Similar conclusions can be drawn about any of
the tools we use. They change us. They change our society.
Therefore, it behooves us to think well before we decide which
tool to use to accomplish a given task. Do we want tools
that usurp power unto themselves, the ones called "non-
convivial" by Illich?

The telephone, a "convivial tool," has remained under   12
control; it has not impinged itself on society or on the individual. Each year it has become more efficient, and it has
not prevented other forms of communication (letter writing,
visits). The world might be poorer without the telephone,
but it would not be grossly different. Telephones do not pol-
lute, are not status symbols, and interact only slightly (if at
all) with one's self-image.

So what about the refrigerator? Or back to the more   13
basic problem to which the refrigerator was a partial answer: what about our supply of food? When did we decide
to convert the emotion-laden threat of starvation from a
shared community problem (of societal structure: farm-
market-home) to a personal one (of storage)? How did we
decide to accept a thawed block taken from a supermarket's
freezer as a substitute for the voluptuous shapes, smells, and
textures of fresh fruits and vegetables obtained from complex individual sources?

The decision for larger refrigerators has been consistent   14
with a change in food-supply routes from highly diversified
"trails" (from small farms to neighborhood markets) to uniform, standardized highways (from large farms to centrally
located supermarkets). Desirable meals are quick and easy
rather than rich and leisurely. Culinary artistry has given
way to efficiency, the efficiency of the big refrigerator.

People have a natural propensity for running good things   15
into the ground. Mass production has been a boon to mankind, but its reliance on homogeneity precludes its being a
paradigm for all areas of human life. Our forebears and
contemporaries have made it possible to mass-produce almost anything. An equally challenging task now lies with
us: to choose which things of this world should be mass-
produced, and how the standards of mass production should
influence other standards we hold dear.

Should houses be mass-produced? Should education?   16
Should food? Which brings us back to refrigerators. How
does one decide how large a refrigerator to buy, considering
one's life, one's society, and the world, and not simply the
question of food storage?

As similar questions are asked about more and more of   17
the things we mass-produce, mass production will become
less of a problem and more of a blessing. As cost begins to
be measured not only in dollars spent and minutes saved,
but in total richness acquired, perhaps smaller refrigerators
will again make good sense. A small step backward along
some of the roads of "technological progress" might be a
large step forward for mankind, and one our age is uniquely
qualified to make.

Comment

If Rodden were trying to persuade West German readers to buy large refrigerators, the benefits they provide would be emphasized. Writing to persuade Americans to give up large refrigerators, he focuses on one cause of their preference for them, the attitude that "time is money." If this attitude is a necessary condition of the American preference—that is, a condition that must be present for this preference to exist—attacking the attitude may help to diminish the incentive. Rodden attacks this attitude by showing the disadvantages of thinking about life in this way; these include the sacrifice of fresh food and the fun of buying it, the gradual disappearance of the small farmer, the use of dangerous pesticides—in general, the limits of choice imposed by technology. There may be other necessary conditions, but Rodden need not identify all of them and does not claim to have done so. The "natural propensity for running good things into the ground" is a necessary condition that would be difficult to eliminate. Writers seldom try to identify all the causes of a situation or attitude—not only because it would be difficult to do so, but because they need not do so to make their point.

Questions for Study and Discussion

1. In what order does Rodden present the costs of large refrigerators?
2. What other causes does Rodden state or imply for the American preference? What is the thesis of the essay, and where is it first stated?
3. Does Rodden explain why Europeans prefer small refrigerators? Is Rodden implying that Americans are more easily captivated by "technological progress"?
4. What in Rodden's comments on storing food and the problem of obesity shows that he is stating only some of the reasons for practices and attitudes, not all of them?
5. Does Rodden assert or imply that the greater efficiency a tool has, the greater control it exerts over people?
6. Do you agree that the telephone is a "convivial tool" and do you agree with Rodden's theory of tools?
7. How formal are the transitions of the essay? What is the overall tone? Do you find shifts in tone?

Vocabulary Study

Find synonyms for the following words: *psychosomatic, transitoriness, corpulence, aesthetic, amenities, homogenization, convivial, usurp, culinary, propensity.*

Suggestions for Writing

1. Analyze your preference for a certain make or size of automobile, or your opinion about the role of the telephone or a comparable tool. Discuss as many causes of your preference or opinion as you can, and present them in the order of their importance.
2. Discuss your eating habits, or those of your family, with attention to the role of the refrigerator in shaping these habits.
3. Discuss a possible change in American eating or consumption habits or recreation that in your opinion would improve the quality of American life. Explain your reasons as Rodden does.

❦
Definition

There are many ways to define a word, each depending on your purpose in writing and on the knowledge of your readers. In defining a cow for a child, it may be enough to point to one in a pasture or picture book. In a formal discussion you may point to a cow through words: first by relating it to the class *animal,* then stating the *specific differences* between the cow and all other animals: "the mature female of domestic cattle (genus *Bos*)" (*Webster's New World Dictionary*). Also, you could explain that *cow* can refer to the female elephant or whale and other female animals.

These definitions are called *denotative* because they point to the object or single it out from all others. *Connotative* definitions by contrast refer to ideas and feelings associated with the word. Denotative definitions are the same for everyone; connotative definitions are not. To some people *cow* suggests laziness, or stupidity; others may associate a cow with feelings of nourishment and contentment.

If you want to explain the origin or derivation of a word, perhaps for the purpose of explaining current meanings, you may state its etymology. The word *coward* derives from the idea of an animal whose tail hangs between its legs. The etymology illuminates one or more connotations of the word. You may, if you wish, propose or stipulate a new word for an idea or discovery. In the thirties Congressman Maury Maverick proposed the word *gobbledygook* as a description for pretentious, involved official writing. Such definitions may gain general acceptance. Some definitions remain in use for years, only to fall into disuse as new discoveries are made and new ideas appear, and better terms are invented to describe them.

How complete the definition is depends on its purpose in the essay, as well as on the reader. For one kind of reader it may not be necessary to point to or single out an object: the writer will assume that the reader knows what the object is, and needs only to be told how it works. Parts of the object (the blade casing of a manual lawn mower) may be defined fully in the course of describing how to care for or fix it; other parts may not be defined because they are unimportant to the process. It may be enough to tell readers of novels written about the 1920s that the Pierce-Arrow is an expensive automobile, or you may give one or two distinctive qualities of the Pierce-Arrow to explain an allusion to it.

August Heckscher

DOING CHORES

August Heckscher, born in 1913 in Huntington, New York, worked for many years as a newspaper editor and as an editorial writer for the *New York Tribune*. He served as director of the Twentieth Century Fund, president of the Woodrow Wilson Foundation, and administrator of recreation and cultural affairs for New York City. His writings include numerous essays and books on public affairs, including *Open Spaces: The Life of American Cities* (1977) and *When LaGuardia Was Mayor: New York's Legendary Years* (1978). His essay on chores is one of several essays in this text concerning the nature of work.

I have been doing chores, being for a brief spell alone   1
in a house that recently was astir with bustle and echoed with the voices of a gathered family. For those who may be in some doubt as to the nature of chores, their variety, their pleasures and their drudgery, I am prepared to deliver a short disquisition.

The first point about chores is that they are repetitive.   2
They come every day or thereabouts, and once done they require after a certain time to be done again. In this regard a chore is the very opposite of a "happening"—that strange sort of event which a few years back was so much in fashion. For a happening was in essence unrepeatable; it came about in ways no one could predict, taking form from vaporous imaginings or sudden impulse. Chores, by contrast, can be foreseen in advance; for better or worse, I know that

tomorrow I must be re-enacting the same small round of ritualistic deeds; and they arise, moreover, from practical necessities, not from poetic flights.

A second point about chores is that they leave no visible mark of improvement or progress behind them. When I am finished, things will be precisely as they were before— except that the fires will have been set, the garbage disposed of, and the garden weeded. In this, they are different from the works which optimistically I undertake. Ozymandias may have been presumptuous, but he was essentially right when he looked about him and said: *"See how my works endure!"* A work, once achieved, leaves a mark upon the world; nothing is ever quite the same again. The page of a book may have been printed or a page of manuscript written; a sketch, a poem, a song composed; or perhaps some happy achievement reached in one of the more evanescent art forms like the dance or cooking. All these have an existence of their own, outside of time, and at least for a little while live on in the mind of their creator and perhaps a few of his friends.

The well-meaning wife, seeing her husband about his chores, will miss the character of his performance. "Henry loves to cut wood," she will say; "he positively dotes on controlling the flow of waste from dinner-table to compost heap." The wife is perhaps trying to appease an unnecessary sense of guilt at seeing her spouse engaged in mundane efforts. The fact is, he doesn't love doing chores. But neither does he feel humiliated or out of sorts for having to do them. The nature of a chore is that it is neither pleasant nor unpleasant in itself; it is entirely neutral—but it is obligatory.

Neutral—and yet I must confess that with their repetition, and perhaps because of their very inconsequence, chores can in the end evoke a mild sort of satisfaction. Here, as in more heroic fields of endeavor, a certain basic craft asserts itself. To do what must be done neatly, efficiently, expeditiously—"without rest and without haste"—lights a small fire deep in the interior being and puts a man in good humor with the world. Santayana described leisure as "being at home among manageable things"; and if he was right we who are

the chore-doers of the world are the true leisure classes. At
least one can be sure that no chore will defeat us; none will
raise insuperable obstacles, or leave us deflated as when the
divine muse abandons her devotee.

A man I know became seduced by the minor pleasure   6
of doing chores—or at any rate by the absence of pain which
they involve—and could be seen from morning till nightfall
trotting about his small domain, putting everything in order,
setting everything to rights that the slow process of time had
disturbed. He was perhaps going too far. To season chores
with work, and to intersperse them with a few happenings,
is the secret of a contented existence. Fortunate the man or
woman who achieves a just balance between these three types
of activity—as I have been able to do by good chance, and
for a little space of time.

Comment

Where Maya Angelou writes concretely about the experience of
work in an Alabama community, Heckscher writes in general terms.
His purpose is to define one kind of happiness. That definition,
coming in the final paragraph, takes the form of a general comment on the three activities discussed in the essay—chores, work,
and happenings: "To season chores with work, and to intersperse
them with a few happenings, is the secret of a contented existence." Heckscher builds to this thesis instead of beginning with
it, because his point about these activities would not be clear without his having defined and illustrated them.

Questions for Study and Discussion

1. What are the differences between chores and work? Has
   Heckscher given a meaning to *work* different from your own?
   Do you ordinarily describe chores as work?
2. How does Heckscher introduce the essay? Does he merely state
   the subject—or does he also hint at his thesis?
3. Could the second point about chores (paragraph 3) have been
   discussed before the first?
4. Is Heckscher writing to a general audience or to a special one—
   perhaps husbands who perform weekend chores? What is his

purpose in writing—to reflect on his personal experience, to inform his readers about work and chores, or to persuade them to change their thinking about work or their way of performing it?

5. Do you agree that chores can provide "a mild sort of satisfaction"?

Vocabulary Study

1. Read Shelley's poem "Ozymandias," and in a short paragraph discuss Heckscher's reference to it in his essay.
2. Compare the dictionary meaning of the italicized word with the word following it in parentheses. Be ready to explain how the parenthesized word changes the meaning of the sentence:

   a. paragraph 1: *disquisition* (sermon)
   b. paragraph 2: *ritualistic* (habitual)
   c. paragraph 3: *presumptuous* (conceited)
   d. paragraph 3: *evanescent* (changing)
   e. paragraph 4: *dotes on* (enjoys)
   f. paragraph 4: *mundane* (ordinary)
   g. paragraph 4: *neutral* (uninteresting)
   h. paragraph 5: *expeditiously* (speedily)
   i. paragraph 5: *deflated* (tired); *devotee* (fan)
   j. paragraph 6: *domain* (household)

Suggestions for Writing

1. Discuss how accurately Heckscher's definitions fit the various kinds of work you perform at home. In the course of your essay, discuss how closely your idea of happiness agrees with Heckscher's.
2. Discuss daily activities at home and at school that you do not consider chores, and explain why.
3. About chores, Heckscher states: "Here, as in more heroic fields of endeavor, a certain basic craft asserts itself." Discuss the "basic craft" of a chore that you perform regularly. Contrast this "craft" with work that you also perform regularly.
4. Write your own definition of a contented existence, comparing your ideas and experiences with Heckscher's if you wish.

Classification and Division

Classification and division are important methods of analysis in exposition. Repair manuals classify various tools into broad groups like drills, then explain the uses of individual drills. When you classify you arrange individual objects into broad groups or classes. Hardware stores, for example, shelve tools according to classes—hammers, drills, wrenches, pliers, and so on.

Division arranges the members of a general class into subclasses according to various principles. The division may be formal or scientific, as in the textbook or dictionary division of fleshy fruits like apples and oranges, drupaceous fruits (those with pits at the center) like cherries and peaches, and dry fruits like peas and nuts. The class to be divided may be as broad as *fruit* or as narrow as *apples* (a member of one of the subclasses of fruit).

The division of the class is made on a single basis or principle. For example, apples can be divided according to color, use, variety, or taste, to cite a few possible divisions:

by color: red apples, green apples, yellow apples, and so on
by use: eating apples, cooking apples, and so on
by variety: Golden Delicious, Jonathan, Winesap, and so on
by taste: sweet, tart, winy, and so on

The principle of division depends on the purpose of the analysis. In instructing people what apples to buy for baking pies, you would divide apples according to variety, then perhaps according to taste. The color of the skin would not be important.

The division need be only as complete as your purpose requires: you might only distinguish tart from sweet and winy apples without naming the varieties. It is sometimes important to note that the division is not exhaustive. You might mention one or two varieties of tart apples like Jonathans and Granny Smiths, noting that other tart varieties are out of season. If you divide apples in more than one way in the course of the essay (for example, dividing according to taste as well as variety), each division should be separate.

Michele Huzicka

ON WAITING IN LINE

Michele Huzicka wrote the following essay in her first year at the University of Akron. She uses informal division simply and effectively, distinguishing types of students and experiences she encountered at various times of the day.

At one time or another, in the course of an average day, all of us must wait in some sort of line. In these lines we can learn much about ourselves and one another before we reach our destination. I wait in line often on campus—most often at meal time in the dining room.

As we all know, there are those who can be called "morning people" and there are those who cannot. Morning people don't mind getting up early. They are cheery, pleasant, organized, and attentive—all without a hair out of place or the least bit of sleep left in their eyes. The non-morning people loathe the morning people for these qualities. When the two come together in a line for breakfast, turbulent feelings may arise. For this reason the breakfast line is relatively quiet, compared to other lines. People would rather not run the risk of sparking ill-feelings so early in the morning. However, if the same people were to meet later in the day, the situation would probably be entirely different.

The lunch line is probably the most pleasant of all the lines we must cope with on campus. The majority of students are now fully awake. The non-morning people no longer feel muddled or groggy; they are now simply "people"— people waiting in line. Idle chatter about one's next class or one's hometown or mutual friends is a good distraction from what would otherwise be a very boring wait. It is here at lunch that we are forced to break away from our little cliques and explore the possibility that there are people different from ourselves. So we meet new people and learn about different classes on campus and about different towns and cities in Ohio. We even listen to trivial details just for the sake of having something to do.

In the dinner line I can see people once again returning   4
to the security of their friends as I join mine. It is always this line that seems to move the fastest as we recap the day's events, gossip about friends, analyze new boyfriends, and plan for the evening ahead. It is not surprising to look around and see other little groups doing very much the same thing. Talk of this sort is the most entertaining of the day.

Other lines, too, weave their way into our everyday lives.   5
Depending upon their location and the time of day, they can most definitely be quite uncomfortable and dull, or they can be adventurous discoveries about other people. Waiting in line at any time of day, we constantly learn new things about ourselves and other people. We are forced to be with masses of people who share one common goal—getting to the start of the line.

Comment

Michele Huzicka might have chosen another basis of division in her essay. Had she noticed differences in how students wait in different kinds of lines, for instance, she might have divided on that basis. Those waiting to register for classes perhaps behave differently from those waiting in a cafeteria. Huzicka began writing her essay with an observation that she wanted to develop and a sense of college life that she wanted to express. Her thesis occurred to her in the act of reporting that observation. At another time, she might have begun her essay with a general idea or thesis that she wished to illustrate and then searched her experience for examples.

Questions for Study and Discussion

1. How does Huzicka introduce her subject? How early in the essay does she state her thesis?

2. Huzicka writes both informatively and expressively. What does she reveal about her personality and interests in characterizing people and lines?
3. In what other ways might Huzicka have divided students standing in line? What other purposes might such divisions have?

Suggestions for Writing

1. Write an essay of your own on the same topic—on standing in line. Use classification or division at some point in the essay or throughout. Use your discussion to develop an idea as Huzicka does.
2. Write an essay characterizing people on another basis, drawing on your personal experience. Use classification or division to develop your essay.
3. Use classification or division to develop an essay on one of the following topics:

    a. On writing essays
    b. On sitting in college classes
    c. On first living away from home
    d. On riding the subway or bus

PART 2

Strategies for Expressive Writing

You have probably scribbled words or made designs in your notebook in an absent moment at home or at school. Perhaps you doodle on the edges of a newspaper or magazine as you listen to the stereo or watch television. Like this absent-minded scrawling, much writing has the purpose of personal expression, the play of the mind for its own sake. For instance, a rambling letter from a friend may jump from one experience to another without obvious transition. Your friend wrote the letter to share feelings and thoughts of the moment, and you may do the same in responding.

Other kinds of expressive writing are more organized. A journal entry, a statement of personal belief, a letter of protest—these are different kinds of personal expression, and they may be organized in various ways for various purposes. For different audiences, you may choose a different order of ideas and details appropriate to a particular audience.

A journal entry, for example, is written for your own use, and that use determines the order in which you record impressions and ideas. You may keep the journal as a strictly chronological record of a trip or a loose compilation of facts collected for a paper. In contrast, a letter of protest is expressive in simply voicing your anger at an unjust law; the order of ideas and details will be shaped by your feelings of the moment—and would probably be quite different from a letter written to urge a change in the law. The statement of personal belief, too, will be shaped by the thoughts and feelings you want to stress as well as by considerations of audience. Writing to a familiar audience, you might include personal details that an unfamiliar audience might neither understand nor appreciate.

In the following essay, Gloria Emerson's purpose in describing her parachute jump is to share the pleasure and surprise of the experience: "Everyone at the center was pleased; in fact, I am sure they were surprised. Perhaps this is what I had in mind all the time." Her purpose is therefore expressive, though she does give us information about sky diving. She presents enough details about the jump to allow us to imagine the experience. But these details are not presented separately from her description of her feelings. The essay focuses on these feelings throughout. Had she wanted merely to give information about sky diving, the focus of her essay would have been different.

No doubt Emerson discovered new feelings and meanings as she wrote. In writing your own essays, you will probably make similar discoveries; indeed, you may discover a purpose you did not have in mind when you began writing. A piece of writing often changes in focus and organization as you put words on paper. Because expressive writing so often incorporates new discoveries and insights, this form of the essay is sometimes more open and organized more loosely than informative and persuasive essays. The writer of the expressive essay wishes to convey the openness of feeling and thought.

Gloria Emerson

TAKE THE PLUNGE . . .

Gloria Emerson worked as a foreign correspondent for the *New York Times* from 1965 to 1972, reporting on Northern Ireland, on the Nigerian Civil War, and, from 1970 to 1972, on Vietnam. She received the 1971 George Polk Award for excellence in her reporting from Vietnam, and the 1978 National Book Award for her book about the Vietnam War, *Winners and Losers.* Her most recent book is *Some American Men* (1985). The feelings she describes in this essay on sky diving require the most careful mounting of detail, and that is what Emerson gives us.

It was usually men who asked me why I did it. Some were amused, others puzzled. I didn't mind the jokes in the newspaper office where I worked about whether I left the building by window, roof or in the elevator. The truth is that I was an unlikely person to jump out of an airplane, being neither graceful, daring nor self-possessed. I had a bad back, uncertain ankles and could not drive with competence because of deficient depth perception and a fear of all buses coming toward me. A friend joked that if I broke my bones I would have to be shot because I would never mend.

I never knew why I did it. It was in May, a bright and dull May, the last May that made me want to feel reckless. But there was nothing to do then at the beginning of the decade that changed almost everything. I could not wait that May for the Sixties to unroll. I worked in women's news; my stories came out like little cookies. I wanted to be brave about something, not just about love, or a root canal, or writing that the shoes at Arnold Constable looked strangely sad.

Once I read of men who had to run so far it burned their chests to breathe. But I could not run very far. Jumping from a plane, which required no talent or endurance, seemed perfect. I wanted to feel the big, puzzling lump on my back that they promised was a parachute, to take serious strides in the absurd black boots that I believed all generals wore.

I wanted all of it: the rising of a tiny plane with the door off, the earth rushing away, the plunge, the slap of the wind, my hands on the back straps, the huge curve of white silk above me, the drift through the space we call sky.

It looked pale green that morning I fell into it, not the baby blue I expected. I must have been crying; my cheeks were wet. Only the thumps of a wild heart made noise; I did not know how to keep it quiet.

That May, that May my mind was as clear as clay. I did not have the imagination to perceive the risks, to understand that if the wind grew nasty I might be electrocuted on high-tension wires, smashed on a roof, drowned in water, hanged in a tree. I was sure nothing would happen, because my intentions were so good, just as young soldiers start out certain of their safety because they know nothing.

Friends drove me to Orange, Massachusetts, seventy miles west of Boston, for the opening of the first U.S. sports parachuting center, where I was to perform. It was the creation, the passion, of a Princetonian and ex-Marine named Jacques Istel, who organized the first U.S. jumping team in 1956. Parachuting was "as safe as swimming," he kept saying, calling it the "world's most stimulating and soul-satisfying sport." His center was for competitions and the teaching of skydiving. Instead of hurtling toward the earth, sky divers maintain a swan-dive position, using the air as a cushion to support them while they maneuver with leg and arm movements until the rip cord must be pulled.

None of that stuff was expected from any of us in the little beginners class. We were only to jump, after brief but intense instruction, with Istel's newly designed parachute, to show that any dope could do it. It was a parachute with a thirty-two-foot canopy; a large cutout hole funneled escaping air. You steered with two wooden knobs instead of having to pull hard on the back straps, or risers. The new parachute increased lateral speed, slowed down the rate of descent, reduced oscillation. We were told we could even land standing up but that we should bend our knees and lean to one side. The beginners jumped at eight A.M., the expert sky divers performed their dazzling tricks later when a crowd came.

Two of us boarded a Cessna 180 that lovely morning, 9 the wind no more than a tickle. I was not myself, no longer thin and no longer fast. The jump suit, the equipment, the helmet, the boots, had made me into someone thick and clumsy, moving as strangely as if they had put me underwater and said I must walk. It was hard to bend, to sit, to stand up. I did not like the man with me; he was eager and composed. I wanted to smoke, to go to the bathroom, but there were many straps around me that I did not understand. At twenty-three hundred feet, the hateful, happy man went out, making a dumb thumbs-up sign.

When my turn came, I suddenly felt a stab of pain for 10 all the forgotten soldiers who balked and were kicked out, perhaps shot, for their panic and for delaying the troops. I was hooked to a static line, an automatic opening device, which made it impossible to lie down or tie myself to something. The drillmaster could not hear all that I shouted at him. But he knew the signs of mutiny and removed my arms from his neck. He took me to the doorway, sat me down, and yelled "Go!" or "Now!" or "Out!" There was nothing to do but be punched by the wind, which knocked the spit from my mouth, reach for the wing strut, hold on hard, kick back the feet so weighted and helpless in those boots, and let go. The parachute opened with a plop, as Istel had sworn to me that it would. When my eyelids opened as well, I saw the white gloves on my hands were old ones from Saks Fifth Avenue, gloves I wore with summer dresses. There was dribble on my chin; my eyes and nose were leaking. I wiped everything with the gloves.

There was no noise; the racket of the plane and wind   11
had gone away. The cold and sweet stillness seemed an astonishing, undreamed-of gift. Then I saw what I had never
seen before, will never see again; endless sky and earth in
colors and textures no one had ever described. Only then
did the parachute become a most lovable and docile toy:
this wooden knob to go left, this wooden knob to go right.
The pleasure of being there, the drifting and the calm, rose
to a fever; I wanted to stay pinned in the air and stop the
ground from coming closer. The target was a huge arrow in
a sandpit. I was cross to see it, afraid of nothing now, for
even the wind was kind and the trees looked soft. I landed
on my feet in the pit with a bump, then sat down for a bit.
Later that day I was taken over to meet General James Gavin,
who had led the 82nd Airborne in the D-day landing at
Normandy. Perhaps it was to prove to him that the least
promising pupil, the gawkiest, could jump. It did not matter
that I stumbled and fell before him in those boots, which
walked with a will of their own. Later, Mr. Istel's mother
wrote a charming note of congratulations. Everyone at the
center was pleased; in fact, I am sure they were surprised.
Perhaps this is what I had in mind all the time.

Questions for Study and Discussion

1. What is Emerson's purpose in writing? Does she state her pur-
    pose directly, or do you discover it from her approach to the
    subject and her focus? What were her motives in making the
    jump?
2. What details does she provide about the operation of the par-
    achute, the descent, and the landing? How are these details
    fitted to the discussion of her feelings at various stages in her
    experience? What are these stages?
3. How does she maintain the focus on her feelings throughout
    the essay? Do these feelings change?
4. Would you have reacted to the parachute jump as Emerson
    did? What comparable experience aroused similar expecta-
    tions and feelings in you?

Vocabulary Study

1. Emerson uses a number of technical terms, among them *rip cord, static line,* and *wing strut.* See whether your dictionary—or an unabridged dictionary—contains these. If you do not find them listed, state how the essay clarifies their meaning. Notice that we do not always require a complete definition of a term to understand its purpose or role in the process. Is that true of these terms?
2. Explain the italicized words and phrases:
   a. "The truth is that I was an unlikely person to jump out of an airplane, being neither graceful, daring nor *self-possessed.*"
   b. "That May, that May my mind was as *clear as clay.*"
   c. "Instead of *hurtling* toward the earth, sky divers maintain a *swan-dive position,* using the air *as a cushion* to support them while they *maneuver with leg and arm movements* until the rip cord must be pulled."

Suggestions for Writing

1. Describe an experience with a complex piece of equipment like a parachute. You might discuss the problems encountered in assembling it, or other difficulties it created for you.
2. Describe an experience comparable to the one Emerson describes. Explain your motives in undertaking the experience, and trace the stages of the experience as Emerson does, giving an account of your feelings at each stage.

Autobiography

In the autobiographical essay, the writer seeks to reach personal understanding by recalling vital experiences of the past. Virginia Woolf tells us that the nineteenth-century English writer Thomas De Quincey, "understood by autobiography the history not only of the external life but of the deeper and more hidden emotions." Woolf defines the art of the autobiographer as follows:

> To tell the whole story of a life the autobiographer must devise some means by which the two levels of existence can be recorded—the rapid passage of events and actions; the slow opening up of single and solemn moments of concentrated emotion.— "De Quincey's Autobiography"

We see this art in the four autobiographical essays that follow. Mary E. Mebane recreates the world of her North Carolina childhood through a description of daily chores and family life; William Flynn recreates the magical world of his Italian grandparents' apartment that he visited as a child. Perri Klass and Leonard Kriegel reach insights about themselves in concentrating upon central experiences in their past.

The autobiographical essay may serve other purposes in addition to expressing personal feelings and insights. In recreating the past, Mebane informs us about growing up black in America. In describing an experience that revealed to her the special bond shared by doctors, students, and patients, Klass informs us about the world of the medical student. Kriegal gives his essay an argumentative edge in questioning values that gave him strength to deal with the crippling effects of polio.

Mary E. Mebane

THE RHYTHM OF LIFE

Born in Durham, North Carolina, in 1933, Mary E. Mebane grew up in a segregated world in which her parents struggled to make a living. Her mother worked in a tobacco factory and did housework; her father farmed and sold junk. Mebane tells us at the end of her autobiography, *Mary:* "I made it the main aim of my life to find someone who was understanding and sensitive, and to find an environment in which I could develop and flourish. Beyond me lay the great world, the white world, the world that I had been taught was my implacable enemy. I didn't know how I was going to get out, but I was going to try. I had to." Encouraged by her aunt, Mebane entered college in Durham, receiving a B.A. from North Carolina College. She later received an M.A. and Ph.D. from the University of North Carolina at Chapel Hill. She has taught at various universities in the United States. In this self-contained section from her autobiography, Mebane describes some of the happy experiences of her childhood. Jesse is her older brother, Ruf Junior her younger brother.

Life had a natural, inexorable rhythm. On weekdays, 1
Mama went to work at a tobacco factory. On Saturdays, early in the morning, we washed clothes. We washed clothes outdoors. First Mama and Jesse drew buckets of water from the well and poured it into the washpot. It was a big iron pot that stood on three legs and was very black from soot. Mama put paper and twigs under it and poured kerosene on them. They blazed up and soon there was blue smoke curling all around the pot. She put all the "white" things in the pot—sheets and pillowcases and underwear—and put Oxydol in with the clothes. I was puzzled because most of the things she put in with the "white" clothes were colored. Our sheets were made from flour sacks and had red or green or blue patterns on them. Some of the underwear was colored, too.

My job was to stand over the pot and "chunk" the 2
clothes down to keep the water from boiling over and putting out the fire. I loved my job. I had a big stick, and some-

times I stood there and "dobbed and dobbed" the clothes up and down all the morning.

Then Mama and Jesse drew water and filled up two large tin tubs. One was to wash clothes in; the other was the first rinse. Then there was a foot tub that was for the second rinse, the one with the bluing in it. Sometimes Mama let me melt the bluing, which came in a long, flat cake. 3

Then there was an even smaller pot, full of starch— cooked flour and water—with a heavy translucent skim on it. It was my job to skim it and throw the heavy part away. I loved that job, too. 4

After the clothes boiled and boiled, Mama would get a big stick and carry them a few at a time from the washpot to the washing and rinsing tubs. Then she would put more clothes in the washpot, add water and more Oxydol, and I would dob some more. Sometimes instead of dobbing I "jugged" the clothes—that is, dobbed from side to side. 5

While the second pot of clothes was boiling, I helped Mama with the wash. There was a big washboard in the first tub and a smaller one in the second tub (that was the first rinse). Mama washed with a big cake of lye soap that she had made, rubbing up and down on the washboard. The lye soap sometimes made tiny holes in her fingers. Then I rubbed the clothes up and down in the first rinse, which got the suds out; next I stirred them around and pulled them up and down in the bluing water. Then Mama wrung them out. Some things she starched. She hung them up high on the clothesline. By that time the second pot of boiling clothes was ready and we started all over again. Later in the morning she put in the "heavy things" to boil—overalls and her blue factory uniforms and the blankets. While they boiled, we ate dinner, the noon meal. 6

For dinner, Mama would send me to the field with a basket over my arm to get a dozen ears of corn, some cucumbers, and tomatoes. I would shuck the corn, pulling the long green hard leaves off, next the lighter green inner leaves, then the silk in long yellow strands. Ruf Junior helped to silk it; then Mama would go over it again. She would let me 7 slice the tomatoes and put mayonnaise on them, and slice the cucumbers and put vinegar, salt, and black pepper on them. But I didn't want to slice the onions because they made me cry, so Mama would slice them in with the cucumbers herself. She sliced the corn off the cob into a big frying pan, full of hot grease. Then we ate the fried corn with tomatoes and cucumber and onions, and a hunk of corn bread, and a big mayonnaise jar full of buttermilk, and a piece of pork.

Sometimes Mama put on a "pot." It cooked a long time 8 on the back of the wood stove. Sometimes it cooked all day. It cooked all the while we were washing, and when we came in we had a steaming plate of turnip greens with tomatoes and cucumbers and onions. Sometimes it was cabbage, yellow from having cooked so long. (I didn't like the yellowish cabbage or the orangey rutabagas.) Sometimes it was string beans. If we didn't have a pot, we had something quick, like fried squash with onions. Mama put on a pot of meat to go with the pot of vegetables. Often it was neck bones or pig feet or pig ears. Sometimes we had pork slices, swimming in red gravy. She would put on a pie at dinner, blackberry or apple, so it would be ready at suppertime; we had lemon meringue pie only on Sunday. We sometimes had sweet-potato custard through the week, also.

After dinner we went back out in the yard. By then the 9 heavy things had boiled, and Mama took them on a large stick to the washtub. The water in the tub was gray now, with a high meringue of foam on it. But she rubbed and I rinsed, and she hung out the clothes high, but now she gave me the socks and sweaters to hang on the bushes. She sent me to see if any of the clothes were "hard," and I went to the line and lowered the stick that was holding it up. I took down the clothes that had been in the sun so long that they were dry and stiff. I took them in the house and put them on the bed. Then Mama went over to the field to look at her crop, leaving me to churn.

I put the gallon jars of sweet milk into the tall churn, 10 using a stick shaped funny at the bottom. Then I jugged it up and down, up and down, looking every few minutes to see if the butter had come. If it hadn't, I jugged some more.

Mama would be over in the field a long time and then she would come and say, "The butter come yet?" And I'd look up and say, "No, ma'am," and churn some more. When the butter came, she scooped it up and shaped it into a cake.

For supper we had what was left in the pot from din- 11 ner, along with a pie Mama had put on then, and a glass of buttermilk, and corn bread.

Before supper, Mama would get out two heavy irons 12 and put them on the hot part of the stove. Then she'd tell me to go sprinkle the clothes. I would take some water and wet the clothes down and then roll them into a ball. That would soften them up some and make the wrinkles come out easier. After supper, Mama would start to iron on a big ironing board that had burned places at the end where the iron stood. I couldn't lift the real heavy iron, but she would let me have the small iron and I would push it up and down a handkerchief or a pair of socks, glad to be a woman like Mama.

She would fold the clothes and put them in a drawer 13 and put the sheets and pillowcases on the beds. By that time the flies and mosquitoes would be buzzing the lamp. When she finished she would go out on the porch and sit in the cool, with the basket of butter beans to be shelled for Sunday dinner. I would take a newspaper and shell right along with her, pausing occasionally to protest when Ruf Junior got a pod that I wanted.

After we finished shelling the beans, my eyes would have 14 sand in them and Mama would tell me to go to bed. I would go into the house and fall asleep while I heard her still moving around.

I helped Mama pick the green tomatoes for chowchow. 15 She cut up the green tomatoes, then a hill of onions while tears ran down her face. She put in green peppers and cup after cup of sugar and a bag of spice. Then she pushed the chowchow far back on the stove and let it cook. In a little while the kitchen and back porch smelled good. It was the chowchow cooking. Mama let it cook and cook until it "cooked down." By nightfall she was ready to put it in the jars that Ruf Junior and I had washed.

She canned vegetables after she came home from work.   16
There were tomatoes, which she put in hot water and scalded,
then peeled; peas and corn; corn and okra; and butter beans
and string beans. She put down cucumbers in a large stone
jar and filled it with brine for pickles. After we finished eating watermelon, I peeled the rinds, front and back, and Mama
cooked them with sugar and we had watermelon preserve.

I washed jars and Ruf Junior washed tops; and row   17
after row of canned goods, looking just like pictures, formed
on the shelves, around the sides of the back porch, and under the house.

When the truck came with the peaches, we stopped   18
everything. If it was Saturday, we didn't wash anymore or
gather vegetables; if it was during the week we worked until
late at night. Everybody had to help because peaches spoiled
so fast. Daddy and Jesse and even Aunt Jo helped. The grown
folks and Jesse had big knives. Ruf Junior and I had small
paring knives. Mama didn't like Ruf Junior and me to peel
because she said we left more of the peach in the peel than
we put in the pot. But she let us peel, too, because if she
didn't we'd holler so loud and beg so hard that she wouldn't
have any peace. She picked out the soft ones, near the bottom, that had bad places on them and let us peel those. We
peeled and ate and peeled and ate and went to bed full of
peaches, sometimes sick.

Slopping the hogs was Jesse's job when Daddy didn't   19
do it. But sometimes if Jesse heard them squealing over in
the pigpen before it was time, he'd let Ruf Junior and me
take them something. We'd get water buckets; I'd take a full
one and Ruf Junior would have half a one, and we'd carry
slops—discarded vegetables cooked with "ship stuff," a coarse
thickening substance about the consistency of sawdust. We'd
pour it through the big spaces between the railings into the
trough and watch them eat. There would always be four or
five, and we'd beat the big ones away with sticks so the little
ones could eat. We were careful not to make too much noise
because Daddy would wonder what was happening to the
hogs if he heard them squealing too much.

Sometimes Mama would get after Ruf Junior and me 20 when she'd hear a chicken squawking and would look out to see a hen flying across the yard with Ruf Junior and me running after it. We didn't want to hurt her; we wanted to play with her; but she didn't understand that and went running for her life.

Daddy and Jesse plowed in the Bottom in the tobacco 21 and cotton. Mama and Aunt Jo hoed in the vegetables. I hoed until I started chopping up too many plants and Mama protested; then I joined Ruf Junior in running up and down the rows, feeling the hot sun on the dry dirt under my feet and the cool wet where the plow had just been. If Ruf Junior and I were good, we could go to the house and get cold water and bring it to the fields in half-gallon jars.

Comment

Autobiographical writing is expressive in purpose. In this section from her autobiography, Mary E. Mebane seeks to give us a sense of herself through the details of her world and also through the experiences of growing up. Like Maya Angelou, Mebane gives us the details of the everyday world so exactly that we are not likely to forget them. Most of her readers probably never washed clothes in a pot or cooked chowchow. She is careful, therefore, to give necessary details, at the same time using these details to evoke the qualities and feelings of Southern life in the 1930s. Description and narrative combine in the essay, as they do in Angelou's.

Questions for Study and Discussion

1. What are the qualities and feelings that Mebane evokes in her description of her childhood world? What is her attitude toward that world?
2. How does her description of washing, preparing food, and other activities illustrate the "natural, inexorable rhythm" of life? How does Mebane show that these activities are inexorable?

3. How different is the impression of Southern black life in Mebane's essay from that in Angelou's? Are there significant similarities?

4. How different from Mebane's was your participation in everyday family activities such as preparing food? Did life have the same "natural, inexorable rhythm" in your growing up?

Vocabulary Study

1. Be ready to explain how Mebane helps us to discover the meaning of the following words: *chunk, dobbed* (paragraph 2); *bluing* (paragraph 3); *jugged* (paragraph 5); *shuck* (paragraph 7); *"pot"* (paragraph 8); *"hard"* (paragraph 9); *chow-chow* (paragraph 15).

2. Examine the following reference books to find out how many of the above words are listed with the meaning they have in the essay:
   a. an unabridged dictionary
   b. *Dictionary of Americanisms on Historical Principles*
   c. *Dictionary of American Slang*
   d. *Dictionary of American English*

Suggestions for Writing

1. Write your own essay on the statement "Life had a natural, inexorable rhythm," drawing on your own childhood experiences. Make all of your details relate to this idea, and give your discussion unity by dealing with one experience at a time.

2. Like Angelou, Mebane tells us much about Southern life in general by focusing on a segment of that life and describing it in detail. Do the same with the world in which you grew up, focusing on a segment of it that you can describe fully in several pages. Define those terms and activities that your audience may not be familiar with.

3. Mebane describes the effect books, magazines, and radio programs had on her in high school: "I lived so intensely what I read in books and what I heard on the radio that even though I knew that it wasn't everyday, it was more real than everyday." Discuss reading and television experiences that had an intense effect on you during high school, and draw a conclusion from these experiences.

William Flynn

THE LOVING WALLS OF GRANDMA'S CASTLE

At the time he wrote this memoir of his grandparents, William Flynn was a student at Westchester Community College, in Valhalla, New York. His essay vividly describes not just the apartment of his grandparents but also a boy's fascination with an exciting world.

One of my favorite places was my grandparents' apartment in a once all-Italian immigrant neighborhood, Park Hill in Yonkers. Spending the day with Grandma in her castle is a cherished memory.

I would dash up the stairs two at a time. By the time I reached the second floor, I would be out of breath, but the thick aroma of an Italian feast would make me run even faster up the next flight of stairs.

When I reached my grandmother's floor, her door was wide open because people from all over the neighborhood would stop in to visit her.

She would say, "Bella Grandma" (meaning "grandma's beautiful one") to me in a sweet Italian accent. Next would come a big kiss and hug. "In one hour, Sal and Grandpa will come home, and then we'll eat," she said.

While Grandma was busy preparing dinner, I would inspect her apartment. The first room was my grandmother's bedroom. It was a big room with a big double bed covered with a snow-white bedspread. On her dresser was a jewelry box I fancied going through. As what I thought were real diamonds, rubies and pearls ran through my fingers, I imagined myself a pirate finding a hidden treasure.

The next room was my Uncle Sal's room. Sal slept in a king-size bed because he was too big for a normal one. Sal's bureau was a mystery to me. I loved going through his top drawer and examining his prized possessions: jewelry, watches, wallets and dollar bills. A closet in Sal's room was another mystery to me. I would look through all his clothes, and I remember the distinctive moth-ball smell. I would put on Sal's long brown, leather jacket and don one of my grandfather's hats. Standing in front of the full-length mirror, I imagined myself a gangster walking down the street and everyone taking a step back as I came through. After fantasizing for a while, I would put everything back neatly.

Next was my favorite part of the house, the back room. The first thing I saw were all the barbells that had made my Uncle Sal so big and strong—bench press, dumbbell, squatting racks and monstrous weights. I put two small weights on either side of an empty bar. I was looking in the mirror trying to get psyched for the big lift. I bent my knees and in one big jerk brought the weight up to my shoulders. I felt my muscles starting to tighten. Next, I noticed the veins in my neck bulge, and my face turned red. I started to push the weight up over my head. At first it felt like too much to handle, but I couldn't give up. I kept pushing for what seemed like forever, and finally my elbows locked over my head. I looked in the mirror satisfied, thinking that some day I'd be as big and strong as Sal.

After successfully pressing 50 pounds, I switched my attention to the most unusual item I knew: Grandma's old Singer sewing machine. I sat down on the chair and started pumping the pedal at the bottom of the machine with my foot. The pedal made the machine needle on top jolt up and down rapidly. The faster I pumped, the faster the needle moved. I was amazed, and I would spend 10 minutes just watching the needle "sew."

My grandmother would break my concentration by calling me to eat. I would rush into the kitchen and greet my grandfather and uncle. Then the time I'd been looking forward to would arrive. Time to eat. The food seemed as if it would last forever: spaghetti with thick rich tomato sauce, the tender veal cutlets, the sweet and hot sausages, the meatballs, red wine and salad. I would feel like a king. Dessert time was another experience in itself. First would come the canoli, éclairs, napoleons and finally the strawberry short cake, my favorite. By the time dinner was over, I would feel ready to burst.

After dinner, I would run downstairs to watch the older   10
guys play stickball. "Hey, there's Sal's nephew," they would
say. I knew most of their names but never could remember
the guys with the funny sounding Italian names, like Nunzio
or Guido.

At night, Grandma and a group of older Italian women   11
would sit on folding chairs in front of her apartment house,
and they would talk in Italian. Grandma would send me
over to the Italian cafe for another favorite, soft Italian ice.

When I returned, the women were ready to leave, and   12
they all gave me a big kiss goodbye. I used to hate kissing
all these strange women dressed in black, but pretended to
like it.

The apartment house my grandparents lived in was a   13
three-story, coldwater flat, and Grandma and Grandpa barely
made enough to get by, but the warmth, love and comfort I
felt with them in their castle is incomparable to any other
feeling I have ever experienced. I shall always remember them,
and the love and security I felt when I was with them.

Comment

Flynn's narrative gives the details of the visit to the apartment moment by moment. Notice how the opening topic sentences identify
each stage and together form a summary of the essay. And notice
how Flynn gives more details on some of his experiences than on
others and how he tells the reader why the back room was his
favorite in the apartment, and why he felt like a king at the dinner
table. An especially fine feature of his essay is the characterization
of people through the objects of their world—the objects in the
uncle's and the grandmother's bedrooms, the contents of the back
room, even the old Singer sewing machine.

Questions for Study and Discussion

1. In what sense of the word was the grandparents' apartment a
    castle? What experiences and words remind the reader that
    Flynn was the inhabitant of a castle during his visit?

2. Why was the back room his favorite, and why did he feel like a king at the dinner table?
3. Flynn states his central idea briefly in the opening paragraph and states it fully in the concluding paragraph. What is that idea? Is Flynn implying anything in addition about his grandparents' world?
4. How might Flynn have narrated the visit other than chronologically? What would be the advantage of a different order of events?

Suggestions for Writing

1. Narrate a childhood visit of your own to the home of a relative. Give the setting and state the occasion in as few words as possible, giving most attention to the most important moments. Use your narrative to develop a central impression or idea and state it in a prominent place in the essay—perhaps in the beginning or in the concluding paragraph.
2. Flynn characterizes his uncle through the details of his bedroom and those of the back room. Characterize a friend or a relative in the same way—through the details of this person's world.

Perri Klass

THE FIRST TIME

Perri Klass, a resident in pediatrics, attended Harvard Medical School. She is also the author of two collections of short stories and a collection of essays on her medical school experiences—*A Not Entirely Benign Procedure: Four Years as Medical Student* (1987). She writes in the introduction: "The experience of writing about medical school while going through it has changed my medical education tremendously. I have found that in order to write about my training so that people outside the medical profession can understand what I am talking about I have had to preserve a certain level of naiveté for myself. I have to hear and see things not only as a doctor, who would take most hospital sights, most medical locutions, completely for granted, but also as a nondoctor." She says of the whole experience: "I didn't kill anyone, and

I didn't crack up, and I didn't lose my sense of humor (though I am afraid it's gotten a little bit twisted), so my worst fears didn't come true either."

There is a first time for everything, of course. For the   1
medical student, back at the very beginning of the long path through medical training, there are terrifying first times for each of any number of small everyday hospital procedures. I think of drawing blood, the most common of these procedures, as a metaphor for much of what we do in the hospital: it involves the direct violation of the body's integrity, the causing of pain, and the removal of ordinarily hidden body substance for examination in the bright light of a microscope.

You wrap the tourniquet around the patient's arm and   2
hope the veins bulge slightly into view. You swab with alcohol. You slide the needle in, as gently as you can, and pull back on the plunger, hoping to see blood rising into the syringe.

For the past two years I have been a medical student,   3
studying my textbooks, sitting in lectures, looking through microscopes at slides, dissecting a cadaver. This summer I did my first "clinical clerkship," working in the hospital. I "followed" a certain number of patients, seeing them every day, doing my best to understand everything that happened to them, reading up on their medical problems. I also did a good deal of what we call "scut," those little jobs, like drawing blood, which inevitably fall down the chain of command to land in the medical student's lap.

And so for the first time I found myself standing next   4
to a sick person with a hypodermic in my hand, while from across the bed an intern said to me, "Okay, see if you can locate a vein."

Patients were remarkably cooperative, which was par-   5
tially the magic of the white coat; wear it and everyone assumes you know what you're doing, no matter how obviously you may be fumbling. Also, the idea of doctors-in-training is very frightening; many patients don't like to face the fact

that the people making decisions about their health may be in some sense just beginners.

The aphorism is "See one, do one, teach one." In theory, someone senior to you should walk you through each procedure slowly the first time, leaving you confident and ready to do it on your own the next time. 6

"With blood gases, for me it's more like see three, try four, miss them all," said a friend of mine. Drawing blood gases means getting blood from the artery instead of the vein. The artery is harder to find than the vein, and the process can be excruciating for the patient—especially if you miss the artery the first couple of times. There was a patient on the ward where I worked for my first few weeks this summer who finally rebelled. We marched in one morning on rounds, the whole crowd of us, one resident, two interns, two medical students. The resident asked the patient how she was doing, listened to her chest, and said to me, "Perri, let's get another blood gas on her." 7

"Oh no," said the patient, "I'm not letting her near me. She tried the other day." 8

"Okay," said the resident, smiling at my apologetic grimace, pointing to the other medical student. "How about him? He's very good." 9

"Oh, no he's not!" said the patient. "He tried too the other day. I'm not letting either of them near me." She pointed to one of the interns. "You do it, you have a light touch." 10

But most patients didn't object, and so I made my way through the summer, drawing blood from veins and arteries as the occasion required, but also putting a tube up someone's nose and down into his stomach for the first time, starting an intravenous line for the first time, and moving on to procedures which are more complex and also genuinely more dangerous—like my first spinal tap. There has to be a first time for everything. 11

There is also the patient's first time, of course. And just as drawing blood, a procedure completely straightforward and routine to the hospital blood technician, can be terrify- 12 ing and extremely complex to the beginning medical student, it is important to remember that procedures and exams which for some patients are not at all traumatic can be tremendously difficult and painful for other patients.

One night early in the summer the intern I was working   13
with asked me to assist her in doing a pelvic exam. The patient was a woman who had come to the hospital because she was feeling a little weak, and who had been discovered to have cancer in several places, cancer which looked metastatic. The problem then was to locate the primary site of her cancer, and the pelvic exam was the first in a series of attempts. The intern, a woman a year or so older than I, actually performed the pelvic; all I did was hold a flashlight—and the patient's hand. She was a woman in her seventies with a sweet face and a gentle smile and, just to complete the picture, an armful of fuzzy knitting. We put her knitting on the bedside table, and, because we had no examining table with stirrups, we propped her up in bed on a bedpan for the exam.

"You probably had one of these exams when you had   14
children," said the intern.

"Oh, no," said the patient, smiling at us, "why, I've   15
never even been married."

"Oh, okay," said the intern. "Well, I want you to know   16
that Perri and I have both had this done to us, and nobody really likes having it done, but we'll be as quick as we can."

And so we did the pelvic, with the poor lady crying out   17
in pain and surprise, because this was something she was not expecting, was not prepared for. In a certain sense this exam, so routine for most women, was an initiation for this woman into a part of her life which will be full of invasive tests, of pain she will be told is necessary, a part of her life she was not expecting. Our white-coated authority offered her no comfort; wanting to help her, we found ourselves reaching for some element of solidarity, reminding her that we had been patients too, that all three of us had a common anatomy.

And in the end, perhaps that is the lesson that comes   18
with experience in those things I do that cause patients pain:

as I become a little more experienced, a little more sure of myself, I become less anxious to retreat behind the barrier of professionalism. Even with drawing blood—the first few times I did it, I was terrified the patient would see how nervous I was and would guess why. "You'll just feel a little stick," I would say cheerfully, trying desperately to find the vein. By now, reasonably sure that I can find the vein if it's there to be found, I am much less afraid to let the patient see if I am puzzled or unsure. "This will hurt a little, but I'll do it as quickly as I can," I say. Perhaps there is an implicit apology in my attitude, and that does not seem to me to be such a bad thing, because surely there ought to be some acknowledgment in such a situation that however necessary the pain may be, I am not the one who has to bear it.

Comment

Perri Klass uses narration and exposition in her autobiographical account of first-time experiences as a medical student. She opens with a general observation—"There is a first time for everything, of course"—but this is not her thesis. She builds slowly toward her thesis, recounting a series of related truths about doctors, students, and patients. Klass might have begun her essay by stating the truths that would then form the thesis of her short essay, but it would be only a generality if presented in that way. To understand its full import, we need to know what Klass experienced. Though she interprets these experiences for us as she presents them, her commentary does not take the place of carefully chosen details or well-focused narration and exposition. Klass tells us much about the life of a medical student in very few paragraphs.

Questions for Study and Discussion

1. Would the essay be different in meaning or effect if Klass had begun with "the patient's first time" and then reported her experiences with drawing blood?
2. What truths does Klass discover through these experiences? How do the details of the essay help us understand these truths?

3. What point is Klass making about the white coats worn by medical students and doctors? Had she wished to make this point the thesis of her essay, what in her experiences with patients would have illustrated it? What might she have omitted from her account?
4. What personal qualities does Klass reveal to us in the course of describing her experiences? Does she refer to or comment on these qualities?

Vocabulary Study

1. Define the following words:
   a. paragraph 2: *tourniquet*
   b. paragraph 3: *dissecting, cadaver, clinical*
   c. paragraph 4: *intern*
   d. paragraph 6: *aphorism*
   e. paragraph 13: *pelvic, stirrups*
   f. paragraph 17: *routine*
   g. paragraph 18: *implicit*
2. Give the dictionary meaning of the following words. Then explain the use Klass makes of the word in the paragraph:
   a. paragraph 1: *metaphor, integrity*
   b. paragraph 12: *traumatic*
   c. paragraph 17: *initiation, authority, solidarity*
   d. paragraph 18: *professionalism*

Suggestions for Writing

1. Give an account of the first time you performed a difficult procedure at work or at school. Then discuss one or more truths that you discovered through this experience.
2. Klass reports the medical aphorism, "See one, do one, teach one." To what extent does this aphorism describe how you were taught a difficult procedure at work or at school?
3. Discuss a truth or lesson about people that cannot be taught— that a person must discover alone. Explain why the truth cannot be taught.
4. Klass discusses "the magic of the white coat." Discuss another uniform and the effect it has upon the person who wears it and upon those whom the person serves or deals with.

Leonard Kriegel

TAKING IT

Leonard Kriegel taught English at City College of New York and is Director of the City College Center for Worker Education. Born in the Bronx, in 1933, Kriegel contracted polio at the age of eleven and spent two years in a hospital recovering from its effects; he later completed grade school and four years of high school through home instruction. In his book *Working Through* (1972), Kriegel states that, upon entering college, "I was far hungrier for education than [my friends]; I was both more expectant and less skeptical of the college experience. I very much wanted to learn, to read whatever was worth reading. It was obvious to me that I knew very little. I was fortunate since, having survived as a cripple, I suspect that I possessed a stronger sense of self and perhaps a better-developed sense of competitiveness than most of my fellow students." Kriegel relates these experiences to the idea of manhood in the following essay, published in 1985.

In 1944, at the age of 11, I had polio. I spent the next   1
two years of my life in an orthopedic hospital, appropriately called a reconstruction home. By 1946, when I returned to my native Bronx, polio had reconstructed me to the point that I walked very haltingly on steel braces and crutches.

But polio also taught me that, if I were to survive, I   2
would have to become a man—and become a man quickly. "Be a man!" my immigrant father urged, by which he meant "become an American." For, in 1946, this country had very specific expectations about how a man faced adversity. Endurance, courage, determination, stoicism—these might right the balance with fate.

"I couldn't take it, and I took it," says the wheel-chair-   3
doomed poolroom entrepreneur William Einhorn in Saul Bellow's "The Adventures of Augie March." "And I *can't* take it, yet I do take it." In 1953, when I first read these words, I knew that Einhorn spoke for me—as he spoke for scores of other men who had confronted the legacy of a maiming disease by risking whatever they possessed of substance in a country that believed that such risks were a man's wagers against his fate.

How one faced adversity was, like most of American life, in part a question of gender. Simply put, a woman endured, but a man fought back. You were better off struggling against the effects of polio as a man than as a woman, for polio was a disease that one confronted by being tough, aggressive, decisive, by assuming that all limitations could be overcome, beaten, conquered. In short, by being "a man." Even a vocabulary of rehabilitation was masculine. One "beat" polio by outmuscling the disease. At the age of 18, I felt that I was "a better man" than my friends because I had "overcome a handicap." And I had, in the process, showed that I could "take it." In the world of American men, to take it was a sign that you were among the elect. An assumption my "normal" friends shared. "You're lucky," my closest friend said to me during an intensely painful crisis in his own life. "You had polio." He meant it. We both believed it.

Obviously, I wasn't lucky. By 19, I was already beginning to understand—slowly, painfully, but inexorably—that disease is never "conquered" or "overcome." Still, I looked upon resistance to polio as the essence of my manhood. As an American, I was self-reliant. I could create my own possibilities from life. And so I walked mile after mile on braces and crutches. I did hundreds of push-ups every day to build my arms, chest, and shoulders. I lifted weights to the point that I would collapse, exhausted but strengthened, on the floor. And through it all, my desire to create a "normal" life for myself was transformed into a desire to become the man my disease had decreed I should be.

I took my heroes where I found them—a strange, disparate company of men: Hemingway, whom I would write of years later as "my nurse"; Pete Reiser, whom I dreamed of replacing in Ebbets Field's pastures and whose penchant for crashing into outfield walls fused in my mind with my own war against the virus; Franklin Delano Roosevelt, who had scornfully faced polio with aristocratic disdain and patrician distance (a historian acquaintance recently disabused me of that myth, a myth perpetrated, let me add, by almost all of Roosevelt's biographers); Henry Fonda and Gary

Cooper, in whose resolute Anglo-Saxon faces Hollywood blended the simplicity, strength and courage a man needed if he was going to survive as a man; any number of boxers in whom heart, discipline and training combined to stave off defeats the body's limitations made inevitable. These were the "manly" images I conjured up as I walked those miles of Bronx streets, as I did those relentless push-ups, as I moved up and down one subway staircase after another by turning each concrete step into a personal insult. And they were still the images when, 15 years later, married, the father of two sons of my own, a Fulbright Professor in the Netherlands, I would grab hold of vertical poles on a train in The Hague and swing my brace-bound body across the dead space between platform and carriage, filled with self-congratulatory vanity as amazement spread over the features of the Dutch conductor.

It is easy to dismiss such images as adolescent. Undoubtedly, they were. But they helped remind me, time and time again, of how men handled their diseases and their pain. Of course, I realized even then that it was not the idea of manhood alone that had helped me fashion a life out of polio. I might write of Hemingway as "my nurse," but it was an immigrant Jewish mother—already transformed into a cliché by scores of male Jewish writers—who serviced my crippled body's needs and who fed me love, patience and care even as I fed her the rhetoric of my rage. 7

But it was the need to prove myself an American man— tough, resilient, independent, able to take it—that pulled me through my war with the virus. I have, of course, been reminded again and again of the price extracted for such ideas about manhood. And I am willing to admit that my sons may be better off in a country in which "Manhood" will mean little more than, say, the name for an after-shave lotion. It is 40 years since my war with the virus began. At 51, even an American man knows that mortality is the only legacy and defeat the only guarantee. At 51, my legs still encased in braces and crutches still beneath my shoulders, my elbows are increasingly arthritic from all those streets 8 walked and weights lifted and stairs climbed. At 51, my shoulders burn with pain from all those push-ups done so relentlessly. And at 51, pain merely bores—and hurts.

Still, I remain an American man. If I know where I'm going, I know, too, where I have been. Best of all, I know the price I have paid. A man endures his diseases until he recognizes in them his vanity. He can't take it, but he takes it. Once, I relished my ability to take it. Now I find myself wishing that taking it were easier. In such quiet surrenders do we American men call it quits with our diseases.

Comment

Kriegel gives us a few details about the onset of his polio and the physical effects of the disease. However, the focus of the essay is on the means by which he learned to cope with the physical effects. Had he given a full account of the onset of the disease and its effects, he would have blurred this focus. He would also have confused the reader about his purpose in writing. Kriegel's style is notable for its vigor and directness. His sentences are often colloquial, but he turns to metaphor in stating important ideas in the final paragraph: "A man endures his diseases until he recognizes in them his vanity." We hear Kriegel speaking to us, but we also get the sense of a person thinking.

Questions for Study and Discussion

1. What ideal of manhood helped Kriegel survive the effects of polio? Does he tell us how he acquired this ideal?
2. How does Kriegel illustrate the effect that this ideal has had upon his character and behavior?
3. What is his attitude toward the ideal? Would a different ideal of manhood have also helped him survive?
4. What does Kriegel mean by the final sentence, "In such quiet surrenders do we American men call it quits with our diseases"?
5. What is Kriegel's thesis? What is Kriegel's purpose in writing this essay, and how do you know?

Vocabulary Study

Explain the following words and phrases:
    paragraph 1: *orthopedic hospital*
    paragraph 2: *stoicism*
    paragraph 3: *poolroom entrepreneur*
    paragraph 4: *question of gender*
    paragraph 5: *inexorably*
    paragraph 6: *perpetrated*
    paragraph 7: *transformed into a cliché*

Suggestions for Writing

1. Kriegel states that when he was growing up the way a man and a woman faced adversity was "like most of American life, a question of gender." Drawing on experiences at home and at school, discuss how you were taught to face adversity and how you do so. State whether your experience suggests that attitudes toward facing adversity have changed from those Kriegel discusses.

2. Discuss your own ideal of manhood or womanhood and how you reached it. Then discuss the effect of this ideal on your relationship with people—perhaps with friends or fellow workers.

3. Write your own essay on the topic, "Taking It." You might focus your essay on experiences at home, at school, or at work. In working out a thesis, you need not draw general conclusions about people or social attitudes. You might draw a specific conclusion about your own ideal of conduct or social attitudes.

Reflection

The reflective essay is more open in its structure than essays bound by the requirements of narration or exposition. For example, it occasionally follows the wanderings of the writer's thought, concluding without tying ideas and details together. This kind of essay comes closest to the trial essay described in the introduction—the loosely organized essay that explores ideas without necessarily bringing the exploration to completion. The sixteenth-century French essayist Michael Montaigne defended these wanderings and unrevised thoughts in his essays, pointing out that his "understanding does not always advance, it also goes backwards. I do not distrust my thoughts less because they are the second or third, than because they are the first, or my present less than my past thoughts. Besides, we often correct ourselves as foolishly as we correct others."

Sometimes the reflective essay is tightly constructed, its ideas built carefully, without continuous revision or restatement. The structure and language of the essay depend on the writer's personality and characteristic manner of thinking. Montaigne describes his own. Writers like Montaigne think as they put words on paper; they revise and correct as they compose. Other writers choose to revise the whole essay and present only their finished thoughts. The reflective essay, more so than other kinds, takes the shape of the writer's thought and feeling.

Henry Beetle Hough

ON SMALL THINGS

Henry Beetle Hough (1896–1985) was born in New Bedford, Massachusetts, and attended Columbia School of Journalism. For more than forty years he was editor and co-publisher (with his wife) of the *Vineyard Gazette*, in Edgartown, Massachusetts. An early book, *History* of *Services Rendered by the American Press,* won the Pulitzer Prize in 1917. Hough is also the author of novels and nonfiction including his autobiography, *Mostly on Martha's Vineyard.* The essay reprinted here is an example of the reflective essay in which Hough excels.

August 7

Dear Jack,

When I dressed this morning I inadvertently put on an   1 old green shirt and the bright blue slacks I bought a few weeks ago at Dave Golart's because my waistline now rebels at the long-familiar Size 36, and because bright blue was about as modest a shade as I could find in this pigment-passionate age. My investment in Size 36 pants is dropping faster and I fear more permanently than the value of the stock portfolios of my betters.

I say this morning's color combination was inadvertent   2 because I think it was, and in that case it was a small thing. If it was not inadvertent, it was probably a big thing, dictate of some enormous reason I shall never learn. Green and bright blue look odd, I know, but they feel all right, and I shall not change until time for the bank directors' meeting this afternoon. The requirements for that are obviously severe.

Assuming my vagary in costume to be a small thing, I   3 remembered on my morning walk with Lochinvar something I had not thought of for years. I quote:

"Neglect of small things is the rock on which the great majority of the human race has split."

I learned this, and the rest of the moral passage, now   4 forgotten, in the Mary B. White School, a red brick building in a graveled yard which stood at the corner of Maxfield and Pleasant streets in New Bedford long ago. It was popularly but incorrectly known as the Maxfield Street School. There were four rooms, two downstairs and two upstairs, and I had a year's schooling in each room. The principal's office was in the turret which surmounted the outside stairs. All public buildings built of brick had turrets. I saw the principal's office only once, and I have forgotten the occasion.

The janitor was Mr. Cochrane. He had a red beard and so far as I can remember always wore a business suit and a derby hat. The boys' urinal in the basement smelled so strong and frightful that I have hardly escaped from it yet, but I suppose Mr. Cochrane considered this normal and acceptable. I tried to hold my breath as I went through, but my lung capacity was usually insufficient.

Once we were let out of school to watch the circus parade pass by on Purchase Street, a block downhill from Pleasant. Across from the school an elderly woman sat on an uncommonly high porch platform attached to the front of a dun-colored house, and just as we were crossing the graveled yard the planks gave way and dropped the elderly woman and her chair ten or twelve feet to the ground. As I remember it, she landed upright, still sitting in the chair. Mr. Cochrane set out on a dead run. I wondered what he was so excited about.

I have forgotten the circus parade in particular; I remember it only in an amalgamated succession of these wonders, mixed up with seeing the circus come in of an early morning at the Pearl Street railroad yards near the Wamsutta Mills. My brother and I used to see the stakes driven and the big tents raised in a lot at the North End near Brooklawn where Daniel Ricketson lived and where he entertained Henry Thoreau. Later the circus went to the West End or the South End, and I lost interest. When something is completely right and wonderful, it shouldn't be changed.

I remember that in my class at the Mary B. White School there were two boys with the given name of Byron.

These various details I supply because if one is going to write of the importance of little things, he had best show he is himself really attentive to them. Maybe the things I have drawn from memory, though small, may not be small enough

to make the desired point. I can't tell. Everything one remembers long enough tends to become fascinating, though
not to a wide public.

The passage I was required to learn, the first sentence   10
of which I have quoted, was written by Dr. Samuel Smiles.
He has seven lines and a fraction in the *Columbia Encyclopedia,* and I learn for the first time that he was Scottish, a
physician, and that his books were mostly devoted to moral
education. I think he is one of the writers of the past century
(1812–1904) who has gone out, and I doubt if he will be
back. There is no use whatever in putting the usual placard
on the door, BACK IN TWENTY MINUTES or even BACK IN A
HUNDRED YEARS.

I suppose the small things Dr. Smiles regarded as im-   11
portant were of an order now outdated: picking up odds
and ends of string, washing behind the ears, painting the
length of fence behind the lilac bush even though no one
will see it, lifting one's hat clear from the scalp instead of
merely tipping the brim, sweeping out the corners with conscience rather than haste, and so on. It was Dr. Smiles who
wrote, "A place for everything and everything in its place,"
but I never had to learn that. It was in Chapter 5 of a piece
called *Thrift.*

This is all I shall say about Dr. Smiles, and it seems an   12
odd beginning for the defense of small things I have set out
to make. He was so moral—so stuffy, I say—that I can hardly
expect to lean upon him or his lavendered philosophy. I must
start out for myself and may as well do so abruptly. I object
to my life being portentous, and especially to the require-
ment that I pretend it to be.

Whatever comes up in the matter of ideas or enterprise,   13
someone says, "Let's broaden it." I don't want to broaden
it. I prefer to narrow it. I can't paint, except for porches,
walls, and things like that, but if I could I would not choose
to paint on a large canvas. I probably wouldn't be able to
reach the top or the sides, and I would only be an over-
blown, pretending artist, not a real one. Another thing—I
don't want to be in the mainstream. The water is muddy,
the pollution great, the vision limited, and too many people

are trying to swim at once, each hitting another over the head.

I suppose what I am getting at principally is what I hope [14] is the small integrity of my point of view. It has to be small, because it is mine, and because I don't want to look out from way up there or way out yonder. I want to look out from here, and "here" happens to be an uncrowded place. Besides, if the ground on which I stand is too large or high I will surely be pushed over.

I think the small things now being importantly ne- [15] glected, that it is so much the fashion to neglect as routine and perfunctory, are the things generally that make life itself and in the end give it the meaning out of which new, fresh, or even grand ideas may spring. Information comes by radio, television, newspaper, magazine, and book, but these are not the country's thinking or the people's thinking. They may be stimulating and they may also be conforming. A man still needs his walking or hammering nails or chopping wood or bowling or shooting pool if he is really to find out what he thinks. The sweeping concept is often not much by itself; it's like the wind that blew over last night, leaving a scatter of debris.

Thoreau said that a man was not born into the world [16] to do everything, but to do something. The opportunities of modern times, puffed and inflated by so many prophets, some real, some false, are over-appreciated; the limitations are undervalued a hundredfold, though they are the intimate companionship of our days and nights, our Sundays and our weekdays.

I suppose, too, that although limitations are generally [17] what they seem and no more, there is always a chance that they may nourish some particular fertility. Most great things nowadays are abstractions, and did not Dr. J. Robert Oppenheimer suggest that some of their puzzling relationships might be brought into understandable order through a small specific?

I argue that we, as ordinary people, ought to neglect [18] great things, even at the cost of appearing presumptuous. I am aware that Dr. Samuel Smiles (there he is again), if he could rise up from his serene bit of God's acre among the yews and willows beside the ivy-mantled church, would be bound to insist that this was not what he had in mind. Maybe, though, he could be persuaded.

I remember how David Copperfield, after his life with Dora, declared that trifles make the sum of life. This is not what Dr. Smiles meant, either; his small things were not trifles. Not to him. But I am of David Copperfield's way of thinking. Life's trifles and trifling are not only its sum but its essence.   19

One small matter of doubt remains, rising from our experience in the newspaper profession. I remember Betty's intent pursuit of trifles: to keep Mrs. Duble's name from appearing in the *Gazette* as Mrs. Deeble, or vice versa; to defeat at all costs that persecuting vulgarity, "Rev. Smith"; to put the apostrophe in exactly and not approximately the correct place. So much of the good health of the paper lay here that, looking backward, I can almost accept the view that there are no minutiae.   20

As a last word in trying for an understanding or even for a compromise with Dr. Smiles, I suggest that if the great majority of the human race is going to split on the rock of neglect of small things, it will at least be too bad for so many of us to split on the rock of the wrong ones.   21

Yours, as ever,

Comment

Hough's letter has the openness and loose structure typical of much expressive writing. The miscellany of details that leads into paragraph 9 seems to illustrate Samuel Johnson's definition of the essay as an "irregular undigested piece." But the details have a purpose, as Hough directly states. That purpose is related to the statement of Samuel Smiles—first quoted in paragraph 3. Throughout the essay Hough gives us a sense of the reflective writer turning over the experiences and sayings that have mattered over a lifetime; Hough discovers a special meaning in writing about them. Out of seemingly small details and ideas concerned with everyday experiences come ideas about life itself.

Questions for Study and Discussion

1. What is the purpose of the miscellany of details that leads into paragraph 9?
2. What is the meaning of the quotation from Samuel Smiles in paragraph 3? How does Hough explain the statement in later paragraphs?
3. Hough discusses how people can live meaningful lives. What paragraphs introduce and develop these ideas?
4. Hough addresses his letter to "Jack"—a particular friend and reader of his newspaper. What features of the essay suggest that Hough has a larger audience in mind?
5. What impression do you get of Hough through his letter? What personal qualities most stand out? What kind of sense of humor does he have?

Vocabulary Study

1. Look up the following words and be ready to discuss how Hough uses them: paragraphs 1–2: *inadvertently, inadvertent;* paragraph 3: *vagary;* paragraph 7: *amalgamated;* paragraph 9: *attentive;* paragraph 12: *portentous;* paragraph 14: *integrity;* paragraph 15: *routine, perfunctory, concept;* paragraph 16: *intimate;* paragraph 18: *presumptuous;* paragraph 19: *trifles;* paragraph 20: *minutiae.*
2. The following words and phrases call a picture or smell to mind. What is that picture, and what does the word or phrase contribute to the meaning of the sentence?
   a. paragraph 12: *lavendered*
   b. paragraph 15: *scatter of debris*
   c. paragraph 16: *puffed, inflated*
   d. paragraph 21: *split, rock of neglect*
3. The words and phrases in question 2 above are metaphors— implied comparisons which attribute the qualities of one thing to another. In paragraph 13 Hough uses another metaphor, *mainstream,* and describes it: "The water is muddy, the pol-

lution great, the vision limited, and too many people are trying to swim at once, each hitting another over the head." What is the implied comparison in *mainstream,* and what other comparisons is Hough making in the sentence?

Suggestions for Writing

Hough gives us a picture of himself through a miscellany of details. He draws no conclusion other than to say that he has paid attention to small details in his life:

a.   Write down quickly a scattering of details that give the reader a picture of your life and interests.

b.   Look carefully at the details, then write down one or two patterns that they suggest. Discuss one of these patterns in a paragraph.

c.   Your paragraph probably contains several ideas. Use one of these ideas as the thesis of an essay that incorporates some or all of the details you recorded. You may wish to add others. Remember that a thesis organizes the details of the essay, giving them direction and purpose.

Phyllis Theroux

BICYCLING TOWARD WISDOM

Phyllis Theroux describes growing up in San Francisco in her memoir of her family, *California and Other States of Graces* (1980). Her essays, some of which appeared in *The Washington Post* and *The New York Times,* are collected in *Peripheral Visions* (1982). In her introduction to this book, Theroux defines the essay as "a short trip in a small boat bearing one or two ideas that the writer hopes to 'get across.'" She explains the title of her collection in the following statement:

> The trick which takes a lifetime to master is to honor the corner of one's eye without losing sight of what lies directly in front of you. Most writers, for instance, have a vision of something they see in the distance. Using the outward circumstances of their lives, they tack back and forth across that line of vision in order to get a closer look. Often, upon drawing nearer, what I saw from a distance was usually far more interesting than originally perceived, at least more interesting to me.

One of the first life decisions I ever made, at an age where causal connections between life and decisions were pretty foggy in my mind, was to switch my college major from English to philosophy.

"Philosophy!" yelled my father over the telephone. "What kind of a job are you going to be able to get with a philosophy major?"

Job? What job? That was a causal connection I hadn't made yet and my father had a point, even though it seemed awfully soiled and commercial.

"The whole point of philosophy," I countered patiently, "is to learn how to *think*. I'll think about a job later." Of course, all indications were that when it came time to find a job, I would have found a husband first, rendering my father's worry moot, but he didn't know about my fallback plan.

"Why don't you be a dietician?" he continued. "There's good money in that, particularly for women." I laughed, told him to relax, and hung up the phone.

Well, as it developed, neither of us was exactly right. The thought of analyzing the nutritional properties of apricot pudding continues to leave a bad taste in my mouth. But to think that one can analyze all of life's problems out of existence by thinking is a fallacy that has trapped me within the Square of Contradiction (a case of freshman logic I never could get straight at the time) too often for comfort. Fortunately, a dazzling little book entitled *A Guide for the Perplexed* by E. F. Schumacher, has recently helped me out.

Mr. Schumacher divides all the problems that assail humankind into two large categories: convergent and divergent. A convergent problem, such as how to build a bicycle, is solved by designing and assembling all the parts and putting them together in the right way. But a divergent problem, such as how to reconcile justice with mercy, doesn't lend itself to this solution. Justice and mercy will contradict each other forever, and the only way to solve the contradiction is to transcend it altogether and wait for wisdom, which sounds quite restful until you think about it.

Everybody is supposed to be waiting for wisdom one   8
way or the other. But how one waits—patiently, impa-
tiently, or in my case, by staring catatonically at a wall plug
and hoping that something will occur to me—separates one
human being from another. Metabolism has something to
do with it, but as the twig is bent, so grows thee.

I come from a family that believed in rising early, sniff-   9
ing the wind, and, after they realized that it was impossible
to reconcile train schedules, golf dates, and my aunt's decision to paint all the wicker furniture before dark, usually
decided to "wait and see what the day will bring forth."
That philosophy dovetailed with what everybody wanted to
do anyway, and while we didn't exactly stand frozen before
the mantelpiece all day, neither did we map out Easter vacation before Thanksgiving, or have a clear idea over breakfast of what was going to happen after lunch.

After all, anything could happen and anything often did,   10
which made life interesting and inclined me to believe that
the best way to deal with life's contradictions was to go into
an empty room and sit with them until I was on the brink
of a nervous breakdown, at which point the telephone would
ring and the person on the other end would clear it up for
me. Only recently have I discovered how anti-American a
belief that is.

Almost no one goes at problems that way, a realization   11
I have been late coming to because most people are too busy
to stop and set you straight. In fact, "being busy" turns out
to be the universal antidote to grief, sorrow, ambivalence,
and general malaise.

When I think of all those philosophy books where   12
"busyness" wasn't even in the index, it is easy to feel cheated.
Perhaps Kierkegaard was driven to write about "leaps of
faith" because he was too whiffle-brained to do anything
more constructive, like clean out the garage.

After listening to enough people tell me that they solved   13
all their problems by sorting through papers, quiltmaking,
even reconciling their bank statements in the midst of heart-
cracking sorrow, I began to think I had it all backward.
Could the general be solved by focusing upon nothing in

particular? It seemed a bit strange to think that one could solve a divergent problem with the tools used to solve convergent problems, but perhaps it was possible. Why not? I, too, would bicycle toward wisdom and give busyness a chance to work its boring magic upon me.

Armed with this new insight, I arose one morning and made a long list of things I would do, purposefully factoring out all light-bulb-staring time in the process. It was a long list filled with such items as "replace windowpane," "call dentist," "deposit check," and "clean out attic." I felt a little like throwing up, but I had no place in my schedule for it, and before 9:30 in the morning I had already cleaned the house, done two loads of wash, called the gas company about an overcharge, watered the flowers, planned dinner, and was moving toward the front door, coat on, ready to attack the town with my stimulated needs. Then the phone rang. 14

Under normal circumstances that would have been a source of joy. Someone at the other end had been moved to solve my life. But these were not normal circumstances. I was impatient to get on with my list, and apprehensive that the crisp, businesslike mantle that I still wore a bit insecurely might slip off my shoulders and leave me staring at the light bulb again. But I answered the phone. 15

"Are you busy?" asked a good friend, not knowing what she was saying. 16

"Well, actually, I was just on my way out the front door." 17

"Okay," she answered. "I'll be over in a few moments," and she hung up. 18

Obviously she had not heard my crisp rejection of her intrusion. Her ears were pretuned to hear what they would hear, and when it didn't materialize she had gone deaf. It made me laugh. I took off my coat, threw my list on the hall table, and went back into my unnaturally clean kitchen to wait for her arrival. 19

She came within the half hour, all smiles and good feelings, carrying a basket of flowers. Her eyes were brimming with divergent problems, and within the hour we had laid some of them out on the kitchen table and made headway 20 with a few. It felt right. There was a close, comradely feeling that had I been at the hardware store, measuring glass, I would have missed for all eternity.

At the end of the morning she rose from her chair, smiling warmly, put her arm around my shoulder, and said semi-apologetically, "I hope I haven't kept you too long."   21

"No," I said. "I'm glad you came. But actually—and I know you won't believe this—I'm supposed to be very busy today."   22

"What do you mean 'supposed to be'?" she said.   23

"Well, I got up this morning and made a list of things I had to do, and when you called I was just on my way out the door to do them."   24

"Oh, I'm sorry," she murmured. "I didn't know."   25

"No," I answered. "Don't be sorry. It wasn't meant to be." And after she left, I sat down at the kitchen table again, stared at the light bulb, and tried to remember where I had put my list. I would have to start again tomorrow, but in the meantime there was nothing left to do but wait and see what the day would bring forth.   26

Comment

The reflective essay usually draws on personal experiences and observations. The essayist may present a series of loosely connected experiences and reflections or may organize them through a central theme or idea. "Bicycling Toward Wisdom" contains a central idea. Theroux does not give it the prominence usually given a philosophical idea in expository and persuasive essays. Instead, she presents the idea as a personal observation—an idea of the moment that she would revise if new experiences and observations warranted.

Questions for Study and Discussion

1. How does the opening dialogue between Theroux and her father introduce the central concern or theme of the essay? What is this concern or theme?

2. What are convergent and divergent problems, and what point does Theroux make about them?
3. What is the anti-American way of solving problems? How is "busyness" different from the anti-American way? What does Theroux discover about busyness as a solution?
4. Why does Theroux give her essay the title "Bicycling Toward Wisdom"? Why not "Driving Toward Wisdom"?

Vocabulary Study

1. Define the following: paragraph 4: *moot*; paragraph 8: *catatonically, metabolism*; paragraph 9: *dovetailed*; paragraph 11: *ambivalence, malaise*; paragraph 14: *factoring out, simulated*.
2. Theroux says the following in paragraph 15:

> I was impatient to get on with my list, and apprehensive that the crisp, businesslike mantle that I still wore a bit insecurely might slip off my shoulders and leave me staring at the light bulb again.

Why does Theroux use the word *apprehensive* rather than *afraid* or *fearful?* What is the "mantle" she wears and why does she describe it as "crisp" and "businesslike"?

Suggestions for Writing

Develop one of the topics or ideas of "Bicycling Toward Wisdom" from your own experience and observation. You might wish to confirm one statement by Theroux, or qualify it, or disagree with the statement completely. In developing your essay, make your central idea prominent and connect your details to it clearly.

Andrew A. Rooney

ELEVATORS

"Andy" Rooney served in the U.S. Army in World War Two, earning the Air Medal and the Bronze Star. He has had a varied career in journalism and television—as a reporter for the Army newspaper *Stars and Stripes,* a newspaper columnist, and a writer and producer for the Columbia Broadcasting System. Since 1978 he has delivered humorous essays on the CBS program *60 Minutes*. Rooney says the following in the preface to *Pieces of My Mind*, a collection of his humorous essays: "Most of the important ideas that we live with aren't new at all. If we're grown up, we've had our personal, political, economic, religious, and philosophical ideas for a long time. They evolved out of some experience we had or they came from someone we were exposed to before we were twenty-five." Ordinary experience and old ideas are the subject of Rooney's essays. "If I never have another really new idea, it won't matter. Enough writers are already exploring the new, the far-out, and the obscure. We don't understand the old ideas yet. I'm satisfied trying to quantify the obvious."

1   If you've ever worked or lived in a building where you had to use an elevator, you know that it becomes part of your life. It's often as much a barrier between you and the ground, or the ground and your office or apartment, as an open drawbridge.

2   No one is ever completely comfortable in an elevator. There's something about them we don't trust. Lurking in the back of our memory is the story we once read about the twelve people who were stuck between the seventh and eighth floors for nine hours. We look around, imagining what it would be like to be stuck with the people now on our elevator.

3   There's an uncertainty in our minds about the engineering principles of an elevator. We've all had little glimpses into the dirty, dark elevator shaft and seen the greasy cables passing each other. They never look totally safe. The idea of being trapped in a small box going up and down on strings induces a kind of phobia in all of us. There we are, standing on a platform, enclosed on all six sides, that could drop to the bottom of the building in an instant if any of the strings and the emergency brakes failed.

4   There's a predictable sequence to the little drama of an elevator ride. If you arrive at the elevator door first and the elevator is on another floor, you press the button and stand there with absolutely nothing to do. Usually someone else arrives before the elevator does. Depending on your relationship with that person, you say nothing, nod or say hello.

Invariably the second person, and subsequent persons 5
who arrive, stand there for ten seconds and then step forward and press the button themselves.

I've never been sure what motivates a person to press 6
the button when I'm already standing there. Does he think
I'm so dumb I was standing there without pressing it
myself?

More often I think it's just a little action that relieves 7
the embarrassment of standing there close to another person
without saying anything. It's something to do. Often it's done
with an impatient gesture, designed to produce a rapport
among the standees, by suggesting a mutual disapproval of
the machinery.

I work on the sixth floor of a building. I know some of 8
the elevator riders well. Others I have only that nodding
acquaintance with and some are total strangers.

I prefer riding with the strangers. Those elevator friends 9
whose names I'm not always sure of aren't comfortable with
the silence, but we don't know each other well enough to
talk about anything of substance. The conversation often turns
to the elevator itself.

If it stops at more than one floor, they'll say, "We've 10
got a local here."

I suppose that remark has been made in my presence in 11
that elevator a thousand times.

Any other conversation is limited to three topics and 12
they begin with a question. Those are:
1—"They keepin' you busy?"
2—"What's new with you?"
3—"Is it hot (cold) enough for you?"

My inclination is to just nod and smile when these are 13
directed at me. I don't want to be unfriendly but I'm not
going to make a fool of myself by answering a question that
wasn't really meant to be one.

Escalators have always been more fun than elevators, 14
although most women approach them gingerly. Years ago I
talked to a hotel architect named William Tabler who had
just designed a new Hilton in New York. He'd put in lots

of elevators but he'd connected three meeting-room floors with escalators.

"They're really slower even if you have to wait for the elevator," he said, "but people like to be moving."   15

This week I've decided to get in shape by walking up   16 and down the six flights in my building. It's something I've decided to do three or four times a year for the last ten years. My resolve disappears in a few days in a fit of heavy breathing and I go back to the elevator.

Comment

As the Hough essay shows, the informal essay has a destination—the unfolding or exploration of a central idea—but it does not always announce its purpose or state the idea, and it may take detours before reaching a conclusion. Rooney explores the general topic of elevators. He begins with a central idea that resembles the thesis of a formal essay. Rooney reflects on our attitude toward elevators, turns to the behavior of people waiting for the elevator, and finishes with a series of random observations. He writes as if conversing: he pauses to consider what he has said and to qualify a statement; in the concluding paragraphs, he turns without transition to other interesting observations.

Questions for Study and Discussion

1. Where does Rooney state his central idea? How does he keep this idea before the reader?
2. In how many ways does Rooney illustrate that idea? Are the ideas of paragraphs 14 through 16 illustrations of the idea, or do they introduce new ideas and observations?
3. Is the tone of the paragraphs 1 through 4 one of amusement or sarcasm? Or is the tone serious and objective—that of an interested and observant spectator? Does the tone change in the remaining paragraphs of the essay?

Vocabulary Study

How would the following substitutions in parentheses change the meaning of the sentence?

paragraph 2: "Lurking [hiding] in the back of our memory. . . ."

paragraph 3: "induces a kind of phobia [fear] in all of us."

paragraph 7: "designed to produce a rapport [agreement] among the standees. . . ."

paragraph 13: "My inclination [wish] is to just nod and smile. . . ."

paragraph 14: "although most women approach them gingerly [suspiciously]."

Suggestions for Writing

1. Describe your own behavior while waiting for an elevator or while riding in one. Use your description to make an observation about yourself or people you have observed.
2. Write an informal essay on a topic suggested in the essay or on one of the following:
   a. on giving directions to a person lost in the city
   b. on riding a crowded bus or train
   c. on sitting in stalled traffic
   d. on walking in a strange neighborhood
   e. on shopping in a crowded supermarket

John Gregory Dunne

QUINTANA

After serving in the United States Army, John Gregory Dunne worked for an advertising agency and a trade magazine in New York City, and he was a staff writer for *Time* magazine for five years. Dunne has written screenplays, essays, and novels, including *True Confessions* (1977), *Dutch Shea, Jr.* (1982), and *The Red, White, and Blue* (1987). His essays are collected in *Quintana and Friends* (1979). His wife is the essayist and novelist Joan Didion (see p. 287). The unusual essay reprinted here describes their relationship with Quintana, their adopted daughter.

Quintana will be eleven this week. She approaches ad-   1
olescence with what I can only describe as panache, but then
watching her journey from infancy has always been like
watching Sandy Koufax pitch or Bill Russell play basketball.
There is the same casual arrogance, the implicit sense that
no one has ever done it any better. And yet it is difficult for
a father to watch a daughter grow up. With each birthday
she becomes more like us, an adult, and what we cling to is
the memory of the child. I remember the first time I saw her
in the nursery at Saint John's Hospital. It was after visiting
hours and my wife and I stood staring through the sound-
proof glass partition at the infants in their cribs, wondering
which was ours. Then a nurse in a surgical mask appeared
from a back room carrying a fierce, black-haired baby with
a bow in her hair. She was just seventeen hours old and her
face was still wrinkled and red and the identification beads
on her wrist had not our name but only the letters "NI."
"NI" stood for "No Information," the hospital's code for
an infant to be placed for adoption. Quintana is adopted.

It has never been an effort to say those three words,   2
even when they occasion the well-meaning but insensitive
compliment, "You couldn't love her more if she were your
own." At moments like that, my wife and I say nothing and
smile through gritted teeth. And yet we are not unaware
that sometime in the not too distant future we face a moment that only those of us who are adoptive parents will
ever have to face—our daughter's decision to search or not
to search for her natural parents.

I remember that when I was growing up, a staple of   3
radio drama was the show built around adoption. Usually
the dilemma involved a child who had just learned by accident that it was adopted. This information could only come
accidentally, because in those days it was considered a radical departure from the norm to inform your son or daughter that he or she was not your own flesh and blood. If such
information had to be revealed, it was often followed by the
specious addendum that the natural parents had died when
the child was an infant. An automobile accident was viewed

as the most expeditious and efficient way to get rid of both parents at once. One of my contemporaries, then a young actress, was not told that she was adopted until she was twenty-two and the beneficiary of a small inheritance from her natural father's will. Her adoptive mother could not bring herself to tell her daughter the reason behind the bequest and entrusted the task to an agent from the William Morris office.

Today we are more enlightened, aware of the psycho- 4 logical evidence that such barbaric secrecy can only inflict hurt. When Quintana was born, she was offered to us privately by the gynecologist who delivered her. In California, such private adoptions are not only legal but in the mid-sixties, before legalized abortion and before the sexual revolution made it acceptable for an unwed mother to keep her child, were quite common. The night we went to see Quintana for the first time at Saint John's, there was a tacit agreement between us that "No Information" was only a bracelet. It was quite easy to congratulate ourselves for agreeing to be so open when the only information we had about her mother was her age, where she was from and a certified record of her good health. What we did not realize was that through one bureaucratic slipup we would learn her mother's name and that through another she would learn ours, and Quintana's.

From the day we brought Quintana home from the hos- 5 pital, we tried never to equivocate. When she was little, we always had Spanish-speaking help and one of the first words she learned, long before she understood its import, was *adoptada*. As she grew older, she never tired of asking us how we happened to adopt her. We told her that we went to the hospital and were given our choice of any baby in the nursery. "No, not that baby," we had said, "not that baby, not that baby . . ." All this with full gestures of inspection, until finally: "That baby!" Her face would always light up and she would say: "Quintana." When she asked a question about her adoption, we answered, never volunteering more than she requested, convinced that as she grew her questions would become more searching and complicated. In terms I hoped she would understand, I tried to explain that adoption offered to a parent the possibility of escaping the prison of the genes, that no matter how perfect the natural child, the parent could not help acknowledging in black moments that some of his or her bad blood was bubbling around in the offspring; with an *adoptada,* we were innocent of any knowledge of bad blood.

In time Quintana began to intuit that our simple para- 6 ble of free choice in the hospital nursery was somewhat more complex than we had indicated. She now knew that being adopted meant being born of another mother, and that person she began referring to as "my other mommy." How old, she asked, was my other mommy when I was born? Eighteen, we answered, and on her stubby little fingers she added on her own age, and with each birthday her other mommy became twenty-three, then twenty-five and twenty-eight. There was no obsessive interest, just occasional queries, some more difficult to answer than others. Why had her other mother given her up? We said that we did not know—which was true—and could only assume that it was because she was little more than a child herself, alone and without the resources to bring up a baby. The answer seemed to satisfy, at least until we became close friends with a young woman, unmarried, with a small child of her own. The contradiction was, of course, apparent to Quintana, and yet she seemed to understand, in the way that children do, that there had been a millennium's worth of social change in the years since her birth, that the pressures on a young unmarried mother were far more in 1966 than they were in 1973. (She did, after all, invariably refer to the man in the White House as President Nixon Vietnam Watergate, almost as if he had a three-tiered name like John Quincy Adams.) We were sure that she viewed her status with equanimity, but how much so we did not realize until her eighth birthday party. There were twenty little girls at the party, and as little girls do, they were discussing things gynecological, specifically the orifice in their mothers' bodies from which they had emerged at birth. "I didn't," Quintana said matter-of-factly. She was sitting in a large wicker fan chair and her pronouncement impelled the other children to silence. "I was adopted." We had often wondered how she would handle this moment with her peers, and we froze, but she pulled it off with such élan and aplomb that in moments the other children were bemoaning their own misfortune in not being adopted, one even claiming, "Well, I was almost adopted."

Because my wife and I both work at home, Quintana has never had any confusion about how we make our living. Our mindless staring at our respective typewriters means food on the table in a way the mysterious phrase "going to the office" never can. From the time she could walk, we have taken her to meetings whenever we were without help, and she has been a quick study on the nuances of our life. "She's remarkably well adjusted," my brother once said about her. "Considering that every time I see her she's in a different city." I think she could pick an agent out of a police lineup, and out of the blue one night at dinner she offered that all young movie directors were short and had frizzy hair and wore Ditto pants and wire glasses and shirts with three buttons opened. (As far as I know, she had never laid eyes on Bogdanovich, Spielberg or Scorsese.) Not long ago an actress received an award for a picture we had written for her. The actress's acceptance speech at the televised award ceremony drove Quintana into an absolute fury. "She never," Quintana reported, "thanked *us*." Since she not only identifies with our work but at times even considers herself an equal partner, I of course discussed this piece with her before I began working on it. I told her what it was about and said I would drop it if she would be embarrassed or if she thought the subject too private. She gave it some thought and finally said she wanted me to write it.

I must, however, try to explain and perhaps even try to justify my own motives. The week after *Roots* was televised, each child in Quintana's fifth-grade class was asked to trace a family tree. On my side Quintana went back to her great-grandfather Burns, who arrived from Ireland shortly after

the Civil War, a ten-year-old refugee from the potato famine, and on her mother's side to her great-great-great-great-
grandmother Cornwall, who came west in a wagon train in
1846. As it happens, I have little interest in family beyond
my immediate living relatives. (I can never remember the
given names of my paternal grandparents and have never
known my paternal grandmother's maiden name. This lack
of interest mystifies my wife.) Yet I wanted Quintana to understand that if she wished, there were blood choices other
than Dominick Burns and Nancy Hardin Cornwall. Over
the past few years, there has been a growing body of literature about adoptees seeking their own roots. I am in general
sympathetic to this quest, although not always to the dogged
absolutism of the more militant seekers. But I would be re-
miss if I did not say that I am more than a little sensitive to
the way the literature presents adoptive parents. We are usually shown as frozen in the postures of radio drama, un-
touched by the changes in attitudes of the last several
generations. In point of fact we accept that our children might
seek out their roots, even encourage it; we accept it as an
adventure like life itself—perhaps painful, one hopes enrich-
ing. I know not one adoptive parent who does not feel this
way. Yet in the literature there is the implicit assumption
that we are threatened by the possibility of search, that we
would consider it an act of disloyalty on the part of our
children. The patronizing nature of this assumption is never
noted in the literature. It is as if we were Hudson and Mrs.
Bridges, below-stairs surrogates taking care of the wee one,
and I don't like it one damn bit.

Often these days I find myself thinking of Quintana's   9
natural mother. Both my wife and I admit more than a passing interest in the woman who produced this extraordinary
child. (As far as we know, she never named the father, and
even more interesting, Quintana has never asked about him.)
When Quintana was small, and before the legalities of adoption were complete, we imagined her mother everywhere, a
wraithlike presence staring through the chain-link fence at
the blond infant sunbathing in the crib. Occasionally today
we see a photograph of a young woman in a magazine—the

mother as we imagine her to look—and we pass it to each other without comment. Once we even checked the name of a model in *Vogue* through her modeling agency; she turned out to be a Finn. I often wonder if she thinks of Quintana, or of us. (Remember, we know each other's names.) There is the possibility that having endured the twin traumas of birth and the giving up of a child, she blocked out the names the caseworker gave her, but I don't really believe it. I consider it more likely that she has followed the fairly well-documented passage of Quintana through childhood into adolescence. Writers are at least semipublic figures, and in the interest of commerce or selling a book or a movie, or even out of simple vanity, we allow interviews and photo layouts and look into television cameras; we even write about ourselves, and our children. I recall wondering how this sentient young woman of our imagination had reacted to four pages in *People*. It is possible, even likely, that she will read this piece. I know that it is an almost intolerable invasion of her privacy. I think it probable, however, that in the dark reaches of night she has considered the possibility of a further incursion, of opening a door one day and seeing a young woman who says, "Hello, Mother, I am your daughter."

Perhaps this is romantic fantasy. We know none of the circumstances of the woman's life, or even if she is still alive. We once suggested to our lawyer that we make a discreet inquiry and he quite firmly said that this was a quest that belonged only to Quintana, if she wished to make it, and not to us. What is not fantasy is that for the past year, Quintana has known the name of her natural mother. It was at dinner and she said that she would like to meet her one day, but that it would be hard, not knowing her name. There finally was the moment: we had never equivocated; did we begin now? We took a deep breath and told Quintana, then age ten, her mother's name. We also said that if she decided to search her out, we would help her in any way we could. (I must allow, however, that we would prefer she wait to make this decision until the Sturm and Drang of adolescence is past.) We then considered the possibility that her mother, for whatever good or circumstantial reasons of her own, might prefer not to see her. I am personally troubled by the militant contention that the natural mother has no right of choice in this matter. "I did not ask to be born," an adoptee once was quoted in a news story I read. "She has to see me." If only life were so simple, if only pain did not hurt. Yet we would never try to influence Quintana on this point. How important it is to know her parentage is a question only she can answer; it is her decision to make.

All parents realize, or should realize, that children are   11
not possessions, but are only lent to us, angel boarders, as it were. Adoptive parents realize this earlier and perhaps more poignantly than others. I do not know the end of this story. It is possible that Quintana will find more reality in family commitment and cousins across the continent and heirloom orange spoons and pictures in an album and faded letters from Dominick Burns and diary entries from Nancy Hardin Cornwall than in the uncertainties of blood. It is equally possible that she will venture into the unknown. I once asked her what she would do if she met her natural mother. "I'd put one arm around Mom," she said, "and one arm around my other mommy, and I'd say, "Hello, Mommies.' "

If that's the way it turns out, that is what she will do.   12

Comment

Though he introduces a central idea in the opening paragraph and builds to his final point that "children are not possessions," Dunne pauses for reflection on the way. He introduces ideas sometimes with formal transition—"Often these days I find myself thinking of Quintana's natural mother," he comments in paragraph 9—and in the preceding paragraph parenthetically mentions his inability to remember certain names. Dunne gives the essay the shape of his thinking and feeling about his adopted child. He shows that his feelings as well as thoughts are sometimes difficult to express. The essay images the writer in this way.

Questions for Study and Discussion

1. Where does Dunne first state the central idea of the essay? How often does he restate it in the whole essay?
2. Is the single-sentence paragraph that concludes the essay another restatement of the thesis, or is it a final reflection?
3. How does the discussion of Quintana's natural mother in paragraphs 9 and 10 develop the thesis?
4. Is Dunne writing to a general audience or to a special one—perhaps to adoptive parents or adopted children? What do you think is his purpose in writing?
5. Possibly we would agree that honesty should guide the relations of parents and children. Do you agree that total honesty is desirable with children of all ages? Is it desirable with adopted children in the circumstances Dunne describes?

Vocabulary Study

The context or surrounding sentences in the text often suggests the meaning of an unfamiliar word or phrase. How much help does the context or use of the following words and phrases give you in understanding them? What additional help do you get from the dictionary?

a. paragraph 1: *panache*
b. paragraph 3: *dilemma, radical departure, specious addendum, expeditious and efficient*
c. paragraph 5: *equivocate*
d. paragraph 6: *parable*
e. paragraph 8: *dogged absolutism, patronizing, surrogates*
f. paragraph 9: *wraithlike, traumas, sentient*
g. paragraph 10: *Sturm and Drang, militant contention*

Suggestions for Writing

1. Dunne writes about parent and child as an adoptive parent and adult. Write an essay of your own on parents and children from your own experience. Limit your topic to a problem you can explore as fully as Dunne explores the problem he and his wife tried to solve. In writing your essay, make your topic sentences direct attention to your thesis as Dunne does.

2. Dunne states in paragraph 11 that "All parents realize, or should realize, that children are not possessions, but are only lent to us, angel boarders, as it were." Use this sentence as the introduction to an essay on the consequences of looking at friends as possessions or a related topic. Explore the problem before you attempt to state a thesis.

PART 3

Strategies for Exposition

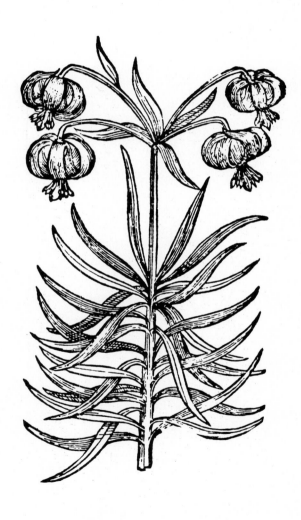

Much writing that you do is for the purpose of giving information. A recipe, directions on how to repair a tire, an explanation of how mules differ from horses, a definition of a molecule, analysis of how the United States became engaged in Vietnam—all these give information. The word *exposition,* meaning explanation or the unfolding or setting forth of an idea, describes this kind of writing.

Exposition may use one or more of the methods of organization discussed in Part One. These include narration, description, example, process, comparison and contrast, cause and effect, definition, and classification and division. In explaining how to repair a tire, you may describe the tire rim and the tire and define and classify the tools needed to do the repair. In explaining Vietnam, you may narrate the events leading to the American engagement, compare the policies of President Kennedy and President Johnson, and trace the effects of these policies. Most of the essays in this section contain more than one method of exposition.

Exposition, in turn, may serve other kinds of writing. Expressive writing often contains information of various kinds; a veteran's personal account of Vietnam probably will include informative details on weapons, terrain, and jungle warfare. Persuasive writing—for example, an essay arguing for or against America's involvement in Vietnam—probably would include details of that involvement as well as an analysis of causes and effects.

The purposes of giving information are obviously many. In the following essay on the need of error in human life, Lewis Thomas is defining the word *human.* Thomas might have developed an abstract definition that a particular audience probably would understand without the observations and details he provides in the essay. Instead, he compares humans with computers and thus draws on experiences most readers have had. The technique of proceeding gradually from known experiences to complex and difficult ideas is a common method in exposition. Many essays do begin with abstract statements, but many essayists prefer to lead into abstract ideas gradually through concrete details. These generate interest in the subject, sometimes through historical background unfamiliar to most readers.

Thomas combines some methods of exposition illustrated in the sections that follow. He bases his exposition on comparison with computers, using the similarities between computers and humans (in particular the programmed error in computers) to define the kind of error that makes human life possible. And he uses analogy, or a point-by-point comparison between unlike things—

here a good laboratory and a good computer—to illustrate why error promotes increased inefficiency and thinking. He also uses contrast between humans and lower animals, which lack the "splendid freedom" of error, to explain why error is essential to human development. Throughout the essay Thomas is concerned with cause and effect—the cause of human progress, the effect of error.

Thomas introduces his thesis early in the essay, following his discussion of computers:

> Mistakes are at the very base of human thought, embedded there, feeding the structure like root nodules. If we were not provided with the knack of being wrong, we could never get anything useful done.

He restates his thesis in the course of his illustration and discussion:

> The capacity to leap across mountains of information to land lightly on the wrong side represents the highest of human endowments.
>
> What we need, then, for moving ahead, is a set of wrong alternatives much longer and more interesting than the short list of mistaken courses that any of us can think up right now.

In this concluding restatement of the thesis, Thomas moves from information to persuasion. But he stops short of developing proposals—ways to encourage acceptance of error, the "splendid freedom" that he earlier suggested animals lack.

This analysis shows that Thomas is organizing the essay according to his judgment of his audience. He is writing as you would converse with a friend—pausing to explain and illustrate ideas when you see that you are not being understood. You repeat your main point to give your explanation a frame but also to be persuasive even when your main purpose is informative. In writing, you must make a judgment about an audience and assess the kind of explanation and information it needs to understand your main point or thesis.

Lewis Thomas

TO ERR IS HUMAN

A graduate of Princeton University and Harvard Medical School, Lewis Thomas has served in a number of medical posts. He has been chairman of pathology and medicine and dean of New York University–Bellevue Medical Center, chairman of pathology and dean of Yale School of Medicine, and president and later chancellor of Sloan–Kettering Cancer Center in New York City. He has also served as professor of medicine and pathology at Cornell Medical School in New York, and as university professor at State University of New York–Stony Brook Health Sciences Center. Thomas describes his medical career in *The Youngest Science: Notes of a Medicine Watcher* (1983). His essays, most of which first appeared in the *New England Journal of Medicine*, have been collected in *Lives of a Cell* (1974), *The Medusa and the Snail* (1979), and *Late Night Thoughts on Listening to Mahler's Ninth Symphony* (1983). Thomas writes on science and medicine for the specialist as well as the general reader. His lucid style is ideal for the exposition of complex ideas.

Everyone must have had at least one personal experi- 1
ence with a computer error by this time. Bank balances are suddenly reported to have jumped from $379 into the millions, appeals for charitable contributions are mailed over and over to people with crazy-sounding names at your address, department stores send the wrong bills, utility companies write that they're turning everything off, that sort of thing. If you manage to get in touch with someone and complain, you then get instantaneously typed, guilty letters from the same computer, saying, "Our computer was in error, and an adjustment is being made in your account."

These are supposed to be the sheerest, blindest acci- 2
dents. Mistakes are not believed to be part of the normal behavior of a good machine. If things go wrong, it must be a personal, human error, the result of fingering, tampering, a button getting stuck, someone hitting the wrong key. The computer, at its normal best, is infallible.

I wonder whether this can be true. After all, the whole 3
point of computers is that they represent an extension of the

human brain, vastly improved upon but nonetheless human, superhuman maybe. A good computer can think clearly and quickly enough to beat you at chess, and some of them have even been programmed to write obscure verse. They can do anything we can do, and more besides.

It is not yet known whether a computer has its own   4
consciousness, and it would be hard to find out about this. When you walk into one of those great halls now built for the huge machines, and stand listening, it is easy to imagine that the faint, distant noises are the sound of thinking, and the turning of the spools gives them the look of wild creatures rolling their eyes in the effort to concentrate, choking with information. But real thinking, and dreaming, are other matters.

On the other hand, the evidences of something like an   5
unconscious, equivalent to ours, are all around, in every mail. As extensions of the human brain, they have been constructed with the same property of error, spontaneous, uncontrolled, and rich in possibilities.

Mistakes are at the very base of human thought,   6
embedded there, feeding the structure like root nodules. If we were not provided with the knack of being wrong, we could never get anything useful done. We think our way along by choosing between right and wrong alternatives, and the wrong choices have to be made as frequently as the right ones. We get along in life this way. We are built to make mistakes, coded for error.

We learn, as we say, by "trial and error." Why do we   7
always say that? Why not "trial and rightness" or "trial and triumph"? The old phrase puts it that way because that is, in real life, the way it is done.

A good laboratory, like a good bank or a corporation   8
or government, has to run like a computer. Almost everything is done flawlessly, by the book, and all the numbers add up to the predicted sums. The days go by. And then, if it is a lucky day, and a lucky laboratory, somebody makes a mistake: the wrong buffer, something in one of the blanks, a decimal misplaced in reading counts, the warm room off

by a degree and a half, a mouse out of his box, or just a misreading of the day's protocol. Whatever, when the results come in, something is obviously screwed up, and then the action can begin.

The misreading is not the important error; it opens the way. The next step is the crucial one. If the investigator can bring himself to say, "But even so, look at that!" then the new finding, whatever it is, is ready for snatching. What is needed, for progress to be made, is the move based on error.   9

Whenever new kinds of thinking are about to be accomplished, or new varieties of music, there has to be an argument beforehand. With two sides debating in the same mind, haranguing, there is an amiable understanding that one is right and the other wrong. Sooner or later the thing is settled, but there can be no action at all if there are not the two sides, and the argument. The hope is in the faculty of wrongness, the tendency toward error. The capacity to leap across mountains of information to land lightly on the wrong side represents the highest of human endowments.   10

It may be that this is a uniquely human gift, perhaps even stipulated in our genetic instructions. Other creatures do not seem to have DNA sequences for making mistakes as a routine part of daily living, certainly not for programmed error as a guide for action.   11

We are at our human finest, dancing with our minds, when there are more choices than two. Sometimes there are ten, even twenty different ways to go, all but one bound to be wrong, and the richness of selection in such situations can lift us onto totally new ground. This process is called exploration and is based on human fallibility. If we had only a single center in our brains, capable of responding only when a correct decision was to be made, instead of the jumble of different, credulous, easily conned clusters of neurones that provide for being flung off into blind alleys, up trees, down dead ends, out into blue sky, along wrong turnings, around bends, we could only stay the way we are today, stuck fast.   12

The lower animals do not have this splendid freedom. They are limited, most of them, to absolute infallibility. Cats,   13 for all their good side, never make mistakes. I have never seen a maladroit, clumsy, or blundering cat. Dogs are sometimes fallible, occasionally able to make charming minor mistakes, but they get this way by trying to mimic their masters. Fish are flawless in everything they do. Individual cells in a tissue are mindless machines, perfect in their performance, as absolutely inhuman as bees.

We should have this in mind as we become dependent on more complex computers for the arrangement of our affairs. Give the computers their heads, I say; let them go their way. If we can learn to do this, turning our heads to one side and wincing while the work proceeds, the possibilities for the future of mankind, and computerkind, are limitless. Your average good computer can make calculations in an instant which would take a lifetime of slide rules for any of us. Think of what we could gain from the near infinity of precise, machine-made miscomputation which is now so easily within our grasp. We would begin the solving of some of our hardest problems. How, for instance, should we go about organizing ourselves for social living on a planetary scale, now that we have become, as a plain fact of life, a single community? We can assume, as a working hypothesis, that all the right ways of doing this are unworkable. What we need, then, for moving ahead, is a set of wrong alternatives much longer and more interesting than the short list of mistaken courses that any of us can think up right now. We need, in fact, an infinite list, and when it is printed out we need the computer to turn on itself and select, at random, the next way to go. If it is a big enough mistake, we could find ourselves on a new level, stunned, out in the clear, ready to move again.

Questions for Study and Discussion

1. To what extent do computers resemble human beings? How does Thomas distinguish the reasoning of each?
2. What is gained in the exposition by the comparison with computers?
3. What consequences of the human kind of reasoning does Thomas explore?

4. What is the thesis of the essay, and where is it stated?
5. Does Thomas explicitly say that nonhuman beings or things cannot possess the human faculty of reasoning?

Vocabulary Study

1. Explain how the italicized words are used in each sentence. Then explain how the word in brackets changes or modifies the meaning:
    a. "The computer, at its *normal* [average] best, is *infallible* [reliable]."
    b. "After all, the whole point of computers is that they represent an *extension* [development] of the human brain. . . ."
    c. "With two sides debating in the same mind, *haranguing* [arguing], there is an *amiable* [mutual] understanding that one is right and the other is wrong."
    d. "It may be that this is a uniquely human gift, perhaps even *stipulated* [arranged for] in our *genetic instructions* [brains]."
    e. "[The lower animals] are limited, most of them, to absolute *infallibility* [predictability]."
    f. "I have never seen a *maladroit* [awkward], clumsy, or *blundering* [muddling] cat."
    g. "Think of what we could gain from the near *infinity* [immensity] of *precise* [exact], machine-made *miscomputation* [misconception] which is now so easily within our grasp."
2. Write a paraphrase of paragraph 12, giving particular attention to the metaphors of the final sentence.

Suggestions for Writing

1. Describe an experience of your own with a computer error. Use your description to develop your own conclusions about the impact of machines on our lives or about some other idea.
2. Discuss an important change that occurred in your life as a result of a mistake you made in thinking about people or about action you intended to take.
3. Explain what Thomas means by *unconscious* in paragraph 5.

Then illustrate the point Thomas is making from your own experience.

4. Discuss the extent to which your own experience with dogs and cats supports the statements Thomas makes about them.

Louis Inturrisi

ON NOT GETTING THERE FROM HERE

Louis Inturrisi is an American who teaches English at the University of Rome. In his essay on the Italian way of giving instructions, he draws on his American–Italian background in interpreting the attitudes and behavior of Italians. Inturrisi makes his points through example. He brings humor and insight to the subject.

Before my first trip to Europe, my grandfather, who was then a very confident 82 and is now a very opinionated 100, poured me a glass of wine and gave me the following instructions: Over there, don't believe anything until three people have told you the same thing. I not only found this advice invaluable for getting around Europe that summer, it has proven useful for traveling in other parts of the world as well. Nowhere, however, has my grandfather's advice been more useful than in his native Italy, where a remarkable enthusiasm to assist foreigners is sometimes overshadowed by a lack of reliable information.

One must start by realizing that in Italy the phrases used when giving directions—such as "go straight," "turn right," "follow this road"—are not to be taken literally. Most of the time they are only suggestions. For example, if you inquire about the location of a museum and are told to go straight—"sempre dritto"—the phrase usually means "go straight *and then ask again.*" Your informant may or may not add the second part, assuming that you are already aware of this vital additional step and will not be dumbfounded or, worse, upset if the museum doesn't appear in front of you in the next 10 minutes.

The trouble comes from thinking that "sempre dritto" means that by trudging ahead you will see what you are looking for. What it really means is that you are probably on the right track, and there is a very good chance that you might find the museum somewhere in this area.

Likewise, the phrase "segua questa strada"—"follow this road"—must be interpreted to mean: "It's around here somewhere, and if you follow this road, you should see it." But do not think that just because you've understood you are within minutes of locating the museum and can start thinking about lunch. You have asked someone who thinks you are on the right track, but it is time to follow my grandfather's advice and ask someone else. If you still don't find the museum, either it is in the other direction or you are standing in front of it.

Another sign of unreliability is the phrase "mi pare"—"I think" or "it seems." A good general rule is to be suspicious of anything starting with the words "mi pare" because what follows will inevitably be too vague to be trusted.

Don't waste time with people who respond to your question by asking *you* a question. This is a strange linguistic habit some Romans have. As a reply to a request for information, some people respond by inquiring, "Is it really around here?" or "Do you know if it's in this area?" These people aren't being perfidious; they're buying time. It's best to say "Grazie. Buona giornata," and move on.

It is important to remember that giving accurate directions is much easier in Manhattan than in Mantua. Many Italian cities are composed of a myriad of tiny streets, many of which are named after people no one has ever heard of. Moreover, the numbering systems change from place to place. In some cities, the numbers, instead of alternating, proceed up one side of the street and then down the other. Piazzas often have an official name and another by which they are popularly known. Often the best any native can do is give an approximation of where you want to go.

What Americans must avoid is a certain Anglo-Saxon rigidity that manifests itself by taking words (especially words in foreign languages) too literally. For example, "laggiù in fondo" literally means "at the end of the street," but it hardly ever means that the building you are looking for is smack dab at the end of the street you are on. It may, in fact, mean that by walking straight on this street you will see what you are looking for. Or that by going straight *in the direction of* the end of the street you will see a sign directing you to your destination.

I have witnessed innocents abroad rush off happily in the direction of a "laggiù in fondo," only to return minutes later more confused than ever. They didn't realize that just before the literal end of the street, they were supposed to make a turn that their informant never mentioned because he never expected to be taken quite so literally.   9

Gestures are another source of misunderstanding. In this culture, gestures have the weight of words, a situation that can cause confusion. For example, there is often a confusing discrepancy between gestures and words, especially as regards the words "destra" ("right") and "sinistra" ("left").   10

Furthermore, Italians don't indicate directions by pointing with their index fingers. Straight ahead, for example, is rendered by a vertical slicing gesture with the open palm outstretched in front of the speaker. But if the person you have asked raises his palm over his head and wiggles it back and forth in the air, it means that you are in big trouble. His reassuring "si si's" may encourage you to continue in the same direction, but his gesture is saying something entirely different. It means something like, "My God! You are nowhere near where you want to go," or "That street is way over on the other side of the city!" If the person should drop both palms to his sides, raise his eyebrows and exhale deeply, you're in the wrong city.   11

There is, of course, always the question of who to ask for instructions. Police officers and taxi drivers are a good choice; newspaper and magazine vendors at sidewalk kiosks are even better. A general rule to follow is to put your trust in whoever answers by mentioning a specific place or landmark, such as, "It's behind Piazza Navona," or "It's next to St. John's Church." Be more than a little suspicious of replies such as, "Over there," or "Two or three streets in that direction."   12

When asking directions in Italy, an inquiry to one in-   13
dividual very soon erupts into a group effort, with everyone
in earshot joining in to offer an opinion. It takes some skill
to extract reliable information from the middle of a heated
debate in dialect, but when such a debate erupts, I tend to
put my faith in the person who seems to be arguing the *least*
vehemently. A fact is a fact to this signora, and she sees no
merit in wasting time or energy proving the existence of the
moon. Or you might wait out the debate until one partici-
pant offers to guide you to your destination to prove to herself and the others she knows what she is talking about.

I once saw a woman on a bus in Naples rescue a Scan-   14
dinavian tourist from a very loud discussion over the best
stop for getting the funicular. Silently, and with mounting
anger, the woman listened to the debate, which involved most
of the passengers as well as the driver, until the bus arrived
at what she knew was the right stop. Abruptly, she stood
up, grabbed the Scandinavian by the arm and gently eased
her off the bus, while her fellow passengers continued to
discuss the issue.

None of this should discourage you from asking ques-   15
tions in your high school or Berlitz Italian. Italians have one
of the healthiest attitudes toward their language of any Europeans. They do not expect you to speak their language
fluently nor are they ecstatic if you mouth a few words correctly. Rarely do they waste time by making you submit to
a grammar lesson in the middle of the street. When they do
correct you, it is more of a conditioned response than an
admonition.

Armed with this advice, as well as your dictionary and   16
a large-scale map, forge forward with a strong sense of adventure, a keen appreciation of the flexibility of words—and
always with my grandfather's advice clearly in the back of
your mind.

Comment

Writing for the travel section of *The New York Times,* Louis Inturrisi tells travelers to Italy what to expect when they ask directions in the street. Inturrisi shows that cultural differences play a

role in everyday situations. In illustrating these differences, he gives us numerous insights into Italians and Italian culture, and into American habits and culture too. Inturrisi also shows that definition often depends on an unspoken contract between people. Asked to define a word, few of us give as much information as the dictionary provides; we usually begin our definition believing that those asking for information possess some knowledge about the word.

Questions for Study and Discussion

1. What mistaken assumptions do Americans hold in receiving directions from Italians? What assumptions do Italians hold in giving directions?
2. What do these differences reveal about the Italian character and Italian life?
3. What do these differences reveal about American character and habits?
4. How does Inturrisi organize his essay? Is he proceeding from less interesting to more interesting facts about Italians, or does he organize the essay in another way?
5. Does Inturrisi describe your own assumptions in asking directions in a strange city? Do you find that age, gender, or ethnic background affects how a person gives directions or receives them?

Vocabulary Study

Describe how each word is used within the sentence: *opinionated* (paragraph 1); *dumbfounded* (paragraph 2); *linguistic, perfidious* (paragraph 5); *myriad, piazza* (paragraph 6); *rigidity* (paragraph 7); *literally* (paragraph 8); *gesture, discrepancy* (paragraph 9); *landmark* (paragraph 11); *dialect, vehemently, signora* (paragraph 12); *fluently, admonition* (paragraph 14); *flexibility* (paragraph 15)

Suggestions for Writing

1. Describe an experience in which confusion resulted after giving or receiving instructions. Then explain what attitudes or assumptions caused the confusion.

2. Characterize a professional class of people or an age group by
   how they give directions or behave in a social situation similar
   to the one presented by Inturrisi. In the course of your discussion, contrast this class with another, as Inturrisi does in comparing Italians with Americans.
3. Show how a lack of information about local customs can lead
   to confusion or misunderstanding between people. Be as specific as you can in illustrating the causes.

Sue Hubbell

FELLING TREES

Born in 1935 in Kalamazoo, Michigan, Sue Hubbell worked for many
years as a librarian in New Jersey and Rhode Island. Since 1973, she has
lived in the Ozark Mountains of southern Missouri, where she is a
commercial beekeeper. She has written about her life in *A Country Life:
Living the Questions* (1986). In describing the process of woodcutting,
Hubbell tells us much about day-to-day country life and the chores at
which everyone must be competent.

I was out in the woods early in the morning cutting 1
firewood for the winter. I do that every day this time of
year. For an hour or two I cut wood, load it into the pickup
and carry it back to my cabin and stack it. It isn't such a
tiring job when I do a bit of it each day, before it gets hot,
and I like being out there at that hour, when the woods are
fresh and fragrant.

This morning I finished sawing up a tree from the place 2
where I had been cutting for the past week. In the process I
lost my screwrench, part screwdriver, part wrench, that I
use to make adjustments on my chain saw. I shouldn't carry
it in my pocket, but the chain had been loose; I had tightened it and had not walked back to the truck to put the
wrench away. Scolding myself for being so careless, I began
looking for another tree to cut and found a big one that had
recently died.

I like to cut the dead trees from my woodlot, leaving 3
the ones still alive to flourish, but this one was bigger than

I feel comfortable about felling. I've been running a chain saw and cutting my own firewood for six years now, but I am still awed by the size and weight of a tree as it crashes to the ground. I have to nerve myself to cut the really big ones. I wanted this tree to fall onto a stretch of open ground that was free of other trees and brush, so I cut a wedge-shaped notch on that side of it. The theory is that the tree, thus weakened, will fall slowly on the side of the notch when the serious cut, slightly above the notch on the other side, is made. The trouble is that trees, particularly dead ones that may have rot on the inside, do not know the theory and may fall in an unexpected direction. That is the way accidents happen.

I was aware of that and was scared, besides, to be cut- 4 ting down such a big tree; as a result, perhaps, I cut too timid a wedge. I started sawing through on the other side, keeping an eye on the treetop to detect the characteristic tremble of a tree about to fall. I did not have time to jam the plastic wedge in my back pocket into the cut to hold it open because the tree began to sway and started to fall in my direction. I killed the engine on the saw and jumped out of the way.

There was no danger, however. Directly in back of where 5 I had been standing were a number of other trees, which was why I had wanted to have the dead one fall the other way, and as it started down, its top branches snagged. I had sawed completely through the tree, but now the butt end had trapped the saw against the stump. I had cut what is descriptively called a widow maker. If I had been cutting with someone else, we could have used the second saw to free mine and perhaps brought the tree down, but it is dangerous and I don't like to do it. I couldn't even free my saw by taking it apart, for I had lost my screwrench, so I drove back to the barn, gathered up the tools I needed, a socket wrench, chains and a portable winch known as a come-along.

The day was warming and I was sweating by the time 6 I got back to the woods, but I was determined to repair the botch I had made. Using the socket wrench, I removed the bar and chain from the saw and set the saw body aside. The weight of the saw gone, I worked the bar and chain free from under the butt of the tree. Then I spat and drank ice water from my thermos and figured out how I was going to pull down the tree with chain and winch.

The come-along is a cheery, sensible tool for a woman. It has a big hook at one end and a hook connected to a steel cable at the other. The cable is wound around a ratchet gear operated by a long handle to give leverage. It divides a heavy job into small, manageable bits that require no more than female strength, and I have used it many times to pull my pickup free from a mudhole. I decided that if I wound a chain around the butt of the widow maker and another chain around a nearby standing tree and connected the two with the come-along, I might be able to winch the felled tree to the ground. I attached the chains and come-along appropriately and began. Slowly, with each pump of the handle against the ratchet gear, the tree sank to the ground. The sun was high, the heat oppressive, and my sweatshirt was soaked with sweat, so I decided to leave the job of cutting up the tree to firewood lengths until tomorrow. I gathered up my tools and, in the process, found the screwrench almost hidden in leaf mold.

I am good friends with a woman who lives across the hollow. She and her husband sell cordwood to the charcoal factory in town. Her husband cuts the logs because a chain saw, in the Ozarks, is regarded as a man's tool, and she helps him load and unload the logs. Even though the wood is going to be turned into charcoal, it is traditional to cut it to four-foot lengths. A four-foot oak log is heavy; a strong man can lift it, but a woman has to use all her strength to do her part. My friend returns from her mornings sick with exhaustion, her head throbbing. She and I talk sometimes about how it would be if women were the woodcutters: the length would be less than four feet. Having to do work beyond her strength makes my friend feel weak, ineffectual, dependent and cross.

My friend, and other Ozark women, often ask me curiously about my chain saw. Most people out here heat with wood, and if families in the suburbs quarrel about taking out the garbage, here the source of squabbles is getting enough firewood cut early in the year so that it can season. Women usually help by carrying the cut wood to the truck, but it is the men who cut the wood, and since the women think they cannot cut it, they frequently worry and sometimes nag about it.

My female Ozark friends envy me having my firewood   10
supply under my own control, and they are interested when I tell them that they have had the hardest part of the job anyway, carrying the wood to the trucks. Cutting the wood into lengths with the chain saw is not hard work, although it does require some skill. So far, however, my friends have not taken up my offer to come over so that I can give them a lesson in using a chain saw. Forty years ago chain saws were heavy and certainly beyond the strength of a woman to use; today they are much improved and light. My saw is a small, light one, but with its 16-inch bar it is big enough to cut any tree I want to fell.

I know that feeling of helplessness and irritation that   11
my friends have, for that is the way I used to be. Like many women my age, I would stand back and let a man change a flat tire. I could press a button on a washing machine but not fix the machine if something failed. I felt uneasy with tools other than a needle, a typewriter or kitchen utensils.

When I began living here alone I had to learn how to   12
break down work into parcels that I could perform with my strength and I had to learn to use tools that I had never used and use them easily. Either that, or I would have had to leave. It was the hardest schooling I've ever taken but the most exhilarating. When there were Things in the world too heavy to move where I wanted them to be and too mysterious to be kept doing what I wanted them to do, I was filled with dissatisfaction and petulance. Those Things controlled me.

I prefer it the other way around.   13

Comment

The personal truth to which Hubbell builds her essay will have no meaning for the reader without the extended example she gives in her account of cutting firewood. To make her experiences clear to the reader who knows nothing about woodcutting, she combines several kinds of exposition: she defines the "come-along," describes the process of cutting down a tree, analyzes why trees fall in unexpected directions, and compares her woodcutting with that of the woman who lives nearby. For the reader experienced in woodcutting, she might have chosen another order of ideas.

Questions for Study and Discussion

1. What is the idea or truth that Hubbell illustrates through the felling of trees? How do the details of the essay illustrate this idea?
2. How different would the effect of the essay be if Hubbell had stated her purpose and central idea at the beginning?
3. Were the essay directed to readers experienced in woodcutting, what might Hubbell have omitted and how might she have reorganized the essay?
4. What personal qualities emerge in the course of the essay— particularly in the description of the tree cuttings? Which of these qualities stand out most?
5. Is Hubbell arguing for a change in attitude toward women like herself, or is she merely contrasting her own life with that of her female neighbors?

Vocabulary Study

Be ready to discuss how the details of the essay or the dictionary help you understand the following terms:

a. *widow maker*
b. *come-along*
c. *screwrench*

Suggestions for Writing

1. Develop the central idea of Hubbell's essay through an extended example of your own. You might build to the idea through your example as Hubbell does or begin the essay with a statement of the idea.

2. Develop one of the following through examples drawn from personal experience:
   a. I have known people to stop and buy an apple on the corner and then walk away as if they had solved the whole unemployment problem.—Heywood Broun
   b. If you have to keep reminding yourself of a thing, perhaps it isn't so.—Christopher Morley
   c. There is no substitute for talent. Industry and all the virtues are of no avail.—Aldous Huxley

Jack Trueblood

FOR A LOVE OF FISHING

Jack Trueblood, an outdoor and conservation writer, for five years was a contributing editor to *Field and Stream Magazine*. A graduate of Boise State University, he writes frequently about southern Idaho where he lives. Trueblood uses process analysis throughout this essay.

Johnson Creek, where it flows into the North Fork of the Boise River, was about three times as wide as a boy is tall when I discovered it. It is a fast creek, cutting its path through granite mountains as it descends from lakes high in Idaho's Sawtooth Wilderness. There are log jams there that have made a great array of holes, pools, backwaters, and riffles, all hiding trout.

One day when we were about fourteen a friend and I fished our way up Johnson Creek, working alternate pools and not concerned with much of anything except the absolute freedom of our situation and the knowledge that we had the ability to catch the wild little cutthroats. When the day was about half used we decided that lunch was in order, so we kept the next four fish and cleaned them while a smokeless willow-twig fire burned to coals on a gravel bar beside the water. Fresh coals were occasionally added from a small fire next to the broiling bed, and the trout we cooked on green willow branches were as good as any fine restaurant could serve. This was an annual event for several years, and the reason it became such a good memory, I think, was not because we could catch the fish, but because we didn't have to.

My parents provided me with the opportunity to be near fishing water from an early age. If you would teach a child to love fishing, do *not* put a rod in his hand and insist that he follow along and imitate you. All too often you find that you have moved into water too rough for the kid to handle, or that the casts required are too long, or that there is nothing for him to do but watch.

Setting is the first necessity in helping a child learn to love fishing. If you live in an area where camping requires a considerable amount of time, perhaps you can find a pond, lake, or creek nearby to use when teaching the elements of casting. If not, a big lawn will do, but a youngster is likely to become impatient and fiddle with the dandelions instead of the rod. Kids usually want to learn to fish, and the value of learning to cast well becomes obvious only after they need the skill.

I've used a fly rod from as early as I can remember, and learned how to handle it while catching crappies from a lake with shores clear of brush. Crappies in season will keep even a novice interested, and it's easy to catch enough to build your confidence. By the time I started fishing seriously on mountain streams I could cast a fly well enough to get by, knew what a strike felt like and how to set up my own tackle. In short, I had passed the primer course in fly fishing before I ever attempted fishing in rough terrain.

My introduction to trout was in places like Granite Creek on the Boise River in Idaho. As trout streams go, Granite isn't much. It wouldn't get mentioned by most of the people who haunt Silver Creek or Henry's Fork of the Snake. But if you and your old man are crouched under willow branches at the edge of a tiny creek while he quietly explains where the trout will be and how to gently flip a fly so that it will pass over them, then Granite Creek is Henry's Fork. Or Silver Creek. Or the Madison. At that moment you are at the center of the world, and all things come to you.

There was a log bridge on Granite Creek, and it was possible for a greenhorn boy to catch wriggling cutthroats just by lying on the bridge and sneaking the tip of his rod over the edge, then easing line out until the fly danced on the water. I soon learned that the same type of sneaking will score on trout from streamside.

A prime ingredient of setting is what the child can do   8
when he tires of fishing. Logging hadn't reached Granite Creek yet, so the road was primitive and there was no traffic. My brother Dan and I were great explorers when we weren't fishing, and an old sheep corral near camp lent itself to all types of boyhood adventures.

My father, who had experience at being a boy, didn't   9
get upset when we wanted to go climbing around the fences rather than fish. Instead he went with us, explaining where the truck had unloaded the sheep and pointing out the trail they had taken into the high country. We were intrigued by his explanation of the nomadic life of a sheepherder and his pack string. The success of his teaching was in letting us pursue our interests.

My age at the time of that trip was less than nine. When   10
I got tired of fishing, there was always something else to do. The point is that you can't teach a kid to love fishing by taking him to a place that is desolate or boring or cold. Go to places that would be good to visit with your kids even if there were no fishing, because he or she is going to be a kid first and then a fisherman.

The abundance of fish is another big factor. Getting   11
enough pan-sized trout for a meal was no problem where we kids fished. In the summertime they weren't finicky feeders, and by the time I was fourteen and needed a license, I knew enough about flies to do quite well. It takes only a few times up a stream with an experienced fisherman for a youngster to learn the basics, and long before I learned about hatches and fly colors I knew that I should carry a few of different types: Black Gnat and Brown Hackle for the times when dark colors were winners, Renegade and Royal Coachman when a splash of white was important, a couple of light-colored dry flies, and a few wet flies. Armed with this selection of a dozen or so, a pocketknife, and a light rod, I soon learned that every likely looking spot usually does hold a trout.

The streams I fished as a boy were not too big to wade, 12
and that's the kind I take my kids to. Pick streams gentle
enough that a child can wade across in most places. Of course
there will be deep holes or rapids that might be dangerous,
but most youngsters won't get foolhardy in these places if
the rest of the stream is something they can handle.

Brush is a thing you should consider too. A kid will be 13
slapped in the face by brush adults can push aside. Streams
completely enclosed by brush should be avoided because they
are too hard for a youngster to approach or to fish.

The tackle a beginner uses is most often like that of his 14
teacher. I was brought up to use a fly rod, though most of
my friends used spinning tackle. Whatever you decide to start
your student with, a few general guidelines are in order.

To begin with, make it light. This will usually mean 15
that it will be more his or her size and less awkward or
burdensome to carry, and that it will transmit the feel of the
fish better than a heavy outfit. Next, make it durable. Kids
often forget about stubbing the rod tip when walking, or
laying the rod down in a careless place. Also, keep it simple.
This will help avoid backlash and tangle problems, and make
it easier to sort out those that do occur. And finally, buy
quality. A nice, well-balanced outfit purchased when a kid
is twelve can be used for the rest of his life, whereas an awkward, poorly made one may discourage the beginner, and in
any case, will have to be upgraded as he becomes a better
caster.

When I was a youngster, my folks took my brother and 16
me on a camping vacation every summer. The "boy trips,"
as they came to be called, were two weeks to a month and
in some of the most scenic places imaginable. It was on these
summertime trips that we both learned about trout fishing,
with camping and mountain lore as an added bonus.

Our favorite stream meandered through willows and 17
provided a multitude of good pools and cut banks in addition to beaver ponds. Kids can learn a lot about trout from
beaver ponds because they can see the fish. I can remember
finding out that trout are frightened by footsteps on quaky
ground. Although it had been explained before, it wasn't
quite believable until I could actually see them dart for cover.

Another thing you can teach a beginner on a beaver   18
pond is how well trout can see. In still water you can point
out how fish are frightened by the shadow of a line, and the
impact of a heavy-handed cast is obvious. Kids learn how
to make a fly drift gently to the water, or if spinning, how
to cast beyond fish and bring the bait or lure to them instead
of bonking them on the head with it. The novice soon realizes that fish can see better through and out of water than
people can into it, and the lessons will carry over whether
the water is rough or smooth.

After the beginner has learned the mechanics of using   19
his tackle, about the best way to help is by leaving yours in
camp. Now you have made him the center of attention, and
he knows that you are really interested. When the youngster
shows signs of tiredness or is catching so many trout that
you just can't stand it, ask if you might use his gear to fish
the next hole. This makes a kid feel important—after all,
the adult wants what he has for a change, instead of the
other way around.

Another advantage of leaving your tackle is that you   20
can give hands-on aid to the beginner. Stand (kneel if your
student is short) immediately behind the learner and grasp
the rod grip just ahead of his hand. You do the work of
casting and the learner just sort of coasts along and learns
from the feel of your cast things that are difficult to put into
words, like the amount of force used and the timing. The
beginner should control the line, letting it out as you in-
struct him to. Soon you apply less and less force and he
naturally puts a little more effort into it, until you just step
back and leave him in control. This often works better than
the clearest of instructions.

Children have an attention span that shortens in direct   21
proportion to their frustration. Probably the greatest frustration to a child is a forceful, nagging, angry teacher. Enjoyment, after all, is the basic reason for sport fishing, and
you have to enjoy your companions as well as your sport.

You can't teach kids to appreciate fishing if you isolate   22
yourself in the adult world and leave them in the child's
world. You must remember that you, too, have experience

at being a boy or girl, and use that experience to communicate the quality of life that is available to you and your kids somewhere along the creek.

Comment

Although his essay is chiefly concerned with giving information about fishing, Trueblood expresses his own love of the sport and tells us much about his background and interests. He also has a point to make about the process he describes. Trueblood might have focused on one of the many topics he discusses—for example, casting on a still pond—and given many more details about this skill. He chooses instead to cover only a few details, presenting those that develop his central point.

Questions for Study and Discussion

1. What is the central point Trueblood is making about children and fishing? How does the process described develop this point?
2. What are the stages of the process? Which stages does Trueblood describe in the most detail, and why?
3. What do you discover about Trueblood as a person through his discussion of his childhood experiences and of fishing?

Vocabulary Study

Plain and untechnical as Trueblood's description of fishing is, some of the steps would require different language or additional details if the essay were addressed to children rather than to parents. Rewrite the following sentences in words children would understand:

a. "Crappies in season will keep even a novice interested and it's easy to catch enough to build your confidence." (paragraph 5)
b. "By the time I started fishing seriously on mountain streams I could cast a fly well enough to get by, knew what a strike felt like and how to set up my own tackle." (paragraph 5)
c. "Kids learn how to make a fly drift gently to the water, or if spinning, how to cast beyond fish and bring the bait

or lure to them instead of bonking them on the head with it." (paragraph 18)

Suggestions for Writing

1. Describe how to teach children a skill similar to fishing. Explain why children will find this skill rewarding, and why it has been rewarding to you.
2. Describe a process you have performed many times—for example, changing a bicycle or an automobile tire or threading and operating a sewing machine. Assume that your reader knows nothing about the necessary tools or machinery. Before writing consider what details you must provide and what terms you must define at each stage of the process.
3. Certain jobs can be performed in more than one way—for example, training a dog not to jump on people. Discuss various ways of doing this or a similar job. Keep these ways distinct for your reader.
4. Trace a historical process like making the decision to attend college. Comment on the implications of some of the stages as you describe the process.

L. Rust Hills

HOW TO EAT AN ICE-CREAM CONE

L. Rust Hills was born in 1924 in Brooklyn, New York, and attended the United States Merchant Marine Academy and Wesleyan University. He was fiction editor of *Esquire* and *The Saturday Evening Post,* has taught writing, and is now a freelance writer. His books include *How to Do Things Right* (1972), *How to Retire at 41* (1973), and *How to Be Good* (1976).

Before you even get the cone, you have to do a lot of planning about it. We'll assume that you lost the argument in the car and that the family has decided to break the automobile journey and stop at an ice-cream stand for cones. Get things straight with them right from the start. Tell them that after they have their cones there will be an imaginary circle six feet away from the car and that no one—man, woman, or especially child—will be allowed to cross the line and reenter the car until his ice-cream cone has been entirely consumed and he has cleaned himself up. Emphasize: Automobiles and ice-cream cones don't mix. Explain: Melted ice cream, children, is a fluid that is eternally sticky. One drop of it on a car-door handle spreads to the seat covers, to trousers, to hands, and thence to the steering wheel, the gearshift, the rearview mirror, all the knobs of the dashboard—spreads *everywhere* and lasts *forever,* spreads from a nice old car like this, which might have to be abandoned because of stickiness, right into a nasty new car, in secret ways that even scientists don't understand. If necessary, even make a joke: "The family that eats ice-cream cones together sticks together." Then let their mother explain the joke and tell them you don't mean half of what you say, and no, we won't be getting a new car.

Blessed are the children who always eat the same flavor   2
of ice cream or always know beforehand what kind they will want. Such good children should be quarantined from those who want to "wait and see what flavors there are." It's a sad thing to observe a beautiful young child who has always been perfectly happy with a plain vanilla ice-cream cone being subverted by a young schoolmate who has been invited along for the weekend—a pleasant and polite visitor, perhaps, but spoiled by permissive parents and scarred by an overactive imagination. This schoolmate has a flair for contingency planning: "Well, I'll have banana if they have banana, but if they don't have banana then I'll have peach, if it's fresh peach, and if they don't have banana or fresh peach I'll see what else they have that's like that, like maybe fresh strawberry or something, and if they don't have that or anything like that that's good I'll just have chocolate marshmallow chip or chocolate ripple or something like that." Then—turning to one's own once simple and innocent child, now already corrupt and thinking fast—the schoolmate invites a similar rigmarole. "What kind are *you* going to have?"

I'm a great believer in contingency planning, but none   3
of this is realistic. Few adults, and even fewer children, are able to make up their minds beforehand what kind of ice-

cream cone they'll want. It would be nice if they could all be lined up in front of the man who is making up the cones and just snap smartly when their turn came, "Strawberry, please," "Vanilla, please," "Chocolate, please." But of course it never happens like that. There is always a great discussion, a great jostling and craning of necks and leaning over the counter to see down into the tubs of ice cream, and much interpersonal consultation—"What kind are *you* having?"— back and forth, as if that should make any difference. Until finally the first child's turn comes and he asks the man, "What kinds do you have?"

Now, this is the stupidest question in the world, be- 4 cause there is always a sign posted saying what kinds of ice cream they have. As I tell the children, that's what they put the sign up there for—so you won't have to ask what kinds of ice cream they have. The man gets sick of telling everybody all the different kinds of ice cream they have, so they put a sign up there that *says*. You're supposed to read it, not ask the man.

"All right, but the sign doesn't say strawberry." 5

"Well, that means they don't have strawberry." 6

"But there *is* strawberry, right there." 7

"That must be raspberry or something." (Look again at 8 the sign. Raspberry isn't there, either.)

When the child's turn actually comes, he says, "Do you 9 have strawberry?"

"Sure" 10

"What other kinds do you have?" 11

The trouble is, of course, that they put up that sign 12 saying what flavors they have, with little cardboard inserts to put in or take out flavors, way back when they first opened the store. But they never change the sign—or not often enough. They always have flavors that aren't on the list, and often they don't have flavors that *are* on the list. Children know this—whether innately or from earliest experience it would be hard to say. The ice-cream man knows it, too. Even grownups learn it eventually. There will always be chaos and confusion and mind-changing and general uproar when ice-cream cones are being ordered, and there has not been, is not, and will never be any way to avoid it.

Human beings are incorrigibly restless and dissatisfied, always in search of new experiences and sensations, seldom content with the familiar. It is this, I think, that accounts for people wanting to have a taste of your cone, and wanting you to have a taste of theirs. "*Do* have a taste of this fresh peach—it's delicious," my wife used to say to me, very much (I suppose) the way Eve wanted Adam to taste her delicious apple. An insinuating look of calculating curiosity would film my wife's eyes—the same look those beautiful, scary women in those depraved Italian films give a man they're interested in. "How's *yours?*" she would say. For this reason, I always order chocolate chip now. Down through the years, all those close enough to me to feel entitled to ask for a taste of my cone—namely, my wife and children—have learned what chocolate chip tastes like, so they have no legitimate reason to ask me for a taste. As for tasting other people's cones, never do it. The reasoning here is that if it tastes good, you'll wish you'd had it; if it tastes bad, you'll have had a taste of something that tastes bad; if it doesn't taste either good or bad, then you won't have missed anything. Of course no person in his right mind ever *would* want to taste anyone else's cone, but it is useful to have good, logical reasons for hating the thought of it.

Another important thing. Never let the man hand you the ice-cream cones for the whole group. There is no sight more pathetic than some bumbling disorganized papa holding four ice-cream cones in two hands, with his money still in his pocket, when the man says, "Eighty cents." What does he do then? He can't hand the cones back to the man to hold while he fishes in his pocket for the money, for the man has just given them to *him*. He can start passing them out to the kids, but at least one of them will have gone back to the car to see how the dog is doing, or have been sent round in back by his mother to wash his hands or something. And even if papa does get them distributed, he's still going to be left with his own cone in one hand while he tries to get his money with the other. Meanwhile, of course, the man is very impatient, and the next group is asking him, "What flavors do you have?"

No, never let the man hand you the cones of others. 15 Make him hand them out to each kid in turn. That way, too, you won't get those disgusting blobs of butter pecan and black raspberry on your own chocolate chip. And insist that he tell you how much it all costs and settle with him *before* he hands you your own cone. Make sure everyone has got paper napkins and everything *before* he hands you your own cone. Get *everything* straight before he hands you your own cone. Then, as he hands you your own cone, reach out and take it from him. Strange, magical, dangerous moment! It shares something of the mysterious, sick thrill that soldiers are said to feel on the eve of a great battle.

Now, consider for a moment just exactly what it is that 16 you are about to be handed. It is a huge, irregular mass of ice cream, faintly domed at the top from the metal scoop, which has first produced it and then insecurely balanced it on the uneven top edge of a hollow inverted cone made out of the most brittle and fragile of materials. Clumps of ice cream hang over the side, very loosely attached to the main body. There is always much more ice cream than the cone could hold, even if the ice cream were tamped down into the cone, which of course it isn't. And the essence of ice cream is that it melts. It doesn't just stay there teetering in this irregular, top-heavy mass; it also melts. And it melts *fast*. And it doesn't just melt—it melts into a sticky fluid that *cannot* be wiped off. The only thing one person could hand to another that might possibly be more dangerous is a live hand grenade from which the pin had been pulled five seconds earlier. And of course if anybody offered you that, you could say, "Oh. Uh, well—no thanks."

Ice-cream men handle cones routinely, and are inured. 17 They are like professionals who are used to handling sticks of TNT; their movements are quick and skillful. An ice-cream man will pass a cone to you casually, almost carelessly. Never accept a cone on this basis! Too many brittle sugar cones (the only good kind) are crushed or chipped or their ice-cream tops knocked askew, by this casual sort of transfer from hand to hand. If the ice-cream man is attempting this kind of brusque transfer, keep your hands at your side, no matter what effort it may cost you to overcome the instinct by which everyone's hand goes out, almost automatically, whenever he is proffered something delicious and expected. Keep your hands at your side, and the ice-cream man will look up at you, startled, questioning. Lock his eyes with your own, and *then*, slowly, calmly, and above all deliberately, take the cone from him.

Grasp the cone with the right hand firmly but gently   18 between thumb and at least one but not more than three fingers, two-thirds of the way up the cone. Then dart swiftly away to an open area, away from the jostling crowd at the stand. Now take up the classic ice-cream-cone-eating stance: feet from one to two feet apart, body bent forward from the waist at a twenty-five-degree angle, right elbow well up, right forearm horizontal, at a level with your collarbone and about twelve inches from it. But don't start eating yet! Check first to see what emergency repairs may be necessary. Sometimes a sugar cone will be so crushed or broken or cracked that all one can do is gulp at the thing like a savage, getting what he can of it and letting the rest drop to the ground, and then evacuating the area of catastrophe as quickly as possible. Checking the cone for possible trouble can be done in a second or two, if one knows where to look and does it systematically. A trouble spot some people overlook is the bottom tip of the cone. This may have been broken off. Or the flap of the cone material at the bottom, usually wrapped over itself in that funny spiral construction, may be folded in a way that is imperfect and leaves an opening. No need to say that through this opening—in a matter of perhaps thirty or, at most, ninety seconds—will begin to pour hundreds of thousands of sticky molecules of melted ice cream. You know in this case that you must instantly get the paper napkin in your left hand under and around the bottom of the cone to stem the forthcoming flow, or else be doomed to eat the cone far too rapidly. It is a grim moment. No one wants to eat a cone under that kind of pressure, but neither does anyone want to end up with the bottom of the cone stuck to a messy napkin. There's one other alternative—one that takes both skill and courage: Forgoing any cradling action, grasp the cone more firmly between thumb and forefinger and extend the other fingers so that they are out of the way of the dripping from the bottom, then increase the waist-bend angle from twenty-five degrees to thirty-five degrees, and then eat the cone, *allowing* it to drip out of the bottom onto the ground in front of you! Experienced and thoughtful cone-eaters enjoy facing up to this kind of sudden challenge.

So far, we have been concentrating on cone problems,   19 but of course there is the ice cream to worry about, too. In this area, immediate action is sometimes needed on three fronts at once. Frequently the ice cream will be mounted on the cone in a way that is perilously lopsided. This requires immediate corrective action to move it back into balance—a slight pressure downward with the teeth and lips to seat the ice cream more firmly in and on the cone, but not so hard, of course, as to break the cone. On other occasions, gobs of ice cream will be hanging loosely from the main body, about to fall to the ground (bad) or onto one's hand (far, far worse). This requires instant action, too; one must snap at the gobs like a frog in a swarm of flies. Sometimes, trickles of ice cream will already (already!) be running down the cone toward one's fingers, and one must quickly raise the cone, tilting one's face skyward, and lick with an upward motion that pushes the trickles away from the fingers and (as much as possible) into one's mouth. Every ice-cream cone is like every other ice-cream cone in that it potentially can present all of these problems, but each ice-cream cone is paradoxically unique in that it will present the problems in a different order of emergency and degree of severity. It is, thank God, a rare ice-cream cone that will present all three kinds of problems in exactly the same degree of emergency. With each cone, it is necessary to make an instantaneous judgment as to where the greatest danger is, and to *act!* A moment's delay, and the whole thing will be a mess

Fig. 1

before you've even tasted it (*Fig. 1*). If it isn't possible to decide between any two of the three basic emergency problems (i.e., lopsided mount, dangling gobs, running trickles), allow yourself to make an arbitrary adjudication; assign a "heads" value to one and a "tails" value to the other, then flip a coin to decide which is to be tended to first. Don't, for heaven's sake, *actually* flip a coin—you'd have to dig in your pocket for it, or else have it ready in your hand before you were handed the cone. There isn't remotely enough time for anything like that. Just decide *in your mind* which came up, heads or tails, and then try to remember as fast as you can which of the problems you had assigned to the winning side of the coin. Probably, though, there isn't time for any of this. Just do something, however arbitrary. Act! *Eat!*

In trying to make wise and correct decisions about the ice-cream cone in your hand, you should always keep the objectives in mind. The main objective, of course, is to get the cone under control. Secondarily, one will want to eat the cone calmly and with pleasure. Real pleasure lies not simply in eating the cone but in eating it *right*. Let us assume that you have darted to your open space and made your necessary emergency repairs. The cone is still dangerous—still, so to speak, "live." But you can now proceed with it in an orderly fashion. First, revolve the cone through the full three hundred and sixty degrees, snapping at the loose gobs of ice cream; turn the cone by moving the thumb away from you and the forefinger toward you, so the cone moves counterclockwise. Then, with the cone still "wound," which will require the wrist to be bent at the full right angle toward you, apply pressure with the mouth and tongue to accomplish overall realignment, straightening and settling the whole mess. Then, unwinding the cone back through the full three hundred and sixty degrees, remove any trickles of ice cream. From here on, some supplementary repairs may be necessary, but the cone is now defused.

At this point, you can risk a glance around you. How badly the others are doing with their cones! Now you can settle down to eating yours. This is done by eating the ice cream off the top. At each bite, you must press down cautiously, so that the ice cream settles farther and farther into the cone. Be very careful not to break the cone. Of course, you never take so much ice cream into your mouth at once

that it hurts your teeth; for the same reason, you never let unmelted ice cream into the back of your mouth. If all these procedures are followed correctly, you should shortly arrive at the ideal—the way an ice-cream cone is always pictured but never actually is when it is handed to you. *(Fig. 2).* The ice cream should now form a small dome whose circumference exactly coincides with the large circumference of the cone itself—a small skullcap that fits exactly on top of a larger, inverted dunce cap. You have made order out of chaos; you are an artist. You have taken an unnatural, abhorrent, irregular, chaotic form, and from it you have sculpted an ordered, ideal shape that might be envied by Praxiteles or even Euclid.

Fig. 2

Now at last you can begin to take little nibbles of the cone itself, being very careful not to crack it. Revolve the cone so that its rim remains smooth and level as you eat both ice cream and cone in the same ratio. Because of the geometrical nature of things, a constantly reduced inverted cone still remains a perfect inverted cone no matter how small it grows, just as a constantly reduced dome held within a cone retains *its* shape. Because you are constantly reshaping the dome of ice cream with your tongue and nibbling at the cone, it follows in logic—and in actual practice, if you are skillful and careful—that the cone will continue to look exactly the same, except for its size, as you eat it down, so that at the very end you will hold between your thumb and forefinger a tiny, idealized replica of an ice-cream cone, a thing perhaps one inch high. Then, while the others are licking their sticky fingers, preparatory to wiping them on their clothes, or going back to the ice-cream stand for more paper napkins to try to clean themselves up—*then* you can hold the miniature cone up for everyone to see, and pop it gently into your mouth.

22

Comment

Hills is writing about the joys of eating ice-cream cones, and he is writing humorously. The problems he describes are real ones, but these are part of the fun of eating ice-cream cones, and he knows that his readers will share this view. Though he gives instructions for each stage in the process, he also knows that his readers are probably familiar with all of the details. The many kinds of analysis—from comparison and contrast to process—can be used for many different purposes, as this delightful essay shows.

Questions for Study and Discussion

1. What in the description of the process depends on the reader's recognition of the problems? How does Hills remind the reader of these problems?
2. What explains the order of the steps in the process? Is Hills moving from the easier to the more difficult steps, or has he chosen another principle of order?
3. What is the overall tone of the essay? How do the drawings contribute to it?
4. Are the various statements about human nature to be taken seriously, though they are presented humorously?
5. The most effective humor develops out of genuine problems and observations—not out of invented ones. Is this true of the humor of this essay?
6. What impression do you get of the writer—his personality, his outlook on life, his sense of humor?

Vocabulary Study

Formal words will often seem humorous in an informal setting: "This schoolmate has a flair for *contingency* planning. . . ." Identify formal words of this sort in the essay, and explain the humor they provide.

Suggestions for Writing

1. Write a humorous description of a process similar to eating an ice-cream cone—perhaps wrapping a large gift, or eating

an unfamiliar food for the first time. Let your details reveal something unusual and important about human beings.

2. Write a set of instructions for a job that involves a number of related processes, for example, changing a flat tire. Keep each of the processes distinct, and be careful to define important terms for the person who has not performed the process before.

Richard Selzer

MY BROTHER SHAMAN

A practicing surgeon and teacher at the Yale School of Medicine, Richard Selzer has written numerous essays on medicine and the art of surgery. Selzer grew up in Troy, New York, the son of a doctor, who, impoverished by the Depression, consoled himself by writing a novel. "It is one of my lifelong regrets," Selzer writes in an essay about his father, "that the manuscript has not been preserved. Now that I too have been reduced to the anguish of writing fiction, it should be my holy scripture, my beacon, and my emblem. As it is, I am a writer unmoored, in search of a heritage, catching at stray ancestors." His fiction and essays are collected in *Rituals of Surgery* (1974), *Mortal Lessons: Notes on the Art of Surgery* (1976), *Confessions of a Knife* (1979), *Letters to a Young Surgeon* (1982), and *Taking the World in for Repairs* (1986). In his fiction and essays, Selzer describes the special qualities of mind and spirit needed by the doctor. In this essay on the doctor and the shaman, he discusses one of his ancestors in the profession of healing.

In the cult of the Bhagavati, as it has been practiced in   1
southern India, there is a ritual in which two entranced shamans dressed in feathered costumes and massive headgear enter a circle of witnesses. All night long in the courtyard of a temple they lunge and thrust at each other, give shouts of defiance, make challenging gestures. It is all done to the sound of drums, conches and horns. Come daybreak, the goddess Kali "slays" the demon Darika, then plunges her hands into the very bowels of Darika, drinking of and smearing herself with blood. At last Kali withdraws from the field of battle having adorned herself with the intestines of the vanquished.

It is a far cry from the bloody trances of shamans to   2
the bloody acts of surgery. Or is it? Take away from Kali
and Darika the disciplinary beat of tautened hide and the
moaning of flutes, and you have . . . an emergency intes-
tinal resection. The technique is there, the bravado, the zeal.
Only lacking in surgery is the ecstasy.

In both surgery and shamanism the business is done   3
largely by the hands of the operator. The surgeon holds his
scalpel, hemostat, forceps; the shaman, his amulet of bone,
wood, metal. For each there is the hieratic honoring of ritual
objects. The handling of these objects induces a feeling of
tranquillity and power. One's mind is nudged from the path
of self-awareness into the pathless glade of the imagination.
The nun, too, knows this. She tells her beads, and her heart
is enkindled. Surely it is true that the handling of instruments is conducive to the kind of possession or devotion
that is the mark of all three—nun, surgeon, shaman. The
surgeon and the shaman understand that one must honor,
revere and entreat one's tools. Both do their handiwork with
a controlled vehemence most dramatically seen in those off-
shoots of Buddhism wherein the shaman ties his fingers in
"knots," giving them a strange distorted appearance. These
priests have an uncanny flexibility of their finger joints, each
of which has a special name. During these maneuvers the
shaman is possessed by finger spirits. He invokes the good
spirits and repels the evil ones. Such hand poses, or mudras,
seen in Buddhist iconography, are used in trancelike rituals
to call down the gods to possess the shaman. In like manner
the surgeon restrains his knife even as he gives it rein. He,
too, is the medium between man and God.

The shaman has his drum which is the river of sound   4
through which he can descend to the Kingdom of Shadows
to retrieve the soul of his tribesfellow. The surgeon listens
to the electronic beep of the cardiac monitor, the regulated
respiration of anesthesia, and he is comforted or warned.
Even the operating table has somewhat the shape and size
of the pagan altars I saw in a tiny sixth-century baptistry in
the Provençal village of Vénasque. Upon these slabs beasts
and, in certain instances, humans were laid open to appease

the gods. Should one of these ancient pagans undergo resurrection and be brought to a modern operating room with its blazing lamps and opulence of linen and gleaming gadgetry, where masked and gowned figures dip their hands in and out of the body of someone who has been plunged into magical sleep, what else would he think but that he has happened upon a ritual sacrifice?

Nor is the toilet of decoration less elaborate for surgeon   5 than for shaman. Take the Washing of the Hands: Behold the surgeon at his ablutions. His lavabo is a deep sink, often of white porcelain, with a central faucet controlled by the knee. The soap he uses is thick and red as iodine. It is held in a nozzled bottle on the wall. The surgeon depresses a pedal on the floor. Once, twice, three times and collects in his cupped palm a puddle of the soap. There it would sit, lifeless, if he did not add a little water from the faucet and begin to brush. Self-containment is part of the nature of soap. Now, all at once, suds break as air and water are incorporated. Here and there in the play of the bristles, bubbles, first one, then another and another, lift from the froth and achieve levitation. For a moment each globule sways in front of the surgeon's dazzled eyes, but only long enough to give him its blessing before winking out. Meanwhile, the stern brush travels back and forth through the slush of forearms, raising wakes of gauze, scratching the skin . . . Oh, not to hurt or abrade, but tenderly, as one scratches the ears of a dog. At last the surgeon thrusts his hands into the stream of water. A dusky foam darkens the porcelain and fades like smoke. A moment later the sink is calm and white. The surgeon too is calm. And purified.

The washing of the hands, then, is at once a rational   6 step in the achievement of sterile technique and a ritual act carried out under the glance of God by which one is made ready to behold, to perform. It is not wholly unlike the whirling of dervishes, or the to and fro rocking of the orthodox Jew at his prayers. The mask, cap, gown and gloves that the surgeon puts on prior to surgery echo, do they not, the phylacteries of this same Jew? Prophetic wisdom, if it will come at all, is most likely to come to one so sacredly trussed. By these simple acts of bathing and adorning, both surgeon and shaman are made receptacular.

Time was when, in order to become a shaman, one had to undergo an initiatory death and resurrection. The aspirant had to be taken to the sky or the netherworld; often he would be dismembered by spirits, cooked in a pot and eaten by them. Only then could he be born again as a shaman. No such rite of passage goes into the making of a surgeon, it is true, but there is something about the process of surgical training that is reminiscent of the sacred ur-drama after all. The modern surgical intern must undergo a long and arduous novitiate during which the subjugation of the will and spirit to the craft is virtually complete. After a number of years of abasement and humiliation he or she is led to a room where no one else is permitted. There is the donning of special raiment, the washing of the hands and, at last, the performance of secret rites before the open ark of the body. In this, surgery remains a hieratic pantomime marked by exorcism, propitiation and invocation. God dwells in operating rooms as He does everywhere. More than once I have surmised a presence . . . something between hearing and feeling. . . .

In the selection of students to enter medical school, I wonder whether the present weight given to academic excellence in organic chemistry is justified. At least as valid a selection would be based upon the presence of a bat-shaped mole on the inner aspect of the thigh, of the aspirant, or a specific conjunction of the planets on his birthday. Neither seems more prophetic than the other in the matter of intuition, compassion and ingenuity which form the trinity of doctorhood.

The shaman's journey through disorder and illness to health has parallels to the surgeon's journey into the body. Both are like Jason setting out in the Argos, weathering many storms to return at last with the Golden Fleece. Or Galahad with the Holy Grail. The extirpated gallbladder, then, becomes the talisman of the surgeon's journey, the symbol of his hard-won manhood. What is different is that the surgeon practices inherited rites, while the shaman is susceptible to visions. Still, they both perform acts bent upon making chaos into cosmos.

Saint John of the Cross alludes to the mystic as a solitary bird who must seek the heights, admit of no companionship even with its own kind, stretch out its beak into the air, and sing sweetly. I think of such a shaman soaring, plummeting, riding ecstatic thermals to the stars, tumbling head over heels, and at last descending among the fog of dreams. If, as it seems, the mark of the shaman was his ability to take flight, soaring to the sky or plummeting to the earth in search of his quarry, only the astronaut or the poet would now qualify. 10

Ever since Nietzsche delivered his stunning pronouncement—"Dead are all the gods"—man has been forced to assume the burden of heroism without divine assistance. All the connections to the ancestral past have been severed. It is our rashest act. For no good can come to a race that refuses to acknowledge the living spirit of ancient kingdoms. Ritual has receded from the act of surgery. Only the flavor of it is left, giving, if not to the performers, then to the patients and to those forbidden to witness these events, a shiver of mysticism. Few and far between are the surgeons who consider what they do an encounter with the unknown. When all is said and done, I am left with the suspicion that we have gone too far in our arrogant drift from the priestly forebears of surgery. It is pleasing to imagine surgeons bending over their incisions with love, infusing them with the impalpable. Only then would the surgeon, like the shaman, turn himself into a small god and re-create the world. 11

Comment

"The machine does not exist that can take the place of the divining physician," Selzer writes in another of his essays, "Textbook." "The physical examination affords the opportunity to touch your patient. It gives the patient the opportunity to be touched by you. In this exchange, messages are sent from one to the other that, if your examination is performed with honesty and humility, will cause the divining powers of the Augurs to be passed on to you—their last heir." The Augurs were the official soothsayers of an-

cient Rome, prophets or diviners who depended on intuitive powers. In this essay on the doctor and the shaman, Selzer compares
the medical doctor and another of his ancestors who drew on special powers of mind and spirit to heal.

Questions for Study and Discussion

1. What details in the ritual described in paragraph 1 suggest to
   Selzer that the goddess Kali is performing an act of healing by
   slaying the demon Darika?
2. What similarities in the use of hands lead Selzer to the conclusion that the surgeon and the shaman act as a "medium between man and God"? What additional support does Selzer
   find for this conclusion in the washing of hands?
3. What other similarities between the surgeon and the shaman
   does Selzer discuss? Does Selzer draw the same conclusion from
   these similarities, or does he draw other conclusions?
4. Does Selzer stress any differences between the surgeon and the
   shaman? Or is he concerned only with similarities?
5. What is Selzer's purpose in making comparisons between the
   surgeon and the shaman and between the surgeon, the nun,
   and the orthodox Jew?
6. What is the thesis of the essay and where does it appear? Does
   Selzer restate the thesis in the course of the essay?
7. Is the comparison developed point by point or in blocks—that
   is, the characteristics of the doctor presented first and then
   those of the shaman?

Vocabulary Study

1. Does the dictionary definition of *shaman* mention qualities that
   Selzer does not discuss? Does Selzer define the word formally,
   or instead assume that his readers know its meaning?
2. Be ready to define the following words: *resection* (paragraph
   2); *hemostat, forceps, amulet* (paragraph 3); *cardiac monitor,
   baptistry* (paragraph 4); *ablutions, lavabo, levitation, abrade*
   (paragraph 5); *phylacteries, trussed* (paragraph 6); *netherworld, novitiate, exorcism, surmised* (paragraph 7); *extirpated*
   (paragraph 9); *thermals* (paragraph 10).
3. Selzer refers to the "hieratic honoring of ritual objects" (paragraph 3). What do the words *hieratic* and *ritual* mean? What

is the "Buddhist iconography" that is referred to in the same paragraph?

4. Use a classical dictionary and other special dictionaries to explain the references to Jason and the Golden Fleece (paragraph 9), Saint John of the Cross (paragraph 10), and Friedrich Nietzsche (paragraph 11).

Suggestions for Writing

1. Selzer defines other qualities of the medical doctor and surgeon in various essays: *Mortal Lessons: Notes on the Art of Surgery, Confessions of a Knife,* and *Taking the World in for Repairs.* After reading an essay in one of these collections, discuss the insight it gives into Selzer's conception of the ideal doctor or surgeon.

2. Discuss significant similarities and differences between one of the following pairs. Use your comparison to develop a thesis:
   a. learning to swim and learning to drive
   b. the experienced and the inexperienced driver
   c. reading a newspaper and reading a novel
   d. listening to a recording and attending a concert
   e. high school and college friends

Don Richard Cox

BARBIE AND HER PLAYMATES

Don Richard Cox was born in Wichita, Kansas, in 1943, and was educated at Wichita State University and the University of Missouri, where he received the Outstanding Graduate Student Teacher Award in 1975. He is the author of two textbooks, *Emblems of Reality* (1973) and *The Technical Reader* (1980), and he now teaches at the University of Tennessee in Knoxville.

The Mattel Corporation's wonder doll, Barbie, is undoubtedly one of the toy phenomena of the second half of the twentieth century. The first of her kind, Barbie helped create a whole new breed of dolls—the fashion dolls. These dolls, all of whom are about eleven or twelve inches tall, are intended to represent attractive, apparently teenaged girls, who, like most teenaged girls, require large wardrobes. These wardrobes are purchased separately from the dolls, of course, and initially most of Barbie's appeal to young purchasers involved the seemingly endless supply of fashions that Barbie and her friends could wear.

One did not simply buy a Barbie doll and stop, for Barbie was not an end in herself but an avenue to a whole world of Barbie accessories. The concept of a doll being primarily a vehicle for the future sale of related merchandise rather than being a terminal product whose marketing success ends with its sale is a concept that has caused Barbie to have the tremendous impact upon the toy industry that she has had and allowed her to survive in a doll market where the average product remains popular only a few years. Barbie's primary social importance as a toy stems from the fact that she is different from the dolls that preceded her; this difference has reshaped our culture's way of looking at dolls and the way children now define their relationship to these dolls that sell in the millions. The sales figures alone are proof of Barbie's attractiveness. There is no doubt that Barbie and her friends have been accepted; they seem to have become a permanent part of twentieth-century life. But now that we have welcomed Barbie into our homes and placed her in our children's bedrooms, we should stop and examine what her presence there means, and what effect it may have. 2

Barbie was first introduced to sell clothes, but her initial role as a vehicle for doll fashions was soon expanded. For example, Barbie's size made her either too large or too small for the conventional doll furniture that had existed, so a new line of doll furniture tailored to her dimensions was created. Barbie's "Dream House" then became one of her first "non-fashion" accessories. Because Barbie was a young and presumably active young lady, her merchandise took on a distinctive character. Barbie was not a "baby" doll and she had no need for baby cribs, high chairs, or other "baby" furniture. So Barbie acquired recreational equipment—a dune buggy, a Volkswagen van, a swimming pool. She also acquired some friends—P.J. and Skipper—and most important 3 of all Barbie found a boyfriend—Ken. With the addition of these friends to share her fun Barbie's need for equipment became as unlimited as the needs of any modern consumer. Barbie could ski, camp, swim, skate, cycle, perform gymnastics, boat, dance, shop, have her hair styled, or just entertain friends in her studio bedroom, her country home, or her penthouse apartment. Almost any activity open to today's teenagers became available to Barbie, and by extension became available to those who brought Barbie into their lives.

The success of the total Barbie market helped initiate   4
several new series of dolls all of whom parlayed the Barbie format to success. Many of these dolls, drawing upon the interest Barbie's Ken had aroused in young boys, turned to a relatively untapped doll market—dolls for the male population. Selling dolls to young boys, however, necessitated a basic change in terminology. Boys' dolls were not called *dolls,* because that word has a distinctly feminine ring. Accordingly we find today that young males are interested in *action figures,* male dolls who are supposedly basically rugged individuals devoted to an outdoor life. "Big Jim," "Johnny West," and most notably "G.I. Joe," all belong to this exclusive club of adventurous spirits who demand enough dune buggies, jeeps, motorcycles, planes, boats, and helicopters to outfit a small mercenary force. Once again we can see what is essentially being marketed here is a sophisticated type of doll "furniture," merchandise that surrounds and supports the original doll vehicles.

The major appeal of the action figures lies in the variety   5
of accessories that can be adapted to them; like Barbie they are not terminal products. The action figures for boys, however, although they represent a direct result of Barbie's impact upon the toy market, do not necessitate a redefinition of the male role in play situations in the same way that Barbie has redefined the female role in these situations. The action figures are distinctly male and they inhabit a world that is exclusively male. A young boy will have to borrow his sister's fashion doll if he wants any feminine intruders invading his all-male play world. In this respect the male action figures do not require an adjustment in the masculine

play role. Although we can label a boy's action figures "dolls," we should understand that as a collection of adult male dolls they might also be seen as simply elaborate toy soldiers, a traditional plaything of boys for generations. Young girls, however, have had their feminine play roles changed significantly by Barbie. Because the consequences of that redefinition could alter a child's basic attitudes toward sex, marriage, or a career, let us examine more closely the value structure implicit in Barbie's world.

We should begin by noting that Barbie's age is not completely clear. Ostensibly she is a teenager and therefore is no more than nineteen years old. Physically, however, as many people have pointed out, Barbie is a rather fully endowed and curvaceous woman possessing a figure few nineteen-year-olds have. Barbie is of course single so her friend Ken is just that—a boyfriend not a husband. Barbie's exact relationship with Ken is noticeably loose. She apparently is free to embark unescorted on all kinds of outings with Ken, including camping overnight (they each have their own sleeping bags, however). Barbie seemingly lives alone in all of her plushly furnished homes although there are certainly enough chairs, couches, and beds to accommodate overnight guests. Again, Ken is free to visit any time he wishes. The point here is not that Barbie is a doll of questionable morals, but we should note that her lifestyle is remarkably uncluttered and free of such complications as nosey little brothers or nagging parents.

Barbie's life is that of the ultimate swinging single. Although she has no parents to cast shadows into her life of constant boating, skiing, and camping, she also does not seem to have a need for them. Total independence is a central characteristic of Barbie. Although she owns an extensive amount of sporting equipment, Barbie seemingly has no need for employment that allows her to purchase this merchandise. There is no such thing as a Barbie office in any of the Barbie equipment, nor are there accessories that remotely suggest a job situation for this carefree doll; although Barbie might be in high school or college there are no accessories that hint at her having to endure the boredom of education.

Life for Barbie appears to be a kind of endless summer vacation, an extended tour of summer homes and resorts, free from school, family, and financial worries.

Barbie's influence upon the minds of the children who 8 share their play hours with her and her expensive wardrobe and recreation equipment is potentially a very strong one. Barbie provides a means of vicarious escape to her young female playmates—a glittering jet trip into a world of leisure and luxury that very few of her young friends will ever actually know. We can see that Barbie is a symbolic escape vehicle, a vicarious toy that encourages fantasy rather than a toy that encourages behavior imitative of normal living patterns.

The dolls that survive outside of the category of fashion 9 dolls are still basically the kind of dolls that existed before Barbie and the fashion dolls came on the scene. These dolls are mostly "baby" dolls, dolls that require young mothers to feed and diaper them. A child who owns such a doll usually assumes a play role that is imitative of her own mother's role. The babies can be loved and cuddled, or punished and put to bed at a young mother's whim. In this play role the child assumes an adult personality, dominating the inferior doll-child just as the youngster herself is dominated. Obviously the work and responsibility involved in being a mother receives a good share of the child's attention in this particular situation. And, although a certain amount of fantasy is involved, presumably these fantasies will one day become more or less true when the child experiences motherhood herself. She in essence is only rehearsing for a future real-life role.

The play role initiated in a child's relationship with 10 Barbie differs considerably from the play role required by a conventional baby doll. First of all Barbie is obviously not a child. She is a teenager and therefore is usually "older" than the child who owns her. The child's personality then is not necessarily a dominant one when she relates with Barbie. Barbie has the clothes, sporting equipment, and most important, freedom, to do as she pleases. The child only directs Barbie in activities that the child herself may not be able to experience. The mother-child relationship that is an inherent part of owning a baby doll is considerably altered. One does not necessarily cuddle or punish a Barbie doll any more than one allows her mother to sit on her lap, or sends her mother to bed without dinner. Barbie's stature in this psychological relationship is not so great that she dominates the child; she does not become a symbolic parent in spite of her independent superiority.

Barbie's independence in fact is just what prevents her from becoming a miniature parent to the child. There are no children in Barbie's life; children, after all, involve responsibility and Barbie is not one to be burdened by such responsibilities. Instead of assuming the duties and pressures of adulthood, Barbie retains the worry-free aura of childhood, becoming a kind of surrogate big sister to the child. This relationship, the interaction between sisters at play, is fundamentally different from the mother-child relationship, and the values inculcated by this interaction are plainly different also.   11

As a model sister, Barbie, who leads a life free from responsibility, is able to stimulate a similar desire for independence in her owners. The degree to which her influence has actually affected children in the sixties and seventies needs to be investigated more closely. Of interest also is Barbie's impact upon future families, the families formed by the young girls of the "Barbie generation." Will they, like Barbie, resist the responsibility of having children, or, following Barbie's lead even more completely, resist the responsibility of marriage and family altogether? There is also the question of the sexual mores of today's Barbie owners. Barbie is a physically attractive woman with no visible permanent attachments. Will she produce a generation of sexually liberated playmates intent on jetting from resort to resort? Will these same playmates become a group of frustrated cynics if their private Barbie fantasies do not come true? Older sisters often set social and marital patterns that their younger sisters attempt to emulate; Barbie is capable of being a dominant model for all her young sisters in this respect.   12

Certainly Barbie's dream world has already affected the sexual lives of her playmates in one way: she has caused girls as young as five or six to confront the problems of   13 teenagers. Very young children, children who might once have been content to feed bottles to their infant dolls, are now exposed to the dating experience. Girls who once spent the second grade believing that boys were generally unpleasant creatures now spend their days escorting Barbie and Ken through idyllic afternoons. Dating and the opposite sex— "those awful boys"—have now become familiar experiences to jaded nine-year-olds who have "accompanied" their "big sister" and her boyfriend on unchaperoned camping trips many times. The accelerating interest of big business in "pre-teenagers" (presumably those children between the ages of seven and twelve) as a potential market for cosmetics, magazines, and phonograph records, is a positive indication of a budding sexual awareness in this age group. The girls who screamed for Elvis in the fifties were seventeen; those who now swoon at Donny Osmond are eleven.

The total impact of Barbie should now begin to make   14
itself visible in her playmates. As each generation finds its own particular fantasy of escape the values of that fantasy become imprinted in the generation itself. Motion pictures, the great escape of the forties and early fifties, provided Hollywood's vision of life for those who grew up munching popcorn in dark theaters. Similarly, it has been proposed that many of the youth protests of the late sixties reflected the desires of a generation that was used to seeing life neatly resolved in sixty-minute segments on a flickering tube. Barbie and her glittering accessories have now been purchased by a generation of children; her fantasy world becomes steadily more elaborate. If Barbie has indeed provided a behavioral model for a segment of the population, the values instilled by her miniature utopia will play an increasing role in the lives of those children who buy her version of the American Dream.

Comment

Cox develops a number of important ideas, all of them related to the impact of the Barbie doll on the girls who own them. These ideas grow out of specific details and analysis, as in paragraph 8:

"We can see that Barbie is a symbolic escape vehicle, a vicarious toy that encourages fantasy rather than a toy that encourages behavior imitative of normal living patterns." Cox builds these ideas to a general thesis, stated late in the essay. One way that Cox develops this and the other ideas of the essay is through comparison with other kinds of dolls—those designed for boys, for example. The relative estimate that emerges from this comparison tells us something important about the cultural attitudes that produced these various dolls and in turn are influenced by them.

Questions for Study and Discussion

1. What background does Cox provide for the reader unacquainted with the Barbie doll? How early does he state the purpose of his analysis?
2. What similarities and differences between Barbie and Ken does Cox discuss and illustrate? What central idea emerges from this relative estimate?
3. What is the point of the comparison with other kinds of dolls? What is gained by building to the comparison instead of introducing it at the beginning of the essay?
4. What have been the effects on children of the Barbie doll, according to Cox? How does he demonstrate these effects?
5. What is Cox's general thesis and where does he state it?
6. What is the overall tone of the essay? Does Cox write as a neutral observer? Or is he obviously approving or disapproving or sarcastic?
7. Cox does not focus on male and female stereotypes, but his essay deals with this idea in the course of the analysis. What other ideas does he deal with indirectly?
8. Do you agree with the conclusion Cox reaches about the impact of the Barbie doll on adolescents? Why or why not?

Vocabulary Study

Explain how the second word in each pair differs from the first, which is Cox's, and how it would change the meaning of the sentence in the paragraph cited:

a. *concept* (paragraph 2), *idea*
b. *terminal* (paragraph 2), *final*

c. *initial* (paragraph 3), *first*
d. *conventional* (paragraph 3), *customary*
e. *necessitated* (paragraph 4), *required*
f. *adapted* (paragraph 5), *fitted*
g. *vicarious* (paragraph 8), *surrogate*
h. *miniature* (paragraph 11), *small*
i. *emulate* (paragraph 12), *imitate*
j. *mores* (paragraph 12), *habits*
k. *unchaperoned* (paragraph 13), *unaccompanied*
l. *idyllic* (paragraph 13), *happy*

Suggestions for Writing

1. Analyze the appeals made in advertisements for cosmetics or clothes or another class of product in a magazine directed to adolescents. Then discuss what similarities and differences you find. Use your analysis to reach a conclusion about the implied values you find or the attitude toward teenagers—their interests and tastes.

2. Compare two magazines—one addressed to adolescents, the second to adults—to determine how different the advertisements for the same product are. Give particular attention to assumptions these ads make about the values, tastes, and interests of their audiences.

3. Test Cox's conclusion that toys promote sexual stereotypes by comparing advertisements for the same class of product—sporting equipment or clothing, for example—in magazines directed to girls and boys, or by comparing books or magazine stories.

Arthur L. Campa

ANGLO VS. CHICANO: WHY?

Arthur L. Campa (1905–1978) was chairman of the Department of Modern Languages at the University of Denver and the director of the Center of Latin American Studies from 1946 to 1978. He served in the U.S. Air Force and the Peace Corps. His several books on Hispanic–American culture include *Treasure of the Sangre de Cristos* and *Hispanic Culture in the Southwest*. Campa depends chiefly on contrast to develop his exposition.

The cultural differences between Hispanic and Anglo-   1
American people have been dwelt upon by so many writers
that we should all be well informed about the values of both.
But audiences are usually of the same persuasion as the
speakers, and those who consult published works are for the
most part specialists looking for affirmation of what they
believe. So, let us consider the same subject, exploring briefly
some of the basic cultural differences that cause conflict in
the Southwest, where Hispanic and Anglo-American cultures meet.

Cultural differences are implicit in the conceptual con-   2
tent of the languages of these two civilizations, and their
value systems stem from a long series of historical circumstances. Therefore, it may be well to consider some of the
English and Spanish cultural configurations before these Europeans set foot on American soil. English culture was basically insular, geographically and ideologically; was more
integrated on the whole, except for some strong theological
differences; and was particularly zealous of its racial purity.
Spanish culture was peninsular, a geographical circumstance
that made it a catchall of Mediterranean, central European
and north African peoples. The composite nature of the
population produced a marked regionalism that prevented
close integration, except for religion, and led to a strong
sense of individualism. These differences were reflected in
the colonizing enterprise of the two cultures. The English
isolated themselves from the Indians physically and cultur-
ally; the Spanish, who had strong notions about *pureza de
sangre* [purity of blood] among the nobility, were not collec-
tively averse to adding one more strain to their racial cock-
tail. Cortés led the way by siring the first *mestizo* in North
America, and the rest of the conquistadores followed suit.
The ultimate products of these two orientations meet today
in the Southwest.

Anglo-American culture was absolutist at the onset; that   3
is, all the dominant values were considered identical for all,
regardless of time and place. Such values as justice, charity,
honesty were considered the superior social order for all men
and were later embodied in the American Constitution. The
Spaniard brought with him a relativistic viewpoint and

saw fewer moral implications in man's actions. Values were looked upon as the result of social and economic conditions.

The motives that brought Spaniards and Englishmen to America also differed. The former came on an enterprise of discovery, searching for a new route to India initially, and later for new lands to conquer, the fountain of youth, minerals, the Seven Cities of Cíbola and, in the case of the missionaries, new souls to win for the Kingdom of Heaven. The English came to escape religious persecution, and once having found a haven, they settled down to cultivate the soil and establish their homes. Since the Spaniards were not seeking a refuge or running away from anything, they continued their explorations and circled the globe twenty-five years after the discovery of the New World.

This peripatetic tendency of the Spaniard may be accounted for in part by the fact that he was the product of an equestrian culture. Men on foot do not venture far into the unknown. It was almost a century after the landing on Plymouth Rock that Governor Alexander Spotswood of Virginia crossed the Blue Ridge Mountains, and it was not until the nineteenth century that the Anglo-Americans began to move west of the Mississippi.

The Spaniard's equestrian role meant that he was not close to the soil, as was the Anglo-American pioneer, who tilled the land and built the greatest agricultural industry in history. The Spaniard cultivated the land only when he had Indians available to do it for him. The uses to which the horse was put also varied. The Spanish horse was essentially a mount, while the more robust English horse was used in cultivating the soil. It is therefore not surprising that the viewpoints of these two cultures should differ when we consider that the pioneer is looking at the world at the level of his eyes while the *caballero* [horseman] is looking beyond and down at the rest of the world.

One of the most commonly quoted, and often misinterpreted, characteristics of Hispanic peoples is the deeply ingrained individualism in all walks of life. Hispanic individualism is a revolt against the incursion of collectivity, strongly asserted when it is felt that the ego is being fenced in. This attitude leads to a deficiency in those social qualities based on collective standards, an attitude that Hispanos do not consider negative because it manifests a measure of resistance to standardization in order to achieve a measure of individual freedom. Naturally, such an attitude has no *reglas fijas* [fixed rules].

Anglo-Americans who achieve a measure of success and security through institutional guidance not only do not mind a few fixed rules but demand them. The lack of a concerted plan of action, whether in business or in politics, appears unreasonable to Anglo-Americans. They have a sense of individualism, but they achieve it through action and self-determination. Spanish individualism is based on feeling, on something that is the result not of rules and collective standards but of a person's momentary, emotional reaction. And it is subject to change when the mood changes. In contrast to Spanish emotional individualism, the Anglo-American strives for objectivity when choosing a course of action or making a decision.

The Southwestern Hispanos voiced strong objections to the lack of courtesy of the Anglo-Americans when they first met them in the early days of the Santa Fe trade. The same accusation is leveled at the *Americanos* today in many quarters of the Hispanic world. Some of this results from their different conceptions of polite behavior. Here too one can say that the Spanish have no *reglas fijas* because for them courtesy is simply an expression of the way one person feels toward another. To some they extend the hand, to some they bow and for the more *intimos* there is the well-known *abrazo*. The concepts of "good or bad" or "right and wrong" in polite behavior are moral considerations of an absolutist culture.

Another cultural contrast appears in the way both cultures share part of their material substance with others. The pragmatic Anglo-American contributes regularly to such institutions as the Red Cross, the United Fund and a myriad of associations. He also establishes foundations and quite often leaves millions to such institutions. The Hispano prefers to give his contribution directly to the recipient so he can see the person he is helping.

A century of association has inevitably acculturated both   11
Hispanos and Anglo-Americans to some extent, but there
still persist a number of culture traits that neither group has
relinquished altogether. Nothing is more disquieting to an
Anglo-American who believes that time is money than the
time perspective of Hispanos. They usually refer to this attitude as the *"mañana* psychology." Actually, it is more of
a "today psychology," because Hispanos cultivate the present to the exclusion of the future; because the latter has not
arrived yet, it is not a reality. They are reluctant to relin-
quish the present, so they hold on to it until it becomes the
past. To an Hispano, nine is nine until it is ten, so when he
arrives at nine-thirty, he jubilantly exclaims: *"¡Justo!"* [right
on time]. This may be why the clock is slowed down to a
walk in Spanish while in English it runs. In the United States,
our future-oriented civilization plans our lives so far in advance that the present loses its meaning. January magazine
issues [including IDs] are out in December; 1973 cars have
been out since October; cemetery plots and even funeral arrangements are bought on the installment plan. To a person
engrossed in living today the very idea of planning his funeral sounds like the tolling of the bells.

It is a natural corollary that a person who is present ori-   12
ented should be compensated by being good at improvising.
An Anglo-American is told in advance to prepare for an
"impromptu speech," but an Hispano usually can improvise
a speech because *"Nosotros lo improvisamos todo"* [we improvise everything].

Another source of cultural conflict arises from the dif-   13
ference between *being* and *doing*. Even when trying to be
individualistic, the Anglo-American achieves it by what he
does. Today's young generation decided to be themselves, to
get away from standardization, so they let their hair grow,
wore ragged clothes and even went barefoot in order to be
different from the Establishment. As a result they all ended
up doing the same things and created another stereotype.
The freedom enjoyed by the individuality of *being* makes it
unnecessary for Hispanos to strive to be different.

In 1963 a team of psychologists from the University of   14
Guadalajara in Mexico and the University of Michigan com-

pared 74 upper-middle-class students from each university. Individualism and personalism were found to be central values for the Mexican students. This was explained by saying that a Mexican's value as a person lies in his *being* rather than, as is the case of the Anglo-Americans, in concrete accomplishments. Efficiency and accomplishments are derived characteristics that do not affect worthiness in the Mexican, whereas in the American it is equated with success, a value of highest priority in the American culture. Hispanic people disassociate themselves from material things or from actions that may impugn a person's sense of being, but the Anglo-American shows great concern for material things and assumes responsibility for his actions. This is expressed in the language of each culture. In Spanish one says, *"Se me cayó la taza"* [the cup fell away from me] instead of "I dropped the cup."

In English, one speaks of money, cash and all related transactions with frankness because material things of this high order do not trouble Anglo-Americans. In Spanish such materialistic concepts are circumvented by referring to cash as *efectivo* [effective] and when buying or selling as something *al contado* [counted out], and when without it by saying *No tengo fondos* [I have no funds]. This disassociation from material things is what produces *sobriedad* [sobriety] in the Spaniard according to Miguel de Unamuno, but in the Southwest the disassociation from materialism leads to *dejadez* [lassitude] and *desprendimiento* [disinterestedness]. A man may lose his life defending his honor but is unconcerned about the lack of material things. *Desprendimiento* causes a man to spend his last cent on a friend, which when added to lack of concern for the future may mean that tomorrow he will eat beans as a result of today's binge. 15

The implicit differences in words that appear to be identical in meaning are astonishing. Versatile is a compliment in English and an insult in Spanish. An Hispano student who is told to apologize cannot do it, because the word doesn't exist in Spanish. *Apologia* means words in praise of a person. The Anglo-American either apologizes, which is a form of retraction abhorrent in Spanish, or compromises, another concept foreign to Hispanic culture. *Compromiso* 16 means a date, not a compromise. In colonial Mexico City, two hidalgos once entered a narrow street from opposite sides, and when they could not go around, they sat in their coaches for three days until the viceroy ordered them to back out. All this because they could not work out a compromise.

It was that way then and to some extent now. Many of 17
today's conflicts in the Southwest have their roots in polarized cultural differences, which need not be irreconcilable when approached with mutual respect and understanding.

Comment

Campa states the subject of his essay in his opening paragraph—the "basic cultural differences that cause conflict in the Southwest." And he states his thesis at the start of his second: "Cultural differences are implicit in the conceptual content of the languages of these two civilizations, and their value systems stem from a long series of historical circumstances." Paragraphs 2 through 6 deal with the second part of this statement, identifying important Hispanic and Anglo-American values and historical circumstances. Paragraphs 7 through 17 explore related values and connect these values to the conceptual content of Hispanic and Anglo-American words and phrases.

Campa depends on formal transitions throughout, sometimes using the opening sentences of his paragraphs as signposts to show the major turns in his analysis:

> A century of association has inevitably acculturated both Hispanos and Anglo-Americans to some extent, but there still persist a number of culture traits that neither group has relinquished altogether. (paragraph 11)

The topic sentence of the paragraph immediately follows:

> Nothing is more disquieting to an Anglo-American who believes that time is money than the time perspective of Hispanos.

Both the transitional and the topic sentences here mark the contrasts Campa is developing. Campa gives emphasis to these contrasts in the opening sentences of most of the paragraphs.

Questions for Study and Discussion

1. What topic does Campa begin his analysis with in paragraph 2? What topic does he turn to in paragraph 3?
2. Campa turns in paragraph 4 to the first of several historical circumstances. Which circumstance does he begin with? How are the circumstances discussed in paragraphs 5 and 6 related to that of paragraph 4?
3. How is Hispanic individualism—introduced in paragraph 7 and explored by contrast in paragraph 8—suggested by the Hispanic equestrian role discussed in paragraph 6?
4. Paragraph 9, which illustrates the differences in Hispanic and Anglo-American individualism, introduces differences in the conceptual content of Spanish and English. What are these concepts?
5. What different values does Campa explore in paragraph 10? How are the different values discussed in paragraph 11 related to these? How does Campa illustrate the differences in these paragraphs? How does paragraph 12 develop the difference discussed in paragraph 11?
6. How do previous differences help to explain that discussed and illustrated in paragraphs 13 through 15?
7. What is the function of paragraphs 16 and 17?
8. Campa develops his essay chiefly by contrast. Which paragraphs open with transitional sentences that mark major turns in the analysis?
9. Are any of the values Campa discusses your own? Is your ethnic background chiefly responsible for them?

Vocabulary Study

1. Find synonyms for the following words. Be ready to discuss what the etymology of the word contributes to your understanding of its use in the paragraph:
   a. paragraph 2: *conceptual, configurations, insular, peninsular, conquistador*
   b. paragraph 5: *peripatetic, equestrian*
   c. paragraph 7: *incursion*
   d. paragraph 10: *pragmatic, myriad*
   e. paragraph 12: *corollary, improvising, impromptu*

    f.   paragraph 15: *circumvented, lassitude, disinterestedness*
    g.   paragraph 16: *abhorrent*
2.   What are the meanings of the words *absolutist* and *relativistic* in paragraphs 3 and 9? What dictionary meanings do these words not have in the essay?

Suggestions for Writing

1.   Contrast values of your own with those of a friend, perhaps referring to some of the values identified by Campa. Then discuss the possible causes of these differences—upbringing, ethnic background, friends, school. Refer to ideas of Campa if these help explain the differences.
2.   Campa states: "Even when trying to be individualistic, the Anglo-American achieves it by what he does." Discuss the extent to which this statement describes your way of being an individual. Compare or contrast your individualism with that of one or more friends. Use your analysis to verify or challenge Campa's analysis of American values.
3.   Contrast the meaning you give particular words relating to money or success with the meaning given them by friends, parents, or teachers. Try to explain these different uses, referring to ideas of Campa if you find them useful.

Sydney J. Harris

CLIMBING THE MOUNTAIN OF SUCCESS

Sydney J. Harris attended the University of Chicago and later taught in its University College. From 1941 to 1978 he was a drama critic and columnist for *The Chicago Daily News*. His column *Strictly Personal* first appeared in the *Daily News* in 1944. Harris is one of the masters of the journalistic essay. Although his essays are brief (most are between 600 and 1000 words), he deals with important social, political, and philosophical issues in simple, exact, and sometimes eloquent words. His essays are collected in *Majority of One* (1957), *For the Time Being* (1972), *Clearing the Ground* (1986), and other books.

It has long struck me that the familiar metaphor of "climbing the ladder" for describing the ascent to success or fulfillment in any field is inappropriate and misleading. There are no ladders that lead to success, although there may be some escalators for those lucky enough to follow in a family's fortunes.

A ladder proceeds vertically, rung by rung, with each rung evenly spaced, and with the whole apparatus leaning against a relatively flat and even surface. A child can climb a ladder as easily as an adult, and perhaps with a surer footing.

Making the ascent in one's vocation or profession is far less like ladder climbing than mountain climbing, and here the analogy is a very real one. Going up a mountain requires a variety of skills, and includes a diversity of dangers, that are in no way involved in mounting a ladder.

Young people starting out should be told this, both to dampen their expectations and to allay their disappointments. A mountain is rough and precipitous, with uncertain footing and a predictable number of falls and scrapes, and sometimes one has to take the long way around to reach the shortest distance.

One needs different tools and the knowledge and skill to use them most effectively—as well as knowing when not to employ them. Most of all, a peculiar combination of daring and prudence is called for, which not all persons possess.

The art of rappelling is important, because sometimes one has to go down a little in order to go up. And the higher one gets, the greater the risk and the greater the fall; there is much exhilaration—but little security and less oxygen—in altitude. As many stars and standouts and company presidents have found to their regret, it is often harder to stay there than to get there.

Then, too, one must learn that there is no necessary relationship between public success and private satisfaction. The top of the ladder is shaky unless the base is firmly implanted and the whole structure is well defended against the winds of envy and greed and duplicity and the demands of one's own ego. The peak of the mountain is even more exposed to a chilling wind, as well as to a pervasive sense of loneliness. Many may have admired the ascent, but many more, eager to make the same endeavor, are waiting at the foot of the slope to witness an ignominious fall. It is easier to extend good will to those who do not threaten our own sense of worth.

People who are not prepared for failure are not prepared for success; if not for failure, at least for setbacks and slides and frustrations, and the acceptance of the deficits that so often accompany the assets. Ambition untempered by realism will never see the missing rung it falls through on that mythical ladder.

8

Comment

A special kind of comparison—analogy—is an important method of exposition and, as Harris points out, a difficult method because of the precision required of the analogy. The writer who uses analogy must be careful that the differences between the two things being compared are unimportant and do not weaken the point the writer is making through significant similarities. Harris begins his essay by criticizing a weak analogy—climbing the ladder of success. He then develops an analogy of his own—with mountain climbing—developing each point of similarity and, at the end of the essay, comparing the weak analogy with which he began to his own.

Questions for Study and Discussion

1. Why is the analogy of climbing the ladder and trying to succeed in one's vocation or profession a weak one? Why does mountain climbing provide a stronger analogy?
2. What similarities between mountain climbing and trying to succeed does Harris discuss? Are these similarities of equal importance, or does Harris stress some more than others?
3. What is the thesis of the essay and where does it appear?
4. Why does Harris return at the end of the essay to the weak analogy criticized at the beginning?

5. Are there other similarities between mountain climbing and trying to succeed that Harris might have discussed? Are there differences that he might have noted? Do these differences weaken the analogy and therefore the thesis of the essay, in your opinion, or are they insignificant?

Vocabulary Study

Define each of the following words, and explain how each differs in meaning from the word immediately following it:

  a. *metaphor* (paragraph 1), *simile*
  b. *precipitous* (paragraph 4), *steep*
  c. *prudence* (paragraph 5), *caution*
  d. *rappelling* (paragraph 6), *ascending*
  e. *duplicity* (paragraph 7), *cunning*
  f. *deficits* (paragraph 8), *hazards*

Suggestions for Writing

Develop a topic of your own by analogy, noting similarities as well as differences between the things being compared. In the course of your discussion, explain why these differences do not weaken the analogy. Here are a few possible topics:

  a. making an enduring friendship
  b. losing a friend
  c. winning an argument fairly
  d. winning an argument unfairly
  e. asking for a raise in salary and getting it

John Garvey

THINKING IN PACKAGES

John Garvey was a columnist for *Commonweal* for many years. Born in 1944 in Decatur, Illinois, he attended Notre Dame University, and after college taught high school and worked as an editor. Garvey writes about contemporary religious and social issues in his column. "There are true and false things," he has said, "and choices which align you with or against the universe." His essay discusses how we think about these things and the dangers of thinking too narrowly.

There is a grave problem which faces those of us who care about ideas. (Notice how I have gathered us all together in a noble little bunch.) It is something I have been paying attention to in a half-conscious way ever since I first started arguing with people, but it has only recently surfaced in all its silly array, probably because Ronald Reagan was elected president. It has to do not so much with ideas as with the way we relate to them. What I have noticed at long last, after years of doing all the wrong things, is embarrassing. It makes me think that everyone—every anarchist, libertarian, conservative, radical, and socialist—ought to take a vow of emotional poverty where ideas are concerned.

We have an investment in our ideas which has nothing to do with the particular worth of our ideas. Our ideas are like clan totems or old school ties. We tend to think that our ideas make us decent. If we have the right opinion about something, it means that we ourselves must be basically good folks; and the other side of this is that those who do not share our feelings on any particular subject are indecent, even perverse. Our ideas become tokens which we shove across the table at one another during conversations to show who we are. They are signals to people we often don't know very well, which we send through the space between us to let them know what to expect of us, and we are delighted when their response is approving: it means they are our sort. If they bat our tokens back at us with a cool stare or, more politely, through careful disagreement, our first impulse is often to assume that their motive for doing so must be base.

I believe, for example, that the arms race is suicidal and that it is almost certainly bound to end in such destruction as the world has never seen. I am putting this as mildly as I can. I also believe that to accept it as a tactical necessity means assuming something which is morally indefensible: the military use of civilian populations, and the willingness to hold them hostage to possible annihilation. I have noticed that people who disagree with me assume all sorts of things I not only have not said, but which I definitely do not believe. They assume that I believe the Soviet Union to be basically trustworthy and decent, not at all bad politically; they assume that I do not object to totalitarianism, and in fact have some sneaky attachment to it, and that I think of America as the world's greatest evil.

The problem is that people on my side of this life and death question do the same sort of thing. Because I agree with them, I tend to forgive them more easily for the moves which, coming from the other side, properly infuriate me. One problem I have always had with *Dr. Strangelove,* much as I enjoyed it, was the sickly consolation it gave to liberals with all of its easy targets. The assumption was that those crazy hawks enjoyed destruction, that they had a romance going with Armageddon. They—our ideological opponents—couldn't honestly believe that unless we met and overtook the Soviets weapon for weapon, we would be faced with a situation in which we might really be forced to accept the domination of a group of people who believe that the Gulag is the proper answer to dissent. They must have a darker reason, something to do with their being anal sorts. They must have had a dreadful relationship with their fathers, or they must have been sexually confused. They couldn't have an honestly different view of the world, a different reading of the same facts.

I disagree with a view of the world which can envision a situation in which our superior strength will force our enemies to back down; we wouldn't be cowed so easily, and it seems naive to suppose that they are that much unlike us. I not only disagree with that view. I think that if it does not kill me off, it will kill my children or grandchildren. Or it may keep them from being killed—at the expense of other people's children and grandchildren. Even if those who defend the arms race as a necessary evil were right in their predictions, I would have to oppose them.

But it is too easy, too self-satisfying, to assume that our own motives in this argument are pure while our opponents are indecent. They are wrong, I think; but to think that they are simply base (or even complicatedly base) involves us in doing several false things. We assume an ulterior motive, which handily keeps us from having to consider seriously the possibility that our opponents could be right. We assume that no other vision of the world could possibly have anything to recommend it, which keeps us from having to examine our own assumptions very closely. And we assume that our having the right idea, which is usually projected at people who already agree with us anyway, ought to gain us support, applause, and moral approval. We do this whether we are on the left or right. And by offering package deals we make it all easier for ourselves. A woman who knew that I opposed the war in Vietnam was shocked to learn that I opposed abortion, because in her package-deal way of thinking a person who opposed war must be in favor of abortion. The left is assumed by its enemies to be predictable, and so is the right. Both sides are right too often. Left and right *are* both pretty predictable, nearly tribal, and ideas and opinions are frequently waved around as signs of respectability within the tribe, as if language had nothing to do with exploring, or with moving towards a truth in a tentative way, or with being doubtful, or with taking a chance at the edge—which means being willing not only to be wrong, because the only thing at stake here is not whether an opinion falls into the true or false column, but also takes into account the possibility that your opponent is a human being as richly complicated and oddly formed as you are.

That does not make your opponent right. One must   7 firmly believe that there are ideas beyond decent debate. Genocide and child molestation are closed issues, I think. It is wrong not to be passionate about the things we care for deeply. I feel as strongly about nuclear war as I do about abortion, and find it difficult to have much sympathy with defenders of capital punishment. If Matthew 25 is right and what is done to the least human being is done to Christ, then capital punishment, abortion, the notion of a war in which whole populations may be destroyed, and the idea that hunger is in some circumstances acceptable, are all under a terrible judgment. But to think of those whose disagreements with us are deep as indecent or base is to put ourselves under the same judgment. An idea must bear fruit; a Christian perception is meant to go out from itself. If we see it as a personal possession we are on the wrong track. As a possession it is something we have to get rid of.

The Quaker saint John Woolman opposed slaveholders   8
and the men who were about to make the Revolutionary War. He thought that their decisions were profoundly wrong, and he let them know that. His life was a lived disagreement—but he always assumed that he was talking to a human being, one loved by God. Even where we believe that there is no room for debate, we must have compassion—which means *suffering with,* which means understanding how a person could arrive at the place where he is—and we must realize that we share the disease of the heart which allows people to wound one another in the name of truth. Erasmus once wrote about one aspect of this universal problem: "There is great obscurity in many matters, and man suffers from this almost congenital disease, that he will not give in once a controversy is started, and after he is warmed up he regards as absolutely true that which he began to sponsor quite casually."

The point is not to become less committed, or to as-   9
sume that all ideas are of equal merit, but to be as clear as we can about our own motives, and to approach those who disagree with us the way Woolman did. We should not allow ourselves the luxury of thinking that our ideas have anything at all to do with our decency. We should realize that Matthew 25 applies to our judgments: the least of the brethren includes our opponents.

Comment

Garvey focuses his discussion on both the causes and effects of "thinking in packages." He begins with causes, as in these sentences of paragraph 2: "Our ideas are like clan totems or old school ties. We tend to think that our ideas make us decent." The transition to the effects occurs in paragraph 6: ". . . but to think that they are simply base (or even complicatedly base) involves us in doing several false things." The concluding paragraphs present a solution to the problem. The basic organization, then, is a movement from problem to solution.

Garvey analyzes causes and effects informally, as we would in ordinary conversation. Indeed, that is how he addresses the reader—as a friend with whom he might on another occasion engage in argument. He talks to the reader as he would like to in an argument: casually, amiably, without heat, and without such a narrow focus on the issues that understanding or honest concession become impossible.

Questions for Study and Discussion

1. In what ways are "our ideas . . . like clan totems or old school ties"? How does Garvey develop these similes?
2. How does he illustrate the causes identified in paragraphs 4 through 6?
3. What are the effects—the "several false things"—that result from "thinking in packages"?
4. Garvey refers in paragraph 6 to the need of examining our assumptions closely. What is an assumption in thinking, and how does Garvey explain and illustrate the term?
5. If there are "ideas beyond decent debate," how can and should they be discussed with those who hold opposite opinions? How does the statement of Erasmus help Garvey to deal with this question? And what use does he make of Matthew 25?

Vocabulary Study

1. Explain the difference between the following words. The first word in each pair is Garvey's:
    a. *investment* (paragraph 2), *interest*
    b. *tactical* (paragraph 3), *diplomatic*
    c. *totalitarianism* (paragraph 3), *dictatorship*
    d. *hawks* (paragraph 4), *fanatics*
    e. *ulterior* (paragraph 6), *deceitful*
    f. *opponents* (paragraph 6), *enemies*
    g. *genocide* (paragraph 7), *murder*

h.   *obscurity* (paragraph 8), *misunderstanding*
i.   *congenital* (paragraph 8), *inborn*

2. Be ready to distinguish between the following words in paragraph 1: *anarchist, libertarian, conservative, radical, socialist.*

Suggestions for Writing

1. Analyze an editorial in a newspaper or newsmagazine, or a letter to the editor, to determine whether the writer is "thinking in packages." In the course of your analysis, explain what Garvey means by this term and what his ideas on thinking are as a whole.

2. Develop one of the following statements from your own experience and point of view. If you disagree with the statement, explain why you do:

    a.   "We have an investment in our ideas which has nothing to do with the particular worth of our ideas."

    b.   "Our ideas are like clan totems or old school ties. We tend to think that our ideas make us decent."

    c.   "And by offering package deals we make it all easier for ourselves."

    d.   "It is wrong not to be passionate about the things we care for deeply. . . . But to think of those whose disagreements with us are deep as indecent or base is to put ourselves under the same judgment."

Michael Nelson

THE DESK

Michael Nelson attended the College of William and Mary and Johns Hopkins University. He has worked as a VISTA volunteer in the Georgia Legal Services Program in Augusta, as a television moderator, and as the editor of *The Washington Monthly*. He has taught at Cornell University and Vanderbilt University, where he is now associate professor of political science. Nelson has published numerous articles on American government and politics and is coeditor (with Charles Peters) of *The Culture of Bureaucracy* (1979); he has also edited several books on the American presidency and political system. This particular essay appeared in *Newsweek* in 1978.

When editorial writers and politicians discuss bureau- 1
cracy, they talk about it with a capital B—the massive, face-
less, redtape-clogged Bureaucracy of chamber of commerce
after-dinner speeches. But when I think of bureaucracy, I
think of Martha.

Martha is a retired woman who lives in Augusta, Geor- 2
gia. She survives, but barely, on a small social-security retirement check. A friend once told her that because her income
was so low, Martha was also eligible for Supplemental Security Income (SSI). Reluctantly—she is a proud woman—
Martha applied.

There is a desk in the Augusta Social Security Admin- 3
istration office; Martha sat down on the "client's" side of
it. She was, she timidly told the caseworker who sat opposite her, at her wit's end. She just couldn't make ends meet,
not with today's prices. She had never asked anyone for
charity before—he had to understand that—but she needed
help and had heard that she was entitled to some.

The caseworker understood. Gently, he asked Martha 4
the questions he needed to fill out her application. Everything was in order—except why did she have this $2,000
savings account? For her burial, she told him. She had always dreaded dying as a ward of the state, so for almost 50
years she had saved—a dollar a week when she had it—to
finance her own funeral.

But, the caseworker said, we aren't allowed to give SSI 5
to people with more than $1,500 in the bank; that's the law.
Don't be silly; the law couldn't apply to burial money, said
Martha, scared and defensive in her embarrassment. The
caseworker saw her point, but there was nothing he could
do; the law did not—and realistically could not—distinguish
between money for funerals and money for high living. Anxious to help, he advised her to go out and blow $500 on a
color television—or anything—just to bring her savings down
to $1,500. Then, he said, she would be eligible for SSI. Ap-
palled by this perverse advice, Martha left.

Martha is one of several dozen people I have talked to 6
over the past three years, ordinary people from a variety of
regions, classes and backgrounds. I talked with them because, as a political scientist and a political journalist, I was

interested in finding out what the world of government and politics looks like from the citizens'-eye view. To my surprise, that world contained little of the issues and personalities that pollsters ask about and pundits fulminate about. Instead, it was a world dominated by bureaucracy—not Bureaucracy, mind you, but rather the specific government agencies that these citizens had to deal with in their personal lives—too often, they felt, and with too little satisfaction.

Most ironic was the image of government that was born 7
of these experiences. As any scholarly treatise on the subject will tell you, the great advantage bureaucracy is supposed to offer a complex, modern society like ours is efficient, rational, uniform and courteous treatment for the citizens it deals with. Yet not only did these qualities not come through to the people I talked with, it was their very opposites that seemed more characteristic. People of all classes—the rich man dealing with the Internal Revenue Service as well as the poor woman struggling with the welfare department—felt that the treatment they had received had been bungled, not efficient; unpredictable, not rational; discriminatory or idiosyncratic, not uniform; and, all too often, insensitive, rather than courteous. It was as if they had bought a big new car that not only did not run when they wanted it to, but periodically revved itself up and drove all around their yards.

Are they right? Would that things were that simple. But 8
we taxpayers can't even make up our minds what the problem is with bureaucrats: are they lazy do-nothings, snoozing afternoons away behind the sports section, or wild-eyed do-everythings who can't *ever* sleep unless they have forced some poor soul to rearrange his life to conform with one of their crazy social theories?

As for the bureaucrats, they seem no less blinded by 9
anger than we. Frequently, they dismiss the unhappy citizens they deal with as sufferers of what one political scientist calls "bureausis"—a childish inability to cope with even the simplest, most reasonable rules and regulations. Like children, they add, we demand a lot but expect somebody else to pay.

Yet there are no callous bureaucrats or "bureautics" in 10
Martha's story, nor were there in most of the stories I heard. What there is, though, is a desk. On one side of it sits the

citizen—a whole person who wants to be treated as a whole person. Special consideration? Of course. Bend the rules a little? Certainly, I'm unique. And she is unique, as is every other person who approaches government from her side of the desk.

Across from her sits the bureaucrat. His perspective is   11
entirely different. He is there not as a friend or neighbor, but purely as the representative of his agency, an agency whose only business is to execute the law. His job is to fit this person across the desk into a category: legally eligible for the agency's services or not; if so, for what and on what terms? He cannot, *must* not, look at the whole person, but only at those features that enable him to transform her into a "case," a "file," a "client" for his agency. That way she can count on getting exactly what any other citizen in her category would get from the government—nothing more, nothing less. And do we really want it any different? Would we rather that low-level bureaucrats had the power to give or refuse public services purely as they saw fit?

The desk, whether physical or metaphorical, is there in   12
every encounter between Americans and their government. It turns unique and deserving citizens into snarling clients, and goodhearted civil servants into sullen automatons. More than anything else, I suspect, it explains why we and our government are at each other's throats—why taxpayers pass Proposition 13s and public employees strike like dock workers. *It* is the bureaucracy problem, and if what I heard from the people I talked with is representative, the bureaucracy problem is the crisis of our age.

I only wish I had the solution.   13

Comment

A reading of only the opening sentences of each paragraph will show that they contain the ideas of the essay in miniature: the reader discovers not only what the essay is about but also what conclusions Nelson draws from the episode he describes. The whole essay builds from an experience—which Nelson considers representative of bureaucracy and its effects—to general conclusions.

Notice that he does not claim to have the solution to the problem of bureaucracy. Identifying the problem is sometimes a step toward a solution; such an identification is his purpose in writing.

Questions for Study and Discussion

1. Do any of the opening or topic sentences state the thesis of the essay? What is that thesis?
2. How does Nelson establish his authority on the subject of bureaucracy? How does he seek to persuade you that Martha's experience is a typical one?
3. What does Nelson mean by *bureaucracy?* Does he define this word formally, or does the episode with Martha, together with other details in the essay, provide an indirect definition?
4. Look up the word *metaphorical.* What does Nelson mean by the statement that the desk is both physical and metaphorical?
5. What distinction is Nelson making in paragraph 6 between *bureaucracy* and *Bureaucracy?* What would the second kind of bureaucracy constitute?
6. Do you believe Nelson is right in saying that "the bureaucracy problem is the crisis of our age"? Have you personally experienced such a problem, whether in government or at school? Do you find similar bureaucratic actions or treatment in institutions outside the government—in school offices, or the public library, and the like?
7. What other current social or political issues has Nelson raised in the course of examining government bureaucracy?

Vocabulary Study

1. Explain the difference in the meaning in the contrasted words in the following sentence: "People of all classes—the rich man dealing with the Internal Revenue Service as well as the poor woman struggling with the welfare department—felt that the treatment they had received had been *bungled,* not *efficient; unpredictable,* not *rational; discriminatory* or *idiosyncratic,* not *uniform;* and, all too often, *insensitive,* rather than *courteous.*"
2. Explain how the word in parentheses changes the meaning of the original sentence:

a. *"Appalled* (surprised) by this *perverse* (mistaken) advice, Martha left."
b. "Most *ironic* (contradictory) was the image of government that was born of these experiences."
c. "Across from her sits the bureaucrat. His *perspective* (attitude) is entirely different."
d. "It turns *unique* (special) and deserving citizens into *snarling* (angry) clients, and goodhearted civil servants into *sullen automatons* (sleepy officials)."

Suggestions for Writing

1. Describe an experience with a government agency or official that shaped or changed your attitude toward government in general. Build from the experience to a statement of its effect on you. Draw some conclusions about the problem of government and the citizen, as Nelson does.
2. Describe a series of experiences that shaped your present attitude to the college you now attend. Vary these experiences as much as you can, instead of writing about only positive or only negative ones. Comment on the motives of the people you encountered.
3. Nelson does not state solutions for the problem, but he does imply some. Discuss what these solutions are—and also any other solutions you would propose.

K. C. Cole

WOMEN AND PHYSICS

A former editor of *Saturday Review* and *Newsday,* K. C. Cole has written on science and on women today for various periodicals. In the preface to her collection of essays *Between the Lines,* Cole states, "But precisely what I find both so rich and so confusing about women's roles today is that so often what seem to be irreconcilable opposites are just two different aspects of the same thing—two different windows on the same rapidly changing world." She adds, "I think there's more to the many sides of today's woman than meets the eye—and more common ground on many 'women's issues' than most people think." Cole deals with the important issue of women and science in *Sympathetic*

Vibrations: Reflections on Physics as a Way of Life (1984) and in this essay, first published in 1981.

I know few other women who do what I do. What I do is write about science, mainly physics. And to do that, I spend a lot of time reading about science, talking to scientists and struggling to understand physics. In fact, most of the women (and men) I know think me quite queer for actually liking physics. "How can you write about that stuff?" they ask, always somewhat askance. "I could never understand that in a million years." Or more simply, "I hate science."

I didn't realize what an odd creature a woman interested in physics was until a few years ago when a science magazine sent me to Johns Hopkins University in Baltimore for a conference on an electrical phenomenon known as the Hall effect. We sat in a huge lecture hall and listened as physicists talked about things engineers didn't understand, and engineers talked about things physicists didn't understand. What *I* didn't understand was why, out of several hundred young students of physics and engineering in the room, less than a handful were women.

Some time later, I found myself at the California Institute of Technology reporting on the search for the origins of the universe. I interviewed physicist after physicist, man after man. I asked one young administrator why none of the physicists were women. And he answered: "I don't know, but I suppose it must be something innate. My 7-year-old daughter doesn't seem to be much interested in science."

It was with that experience fresh in my mind that I attended a conference in Cambridge, Massachusetts, on science literacy, or rather the worrisome lack of it in this country today. We three women—a science teacher, a young chemist and myself—sat surrounded by a company of august men. The chemist, I think first tentatively raised the issue of science illiteracy in women. It seemed like an obvious point. After all, everyone had agreed over and over again that scientific knowledge these days was a key factor in economic power. But as soon as she made the point, it became clear that we women had committed a grievous social error. Our genders were suddenly showing; we had interrupted the serious talk with a subject unforgivably silly.

For the first time, I stopped being puzzled about why there weren't any women in science and began to be angry. Because if science is a search for answers to fundamental questions then it hardly seems frivolous to find out why women are excluded. Never mind the economic consequences.

A lot of the reasons why women are excluded are spelled out by the Massachusetts Institute of Technology experimental physicist Vera Kistiakowsky in a recent article in *Physics Today* called "Women in Physics: Unnecessary, Injurious and Out of Place?". The title was taken from a 19th-century essay written in opposition to the appointment of a female mathematician to a professorship at the University of Stockholm. "As decidedly as two and two make four," a woman in mathematics is a "monstrosity," concluded the writer of the essay.

Dr. Kistiakowsky went on to discuss the factors that make women in science today, if not monstrosities, at least oddities. Contrary to much popular opinion, one of those is *not* an innate difference in the scientific ability of boys and girls. But early conditioning does play a stubborn and subtle role. A recent Nova program, "The Pinks and the Blues," documented how girls and boys are treated differently from birth—the boys always encouraged in more physical kinds of play, more active explorations of their environments. Sheila Tobias, in her book, *Math Anxiety,* showed how the games boys play help them to develop an intuitive understanding of speed, motion and mass. The main sorting out of the girls from the boys in science seems to happen in junior high school. As a friend who teaches in a science museum said, "By the time we get to electricity, the boys already have had some experience with it. But it's unfamiliar to the girls." Science books draw on boys' experiences. "The examples are all about throwing a baseball at such and such a speed," said my step daughter, who barely escaped being a science drop-out.

The most obvious reason there are not many more 8
women in science is that women are discriminated against
as a class, in promotions, salaries and hirings, a conclusion
reached by a recent analysis by the National Academy of
Sciences.

Finally, said Dr. Kistiakowsky, women are simply made 9
to feel out of place in science. Her conclusion was supported
by a Ford Foundation study by Lynn H. Fox on the problems of women in mathematics. When students were asked
to choose among six reasons accounting for girls' lack of
interest in math, the girls rated this statement second: "Men
do not want girls in the mathematical occupations."

A friend of mine remembers winning a Bronxwide 10
mathematics competition in the second grade. Her friends—
both boys and girls—warned her that she shouldn't be good
at math: "You'll never find a boy who likes you." My friend
continued nevertheless to excel in math and science, won
many awards during her years at the Bronx High School of
Science, and then earned a full scholarship to Harvard. After
one year of Harvard science, she decided to major in English.

When I asked her why, she mentioned what she called 11
the "macho mores" of science. "It would have been O.K. if
I'd had someone to talk to," she said. "But the rules of comportment were such that you never admitted you didn't understand. I later realized that even the boys didn't get
everything clearly right away. You had to stick with it until
it had time to sink in. But for the boys, there was a payoff
in suffering through the hard times, and a kind of punishment—a shame—if they didn't. For the girls it was O.K. not
to get it, and the only payoff for sticking it out was that
you'd be considered a freak."

Science is undeniably hard. Often, it can seem quite 12
boring. It is unfortunately too often presented as laws to be
memorized instead of mysteries to be explored. It is too often
kept a secret that science, like art, takes a well developed
esthetic sense. Women aren't the only ones who say, "I hate
science." That's why everyone who goes into science needs

a little help from friends. For the past ten years, I have been getting more than a little help from a friend who is a physicist. But my stepdaughter—who earned the highest grades ever recorded in her California high school on the math Scholastic Aptitude Test—flunked calculus in her first year at Harvard. When my friend the physicist heard about it, he said, "Harvard should be ashamed of itself."

What he meant was that she needed that little extra   13
encouragement that makes all the difference. Instead, she got that little extra discouragement that makes all the difference. "In the first place, all the math teachers are men," she explained. "In the second place, when I met a boy I liked and told him I was taking chemistry, he immediately said: 'Oh, you're one of those science types.' In the third place, it's just a kind of social thing. The math clubs are full of boys and you don't feel comfortable joining."

In other words, she was made to feel unnecessary, and   14
out of place.

A few months ago, I accompanied a male colleague from   15
the science museum where I sometimes work to a lunch of the history of science faculty at the University of California. I was the only woman there, and my presence for the most part was obviously and rudely ignored. I was so surprised and hurt by this that I made an extra effort to speak knowledgeably and well. At the end of the lunch, one of the professors turned to me in all seriousness and said: "Well, K. C., what do the women think of Carl Sagan?" I replied that I had no idea what "the women" thought about anything. But now I know what I should have said: I should have told him that his comment was unnecessary, injurious and out of place.

Comment

The issue that Cole explores—whether women lack ability in science and mathematics—is related to a broader issue considered briefly in paragraphs 6 and 7. This is whether males and females differ innately in scientific ability. Cole reviews some recent evidence, then presents personal experiences that support the view that social conditioning plays a decisive role; she wishes to show, mainly, that girls are discouraged from excelling in science and mathematics. The evidence she presents is not, and cannot be, conclusive; but it is strong enough to answer the question she poses at the beginning of the essay—"why, out of several hundred young students of physics and engineering in the room, less than a handful were women." Her question cannot yet be answered definitely, but the evidence she assembles from various sources provides what she believes is a highly probable answer.

Questions for Study and Discussion

1. How various is the evidence Cole presents for the conclusion she reaches? Where does she state that conclusion?
2. How many causes does she distinguish for the failure of many women to excel in science and mathematics?
3. Does Cole say that innate differences in scientific ability do not exist between males and females, or does she reach a limited or qualified conclusion?
4. What other kind of evidence might be presented in consideration of the issue of innate scientific ability? For what kind of audience would this evidence have to be presented? For what audience is Cole writing?
5. Does your personal experience support the idea that ability in science and mathematics depends on encouragement and social conditions? Or do you have reason to believe that such ability is inborn?
6. How persuasive do you find the evidence Cole presents in support of her ideas?

Vocabulary Study

Explain the specific use Cole makes of the italicized words:

a. "Our *genders* were suddenly showing; we had interrupted the serious talk with a subject unforgivably *silly*" (paragraph 4).
b. "Dr. Kistiakowsky went on to discuss the *factors* that make women in science today, if not *monstrosities,* at least *oddities*" (paragraph 7).
c. "When I asked her why, she mentioned what she called the '*macho mores*' of science" (paragraph 11).

d.   "But the rules of *comportment* were such that you never admitted you didn't understand" (paragraph 11).

Suggestions for Writing

1. Discuss your own experiences in learning science and mathematics, giving attention to the conditioning and encouragement you received, and in general the reasons for your good or bad or just average performance in them. Use your discussion to reach a limited conclusion or opinion on the issue Cole discusses.
2. Discuss the extent to which your personal experience supports one of the following statements:
    a.   "The games boys play help them to develop an intuitive understanding of speed, motion and mass."
    b.   "The main sorting out of the girls from the boys in science seems to happen in junior high school."
    c.   "But the rules of comportment were such that you never admitted you didn't understand."
    d.   "Science is undeniably hard. Often, it can seem quite boring. It is unfortunately too often presented as laws to be memorized instead of mysteries to be explored."

Lewis Yablonsky

THE VIOLENT GANG

Lewis Yablonsky has written much about juvenile crime. He was born in 1924 in Irvington, New Jersey, and studied at Rutgers and New York University, where he received his Ph.D. in 1957. He has taught at several universities, including the University of Massachusetts and the University of California at Los Angeles, and he is now professor of sociology at California State University in Northridge. This essay was first published in 1960.

It is a truism that criminal organizations and criminal   1
activities tend to reflect social conditions. Just as surely as
the Bowery gang mirrored aspects of the 1900's, the Capone
mob aspects of the twenties, and the youth gangs of the

depression elements of the thirties, so do the delinquent gangs that have developed since the 1940's in the United States reflect certain patterns of our own society.

The following quotations indicate the tone and ethos of [2] a representative gang of today, the so-called Egyptian Kings, whose members beat and stabbed to death a fifteen-year-old boy named Michael Farmer in a New York City park not long ago. Michael Farmer, who had been crippled by polio, was not known to the Kings before the killing, nor had he been acquainted with any members of the gang.

> He couldn't run any way, 'cause we were all around him. So then I said, "You're a Jester," and he said "Yeah," and I punched him in the face. And then somebody hit him with a bat over the head. And then I kept punchin' him. Some of them were too scared to do anything. They were just standin' there, lookin'.

> I was watchin' him. I didn't wanna hit him, at first. Then I kicked him twice. He was layin' on the ground, lookin' up at us. I kicked him on the jaw, or some place; then I kicked him in the stomach. That was the least I could do, was kick 'im.

> I was aimin' to hit him, but I didn't get a chance to hit him. There was so many guys on him—I got scared when I saw the knife go into the guy, and I ran right there. After everybody ran, this guy stayed, and started hittin' him with a machete.

> Somebody yelled out, "Grab him. He's a Jester." So then they grabbed him. Magician grabbed him, he turned around and stabbed him in the back. I was . . . I was stunned. I couldn't do nuthin'. And then Magician—he went like that and he pulled . . . he had a switch blade and he said, "You're gonna hit him with the bat or I'll stab you." So I just hit him lightly with the bat.

> Magician stabbed him and the guy he . . . like hunched over. He's standin' up and I knock him down. Then he was down on the ground, everybody was kickin' him, stompin' him, punchin' him, stabbin' him so he tried to get back up and I knock him down again. Then the guy stabbed him in the back with a bread knife.

The attitudes toward homicide and violence that emerge from these statements led to eleven gang killings last summer and can be expected to produce an even greater number from now on.

One important difference between the gangs of the past 3 and those that now operate on our city streets is the prevalence of the psychopathic element in the latter. The violent gangs of the twenties contained psychopaths, but they were used to further the profitmaking goal of the gang, and were themselves paid for their violence. Here, for example, is how Abe "Kid Twist" Reles—who informed on Murder, Inc., and confessed to having committed over eighteen murders himself—described the activities of the Crime Trust to a writer in the *Nation:*

> The Crime Trust, Reles insists, never commits murders out of passion, excitement, jealousy, personal revenge, or any of the usual motives which prompt private unorganized murders. It kills impersonally and solely for business considerations. No gangster may kill on his own initiative; every murder must be ordered by the leaders at the top, and it must serve the welfare of the organization. . . . Any member of the mob who would dare kill on his own initiative or for his own profit would be executed. . . . The Crime Trust insists that murder must be a business matter organized by the chiefs in conference and carried out in a disciplined way.

Frederic Thrasher's famous analysis of Chicago gangs 4 in the mid-twenties describes another group that bears only a limited resemblance to the violent gangs of today. Thrasher's gangs

> . . . broke into box cars and "robbed" bacon and other merchandise. They cut out wire cables to sell as junk. They broke open telephone boxes. They took autos for joy-riding. They purloined several quarts of whiskey from a brewery to drink in their shack. . . .

Nor do the gangs of the thirties and early forties de- 5 scribed by W. F. Whyte in *Street Corner Society* bear much resemblance to the violent gang of today. The difference becomes strikingly evident when we compare the following comments by two Egyptian Kings with those of Doc, the leader of Whyte's Norton Street gang.

I just went like that, and I stabbed him with the bread knife. You know I was drunk so I stabbed him. *[Laughs]* He was screamin' like a dog. He was screamin' there. And then I took the knife out and told the other guys to run. . . .

The guy that stabbed him in the back with the bread knife, he told me that when he took the knife out o' his back, he said, "Thank you."

Now Doc, leader of the Norton Street gang:

Nutsy was a cocky kid before I beat him up. . . . After that, he seemed to lose his pride. I would talk to him and try to get him to buck up. . . . I walloped every kid in my gang at some time. We had one Sicilian kid on my street. When I walloped him, he told his father and the father came out looking for me. I hid up on a roof, and Nutsy told me when the father had gone. When I saw the kid next, I walloped him again—for telling his father on me. . . . But I wasn't such a tough kid, Bill. I was always sorry after I walloped him.

Doc's comments about beating up Nutsy—"I would talk to him and try to buck him up"—or about fighting the other kids—"I was always sorry after I walloped them"—are in sharp contrast to the post-assault comments of the Egyptian Kings. Here is how one of the Kings who stabbed Farmer replied to my questions about his part in the homicide. The interview took place in a reformatory.

> KING: "I stab him with the butcher—I mean the bread-knife and then I took it out."
>
> QUESTION: "What were you thinking about at the time, right then?"
>
> KING: "What was I thinking? *[Laughs]* I was thinking whether to do it again."
>
> QUESTION: "Are you sorry about what happened?"
>
> KING: "Am I sorry? Are you nuts; of course, I'm sorry. You think I like being locked up?"

The element of friendship and camaraderie—one might almost call it cooperativeness—that was central to the Norton Street gang and others like it during the depression is entirely absent from the violent gang of today. To be sure, "candy store" or corner hang-out groups similar to those described by Whyte still exist, but it is not such groups who are responsible for the killings and assaults that have caused so much concern in our major cities in recent years.

Today's violent gang is, above all, characterized by flux. 7 It lacks all the features of an organized group, having neither a definite number of members, nor specific membership roles, nor a consensus of expected norms, nor a leader who supplies directive for action. It is a moblike collectivity which forms around violence in a spontaneous fashion, moving into action—often on the spur of an evening's boredom—in search of "kicks." Violence ranks extremely high in the loose scheme of values on which such gangs are based. To some boys it acts as a kind of existential validation, proving (since they are not sure) that they are alive. Others, clinging to membership in this marginal and amorphous organization, employ violence to demonstrate they are "somebody." But most members of the gang use violence to acquire prestige or to raise their "rep."

> I didn't want to be like . . . you know, different from the other guys. Like they hit him, I hit him. In other words, I didn't want to show myself as a punk. You know, ya always talkin', "Oh, man, when I catch a guy, I'll beat him up," and all of that, you know. And after you go out and you catch a guy, and you don't do nothin' they say, "Oh, man, he can't belong to no gang, because he ain't gonna do nothin'."

> Momentarily I started to thinking about it inside: I have my mind made up I'm not going to be in no gang. Then I go on inside. Something comes up, den here come all my friends coming to me. Like I said before, I'm intelligent and so forth. They be coming to me—then they talk to me about what they gonna do. Like, "Man, we'll go out here and kill this cat." I say, "Yeah." They kept on talkin'. I said, "Man, I just gotta go with you." Myself, I don't want to go, but when they start talkin' about what they gonna do, I say, "So, he isn't gonna take over my rep.

I ain't gonna let him be known more than me." And I go ahead just for selfishness.

If I would of got the knife, I would have stabbed him. That would have gave me more of a build-up. People would have respected me for what I've done and things like that. They would say, "There goes a cold killer."

It makes you feel like a big shot. You know some guys think they're big shots and all that. They think, like you know, they got the power to do everything they feel like doing. They say, like, "I wanna stab a guy," and then the other guy says, "Oh, I wouldn't dare to do that." You know, he thinks I'm acting like a big shot. That's the way he feels. He probably thinks in his mind, "Oh, he probably won't do that." Then, when we go to fight, you know, he finds out what I do.

The structure of the violent gang can be analyzed into three different levels. At the center, on the first level, are the leaders, who—contrary to the popular idea that they could become "captains of industry if only their energies were re-directed"—are the most psychologically disturbed of all the members. These youths (who are usually between eighteen and twenty-five years old) need the gang more than anyone else, and it is they who provide it with whatever cohesive force it has. In a gang of some thirty boys there may be five or six such leaders who desperately rely on the gang to build and maintain a "rep," and they are always working to keep the gang together and in action. They enlist new members (by force), plot, and talk gang warfare most of their waking hours.

At the second level, there are youths who claim affiliation to the gang but only participate in it sporadically. For example, one of the Egyptian Kings told me that if his father had not given him a "bad time" and kicked him out of the house the night of the homicide, he would not have gone to the corner and become involved in the Michael Farmer killing. The gang was for this boy, on that night, a vehicle for acting out aggressions related to another area of his life. Such a "temporal" gang need, however, is a common phenomenon.

At the third level are boys who occasionally join in with   10
gang activity but seldom identify themselves as members of
the gang at any other time. One boy, for instance, went along
with the Egyptian Kings and participated in the Farmer killing, as he put it, "for old time's sake." He never really "belonged" to the gang: he just happened to be around that
night and had nothing else to do.

The "size" of violent gangs is often impossible to deter-   11
mine. If a leader feels particularly hemmed in at a given moment, he will say—and believe—that his gang is very large.
But when he is feeling more secure, he will include in his
account of the gang's size only those members he actually
knows personally. In the course of a one-hour interview, for
example, a gang leader variously estimated the size, affilia-
tions, and territory of his gang as follows: membership
jumped from one hundred to four thousand, affiliation from
five brother gangs or alliances to sixty, and territorial control from about ten square blocks to jurisdiction over the
boroughs of New York City, New Jersey, and part of Philadelphia. To be sure, gangs will often contact one another
to discuss alliances, and during the street-corner "negotia-
tions," the leaders will brag of their ability to mobilize vast
forces in case of a fight. On a rare occasion, these forces
will actually be produced, but they generally appear quite
spontaneously—the youths who participate in such alliances
have very little understanding of what they are doing.

The meaning of gang membership also changes accord-   12
ing to a boy's needs of the moment. A youth will belong
one day and quit the next without necessarily telling any
other member. To ask certain gang boys from day to day
whether they are Dragons or Kings is comparable to asking
them, "How do you feel today?" So, too, with the question
of role. Some boys say that the gang is organized for protection and that one role of a gang member is to fight—how,
when, whom, and for what reason he is to fight are seldom
clear, and answers vary from member to member. One gang
boy may define himself more specifically as a protector of
the younger boys in the neighborhood. Another will define
his role in the gang by the statement, "We are going to

get all those guys who call us Spics." Still others say their participation in the gang was forced upon them against their will.

Despite these differences, however, all gang members believe that through their participation they will acquire prestige and status; and it is quite clear, furthermore, that the vagueness which surrounds various aspects of gang life and organization only enables the gang to stimulate such expectations and, in some respects, actually helps it to fulfill them. Similarly, if qualifications for membership were more exact, then most gang members would not be able to participate, for they lack the ability to assume the responsibilities of more structured organizations.   13

The background out of which the violent gang has emerged is fairly easy to sketch. In contemporary American society, youth is constantly bombarded by images—from the media, schools, and parents—of a life of ownership and consumption, but for the great majority of young people in this country, and especially for those from depressed social and economic backgrounds, the means of acquiring such objectives are slim. Yet something more definite than class position or the inadequate relation between means and ends disturbs young people. It is the very fact of their youth which places them at an immediate disadvantage; objects and goals that adults take for granted are, for them, clearly unattainable. As a consequence, many young people step beyond the accepted social boundaries in an attempt to find through deviant means a dramatic short-cut to an immediate feeling of success.[1]   14

Drugs and alcohol are two possible short cuts; another characteristic deviant path is the search for thrills or "kicks." The violent gang, especially because it is both flexibly organized and amenable to the distortions of fantasy, is an obvious vehicle for acting out the desire for ownership and status. In the gang, a youth can be "president" and control   15

---

[1] This statement is a gross oversimplification of conceptual developments of Emile Durkheim, Robert Merton, and others, who have examined the means-goal dislocation.

vast domains, while the members can reinforce one another's fantasies of power—"Don't call my bluff and I won't call yours." In the gang, it is only necessary to talk big and support the talk with some violent action in order to become a "success," the possessor of power and status: "We would talk a lot and like that, but I never thought it would be like this. Me here in jail. It was just like fun and kidding around and acting big."

The choice of violence as a means toward achieving "social" success seems to be the result in part of the past two decades of war as well as the international unrest that filters down to the gang boy and gives him the same feelings of uneasiness that the average citizen experiences. At this level of analysis, direct casual relations are by *no means* precise; yet a number of connections do seem apparent.   16

A considerable amount of explicit data indicates that recent wars and current international machinations serve as models for gang warfare. For example, one form of gang battle is called a "Jap": "a quick stomp where a group of guys go into an enemy's territory, beat up some of their guys and get out fast. The thing is not to get caught." "Drafting" members is another common gang practice. The boys themselves freely use such terms as "drafting," "allies" (brother gangs), "war counselor," "peace treaty," etc., and they often refer, both directly and indirectly, to more complex patterns of conflict and structure. Here is one Egyptian King talking about a territorial dispute: 17

> You have a certain piece of land, so another club wants to take over your land, in order to have more space, and so forth. They'll fight you for it. If you win, you got your land; if you don't win, then they get your land. The person that loses is gonna get up another group, to help out, and then it starts all over again. Fight for the land again.

Here is another discussing gang organization:

> First, there's the president. He got the whole gang; then there comes the vice president, he's second in command; then there's the war counselor, war lord, whatever you're gonna call it—

that's the one that starts the fights; then there's the prime minister—you know, he goes along with the war counselor to see when they're gonna fight, where they're gonna fight. And after that, just club members.

Murder, Inc., Thrasher's gangs, and Whyte's Norton Street gang did not have the "divisions," "war lords," and "allies" typical of the contemporary violent gang.

In addition to this international model, it is important [18] to note that many weapons now used by gangs were brought to this country by veterans of recent wars. Where in former years, gang wars were more likely to be fought with sticks, stones, and fists, today abandoned World War II weapons such as machetes (one was used in the Michael Farmer killing) and Lugers consistently turn up. The returning soldiers also brought back stories of violence to accompany the weapons. War and violence dominated not only the front pages of the press, but everyday family discussion, and often it was a father, an uncle, or an older brother whose violent exploits were extolled.

Another aspect of international events which gang youths [19] may have absorbed, and which they certainly now emulate, is the authoritarian-dictatorial concept of leadership. Earlier gangs sometimes utilized democratic processes in appointing leaders. But, today, in the violent gang, the leader is usually supreme and gang members tend to follow him slavishly. In recent years, in fact, there have been many abortive attempts—several on the Upper West Side of New York City—to pattern gangs specifically upon the model of Hitler and the Nazi party.

What finally confronts the youth of today is the possi- [20] bility of total destruction by atomic power—everyone is aware of this on some level of consciousness—and the possibility of induction into the army at a point when he might be establishing himself in the labor force. In short, the recent history of international violence, the consequences of the past war, and the chance of total annihilation, establish a framework which may not only stimulate the formation of gangs but in some respects may determine its mode of behavior—in other words, its violence.

But such background factors, however much they cre- 21
ate an atmosphere that gives implicit social approval to the
use of violence, cannot actually explain how violence functions for the gang boy. As I have already indicated, gang
youths feel extremely helpless in their relations to the "outside" world. The gang boy considers himself incapable of
functioning in any group other than the gang, and is afraid
to attempt anything beyond the minimal demands of gang
life. One interesting indication of this is the way gang boys
respond to flattery. They invariably become flustered and
confused if they are complimented, for the suggestion that
they are capable of more constructive activity upsets their
conviction of being unfit for the hazards of a life outside the
protective circle of the gang.

Given this low self-estimate, the gang boy has carved 22
out a world and a system of values which entail only the
kind of demands he can easily meet. Inverting society's norms
to suit himself and the limits of his partly imagined and partly
real potential, he has made lying, assault, theft, and unpro-
voked violence—and especially violence—the major activities of his life.

The very fact that it is *senseless* rather than premedi- 23
tated violence which is more highly prized by the gang, tells
us a great deal about the role violence plays for the gang
boy. He is looking for a quick, almost magical way of
achieving power and prestige, and in a single act of unpre-
meditated intensity he at once establishes a sense of his own
existence and impresses this existence on others. No special
ability is required—not even a plan—and the anxiety atten-
dant upon executing a premeditated (or "rational") act of
violence is minimized in the ideal of a swift, sudden, and
"meaningless" outbreak. (To some extent, the public's reaction to this violence, a reaction, most obviously of horror,
also expresses a sort of covert aggrandizement—and this the
gang boy instinctively understands.)

Thus the violent gang provides an alternative world for 24
the disturbed young who are ill-equipped for success in a
society which in any case blocks their upward mobility. The
irony is that this world with its nightmare inversion of the

official values of our society is nevertheless constructed out of elements that are implicitly (or unconsciously) approved—especially in the mass media—and that its purpose is to help the gang boy achieve the major value of respectable society: success. "I'm not going to let anybody be better than me and steal my 'rep' . . . when I go to a gang fight, I punch, stomp, and stab harder than anyone."

Comment

Division is an important method of exposition in Yablonsky's essay. First Yablonsky classifies gangs of the past and gangs of the present, then defines their purpose and structure. Second, he divides gangs of the present—the violent street gangs—according to their "levels." This division is, in fact, a more detailed analysis of the structure of the gang, for Yablonsky's earlier dicussion of that structure is concerned only with its general features. The three levels reveal the various motives of the gang members. Reflecting the values of the fifties, the violent gang shows how people are directed by forces beyond their control. Yablonsky's concern over the death of Michael Farmer is in part a concern over wanton acts by boys who did not know their victim or themselves. He returns to this point at the end. His essay shows how an episode (the murder of Michael Farmer) can be used to say much about a society—its values, its structure, the motives of acts that seem "senseless."

Questions for Study and Discussion

1. How does Yablonsky explain the difference between gangs of the past and the violent gang of the fifties?
2. By what other principles might the violent gang be divided? To what use could these divisions be put in another essay?
3. Yablonsky states: "In contemporary American society, youth is constantly bombarded by images—from the media, schools, and parents," and he identifies those images and their effect. Yablonsky was writing in 1960. Do you believe youth in the late eighties is bombarded by the same images? Are the effects of images the same today?
4. What does Yablonsky mean in paragraph 14 by "the inade-

quate relation between means and ends"? How does the context of the statement help to explain it?

5. The phrase "society's norms" (paragraph 22) refers to the values or standards by which people live. How does Yablonsky show that not all of these "norms" are admitted or recognized by the people who live by them?

6. What is Yablonsky's thesis and where is it first stated? How does he restate it in the course of the essay?

7. To what extent does Yablonsky depend on formal transitions?

8. Yablonsky cites the Second World War and the atomic bomb as causes of certain attitudes and behavior in youth of the fifties. Do you believe war and fear of destruction are a major cause of juvenile crime today, as reported in *Newsweek* (March 28, 1988) and other recent periodicals? Do you believe the pressures to conform are as strong today as they were in the fifties?

Vocabulary Study

Complete the following sentences, using the italicized word according to one of its dictionary meanings:

a. It is a *truism* of life that
b. One *aspect* of the energy crisis is
c. There was no *consensus*
d. The *phenomenon* of flying saucer reports
e. The teacher was *amenable* to
f. She could distinguish between *fantasy* and
g. They could not *emulate*
h. The contract *entails*
i. There was a *covert* recognition

Suggestions for Writing

1. Analyze the attitudes and organization of a group you belong to. Use your analysis to develop a thesis, relating perhaps to how people behave in groups.

2. Support or argue against one of Yablonsky's conclusions, drawing on your own experiences and observations.

Robert Coles

SETTLING IN

Robert Coles is Professor of Psychiatry and Medical Humanities at
Harvard University. A psychiatrist concerned with children, he has
served on various boards, commissions, and foundations devoted to the
education and welfare of children. Coles has written a series of books
on American children under the general title *Children of Crisis,* the first
of these appearing in 1967; the second and third volumes—*Migrants,
Sharecroppers, Mountaineers* and *The South Goes North*—were
awarded the Pulitzer Prize in 1973. With Jane Hallowell Coles, he wrote
another series under the general title *Women of Crisis.* Coles is also the
author of books on American Eskimos, children of migrant farm
workers, the moral life and political life of children, and the fiction and
poetry of some American and English writers. The essay reprinted here
is taken from *The South Goes North,* a study of Southern rural people
living in Northern cities. Ellen Goodman, Kathy Seelinger, and George
F. Will discuss small town and city life later in parts 4 and 5.

Automobiles are hardly anything new to America's youth.   1
Up the remotest hollows one can find them, often enough
broken down and abandoned. But they are used, too—and
in the course of my work with young Appalachian men I
have often wondered what we would have talked about had
there not been an automobile to mention, then discuss at
some length, then go over and look at, and finally drive in.
I suppose before there were cars, men talked about horses.
When one first begins to spend time in Kentucky or West
Virginia the roads seem thoroughly dangerous. If one is like
me, possessed of and sometimes victimized by a particular
vocabulary, thoughts begin to assert themselves: am I crazy
or suicidal to be on these roads with these drivers, or are
they all crazy or suicidal—or "aggressive" or "antisocial"?
The roads are narrow and winding and at times tortuous
beyond all others in the nation. Asphalt can without warn-
ing turn into sand or mud. And the drivers: they seem so
casual and vigorous; they move along as though lanes and
lanes of road were on either side of them, and no cars were
in sight for miles ahead—even when only a few inches

separate them from the steepest of hills, or a curve approaches around which totally unseen, a car or huge coal truck may be coming in the opposite direction. Yet throughout the years of my work in Appalachia, I have never seen an accident—which is not to say accidents don't occur, but simply to suggest that my fearfulness must have had something to do with the limitations of my own experience: as a driver I took for granted certain road conditions, consequently I was made nervous when I found them lacking.

By the same token a youth from, say, Leslie County, Kentucky, can find superhighways and most especially city traffic puzzling if not terrifying. All that space and all those cars and all those traffic lights and traffic signs! So many distractions: horns blowing, stores with things in the window and pictures of wine and women! And the turnoffs, the constant intersections, the warnings which insist this highway has now become something else, or is about to join with yet another road—all of that is confusing, as are those constant reminders that one is so-and-so miles from such-and-such a town or city, not to mention from some state line. Then, there are the restaurants and gas stations: how can they all stay open? How can there be so many people eager to use such places? How can there be so many people at all?

For Larry Walker, age seventeen and a half, who is originally from a creek near Thousand-Sticks, Leslie County, Kentucky, but now lives in Dayton, Ohio, those questions are not openly asked. They are very much on his mind, though; and after a beer or two they come to expression. Larry has been in Dayton for five years, but he is not *from* Dayton. His little brother and sister may have the notion at times that they are from Ohio, that Dayton is their home, that their future is to be found in a growing city, but not Larry: "I'm from Leslie County, and I'll always say that's where my home is. When I turn eighteen I'll probably go into the Army. I hurt my arm once, broke it, but I don't think they will hold that against me. They'd be fools to; I'd make a good soldier, I believe. I've always dreamed I might one day go into the service and maybe stay there for a while.

If you stay in twenty years, you can retire, and you have a good pension, and then you can go back to Leslie County and there's no ache over money. We only left the county because we had to leave. My father's brother left first, my Uncle Jim. He got a job here in a factory, and he came back with all those green bills in his hand and told my father he had to come up to Ohio, too; so here we are. My mother says it's like in the stories you see on television: people go away for a while, but then they come home, and they're glad. She means they go on vacation. Like my dad says: it's a vacation having a job and money; you don't have to stand around all the time and worry if you're going to survive the winter.

"If I had my choice, I'd go into the Navy. I know it's strange, because I've never seen the ocean, only a lake or two in Kentucky. But I saw a movie once about the Navy when I was real little, maybe seven, I'd say. I've wanted ever since to join the Navy. The Navy people might decide I'm no good, being from the mountains. I'd probably get seasick. I'm going to wait to be drafted; I'll have a chance to go back to Leslie County then and take my physical. The government will pay for my travel home, I believe. The Army can tell me where they want me to go, and I'll be glad to serve my country—even if it means Vietnam. There's too many people these days who don't salute the flag the way they should. This is the greatest country in the world, and if there's going to be a great country, there has to be a great Army.

"Until we moved to Ohio I never realized how *big* the country is, and how you can go from one place to another, and it all changes. I knew we had these cities, these big cities, but like I tell my friends when we go back home and I can talk with them: seeing is believing. If I'd stayed there and seen pictures of Dayton on the television, I wouldn't know much, not compared to what I know now. I mean, you have to drive in a city to know it. You can't believe it's like it is until you try to drive from one place to another, one street to another; then you find out. The guys back home, kids I grew up with, they say a road is a road, and that's all there is to it. I tell them they don't know what they're talking about. I have my car, and I've got to keep my foot on the brake more than on the gas—that's what it means to live in the city. Living in the city for a guy like me is learning to brake the car all the time, and wearing the clutch out, and using gas like it's water that's come down the mountain and is waiting to be picked up in buckets and poured into the tank. Living in the city means you have to turn your head every other minute you're driving and keep your eye out for almost anything—when all you want to do is push that gas pedal to the floor and take off.

"I love my car. She's a beauty. She's a Chevy, the best ⁶ car there is. The motor is good. The tires are good. I think there's no use driving a car if you can't have good tires. Have you ever had a flat on a city street? That's no fun. I'd rather have to fix a flat right in the middle of a curve up one of those hills; there I could hear the car coming and flag it down. Here in Dayton no one pays any attention to the next guy driving, and it is so noisy you can't hear your own voice speaking. They tell me it's even worse in Cleveland. I can get around here, though; now I can. And if my car goes bad, I can take it off the road and fix it myself. I've learned everything I can about car engines. I like new cars and I like old cars. Don't you love the old Thunderbirds? They were some car—1955 or 1956, I believe. I was only a baby then. When I was a little older and just beginning to go to school I remember a big shot, someone from Hazard, coming up to the little schoolhouse we had; and it was a Thunderbird he drove. I think they were talking about closing down the school and sending us someplace else. I think a mine company bought the hill nearby, and they were going to tear it up for coal. I recall telling my friend Carl—he was my best friend—that I hoped one day I could drive a car like that, a Thunderbird; then I'd have everything I wanted. I still don't have a Thunderbird, but now I don't think I'd buy one even if I had a huge bankroll on me. I'd buy a Mustang or a Cougar, maybe. But for a beginner like me, this old Chevy is a good car to have.

"I've taken the motor apart three times. I painted the　7
car myself. I know how. I know how to spray the right way.
If I go into the Army, I hope I can be near some of those
jeeps and trucks. I wouldn't mind driving them; I hear they're
something to drive all right! I'd rather work on the motors,
though; that way I could learn more about the different kinds
and how they all work. If I could only get a job back home
working in a garage or a gas station! But it's not easy to do.
I don't know anyone who owns a gas station, and if I did
he'd want to use his own son, I'm sure. Jobs are scarce back
home. That's why we drove here, and that's why my car is
going to spend most of its life in Ohio. The poor car will
suffer plenty on that account, but that's just how it works
out. I'll be driving—and stopping and starting and stopping
and starting—and I can hear the motor saying: stop it, and
get me out of here, fast. So, I just talk back to it. I say:
motor, take it easy and just keep going, because there's not
a thing in the world you or I can do anyway, except keep
going. Then I baby her a bit; I go easy on the brakes and
try not to shift more times than I have to—and the old motor seems happier.

"I get nervous when I'm in a crowd of cars; that's when　8
I guess I keep shifting the gears back and forth, and it's not
good to do. But how are you supposed to live with all those
other cars? I never knew there were so many real, live,
honest-to-goodness people in America until we came up here.
To this day I can hardly believe it. In school they taught us
that it was New York City that was most crowded, and next
Chicago. But I asked the teacher if it could get much more
crowded than Dayton, Ohio, when the factories were letting
out, and she said no, she was sure it couldn't, because there
are hundreds and hundreds of cars all over the road, and
they're coming in and turning off and switching from one
lane to the other, and the horns are going, and you get the
meanest looks, and all you're trying to do is mind your own
business and not get yourself in a giant of a wreck.

"I've had two accidents. If I'd have been driving only　9
in Kentucky I'm sure I wouldn't have any accidents to my

name. They weren't big accidents, just small ones, a fender each time. I fixed them myself, did the straightening and sanding and painting. I knew how to do that from watching my dad. He learned as a boy himself. He'd hit the car into a tree going up or down the creek sometimes. Mostly he's a good driver, though. He never had an accident in Leslie County, but he's had one up here, and that makes three in the family—two for me and one for him. It's different, driving in Kentucky. There aren't all the other cars. There aren't a lot of signs every mile or so, confusing you, always confusing you. They'll drive me to wearing glasses, those signs will, I do believe. And I don't mean to say anything against the people up here, but I think it's friendlier back in Leslie County, and it comes out on the road, because at home people will be more helpful to each other.

"I'll drive out away from Dayton sometimes. I'm not 10 going anyplace special. I'm not going to see someone. I just want to give my Chevy a rest from the city. I want to give her a good time. I want to take her on a road and let her roll along, and not stop and start. I don't want to have to clutch her and shift her and break her and idle her and get her so tired and hot she's ready to explode or go dead on me. Out in the country I can bring her up to sixty or seventy pretty fast. She holds the road good. She's no new racing car. She's no big new car. She's light and six years old. But she's got pep in her, a lot of life in her. I hope I'll be like her when I'm that old. A car is like a dog, you know. Each year is six or seven. I figure my car is getting on to forty-five, and that's old.

"My dad says it is not old, forty-five, but to me that's 11 a long way off. I can't picture what it's like to be twenty-five, never mind forty or forty-five. You must begin to feel real tired. I get tired myself. I'll be in the stockroom, handling all those crates, from eight in the morning to five in the afternoon. When I punch my card, and it says five minutes after five, I ask myself where the day has gone to, and my muscles answer that they can tell me, they surely can. Then I come home and have my supper, and I go and drive around. I rest that way. I'm sitting in my car, and I have a

good, soft blanket on the seat, and that rests my back. I
have some friends I take for a ride—a few of the guys I
know up here. And I have two girls I take out. I switch to
one, then I switch to the other; they're both from Ohio,
born here, and I don't know if I want to get serious with a
girl who isn't from Kentucky. I don't have to marry a girl
from Leslie County, but Kentucky is my home state, and I
want to be going back there someday, so I don't see why
I should get myself married to a girl who has other ideas in
her head, you know. I've heard them talk, the girls from
around here. A lot of them are spoiled. They want everything. They *expect* everything.

"I went to school until last year, until I was sixteen. I   12
didn't graduate from high school, but I went there, and you
get taught a lot. My friends back home, a lot of them never
bothered going beyond sixth or seventh grade. They said:
what's the reason to? I can see how they think that way. I
wish I'd gone and finished high school. It's just that I had
this chance for a job, and I couldn't turn a good job down.
The job means money for all of us, and I save some for a
new car. In school that's all the girls wanted, a guy with a
new car; they didn't care much what the guy himself was
like. I always thought it showed something about the girls,
the way they looked at you for your car and not yourself. I
don't believe a girl in Leslie County would be like that, though
my mother and dad say they would, because it's only natural. I guess a girl is going to like a car, just like a toy, and
that's why they ask you right away: what are you driving?

"They want to know your *plans,* the girls do. I tell them   13
I don't have any. I tell them I may one day get into my car
and drive and drive and fill the tank and empty it, until the
road ends, and I'm somewhere, but I don't know where.
Then, wherever it is I stop, I'll settle down. I'll get settled
in, settled into a house, and there'll be a garage for my Chevy,
and another garage in case I decide to get a second car, and
I'll work in a job—I don't know what kind. The girl will be
waiting for me to mention her. They don't know how much
they tell about what's on their mind by the way they look.
I try to keep myself from laughing, and I keep talking—but

I never mention getting married. They always ask me why I may get myself a second car, and I tell them it's nice to give one car a rest and use the other, and then switch back again. You can get attached to a car. You have driven it so long and worked on it all that time, so it's yours, and you don't want to lose what's yours. The nice thing about living in Dayton is you stand a chance of making money, all the money you need. Then you can treat your car right!"

He thinks about it more than he talks about it, the money   14
Dayton, Ohio, permits him to make, the money he cannot make in Leslie County, Kentucky. With each year he is more and more a city dweller, an owner of property, a worker— hence, less likely to return for very long to his home in the mountains, unless things should drastically change there, which is highly unlikely. He is no longer a child, yet not quite a grown-up. Almost half his childhood has been spent in Ohio, but with each month the balance changes, and he feels increasingly "settled in." He often uses that term "set-tled in," uses it as he did just above, in connection with what I suppose can be called a daydream or a fantasy—or an utterly exact way of describing what is on his mind and what he at least presently intends to do. He cannot really go back home, he knows that, yet he is not very happy living in even a medium-sized city like Dayton. He dreams of the West, the open and endless West, perhaps in the way his ancestors dreamed of what stretched ahead as they left the eastern seaboard. But he may actually spend the rest of his life in Ohio.

As one talks with him it becomes quite apparent that   15
he finds a life without automobiles inconceivable, and a life without a decent home and a garage and suitable clothes and enough food also impossible to contemplate. He very much enjoys buying himself a sporty new jacket, unworn by someone else, not handed down to him to be used for a while and then in turn handed over to a brother or a cousin. And he likes to do other things that in sum reassure him how well he is coming along, how able he is to take care of himself, put away a little cash, and feel like what he calls "a going business." His father always had wished he could raise

the money to have just that, a gas station or a garage, "a going business," he also puts it when he reminisces. The son now has those same dreams, but of course knows that if his business is going to grow, or even survive, Dayton will have to be the address and not some very small town in Leslie County.

So, step by step, innocently but decisively, the young man thinks things and dreams things and says things and decides things that commit him more and more to the life of a northern city, or maybe a far western one—and commit him, perhaps, to a girl who does not come from home, from the mountain country of eastern Kentucky. He does not say out and out what I have just written. How many of us at seventeen (maybe at any age) want to say exactly what we will be doing, come five or ten years? But we do at all times have certain assumptions, silent but influential, and during his five or so years in the city Larry Walker has become a different youth than he would be had he not been brought to Ohio as a child by his parents. He especially notices those various differences when he goes back home on a visit, and when he returns to Dayton he is most likely to talk about such matters. He is most likely to observe what he does in the day, and contrast all of his activities with those of his friends he knew as a small child. He is most likely to notice the way he dresses and the way others who live near Thousand-Sticks, Kentucky, dress. And yes, he is most likely to look at those girls he once knew and had crushes on and fought with and felt close to, and then think of the girls he met when he went to school in Dayton, three or four of whom he has courted in an offhand fashion, then forsaken, then gone back to, then again withdrawn from.

What distinguishes those girls from the girls in Kentucky, what distinguishes him from the boys in Kentucky, is something he finds hard to find words for, yet very much wants to clarify in his mind—hence the effort of language: "It's my home, my folks' home, Leslie County is. When I go back there I feel like I'm back where I belong. I can sit back and enjoy myself with the best people the Lord ever made. But after a few days I don't mind it too much if I have to leave. I begin to hear myself saying: it's near time to go, Larry, it's near time. There will even be a time when I start having a talk with myself. I say I'm ready to leave. Then I say why on earth are you actually looking forward to going, when you know full well how you'll soon be complaining about Dayton?

"I guess that the more you live in a place, the more it grows on you. I don't mean to say I like living here in the city rather than up in the hills, but a man has to earn a living, like my dad says. And if I'm going to get married and have kids, I can't see being so down and out, the way a lot of people in Kentucky are. I don't want my son to see me just sitting on a porch and carving wood and maybe picking on my guitar. My dad said he'd never have stayed alive, if he had kept on spending his days like that. He came up here, instead, and he was lucky to get a job for himself and hold on to it, and I've been lucky to get a job for myself and hold on to it—and that's why I don't think either of us can go back to Leslie County for more than a few days. There's no work, compared to the work you get here. 18

"But I do admit work isn't the only thing good up here. I talk a lot about my job, because I'm grateful to have it, and the money is good; it's sweet, real sweet, that money. I like Dayton, though. There are the movies, all of them; I've never seen the number of movie houses we have here in all of Kentucky I've been through, not just Leslie County. There are restaurants, good ones. You can live it up here. You can take a girl out on the town. You can have a good supper, any kind you want, then go to a movie, almost any kind you want. You can go bowling and you can go play pool and you can hear a good singer in a club and have a few drinks. It's not bad living in a city. There's a lot you miss, but there's a lot you have, too. I guess it's a matter of what your philosophy is, and where you can get the money. 19

"I'm not sure I could bring a girl up here from Kentucky, though. It might be real hard on someone to live here— a person who hasn't grown into the place, like I have. I think the kids I grew up with, they'd have a hard time coming up here now. The reason I don't mind a lot of things, 20

and like living here, at times, anyway, is that I was brought
up here when I was much younger. I wasn't a baby. I was
over twelve. I was growing fast. I was outgrowing everything, I can recall my mother saying. But I was still a kid,
and I wasn't set in my ways. I'm getting set now; my dad
says so, and he's right. I might want to get married soon,
except that I may go into the service in a few months. Sometimes I think I'd be smarter to come back to Dayton after
two years in the Army, rather than make a career of it, go
regular. I'll have to wait and see.

"If I meet a real nice, pretty girl from here in Dayton, I 21
might just marry her, if she'd have me. I once asked my
favorite girl in Leslie County, Sylvia is her name, if she'd
think of coming back with me, just for a week or so. I told
her she could stay with us, and she knows my folks. She's
distant kin to us, I believe. No, she said; she didn't want to
leave the county. I asked her why. She said she didn't have
anything against me or my folks, no sir; she'd love to stay
with us, she said, and for longer than a week, she said. But
to go all the way up to Dayton, out of the county and out
of the state, that was too much for her, she said. She gave
me a long look, right into my eyes, and I could see she really
wanted me to propose marriage to her then and there, but I
believe she knew, like I did, that I had to go back up North,
and there wasn't any two ways about it. I said to her: Sylvia, just come and give it a try; come and travel through
Kentucky and cross the river, the Ohio River, and look at
Cincinnati, and then go up into the state of Ohio and get to
know Dayton a little. But she kept on shaking her head. She
didn't answer me. She just turned her head to the left and
to the right, and I knew what she was telling me. Maybe the
reason she couldn't speak her thoughts out loud was that
she really did want to go with me, and she couldn't bear
hearing herself say she wouldn't.

"I came home and told my folks what I'd said to Sylvia 22
and what her answer had been. I never mentioned the word
marriage, or anything like that, but my mother said she
thought that since we all are settling in, me included, and
we're not going to leave Dayton for a long time, then I might

have better luck if I chose a girl from Dayton, provided she's a good girl, for my wife than someone like Sylvia from back home. I was mad as I've ever been. I told my mother she was talking out of her head, because I wasn't thinking of getting married now, and when I did think of marriage, that would be the time I would go home to Kentucky and by God I'd stay there until I found a wife, and if my wife wanted to stay there and never leave, I'd stay that long myself and be glad to do it. Then my mother told me to cool myself down, and she said the way I was talking, she was sure I wasn't going to get married in a long, long time, not if I meant every word I'd said to her. Well, I had to smile then. I saw what she meant."

He not only saw what his mother meant; he knew it in   23 his bones, her message. He is glad in so many ways to be in Dayton, bothersome as its traffic is, hard as his car finds the going, crowded and anonymous and noisy as the city, any city, can always be. He is glad that he is not living in a cabin up a hollow or creek. He is glad he does not live in a small town whose "unemployment problem" is severe and chronic and to a youth like him discouraging beyond the power of words to convey. Still, he does straddle two worlds, does go back and forth, feel divided loyalties, dream of one place while he lives in another. At seventeen nostalgia can be as powerful and summoning as at any other age, but at seventeen the meaning of a job and money is no less influential. What an observer like me has to watch very closely is the temptation to take a young man like Larry Walker too seriously *at any one moment in his life.* One day he can sound utterly convinced that he will soon, very soon, be a mountaineer again—a real one, not a distant, would-be one. The next time we talk, all of that seems not gone or buried or forgotten or "repressed" or denied or contradicted, but gently and tactfully put aside.

It is in such moments of "adjustment" to Dayton that   24 a youth like Larry feels most alert, most challenged, most sure of himself—and most at loose ends. What indeed will he do and where—now that he has ("sort of") decided that his destiny is to be found in Ohio's industrial cities, or perhaps in Illinois, or (who knows?) California, to which the Army might one day order him? And will he, therefore, slowly lose contact with Leslie County? Will he less and less think of those hills and valleys, those waterfalls and high trees and soaring birds, those clever animals and those dumb animals, those innocent but ever so swift and elusive fish? Will his car lose forever the feel of a narrow mountain road, with the sharp rises and the sudden falls, with the exciting twists and turns and curves? Will traveling by car become a bore, a nuisance, a tedious necessity? Will he one day say good-bye to that Chevy and good-bye to the notion that motors are wonderful, demanding, endlessly stimulating puzzles—objects of interest, exploration, and passion? Will he instead find his woman, his wife; find his job that lasts and lasts; find his nice, comfortable home, near others, near dozens and dozens of others? And for his two cars will he have no proud old two-door Chevy, no Mustang or Cougar, but a station wagon and perhaps a brand new Chevy four-door sedan? At seventeen one often doesn't *ask* such questions; instead, one does things—and so Larry's actions gradually will supply the answers to those questions.

Comment

Coles might have summarized his interview with the young man from an economically depressed Kentucky mountain community to give one example of the process of adjustment to Northern urban life. Coles chooses instead to let us hear Larry Walker talk about his life in Dayton, Ohio, and his much different life in Leslie County, Kentucky. Verbatim testimony helps us discover the conflict in attitudes and values that a witness like Larry is experiencing. Larry is typical for Coles of many young Southerners who do not want to lose the world that economic necessity has forced them to give up; Coles might therefore have stated his conflict in the abstract language of the sociologist or social psychologist. But Larry is an individual and his conflict is a personal one. Coles does not want us to forget that although people belong to classes, they are also individuals.

Questions for Study and Discussion

1. What is the personal conflict that Larry is experiencing? How does Larry express that conflict?
2. What point does Coles make through Larry about southern people who live in northern cities? Why does he title his essay "Settling In"?
3. What personal qualities emerge in Larry's account of his life? What most distinguishes him as a person?
4. Is Larry's love of his Chevy typical only of the American teenager's love of cars? Or does Coles want us to see something more than this general attitude?
5. Is Sylvia typical for Coles of young Southern women? Or does she represent one set of attitudes only?

Suggestions for Writing

1. Describe the experience of living in two different worlds— perhaps a small town and a large city. Then discuss an important change in attitude or values, or a conflict in attitudes, that resulted from this experience. Use your discussion to develop a thesis.
2. Coles says the following about Larry Walker and people generally:

    > How many of us at seventeen (maybe at any age) want to say exactly what we will be doing, come five or ten years? But we do at all times have certain assumptions, silent but influential, and during his five or so years in the city Larry Walker has become a different youth than he would be had he not been brought to Ohio as a child by his parents. (paragraph 16)

    Discuss one or two assumptions that shape your own attitudes and life at the present time. Discuss the possible origin of these assumptions. In the course of your discussion, compare them with the assumptions of Larry or Sylvia.

William Safire

DEMAGOGUE

William Safire began his career in journalism as a reporter for the *New York Herald Tribune*. From 1968 to 1972, he was a senior speechwriter for President Richard M. Nixon; he describes his White House experience in *Before the Fall: An Inside View of the Pre-Watergate White House*. Since 1973 Safire has been a columnist for the *New York Times*; he was awarded the Pulitzer Prize for Commentary in 1978. Safire is also a novelist and the author of several books on English words and phrases. His essay on the word *demagogue* is from *Safire's Political Dictionary*, a book showing that the "new, old, and constantly changing language of politics is a lexicon of conflict and drama, of ridicule and reproach, of pleading and persuasion. Color and bite permeate a language designed to rally many men, to destroy some, and to change the minds of others."

Demagogue—one who appeals to greed, fear, and hatred; a spellbinding orator, careless with facts and a danger to rational decision. 1

This is one of the enduring, slashing attack words of politics, in use since the American republic began. John Adams in 1808: "It is to no purpose to declaim against 'demagogues.' . . . Milo was as much an agitator for the patricians as Clodius for the plebeians; and Hamilton was as much a demagogue as Burr." 2

Being denounced as a demagogue is a sure sign to a speaker that he is making powerful points with some part of the public. In different historical periods, those most often denounced were Ben Butler, William Jennings Bryan, Huey Long, and Senator Joseph McCarthy. Reverend Thomas Dixon's attack on Bryan was typical: "a slobbering, mouthing demagogue, whose patriotism is in his jawbone." At one time, "slobber" was an operative verb for demagogue's noun. When Wilson's Secretary of War Newton Baker appealed for support of the League of Nations by referring to "the closed eyes of soldiers in American uniform who were dying and who whispered to me messages to bring to their 3 mothers," Senator Key Pittman of Nevada replied, "The speaker who spoke before here, with his wild burst of oratory, with tears in his eyes and his brokendown, slobbering body across this rail, is trying to appeal to your sympathies, not to your judgment."

Theodore Roosevelt and William Howard Taft, after their falling-out, exchanged charges of "fathead" and "demagogue." Roosevelt observed in a letter to Henry Cabot Lodge: "When there is a great unrest, partly reasoning and partly utterly unreasoning and unreasonable, it becomes extremely difficult to beat a loud-mouthed demagogue, especially if he is a demagogue of great wealth."

The appeal to emotion is not the only hallmark of the   5
demagogue; an appeal to class is often included. When Democrat Al Smith broke with FDR, he made this point in words reminiscent of the earlier Roosevelt-Taft break: "I will take off my coat and fight to the end against any candidate who persists in any demagogic appeal to the masses of the working people of this country to destroy themselves by setting class against class and rich against poor!"

The word has had its defenders. It is from the Greek   6
demagogos (leader of the people), which referred to the popular leaders who appeared in Athens during its period of decay. English journalist George Steevens, writing about the U.S. in 1897, held that "in a free country every politician must be something of a demagogue. Disraeli and Gladstone were both finished demagogues, and until we have two more great demagogues in England, politics will continue to be as dishwater." Muckraker Lincoln Steffens wrote in his autobiography: "I had begun to suspect that, whenever a man in public life was called a demagogue, there was something good in him, something dangerous to the system."

But the popular conception of the word was given most   7
eloquently by a President not known for his eloquence, Calvin Coolidge: ". . . the final approval of the people is given not to demagogues, slavishly pandering to their selfishness, merchandising with the clamor of the hour, but to statesmen, ministering to their welfare, representing their deep, silent, abiding convictions."

The word has retained all of its original sting. Relations 8
between Presidents Truman and Eisenhower permanently
cooled when Truman referred to Eisenhower's "I shall go to
Korea" statement as "a piece of demagoguery."

The final *g* in the adjective *demagogic* is soft; the more 9
difficult-to-pronounce and spell *demagoguery*, with its final
g hard, is more commonly used in the U.S. than *demagogy*,
final *g* soft, which is British usage.

Comment

The *Oxford English Dictionary* (or *New English Dictionary*) and
Dictionary of American English and other historical dictionaries
trace the history and use of words like *demagogue*. Unabridged
and abridged dictionaries of contemporary usage like *Webster's
Third New International Dictionary, The Random House Dictionary of the English Language, Webster's Ninth New Collegiate
Dictionary,* and *Webster's New World Dictionary of the English
Language* give current meanings but also cite obsolete and rare
uses of words. Special dictionaries and reference works like the
Dictionary of American Biography and *Encyclopedia of American
History* give additional information and background. In his specialized political dictionary, William Safire gives the contemporary
meaning of the word as well as a full discussion of its political
contexts. The essay form allows Safire to explore the historical
and political background of the word and give other information
about it.

Questions for Study and Discussion

1. Does Safire include all of the meanings of *demagogue* cited in
   the *Oxford English Dictionary* and the *Dictionary of American English?* Are any of these meanings obsolete, according
   to Safire? Are any of the meanings rare?
2. What is the etymology of *demagogue* and where in the essay
   does Safire discuss it?
3. How does Safire distinguish the popular denotative meaning
   of the word from its political connotations?
4. How much information does Safire assume his readers possess
   about American history and politics? Does he provide the same

amount of detailed information on the various eras of American history he discusses?

Vocabulary Study

1. Who were the *patricians* and the *plebeans*, and why does John Adams distinguish between them in the statement quoted in paragraph 2?
2. What are the denotative and connotative meanings of *slobber*? Why does Safire discuss this word in paragraph 3?
3. Look up two of the following politicians—Ben Butler, William Jennings Bryan, Huey Long, Joseph McCarthy—in the *Dictionary of American Biography, Encyclopedia of American History,* and other reference books. What details explain why they were accused of demagoguery in their time?
4. How is *demagogue* different denotatively or connotatively from the following words?
   a. agitator
   b. grandstander
   c. hate-monger
   d. rabble-rouser
   e. spellbinder

Suggestions for Writing

1. Safire states in the introduction to the 1968 edition of his political dictionary that he records "words and phrases that have misled millions, blackened reputations, held out false hopes, oversimplified ideas to appeal to the lowest common denominator, shouted down inquiry, and replaced searching debate with stereotypes that trigger approval or hatred." His dictionary also shows "how the choice of a word or metaphor can reveal sensitivity and genius, crystallize a mood and turn it to action; some political language captures the essence of an abstraction and makes it understandable to millions." Discuss how you discovered the purpose of his definition of *demagogue.*
2. Use the *Oxford English Dictionary* and other sources to write a history of one of the following musical instruments. Give enough details about the instrument to distinguish it from

similar ones, and discuss the special qualities or effects associated with it. Include information about its etymology:

a. bassoon
b. cello
c. English horn
d. flute
e. French horn
f. harmonica
g. harpsichord
h. oboe
i. piano
j. violin

Robert Ramirez

THE WOOLEN SARAPE

Robert Ramirez was born in Edinburg, Texas, in 1950. He graduated from Pan American College, where he later taught freshman composition. He also taught elementary school and has worked as a photographer, a reporter, and an announcer for a television news department in Texas. His essay on the barrio illustrates a special kind of definition.

The train, its metal wheels squealing as they spin along the silvery tracks, rolls slower now. Through the gaps between the cars blinks a streetlamp, and this pulsing light on a barrio streetcorner beats slower, like a weary heartbeat, until the train shudders to a halt, the light goes out, and the barrio is deep asleep. 1

Throughout Aztlán (the Nahuatl term meaning "land to the north"), trains grumble along the edges of a sleeping people. From Lower California, through the blistering Southwest, down the Rio Grande to the muddy Gulf, the darkness and mystery of dreams engulf communities fenced off by railroads, canals, and expressways. Paradoxical communities, isolated from the rest of the town by concrete col- 2 umned monuments of progress, and yet stranded in the past. They are surrounded by change. It eludes their reach, in their own backyards, and the people, unable and unwilling to see the future, or even touch the present, perpetuate the past.

Leaning from the expressway or jolting across the tracks, one enters a different physical world permeated by a different attitude. The physical dimensions are impressive. It is a large section of town which extends for fifteen blocks north and south along the tracks, and then advances eastward, thinning into nothingness beyond the city limits. Within the invisible (yet sensible) walls of the barrio, are many, many people living in too few houses. The homes, however, are much more numerous than on the outside.   3

Members of the barrio describe the entire area as their home. It is a home, but it is more than this. The barrio is a refuge from the harshness and the coldness of the Anglo world. It is a forced refuge. The leprous people are isolated from the rest of the community and contained in their section of town. The stoical pariahs of the barrio accept their fate, and from the angry seeds of rejection grow the flowers of closeness between outcasts, not the thorns of bitterness and the mad desire to flee. There is no want to escape, for the feeling of the barrio is known only to its inhabitants, and the material needs of life can also be found here.   4

The *tortillería*[1] fires up its machinery three times a day, producing steaming, round, flat slices of barrio bread. In the winter, the warmth of the tortilla factory is a wool *sarape*[2] in the chilly morning hours, but in the summer, it unbearably toasts every noontime customer.   5

The *panadería*[3] sends its sweet messenger aroma down the dimly lit street, announcing the arrival of fresh, hot sugary *pan dulce*.[4]   6

The small corner grocery serves the meal-to-meal needs   7

---

[1] *tortillería:* tortilla bake shop
[2] *sarape:* blanket or shawl
[3] *panadería:* bakery
[4] *pan dulce:* sweet bread or roll

of customers, and the owner, a part of the neighborhood, willingly gives credit to people unable to pay cash for food-stuffs.

The barbershop is a living room with hydraulic chairs, radio, and television, where old friends meet and speak of life as their salted hair falls aimlessly about them.   8

The pool hall is a junior level country club where *'chu-cos,*[5] strangers in their own land, get together to shoot pool and rap, while veterans, unaware of the cracking, popping balls on the green felt, complacently play dominoes beneath rudely hung *Playboy* foldouts.

The *cantina*[6] is the night spot of the barrio. It is the country club and the den where the rites of puberty are en-acted. Here the young become men. It is in the taverns that a young dude shows his *machismo*[7] through the quantity of beer he can hold, the stories of *rucas*[8] he has had, and his willingness and ability to defend his image against hardened and scarred old lions.   10

No, there is no frantic wish to flee. It would be absurd to leave the familiar and nervously step into the strange and cold Anglo community when the needs of the Chicano can be met in the barrio.   11

The barrio is closeness. From the family living unit, fa-milial relationships stretch out to immediate neighbors, down the block, around the corner, and to all parts of the barrio. The feeling of family, a rare and treasurable sentiment, per-vades and accounts for the inability of the people to leave. The barrio is this attitude manifested on the countenances of the people, on the faces of their homes, and in the gaiety of their gardens.   12

The color-splashed homes arrest your eyes, arouse your curiosity, and make you wonder what life scenes are being played out in them. The flimsy, brightly colored, wood-frame houses ignore no neon-brilliant color. Houses trimmed in   13

---

[5] *'chucos: pachuco,* or Mexican (derogatory term)
[6] *cantina:* tavern or saloon
[7] *machismo:* manhood
[8] *rucas:* girls

orange, chartreuse, lime-green, yellow, and mixtures of these and other hues beckon the beholder to reflect on the peculiarity of each home. Passing through this land is refreshing like Brubeck, not narcoticizing like revolting rows of similar houses, which neither offend nor please.

In the evenings, the porches and front yards are occupied with men calmly talking over the noise of children playing baseball in the unpaved extension of the living room, while the women cook supper or gossip with female neighbors as they water the *jardines*.[9] The gardens mutely echo the expressive verses of the colorful houses. The denseness of multicolored plants and trees gives the house the appearance of an oasis or a tropical island hideaway, sheltered from the rest of the world.

Fences are common in the barrio, but they are fences and not the walls of the Anglo community. On the western side of town, the high wooden fences between houses are thick, impenetrable walls, built to keep the neighbors at bay. In the barrio, the fences may be rusty, wire contraptions or thick green shrubs. In either case you can see through them and feel no sense of intrusion when you cross them.

Many lower income families of the barrio manage to maintain a comfortable standard of living through the communal action of family members who contribute their wages to the head of the family. Economic need creates interdependence and closeness. Small barefooted boys sell papers on cool, dark Sunday mornings, deny themselves pleasantries, and give their earnings to *mamá*. The older the child, the greater the responsibility to help the head of the household provide for the rest of the family.

There are those, too, who for a number of reasons have not achieved a relative sense of financial security. Perhaps it results from too many children too soon, but it is the homes of these people and their situation that numbs rather than charms. Their houses, aged and bent, oozing children, are fissures in the horn of plenty. Their wooden homes may have

14

15

16

17

---

[9] *jardines:* gardens

brick-pattern asbestos tile on the outer walls, but the tile is not convincing.

Unable to pay city taxes or incapable in influencing the city to live up to its duty to serve all the citizens, the poorer barrio families remain trapped in the nineteenth century and survive as best they can. The backyards have well-worn paths to the outhouses, which sit near the alley. Running water is considered a luxury in some parts of the barrio. Decent drainage is usually unknown, and when it rains, the water stands for days, an incubator of health hazards and an avoidable nuisance. Streets, costly to pave, remain rough, rocky trails. Tires do not last long, and the constant rattling and shaking grind away a car's life and spread dust through screen windows.   18

The houses and their *jardines,* the jollity of the people in an adverse world, the brightly feathered alarm clock pecking away at supper and cautiously eyeing the children playing nearby, produce a mystifying sensation at finding the noble savage alive in the twentieth century. It is easy to look at the positive qualities of life in the barrio, and look at them with a distantly envious feeling. One wishes to experience the feelings of the barrio and not the hardships. Remembering the illness, the hunger, the feeling of time running out on you, the walls, both real and imagined, reflecting on living in the past, one finds his envy becoming more elusive, until it has vanished altogether.   19

Back now beyond the tracks, the train creaks and groans, the cars jostle each other down the track, and as the light begins its pulsing, the barrio, with all its meanings, greets a new dawn with yawns and restless stretchings.   20

Comment

Robert Ramirez defines the barrio denotatively and connotatively through his details of barrio life. In doing so, he defines not only a place but a culture: the quality of life that distinguishes the barrio from other cultural worlds in the United States. So detailed a description might have become disunified; instead, Ramirez achieves unity in his description by letting us see the barrio as a stranger would. Once he establishes his point of view, with the reference to the train that approaches the barrio, he does not stray from it. Each part of the scene Ramirez describes is dealt with fully before he turns to another. The concluding paragraph reminds us that the barrio is a world set apart physically and emotionally from the world outside.

Questions for Study and Discussion

1. What statements and details show that Ramirez is writing to an audience unfamiliar with the barrio?
2. What qualities do the people of the barrio share? Does Ramirez show qualities or attitudes that mark them as individuals—as separate people living in the same neighborhood?
3. How does he introduce these qualities without disturbing his focus on the physical qualities of the barrio?
4. In what order are those physical qualities presented? Once the physical point of view is established, how does Ramirez remind us of it as the essay progresses?
5. What details of barrio life do you recognize in your own neighborhood, town, or city? In general, what similarities and differences are there between the barrio and your world?

Vocabulary Study

Write sentences of your own, using the following words to reveal their dictionary meanings: *paradoxical, permeated, stoical, pariahs, mutely, adverse.*

Suggestions for Writing

1. Discuss how the title of the essay contributes to the overall tone and point of view. Then analyze the order of ideas and development of the thesis.
2. Describe the prevailing culture, or variety of cultures, in a neighborhood or community you know well. Include the extent to which people of the neighborhood share a common language, perhaps a slang that protects them from the world outside. Give particular attention to their feelings and attitudes toward that outside world.

Susan Allen Toth

CINEMATYPES

Susan Allen Toth was born in Ames, Iowa, and attended Smith College, the University of California at Berkeley, and the University of Minnesota. She has taught English at Macalester College in St. Paul, Minnesota, since 1969. As a writer, she is particularly interested in the education and changing roles of American women, subjects of her books, *Blooming: A Small-Town Girlhood* (1981) and *Ivy Days: Making My Way Out East* (1985).

Aaron takes me only to art films. That's what I call them, anyway: strange movies with vague poetic images I don't always understand, long dreamy movies about a distant Technicolor past, even longer black-and-white movies about the general meaninglessness of life. We do not go unless at least one reputable critic has found the cinematography superb. We went to *The Devil's Eye,* and Aaron turned to me in the middle and said, "My God, this is *funny.*" I do not think he was pleased.

When Aaron and I go to the movies, we drive our cars separately and meet by the box office. Inside the theater he sits tentatively in his seat, ready to move if he can't see well, poised to leave if the film is disappointing. He leans away from me, careful not to touch the bare flesh of his arm against the bare flesh of mine. Sometimes he leans so far I am afraid he may be touching the woman on his other side. If the movie is very good, he leans forward, too, peering between the heads of the couple in front of us. The light from the screen bounces off his glasses; he gleams with intensity, sitting there on the edge of his seat, watching the screen. Once I tapped him on the arm so I could whisper a comment in his ear. He jumped.

After *Belle de Jour* Aaron said he wanted to ask me if he could stay overnight. "But I can't," he shook his head mournfully before I had a chance to answer, "because I know I never sleep well in strange beds." Then he apologized for asking. "It's just that after a film like that," he said, "I feel the need to assert myself."

Pete takes me only to movies that he thinks have re-   4
deeming social value. He doesn't call them "films." They tend to be about poverty, war, injustice, political corruption, struggling unions in the 1930s, and the military-industrial complex. Pete doesn't like propaganda movies, though, and he doesn't like to be too depressed, either. We stayed away from *The Sorrow and the Pity;* it would be, he said, just too much. Besides, he assured me, things are never that hopeless. So most of the movies we see are made in Hollywood. Because they are always topical, these movies offer what Pete calls "food for thought." When we saw *Coming Home,* Pete's jaw set so firmly with the first half-hour that I knew we would end up at Poppin' Fresh Pies afterward.

When Pete and I go to the movies, we take turns driv-   5
ing so no one owes anyone else anything. We leave the car far from the theater so we don't have to pay for a parking space. If it's raining or snowing, Pete offers to let me off at the door, but I can tell he'll feel better if I go with him while he finds a spot, so we share the walk too. Inside the theater Pete will hold my hand when I get scared if I ask him. He puts my hand firmly on his knee and covers it completely with his own hand. His knee never twitches. After a while, when the scary part is past, he loosens his hand slightly and I know that is a signal to take mine away. He sits companionably close, letting his jacket just touch my sweater, but he does not infringe. He thinks I ought to know he is there if I need him.

One night, after *The China Syndrome,* I asked Pete if   6
he wouldn't like to stay for a second drink, even though it was past midnight. He thought a while about that, considering my offer from all possible angles, but finally he said no. Relationships today, he said, have a tendency to move too quickly.

Sam likes movies that are entertaining. By that he means   7
movies that Will Jones in the *Minneapolis Tribune* loved and either *Time* or *Newsweek* rather liked; also movies that do not have sappy love stories, are not musicals, do not have

subtitles, and will not force him to think. He does not go to movies to think. He liked *California Suite* and *The Seduction of Joe Tynan,* though the plots he said, could have been zippier. He saw it all coming too far in advance, and that took the fun out. He doesn't like to know what is going to happen. "I just want my brain to be tickled," he says. It is very hard for me to pick out movies for Sam.

When Sam takes me to the movies, he pays for everything. He thinks that's what a man ought to do. But I buy my own popcorn, because he doesn't approve of it; the grease might smear his flannel slacks. Inside the theater, Sam makes himself comfortable. He takes off his jacket, puts one arm around me, and all during the movie he plays with my hand, stroking my palm, beating a small tattoo on my wrist. Although he watches the movie intently, his body operates on instinct. Once I inclined my head and kissed him lightly just behind his ear. He beat a faster tattoo on my wrist, quick and musical, but he didn't look away from the screen.

When Sam takes me home from the movies, he stands outside my door and kisses me long and hard. He would like to come in, he says regretfully, but his steady girlfriend in Duluth wouldn't like it. When the *Tribune* gives a movie four stars, he has to save it to see with her. Otherwise her feelings might be hurt.

I go to some movies by myself. On rainy Sunday afternoons I often sneak into a revival house or a college auditorium for old Tehcnicolor musicals, *Kiss Me Kate, Seven Brides for Seven Brothers, Calamity Jane,* even, once, *The Sound of Music.* Wearing saggy jeans so I can prop my feet on the seat in front, I sit toward the rear where no one will see me. I eat large handfuls of popcorn with double butter. Once the movie starts, I feel completely at home. Howard Keel and I are old friends; I grin back at him on the screen. I know the sound tracks by heart. Sometimes when I get really carried away I hum along with Kathryn Grayson, remembering how I once thought I would fill out a formal like that. I am rather glad now I never did. Skirts whirl, feet tap, acrobatic young men perform impossible feats, and then the camera dissolves into a dream sequence I know I can comfortably follow. It is not, thank God, Bergman.

If I can't find an old musical, I settle for Hepburn and   11
Tracy, vintage Grant or Gable, on adventurous days Claudette Colbert or James Stewart. Before I buy my ticket I make sure it will all end happily. If necessary, I ask the girl at the box office. I have never seen *Stella Dallas* or *Intermezzo*. Over the years I have developed other peccadilloes: I will, for example, see anything that is redeemed by Thelma Ritter. At the end of *Daddy Long Legs* I wait happily for the scene when Fred Clark, no longer angry, at last pours Thelma a convivial drink. They smile at each other, I smile at them, I feel they are smiling at me. In the movies I go to by myself, the men and women always like each other.

Comment

Toth uses division to organize her simple, richly detailed essay; she also depends on contrast. Out of her division and contrast emerges a similarity that Toth hints at in her concluding statements—a quality shared by the men described. The humor of the essay arises in part from our not immediately realizing what she is doing and in part from the details of her experiences. Her thesis is implicit in these details and her comments on the movies she attends. Toth shows that much can be said through details alone if they are carefully arranged.

Questions for Study and Discussion

1. What are the differences that Toth stresses in the male "cinematypes" she describes? What do we discover at the end of the essay that they have in common?
2. How does Toth use contrast with her own movie-going to lead up to this similarity? What is this point or thesis?
3. The class that Toth divides is *cinematypes*. What is her principle of division?

4. What does Toth gain by omitting a formal introduction and formal transitions?

5. Has Toth exhausted the types of moviegoers, or are there others she might have included?

Vocabulary Study

1. What is the difference for some people between *films* and *movies,* and what point is Toth making about this distinction?

2. What is the tone of the following sentence—"We do not go unless at least one reputable critic has found the cinematography superb"? What does the word *cinematography* contribute to the tone?

3. What words in paragraph 6 contribute most to the tone? What is that tone?

4. Toth says in paragraph 11: "Over the years I have developed other peccadilloes." How would the meaning change if she had "developed other bad habits" instead?

Suggestions for Writing

1. Write an essay dividing one of the following classes, illustrating each type in your division simply but in detail, as Toth does, and using your analysis to develop a point or thesis. Save this thesis for later in the essay, perhaps building to it as Toth does. Divide the class consistently, in a single way:
   a. concertgoers
   b. automobile drivers
   c. television addicts
   d. boyfriends
   e. girlfriends

2. Divide one of the following in more than one way—for example, by variety and use. Then use your analysis to make a point:
   a. musical comedies
   b. horror movies
   c. romantic comedies
   d. soap operas
   e. adventure or detective movies

Robert J. Samuelson

COMPUTER COMMUNITIES

Robert J. Samuelson writes a column on economics for *Newsweek*. He is particularly interested in federal economic policy and its effects. His column on computer communities deals with changes in marketing and consumption that has led to a "massive paradox." Samuelson explores the implications of these changes for the American consumer and marketer.

This holiday season is also the high season for catalogs. I'm sitting with 30 of them, offering everything from teddy bears to electronic scrabble games. They all arrived at our house in recent months. My wife tells me we get about 100 a year. This bothered me. Were we such lavish consumers to attract every selling organization in America? I checked it out. We're about average. There are roughly 10 billion catalogs mailed out annually, which is more than 50 for every American over 18, and the number has more than doubled since 1978.

Historian Daniel Boorstin's apt phrase—consumption communities—describes people connected by what they buy, not where they live. The modern analogue is computer communities. We are, in part, defined by the computer lists we're on: the lists for catalogs, magazines, credit cards, alumni associations, unions and trade groups. They are windows to our pocketbooks, and almost all can be rented. Bob Castle, a major list broker, offers 40,000 lists. His biggest has 165 million Americans by age and address, but for a client selling an executive jet, "I once rented a list of 40 oil sheiks living in America."

Our language overflows with marketing jargon: "niches," "segments" and "clusters." We're coded according to age, income, education, reading habits and spending patterns, even if these things are inferred from the census tract where we live. Lists are run against each other to produce new lists with more information. Suitably grouped, we're fair game for catalogs, charitable solicitations, political appeals and advertising fliers. We're peddled mutual funds, insurance policies and vacations. In 1985, third-class—alias "junk"—mail totaled 52 billion pieces; it's growing four times faster than other mail.

This direct-mail boom is said to cater to working women. 4 Shopping time is scarce. Nearly 60 percent of people who order by mail or phone are women. This pop theory, though true, is much overrated. Computers have been the dominant agent of change by making it cheaper to analyze and address Americans by groups. Direct mail's rise, for example, does not parallel the gradual increase of working women. The explosive growth was triggered in 1979 by cuts in bulk-mail rates, based on computerized presorting of letters to individual postal routes. Some third-class mail rates are now lower than in 1978.

The computers are trying to straddle a huge schism in 5 national culture. Americans exalt individuality, but our economic success rests on a mass market that stresses commonality. By creating huge new groups—big enough to produce economies of scale, but small enough to seem personal—the computers seek to skirt this conflict. Magazines and television audiences are dissected by the same computerized scanning to determine which are best for cameras and which for beer. All advertisers want the right niche, which sounds like a cozy group. The mass market is supposed to be dead, but, of course, any niche worth selling has hundreds of thousands, usually millions, of customers.

This hypocrisy—marketers trying to make us feel select, 6 when we're not—offends some. Columnist Richard Cohen of The Washington Post recently unleashed this splendid tirade against the direct-mail avalanche: "Every day, I come home to open a newly arrived stack of lies. . . . The Book-of-the-Month Club tells me, in the manner of the Marines, that it is seeking 'a few people in Washington,' when, of course, it will take anyone it can get. . . . I get letters in which my name [is] misspelled each and every time: 'Yes, Rojhard Cohen, the whales are in danger.' "

Well Rojhard, it's an old story. The early mail-order 7 houses—Montgomery Ward (1872) and Sears (1888)—succeeded in part by cultivating a personal bond with their customers. Confidence was essential, notes historian Boorstin, "to induce farmers to buy goods sight unseen from a distant warehouse." Many customers wrote personal letters that were answered. "I suppose you wondered why we haven't ordered anything from you since the fall," one letter to Ward's founder said. "Well, the cow kicked my arm and broke it and besides my wife was sick, and there was the doctor bill."

The pretense of exclusivity doesn't fool most of us. We tolerate or enjoy the obvious deceptions of advertising, including direct mail. For all the excesses, we secretly appreciate the attention. Even throwing the stuff away unopened provides a perverse satisfaction that someone wants our business. A friend of mine peruses catalogs while pedaling an exercise bike. She is surely treated to the constant surprises of the commercial imagination. A place in Maine will send you a telephone shaped like a piano (you dial on the keyboard) for $59, and then there's the $39 Snore Stopper from California: 8

"A snoring sleeper can cause a loving bedmate to endure many a sleepless night. . . . The static electrical pulse which Snore Stopper emits, each time you snore, is very light—and it goes on for only 5/100 of a second. . . . [B]ut it will stop even the heaviest sleeper from snoring."   9

But the result of all this computerized marketing—the obsession with niche building—is a massive paradox. The point of splintering consumers into finer subdivisions is to give vent to individual differences and choices. In fact, our high-tech marketing simply fosters new, more variegated styles of conformity. What the marketers call niches and segments, you and I call friends. People don't compare themselves with strangers. They look at their peers: people like themselves. Most of us—along with our friends—are being bombarded by the same appeals for the same specialized products.   10

There's a shortening of the half-lives of fads and fashions. Nothing remains novel very long, because the tools of mass marketing accelerate the introduction of new products aimed at particular groups: whether Yuppies, prosperous retirees or skiing buffs. Our marketers pander to the rhetoric of individuality, but in our new computer communities,   11 differences are still hard to detect. The more refined customer markets become, the faster the spread of new products. The ultimate irony of computerized merchandising is that it's made being a snob a more exhausting and exacting exercise than ever.

Comment

In his discussion of Americans as consumers, Samuelson depends chiefly on classification and division to develop his thesis. He first shows how advertisers put consumers into a broad class, defined by Daniel Boorstin as "consumption communities." Samuelson then divides this class in various ways, and draws a number of conclusions about consumer attitudes and marketing technology. Comparison and causal analysis also play an important part in describing this technology. Samuelson uses his analysis to say something important about advertising and marketing today.

Questions for Study and Discussion

1. Into what groups do mail advertisers divide consumers?
2. Why do advertisers seek to create "huge new groups" of consumers? Why must these groups not be too big?
3. What point is Samuelson making in his comparison of consumption communities and computer communities (paragraph 2)? Where else does he use comparison, and what point does he make through this comparison?
4. What is the "massive paradox" that results from computerized marketing? What point is Samuelson making through discussion of this paradox? What is the "ultimate irony" of computerized marketing?
5. Samuelson is writing to increase our understanding of mail advertising. Does he have another purpose in writing—for example, to encourage readers of his *Newsweek* column to change their buying habits?

Vocabulary Study

Give the dictionary meaning of the following words. Then explain how Samuelson uses the word in the paragraph:

a. paragraph 2: *analogue*
b. paragraph 3: *inferred*
c. paragraph 5: *schism, dissected, niche*
d. paragraph 8: *exclusivity, perverse*
e. paragraph 10: *paradox*
f. paragraph 11: *irony*

Suggestions for Writing

1. Samuelson states: "The pretense of exclusivity doesn't fool most of us. We tolerate or enjoy the obvious deceptions of advertising, including direct mail. For all the excesses, we secretly appreciate the attention." Discuss the extent to which this statement describes your attitude toward mail advertising.
2. Discuss the extent to which the advertising of a particular product—for example, automobiles—illustrates one of the following statements in paragraph 11:
    a. "There's a shortening of the half-lives of fads and fashions."
    b. "Nothing remains novel very long, because the tools of mass marketing accelerate the introduction of new products aimed at particular groups. . . ."
    c. "Our marketers pander to the rhetoric of individuality, but in our new computer communities, differences are still hard to detect."

Wendell Berry

THE RISE

Wendell Berry taught English at the University of Kentucky from 1964 to 1977. He has written about his native Kentucky in numerous poems, novels, and essays. His *Collected Poems* was published in 1985; his novels include *Nathan Coulter* (1960) and *The Memory of Old Jack* (1974); his essays appear in *The Long-Legged House* (1969) and other books. Berry has long been associated with the environmental movement and its effort to preserve wilderness areas throughout the United States. "The Rise" describes such an area in Kentucky.

We put the canoe in about six miles up the Kentucky   1
River from my house. There, at the mouth of Drennon Creek,
is a little colony of summer camps. We knew we could get
down to the water there with some ease. And it proved easier than we expected. The river was up maybe twenty feet,
and we found a path slanting down the grassy slope in front
of one of the cabins. It went right into the water, as perfect
for launching the canoe and getting in as if it had been worn
there by canoeists.

To me that, more than anything else, is the excitement   2
of a rise: the unexpectedness, always, of the change it makes.
What was difficult becomes easy. What was easy becomes
difficult. By water, what was distant becomes near. By land,
what was near becomes distant. At the water line, when a
rise is on, the world is changing. There is an irresistible sense
of adventure in the difference. Once the river is out of its
banks, a vertical few inches of rise may widen the surface
by many feet over the bottomland. A sizable lagoon will
appear in the middle of a cornfield. A drain in a pasture will
become a canal. Stands of beech and oak will take on the
look of a cypress swamp. There is something Venetian about
it. There is a strange excitement in going in a boat where
one would ordinarily go on foot—or where, ordinarily, birds
would be flying. And so the first excitement of our trip was
that little path; where it might go in a time of low water
was unimaginable. Now it went down to the river.

Because of the offset in the shore at the creek mouth,   3
there was a large eddy turning in the river where we put in,
and we began our drift downstream by drifting upstream.
We went up inside the row of shore trees, whose tops now
waved in the current, until we found an opening among the
branches, and then turned out along the channel. The current took us. We were still settling ourselves as if in preparation, but our starting place was already diminishing behind us.

There is something ominously like life in that. One would   4
always like to settle oneself, get braced, say "Now I am going
to begin"—and then begin. But as the necessary quiet seems
about to descend, a hand is felt at one's back, shoving. And

that is the way with the river when a current is running: once the connection with the shore is broken, the journey has begun.

We were, of course, already at work with the paddles. But we were ahead of ourselves. I think that no matter how deliberately one moved from the shore into the sudden fluid violence of a river on the rise, there would be bound to be several uneasy minutes of transition. It is another world, which means that one's senses and reflexes must begin to live another kind of life. Sounds and movements that from the standpoint of the shore might have come to seem even familiar now make a new urgent demand on the attention. There is everything to get used to, from a wholly new perspective. And from the outset one has the currents to deal with.

It is easy to think, before one has ever tried it, that nothing could be easier than to drift down the river in a canoe on a strong current. That is because when one thinks of a river one is apt to think of *one* thing—a great singular flowing that one puts one's boat into and lets go. But it is not like that at all, not after the water is up and the current swift. It is not one current, but a braiding together of several, some going at different speeds, some even in different directions. Of course, one *could* just let go, let the boat be taken into the continuous mat of drift—leaves, logs, whole trees, cornstalks, cans, bottles, and such—in the channel, and turn and twist in the eddies there. But one does not have to do that long in order to sense the helplessness of a light canoe when it is sideways to the current. It is out of control then, and endangered. Stuck in the mat of drift, it can't be maneuvered. It would turn over easily; one senses that by a sort of ache in the nerves, the way bad footing is sensed. And so we stayed busy, keeping the canoe between the line of half-submerged shore trees and the line of drift that marked the channel. We weren't trying to hurry—the currents were carrying us as fast as we wanted to go—but it took considerable labor just to keep straight. It was like riding a spirited horse not fully bridle-wise: We kept our direction *by inten-*

tion; there could be no dependence on habit or inertia; when our minds wandered the river took over and turned us according to inclinations of its own. It bore us like a consciousness, acutely wakeful, filling perfectly the lapses in our own.

But we did grow used to it, and accepted our being on it as one of the probabilities, and began to take the mechanics of it for granted. The necessary sixth sense had come to us, and we began to notice more than we had to.   7

There is an exhilaration in being *accustomed* to a boat on dangerous water. It is as though into one's consciousness of the dark violence of the depths at one's feet there rises the idea of the boat, the buoyancy of it. It is always with a sort of triumph that the boat is realized—that it goes *on top of the water,* between breathing and drowning. It is an ancient -feeling triumph; it must have been one of the first ecstasies. The analogy of riding a spirited horse is fairly satisfactory; it is mastery over something resistant—a buoyancy that is not natural and inert like that of a log, but desired and vital and to one's credit. Once the boat has fully entered the consciousness it becomes an intimate extension of the self; one feels as competently amphibious as a duck, whose feet are paddles. And once we felt accustomed and secure in the boat, the day and the river began to come clear to us.   8

It was a gray, cold Sunday in the middle of December. In the woods on the north slopes above us we could see the black trunks and branches just faintly traced with snow, which gave them a silvery, delicate look—the look of impossibly fine handwork that nature sometimes has. And they looked cold. The wind was coming straight up the river into our faces. But we were dressed warmly, and the wind didn't matter much, at least not yet. The force that mattered, that surrounded us, and inundated us with its sounds, and pulled at or shook or carried everything around us, was the river.   9

To one standing on the bank, floodwater will seem to be flowing at a terrific rate. People who are not used to it will commonly believe it is going three or four times as fast as it really is. It is so all of a piece, and so continuous. To   10 one drifting along in a boat this exaggerated impression of speed does not occur; one is going the same speed as the river then and is not fooled. In the Kentucky when the water is high a current of four or five miles an hour is about usual, I would say, and there are times in a canoe that make that seem plenty fast.

What the canoeist gets, instead of an impression of the   11
river's speed, is an impression of its power. Or, more exactly, an impression of the *voluminousness* of its power. The sense of the volume alone has come to me when, swimming in the summertime, I have submerged mouth and nose so that the plane of the water spread away from the lower eyelid; the awareness of its bigness that comes then is almost intolerable; one feels how falsely assuring it is to look down on the river, as we usually do. The sense of the power of it came to me one day in my boyhood when I attempted to swim ashore in a swift current, pulling an overturned rowboat. To check the downstream course of the boat I tried grabbing hold of the partly submerged willows along the shore with my free hand, and was repeatedly pulled under as the willows bent, and then torn loose. My arms stretched between the boat and the willow branch might have been sewing threads for all the holding they could do against that current. It was the first time I realized that there could be circumstances in which my life would count for nothing, absolutely nothing—and I have never needed to learn that again.

Sitting in a canoe, riding the back of the flooding river   12
as it flows down into a bend, and turns, the currents racing and crashing among the trees along the outside shore, and flows on, one senses the volume and the power all together. The sophistications of our age do not mitigate the impression. To some degree it remains unimaginable, as is suggested by the memory's recurrent failure to hold on to it. It can never be remembered as wild as it is, and so each new experience of it bears some of the shock of surprise. It would take the mind of a god to watch it as it changes and not be surprised.

These long views that one gets coming down it show it
to move majestically. It is stately. It has something of the
stylized grandeur and awesomeness of royalty in a Sophoclean tragedy. But as one watches, there emanates from it,
too, an insinuation of darkness, implacability, horror. And
the nearer look tends to confirm this. Contained and borne
in the singular large movement are hundreds of smaller ones:
eddies and whirlpools, turnings this way and that, cross-
currents rushing out from the shores into the channel. One
must simplify it in order to speak of it. One probably simpli-
fies it in some way in order to look at it.   13

There is something deeply horrifying about it, roused.
Not, I think, because it is inhuman, alien to us; some of us
at least must feel a kinship with it, or we would not loiter
around it for pleasure. The horror must come from our sense
that, so long as it remains what it is, it is not subject. To
say that it is indifferent would be wrong. That would imply
a malevolence, as if it could be aware of us if only it wanted
to. It is more remote from our concerns than indifference. It
is serenely and silently not subject—to us or to anything else
except the other natural forces that are also beyond our control. And it is apt to stand for and represent to us all in
nature and in the universe that is not subject. That is its
horror. We can make use of it. We can ride on its back in
boats. But it won't stop to let us get on and off. It is not a
passenger train. And if we make a mistake, or risk ourselves
too far to it, why then it will suffer a little wrinkle on its
surface, and go on as before.   14

That horror is never fully revealed, but only sensed
piecemeal in events, all different, all shaking, yet all together
falling short of the full revelation. The next will be as unexpected as the last.   15

A man I knew in my boyhood capsized his motorboat
several miles upriver from here. It was winter. The river was
high and swift. It was already nightfall. The river carried
him a long way before he drowned. Farmers sitting in their
houses in the bottoms heard his cries passing down in the
darkness, and failed to know what to make of them. It is   16

hard to imagine what they could have done if they had known.

I can't believe that anyone who has heard that story [17] will ever forget it. Over the years it has been as immediate to me as if I had seen it all—almost as if I had *known* it all: the capsized man aching and then numb in the cold water, clinging to some drift log in the channel, and calling, seeing the house lights appear far off across the bottoms and dwindle behind him, the awful power of the flood and his hopelessness in it finally dawning on him—it is amazingly real; it is happening to him. And the families in their lighted warm kitchens, eating supper maybe, when the tiny desperate outcry comes to them out of the darkness, and they look up at the window, and then at each other.

"Shhh! Listen! What was that?" [18]

"By God, it sounded like somebody hollering out there [19] on the river."

"But it *can't* be." [20]

But it makes them uneasy. Whether or not there *is* [21] somebody out there, the possibility that there *may* be reminds them of their lot; they never know what may be going by them in the darkness. And they think of the river, so dark and cold.

The history of these marginal places is in part the his- [22] tory of drownings—of fisherman, swimmers, men fallen from boats. And there is the talk, the memory, the inescapable *feeling* of dragging for the bodies—that terrible fishing for dead men lost deep in the currents, carried downstream sometimes for miles.

Common to river mentality, too, are the imaginings: [23] stepoffs, undertows, divers tangled in sunken treetops, fishermen hooked on their own lines.

And yet it fascinates. Sometimes it draws the most fear- [24] ful to it. Men must test themselves against it. Its mystery must be forever tampered with. There is a story told here of a strong big boy who tried unsuccessfully to cross the river by walking on the bottom, carrying an iron kettle over his head for a diving bell. And another story tells of a young man who, instead of walking under it, thought he would walk *on* it, with the help of a gallon jug tied to each foot. The miracle failing, of course, the jugs held his feet up, and his head under, until somebody obliged him by pulling him out. His pride, like Icarus', was transformed neatly into his fall—the work of a river god surely, *hybris* being as dangerous in Henry County as anywhere else.

To sense fully the power and the mystery of it, the eye must be close to it, near to level with the surface. I think that is the revelation of George Caleb Bingham's painting of trappers on the Missouri. The painter's eye, there, is very near the water, and so he sees the river as the trappers see it from their dugout—all the space coming down to that vast level. One feels the force, the aliveness, of the water under the boat, close under feet of the men. And there they are, isolated in the midst of it, with their box of cargo and their pet fox—men and boat and box and animal all so strangely and poignantly coherent on the wild plain of the water, a sort of island. [25]

But impressive as the sights may be, the river's wildness is most awesomely announced to the ear. Along the channel, the area of the most concentrated and the freest energy, there is silence. It is at the shore line, where obstructions are, that the currents find their voices. The water divides around the trunks of the trees, and sucks and slurs as it closes together again. Trunks and branches are ridden down to the surface, or suddenly caught by the rising water, and the current pours over them in a waterfall. And the weaker trees throb and vibrate in the flow, their naked branches clashing and rattling. It is a storm of sound, changing as the shores change, increasing and diminishing, but never ceasing. And between these two storm lines of commotion there is that silence of the middle, as though the quiet of the deep flowing rises into the air. Once it is recognized, listened to, that silence has the force of a voice. [26]

After we had come down a mile or two we passed the house of a fisherman. His children were standing on top of the bank, high at that place, waiting for him to come in off [27] the river. And on down we met the fisherman himself, working his way home among the nets he had placed in the quieter water inside the rows of shore trees. We spoke and passed, and were soon out of sight of each other. But seeing him there changed the aspect of the river for us, as meeting an Arab on a camel might change the aspect of the desert. Problematic and strange as it seemed to us, here was a man who made a daily thing of it, and went to it as another man would go to an office. That race of violent water, which would hang flowing among the treetops only three or four days, had become familiar country to him, and he sunk his nets in it with more assurance than men sink wells in the earth. And so the flood bore a pattern of his making, and he went his set way on it.

And he was not the only creature who had made an   28
unexpected familiarity with the risen water. Where the drift had matted in the shore eddies, or caught against trees in the current, the cardinals and chickadees and titmice foraged as confidently as on dry land. The rise was an opportunity for them, turning up edibles they would have found with more difficulty otherwise. The cardinals were more irresistibly brilliant than ever, kindling in the black-wet drift in the cold wind. The sight of them warmed us.

The Kentucky is a river of steep high banks, nearly   29
everywhere thickly grown with willows and water maples and elms and sycamores. Boating on it in the summer, one is enclosed in a river-world, moving as though deep inside the country. One sees only the river, the high walls of foliage along the banks, the hilltops that rise over the trees first on one side and then the other. And that is one of the delights of this river. But one of the delights of being out on a winter rise is in seeing the country, and in seeing it from a vantage point that one does not usually see it from. The rise, that Sunday, had lifted us to the bank tops and higher, and through the naked trees we could look out across the bottoms. It was maybe like boating on a canal in Holland, though we had never done that. We could see the picked cornfields, their blanched yellow seeming even on that cloudy day to give off a light. We could see the winter grain spiking

green over the summer's tobacco patches, the thickly wooded hollows and slews, the backs of houses and farm buildings usually seen only by the people who live there.

Once, before the man-made floods of modern times, and before the automobile, all the river country turned toward the river. In those days our trip would probably have had more witnesses than it did. We might have been waved to from house windows, and from barn doors. But now the country has turned toward the roads, and we had what has come to be the back view of it. We went by mostly in secret. Only one of the fine old river houses is left on this side of the river in the six miles of our trip, and it is abandoned and weathering out; the floods have been in it too many times in the last thirty-five years, and it is too hard to get back to from the road. We went by its blank windows as the last settlers going west passed the hollow eyes of the skulls of their predecessors' oxen.

The living houses are all out along the edges of the valley floor, where the roads are. And now that all the crops had been gathered out of the bottoms, men's attention had mostly turned away. The land along the river had taken on a wildness that in the summer it would not have. We saw a pair of red-tailed hawks circling low and unafraid, more surprised to see us than we were to see them.

Where the river was over the banks a stretch of comparatively quiet water lay between the trees on the bank top and the new shore line. After a while, weary of the currents, we turned into one of these. As we made our way past the treetops and approached the shore we flushed a bobwhite out of a brush pile near the water and saw it fly off downstream. It seemed strange to see only one. But we didn't have to wait long for an explanation, for presently we saw the dogs, and then the hunters coming over the horizon with their guns. We knew where their bird had gone, but we didn't wait to tell them.

These men come out from the cities now that the hunting season is open. They walk in these foreign places, unknown to them for most of the year, looking for something to kill. They wear and carry many dollars' worth of equipment, and go to a great deal of trouble, in order to kill some small creature that they would never trouble to know alive, and that means little to them once they have killed it. If those we saw had killed the bobwhite they would no doubt have felt all their expense and effort justified, and would have thought themselves more manly than before. It reminds one of the extraordinary trouble and expense governments go to in order to kill men—and consider it justified or not, according to the "kill ratio." The diggers among our artifacts will find us to have been honorable lovers of death, having been willing to pay exorbitantly for it. How much better, we thought, to have come upon the *life* of the bird as we did, moving peaceably among the lives of the country that showed themselves to us because we were peaceable, than to have tramped fixedly, half oblivious, for miles in order to come at its death.

We left the hunters behind and went down past a green 34 grainfield where cattle were grazing and drinking at the waterside. They were not disturbed that the river had come up over part of their pasture, no more troubled by the height of today's shore line than they were by the height of yesterday's. To them, no matter how high it was, so long as the ground was higher it was as ordinary as a summer pond. Surely the creatures of the fifth day of Creation accepted those of the sixth with equanimity, as though they had always been there. Eternity is always present in the animal mind; only men deal in beginnings and ends. It is probably lucky for man that he was created last. He would have got too excited and upset over all the change.

Two mallards flew up ahead of us and turned downriv- 35 er into the wind. They had been feeding in the flooded corn rows, reminding us what a godsend the high water must be for ducks. The valley is suddenly full of little coves and havens, so that they can scatter out and feed safer and more hidden, and more abundantly too, than they usually can, never having to leave the river for such delicacies as the shattered corn left by the pickers. A picked cornfield under a few inches of water must be the duck Utopia—Utopia being, I assume, more often achieved by ducks than by men.

If one imagines the shore line exactly enough as the division between water and land, and imagines it rising—it comes up too slowly for the eye usually, so one *must* imagine it—there is a sort of magic about it. As it moves upward it makes a vast change, far more than the eye sees. It makes a new geography, altering the boundaries of worlds. Above it, it widens the freehold of the birds; below it, that of the fish. The land creatures are driven back and higher up. It is a line between boating and walking, gill and lung, standing still and flowing. Along it, suddenly and continuously, all that will float is picked up and carried away: leaves, logs, seeds, little straws, bits of dead grass. 36

And also empty cans and bottles and all sorts of buoyant trash left behind by fishermen and hunters and picnickers, or dumped over creek banks by householders who sometimes drive miles to do it. We passed behind a house built on one of the higher banks whose backyard was simply an avalanche of kitchen trash going down to the river. Those people, for all I know, may be champion homebodies, but their garbage is well-traveled, having departed for the Gulf of Mexico on every winter rise for years. 37

It is illuminating and suitably humbling to a man to recognize the great power of the river. But after he has recognized its power he is next called upon to recognize its limits. It can neither swallow up nor carry off all the trash that people convenience themselves by dumping into it. It can't carry off harmlessly all the sewage and pesticides and industrial contaminants that we are putting into it now, much less all that we will be capable of putting into it in a few years. We haven't accepted—we can't really believe—that the most characteristic product of our age of scientific miracles is junk, but that is so. And we still think and behave as though we face an unspoiled continent, with thousands of acres of living space for every man. We still sing "America the Beautiful" as though we had not created in it, by strenuous effort, at great expense, and with dauntless self-praise, an unprecedented ugliness. 38

The last couple of miles of our trip we could hear off in the bottoms alongside us the cries of pileated woodpeck- 39 ers, and we welcomed the news of them. These belong to the big trees and big woods, and more than any other birds along this river they speak out of our past. Their voices are loud and wild, the cries building strongly and then trailing off arrhythmically and hesitantly as though reluctant to end. Though they never seemed very near, we could hear them clearly over the commotion of the water. There were probably only a pair or two of them, but their voices kept coming to us a long time, creating beyond the present wildness of the river, muddy from the ruin of mountainsides and farmlands, the intimation of another wildness that will not overflow again in *our* history.

The wind had finally made its way into our clothes, and   40
our feet and hands and faces were beginning to stiffen a little with the cold. And so when home came back in sight we thought it wasn't too soon. We began to slant across the currents toward the shore. The river didn't stop to let us off. We ran the bow out onto the path that goes up to my house, and the current rippled on past the stern as though it were no more than the end of a stranded log. We were out of it, wobbling stiff-legged along the midrib on our way to the high ground.

With the uproar of the water still in our ears, we had   41
as we entered the house the sense of having been utterly outside the lives we live as usual. My warm living room was a place we seemed to have been away from a long way. It needed getting used to.

Comment

Some essays are solely informative, widening our knowledge of the world. Other essays are solely expressive or persuasive in aim. "The Rise" is both expressive and informative, and toward the end Berry seeks to persuade us to take action on a matter of concern. Combining description with narration, he informs us what it is like to ride a canoe on a swiftly flowing river. He gives us vivid details of the river and the shore in the course of narrating the journey. Berry also uses various methods of exposition to explain what is happening. In paragraphs 7 and 8, for example, he analogizes the canoeist to the rider of a spirited horse. In the same paragraph, he expresses his feelings about riding upon and swimming in the river. Throughout the essay he expresses what the river has meant to him in his life.

Questions for Study and Discussion

1. Where does Berry first state what the rising river means to him? What has the river meant to him in his life, and how does Berry reveal this meaning?
2. What use does Berry make of analogy and comparison?
3. How does he use example to inform us about the power of the river? Does he explain the cause of this power?
4. What action does Berry persuade us to take in later paragraphs? What methods of persuasion does he use?
5. What truths about people and nature does Berry develop in the essay?
6. What effect did the essay have upon you in reading it? What in the essay produced this effect?
7. What impression of Berry emerges while reading the essay? What details or statements most contribute to this impression?

Vocabulary Study

Use your dictionary to explain the following words and phrases in the context of the paragraph. You will need to consult reference books like *The Columbia Encyclopedia* and *The Oxford Classical Dictionary* on some of the following:

paragraph 4: *ominously*
paragraph 6: *eddies*
paragraph 8: *exhilaration, buoyancy, amphibious*
paragraph 11: *voluminousness*
paragraph 12: *sophistications, mitigate*
paragraph 13: *stylized, Sophoclean tragedy, insinuation, implacability*
paragraph 14: *kinship, subject*
paragraph 24: *Icarus, hybris* (or *hubris*)
paragraph 25: *poignantly, coherent*
paragraph 28: *kindling*
paragraph 29: *blanched, spiking, hollows, slews*
paragraph 32: *flushed*

paragraph 33: *artifacts, exorbitantly*
paragraph 34: *equanimity*
paragraph 35: *Utopia*
paragraph 40: *midrib*

Suggestions for Writing

1. Narrate an experience in nature that made you aware of its power or revealed an important truth to you. Give sufficient details of the experience to help the reader understand what you felt.
2. Berry states in paragraph 8: "There is an exhilaration in being *accustomed* to a boat on dangerous water." Discuss a similar experience in which you felt exhilaration in a position of danger. Give sufficient details to let the reader experience what you did. Explain the causes.

PART 4

Effective Sentences
and Diction

The sentences we speak and write derive from sentences we hear and read from day to day. The same is true of the words we use. We adopt new words and new turns of phrase and ways of giving ideas emphasis usually without realizing we have done so. And usually the change is slight, for habits of speech and writing are established early and are not easy to change. Adopting new words is, however, easier for us than adopting new sentence patterns.

How conscious we are of language depends on the formality of the speaking or writing situation. Each of us has an informal and a formal way of speaking—each appropriate to different occasions, each expressive and useful. We make adjustments in our spoken language usually without realizing we are doing so. Writing calls for more deliberate choice, particularly in tightening sentences that derive from our informal speech.

The following is a transcription of spoken English:

> In the minor leagues we spent a lot of hours riding in buses, and they were so hot and you didn't have too many stops to eat. You ate poorly because you had bad meal money. We got $1.50 a day. But you were young. When I was with a class B league, I got a long distance call. My wife went to the hospital in labor. It was the first baby. I had to get home. The ticket was forty-some dollars. We didn't have it between us—the manager, everybody. I got there a day late.—Studs Terkel, *Working*

These informal sentences are expressive despite the loose organization and the looseness of the first sentence and the fragmented sound of the short sentences that follow. Informal writing usually follows the same loose patterns of speech and uses familiar phrases, colloquial words, and contracted words:

> The excitement of the rodeo comes not so much from the competition between the cowboys themselves as from the competition between man and animal. The fans, of course, are partisans; they root for their own species. The crowd always cheers when a cowboy wins even if they've never heard of the chap. But the animals must be good, or the contest will be no fun. The horses, bulls, steers, and calves are thus all bred and raised especially for their spunk.—Ray Raphael, *Edges*

At its best, as in this statement on rodeos, informal writing stays close to colloquial patterns. It becomes inexpressive and monotonous, however, when most of the sentences are short or loosely strung together.

To convey meaning when we speak, we depend on voice pitch and inflection. The baseball player above probably stressed particular words in the series of short sentences that conclude his statement. These resources in speech are not available to the writer. Written sentences therefore must be tighter than the fragmented or run-on sentences we sometimes speak. In our formal writing as in our formal speech, we give even more attention to precision and emphasis. When formal writing deals with ideas, it uses a large number of abstract words and words that are also chosen for their exactness:

> Lincoln was a pre-eminent example of that self-help which Americans have always so admired. He was not, of course, the first eminent American politician who could claim humble origins, nor the first to exploit them. But few have been able to point to such a sudden ascent from relative obscurity to high eminence; none has maintained so completely while scaling the heights the aspect of extreme simplicity; and none has combined with the attainment of success and power such an intense awareness of humanity and moral responsibility.—Richard Hofstadter, *The American Political Tradition*

The coordination of clauses in the first sentence of this formal passage is tighter than that in the statement on rodeos. The diction is also frequently abstract (*the aspect of extreme simplicity, the attainment of success and power, awareness of humanity and moral responsibility*) and the choice of words is exact (*ascent* rather than the informal *rise, high eminence* rather than *fame*). Formal writing, it should also be noted, sometimes depends on the passive voice more than informal writing does:

> Evidently nature can no longer be seen as matter and energy alone. Nor can all her secrets be unlocked with the keys of chemistry and physics, brilliantly successful as these two branches of science have been in our century. A third component is needed for any explanation of the world that claims to be complete. To the powerful theories of chemistry and physics must be added a late arrival: a theory of information. Nature must be interpreted as matter, energy, and information.—Jeremy Campbell, *Grammatical Man*

An abstract subject such as information theory invites a formal style, a concrete subject like the rodeo an informal style; but both subjects might be written about in informal and formal language. Much depends on what style the writer believes is suited to a particular audience or its expectations.

Much writing today avoids the extremes of highly formal or highly informal English. General English is the term given to a spoken and written standard that shares characteristics of both. General English is much tighter than informal spoken English, but it is looser than the formal sentences just quoted—conveying the rhythm of ordinary speech, more often the rhythm of the active voice than the passive. It uses a plain vocabulary where possible, depending on abstract and technical words only when simpler words will not express the intended ideas.

The Joan Didion essay on bureaucrats that follows illustrates General English, and so do most of the essays in this book. Compare Terkel's statement (p. 283) with the following from Didion's essay:

> Mere driving on the freeway is in no way the same as participating in it. Anyone can "drive" on the freeway, and many people with no vocation for it do, hesitating here and resisting there, losing the rhythm of the lane change, thinking about where they came from and where they are going. Actual participants think only about where they are. Actual participation requires a total surrender, a concentration so intense as to seem a kind of narcosis, a rapture-of-the-freeway. *The mind goes clean. The rhythm takes over.* A distortion of time occurs, the same distortion that characterizes the instant before an accident. [italics added]

Didion varies these sentences to considerable effect. The italicized short sentences make the impact they do because Didion uses them sparingly. Short sentences need not be as dramatic as these; the effect depends on the ideas they express.

At the same time, sentences that depart markedly from patterns of speech may sound stilted. In speaking, we usually begin with the main idea and add to it supporting details and other modifiers, or link the main idea to another as Didion does in the passage above:

> Anyone can "drive" on the freeway, and many with no vocation for it do, hesitating here and resisting there, losing the rhythm of the lane change, thinking about where they came from and where they are going.

Because so many spoken sentences open with the main clause, variation from this pattern catches the reader's attention:

> The closed door upstairs at 120 Spring Street in downtown Los Angeles is marked OPERATIONS CENTER. In the windowless room beyond the closed door a reverential hush prevails. From six A.M. until seven P.M. in this windowless room men sit at consoles watching a huge board flash colored lights.

The second and third sentences—called *periodic* because the subject and verb of the main clause come at the end—catch our attention because of the dramatic build up from the opening modifiers. Sentences such as these make their impact because Didion varies them to catch the pauses, interruptions, and nuances of talk.

Informal, Formal, and General English use concrete and abstract words, specific and general ones. The passages quoted from Didion contain all of these. And writing at these three levels also contains metaphors and other figures of speech. In expressive writing like Annie Dillard's on the coming of spring (p. 353), metaphor dramatically expresses the special feelings and perceptions of the writer:

> This is the hoop of flame that shoots the rapids in the creek or spins across the dizzy meadows; this is the arsonist of the sunny woods. . . .

In informative writing, as in David R. Scott's description of his moon walk (p. 344), figurative language is often not so obvious:

> The flowing moonscape, unmarred by a single jagged peak, reminds me of earth's uplands covered by a heavy blanket of fresh snow.

Every style has its hazards. Formal sentences that depart too far from colloquial English become hard to understand. Technical words or jargon are often essential in writing about technical subjects; usually only the special audience knows the meaning of these terms. The formal writer wants to be precise, but precision can become a fault as in the following sentence:

> But already at a point in economic evolution far antedating the emergence of the lady, specialized consumption of goods as an evidence of pecuniary strength had begun to work out in a more or less elaborate system.—Thorstein Veblen, *Theory of the Leisure Class*

This overprecise sentence uses abstract, theoretical terms to state simple ideas. "Pecuniary strength" means nothing more than having money; "specialized consumption of goods" means buying things because they look expensive. In colloquial English, people are "putting on the dog."

At the three levels, overused phrases can make writing sound stale. A phrase like "putting on the dog"—a popular colloquialism—loses its color in writing through overfamiliarity. We refer to phrases of this kind as clichés. A piece of writing may also seem too colorful—overcrowded with metaphor and other figures. But deciding what is overfamiliar or overcolorful is not easy. There are no rules for deciding what sentence style or kind of diction is appropriate to particular subjects or audiences. A sense of appropriateness comes only with wide reading and the awareness that writers achieve different effects with different means and in no predictable ways.

Joan Didion

BUREAUCRATS

Joan Didion has had a varied career in writing since her graduation from the University of California at Berkeley in 1956. She has been an editor of *Vogue* and a columnist for *The Saturday Evening Post*. She reported on the Salvadoran civil war in *Salvador* (1983). She has also written screenplays, numerous essays, and novels about contemporary American life including *Play It as It Lays* (1971), *The Book of Common Prayer* (1977), and *Democracy* (1984). "Bureaucrats" shows her concern with urban problems today and, in particular, her ironic view of the workings of government. It is reprinted from *The White Album* (1979), a collection of Didion's essays.

The closed door upstairs at 120 South Spring Street in downtown Los Angeles is marked OPERATIONS CENTER. In the windowless room beyond the closed door a reverential hush prevails. From six A.M. until seven P.M. in this windowless room men sit at consoles watching a huge board flash colored lights. "There's the heart attack," someone will murmur, or "we're getting the gawk effect." 120 South Spring is the Los Angeles office of Caltrans, or the California Department of Transportation, and the Operations Center is where Caltrans engineers monitor what they call "the 42-Mile Loop." The 42-Mile Loop is simply the rough triangle formed by the intersections of the Santa Monica, the San Diego and the Harbor freeways, and 42 miles represents less than ten per cent of freeway mileage in Los Angeles County alone, but these particular 42 miles are regarded around 120 South Spring with a special veneration. The Loop is a "demonstration system," a phrase much favored by everyone at Caltrans, and is part of a "pilot project," another two words carrying totemic weight on South Spring.

The Loop has electronic sensors embedded every half-mile out there in the pavement itself, each sensor counting the crossing cars every twenty seconds. The Loop has its own mind, A Xerox Sigma V computer which prints out, all day and night, twenty-second readings on what is and is not moving in each of the Loop's eight lanes. It is the Xerox Sigma V that makes the big board flash red when traffic out there drops below fifteen miles an hour. It is the Xerox Sigma V that tells the Operations crew when they have an "incident" out there. An "incident" is the heart attack on the San Diego, the jackknifed truck on the Harbor, the Camaro just now tearing out the Cyclone fence on the Santa Monica. "Out there" is where incidents happen. The windowless room at 120 South Spring is where incidents get "verified." "Incident verification" is turning on the closed-circuit TV on the console and watching the traffic slow down to see (this is "the gawk effect") where the Camaro tore out the fence. 2

As a matter of fact there is a certain closed-circuit aspect to the entire mood of the Operations Center. "Verifying" the incident does not after all "prevent" the incident, which lends the enterprise a kind of tranced distance, and on the day recently when I visited 120 South Spring it took considerable effort to remember what I had come to talk about, which was that particular part of the Loop called the Santa Monica Freeway. The Santa Monica Freeway is 16.2 miles long, runs from the Pacific Ocean to downtown Los 3

Angeles through what is referred to at Caltrans as "the East–
West Corridor," carries more traffic every day than any other
freeway in California, has what connoisseurs of freeways
concede to be the most beautiful access ramps in the world,
and appeared to have been transformed by Caltrans, during
the several weeks before I went downtown to talk about it,
into a 16.2-mile parking lot.

The problem seemed to be another Caltrans "demon-   4
stration," or "pilot," a foray into bureaucratic terrorism they
were calling "The Diamond Lane" in their promotional literature and "The Project" among themselves. That the promotional literature consisted largely of schedules for buses
(or "Diamond Lane Expresses") and invitations to join a car
pool via computer ("Commuter Computer") made clear not
only the putative point of The Project, which was to encourage travel by car pool and bus, but also the actual point,
which was to eradicate a central Southern California illusion, that of individual mobility, without anyone really noticing. This had not exactly worked out. "FREEWAY
FIASCO," the *Los Angeles Times* was headlining page-one
stories. "THE DIAMOND LANE: ANOTHER BUST BY
CALTRANS." "CALTRANS PILOT EFFORT ANOTHER
IN LONG LIST OF FAILURES." "OFFICIAL DIAMOND
LANE STANCE: LET THEM HOWL."

All "The Diamond Lane" theoretically involved was re-   5
serving the fast inside lanes on the Santa Monica for vehicles
carrying three or more people, but in practice this meant
that 25 per cent of the freeway was reserved for 3 per cent
of the cars, and there were other odd wrinkles here and there
suggesting that Caltrans had dedicated itself to making all
movements around Los Angeles as arduous as possible. There
was for example the matter of surface streets. A "surface
street" is anything around Los Angeles that is not a freeway
("going surface" from one part of town to another is generally regarded as idiosyncratic), and surface streets do not
fall directly within the Caltrans domain, but now the engi-
neer in charge of surface streets was accusing Caltrans of
threatening and intimidating him. It appeared that Caltrans

wanted him to create a "confused and congested situation" on his surface streets, so as to force drivers back to the freeway, where they would meet a still more confused and congested situation and decide to stay home, or take a bus. "We are beginning a process of deliberately making it harder for drivers to use freeways," a Caltrans director had in fact said at a transit conference some months before. "We are prepared to endure considerable public outcry in order to pry John Q. Public out of his car. . . . I would emphasize that this is a political decision, and one that can be reversed if the public gets sufficiently enraged to throw us rascals out."

Of course this political decision was in the name of the greater good, was in the interests of "environmental improvement" and "conservation of resources," but even there the figures had about them a certain Caltrans opacity. The Santa Monica normally carried 240,000 cars and trucks every day. These 240,000 cars and trucks normally carried 260,000 people. What Caltrans described as its ultimate goal on the Santa Monica was to carry the same 260,000 people, "but in 7,800 fewer, or 232,200 vehicles." The figure "232,200" had a visionary precision to it that did not automatically create confidence, especially since the only effect so far had been to disrupt traffic throughout the Los Angeles Basin, triple the number of daily accidents on the Santa Monica, prompt the initiation of two lawsuits against Caltrans, and cause large numbers of Los Angeles County residents to behave, most uncharacteristically, as an ignited and conscious proletariat. Citizen guerrillas splashed paint and scattered nails in the Diamond Lanes. Diamond Lane maintenance crews expressed fear of hurled objects. Down at 120 South Spring the architects of the Diamond Lane had taken to regarding "the media" as the architects of their embarrassment, and Caltrans statements in the press had been cryptic and contradictory, reminiscent only of old communiqués out of Vietnam.

To understand what was going on it is perhaps necessary to have participated in the freeway experience, which is the only secular communion Los Angeles has. Mere driving on the freeway is in no way the same as participating in it. Anyone can "drive" on the freeway, and many people with no vocation for it do, hesitating here and resisting there, losing the rhythm of the lane change, thinking about where they came from and where they are going. Actual participants think only about where they are. Actual participation requires a total surrender, a concentration so intense as to seem a kind of narcosis, a rapture-of-the-freeway. The mind goes clean. The rhythm takes over. A distortion of time occurs, the same distortion that characterizes the instant before an accident. It takes only a few seconds to get off the Santa Monica Freeway at National-Overland, which is a difficult exit requiring the driver to cross two new lanes of traffic streamed in from the San Diego Freeway, but those few seconds always seem to me the longest part of the trip. The moment is dangerous. The exhilaration is in doing it. "As you acquire the special skills involved," Reyner Banham observed in an extraordinary chapter about the freeways in his 1971 *Los Angeles: The Architecture of Four Ecologies,* "the freeways become a special way of being alive . . . the extreme concentration required in Los Angeles seems to bring on a state of heightened awareness that some locals find mystical."

Indeed some locals do, and some nonlocals too. Reduc- 8 ing the number of lone souls careering around the East–West Corridor in a state of mechanized rapture may or may not have seemed socially desirable, but what it was definitely not going to seem was easy. "We're only seeing an initial period of unfamiliarity," I was assured the day I visited Caltrans. I was talking to a woman named Eleanor Wood and she was thoroughly and professionally grounded in the diction of "planning" and it did not seem likely that I could interest her in considering the freeway as regional mystery. "Any time you try to rearrange people's daily habits, they're apt to react impetuously. All this project requires is a certain rearrangement of people's daily planning. That's really all we want."

It occurred to me that a certain rearrangement of peo- 9 ple's daily planning might seem, in less rarefied air than is breathed at 120 South Spring, rather a great deal to want, but so impenetrable was the sense of higher social purpose there in the Operations Center that I did not express this reservation. Instead I changed the subject, mentioned an earlier "pilot project" on the Santa Monica: the big electronic message boards that Caltrans had installed a year or two before. The idea was that traffic information transmitted from the Santa Monica to the Xerox Sigma V could be translated, here in the Operations Center, into suggestions to the driver, and flashed right back out to the Santa Monica. This operation, in that it involved telling drivers electronically what they already knew empirically, had the rather spectral circularity that seemed to mark a great many Caltrans schemes, and I was interested in how Caltrans thought it worked.

"Actually the message boards were part of a larger pilot project," Mrs. Wood said. "An ongoing project in incident management. With the message boards we hoped to learn if motorists would modify their behavior according to what we told them on the boards."   10

I asked if the motorists had.   11

"Actually no," Mrs. Wood said finally. "They didn't react to the signs exactly as we'd hypothesized they would, no. *But.* If we'd *known* what the motorist would do . . . then we wouldn't have needed a pilot project in the first place, would we."   12

The circle seemed intact. Mrs. Wood and I smiled, and shook hands. I watched the big board until all lights turned green on the Santa Monica and then I left and drove home on it, all 16.2 miles of it. All the way I remembered that I was watched by the Xerox Sigma V. All the way the message boards gave me the number to call for CAR POOL INFO. As I left the freeway it occurred to me that they might have their own rapture down at 120 South Spring, and it could be called Perpetuating the Department. Today the California Highway Patrol reported that, during the first six weeks of the Diamond Lane, accidents on the Santa Monica, which normally range between 49 and 72 during a six-week period, totaled 204. Yesterday plans were announced to extend the Diamond Lane to other freeways at a cost of $42,500,000.   13

Questions for Study and Discussion

1. What variations of sentence length do you find in paragraphs 1–6?
2. How many sentences in paragraphs 1–6 are built by addition of detail? How many are built by qualification and modification?
3. The greater the number of simple and compound sentences, the greater the informality of the essay. How informal is this essay?
4. Does Didion state her attitude toward Caltrans directly, or instead imply it through her details?
5. In what ways is the Los Angeles Freeway symbolic of Los Angeles life? Does Didion see the freeway as symbolic or representative of California or perhaps American life, generally?

Vocabulary Study

1. What is Didion saying about the word *verified* and the other forms of it she cites in paragraphs 2 and 3?
2. What points is she making about other special terms she discusses—for example, *surface street*?
3. Why does she use the word *proletariat* rather than *population* or *citizenry* in paragraph 6?
4. Why does she use the phrase *secular communion* instead of *being together*—"the only way of being together that Los Angeles has"—in paragraph 7?
5. Explain the italicized words:

   This operation, in that it involved telling drivers electronically what they already knew *empirically,* had the rather *spectral circularity* that seemed to mark a great many Caltrans schemes. . . .

Suggestions for Writing

1. Didion is describing a different experience with bureaucracy from Nelson's ("The Desk," p. 209). Discuss the differences in the experiences and the conclusions reached about bureaucracy.

2. Use the traffic of your hometown or city to comment on its quality of life or atmosphere. Make your details as specific as you can.

3. Discuss an "improvement" that in your opinion has worsened the situation it was intended to make better. Describe the situation in detail.

Emphasis

Giving ideas exact emphasis requires attention to sentence coordination and subordination. When you *coordinate* you use the words *and, but, for, or, nor,* and *yet* to connect words, phrases, and clauses of the same weight and importance. The three opening clauses in the following sentence are independent and coordinate:

> The cold night had come, *and* Ukwane in the frosty grass was shivering, *yet* he sat for an hour keeping his patience, putting his hands into the cold blood of the springbok to trace veins to their source, prefacing all his answers with positive, qualifying remarks.—Elizabeth Marshall Thomas, *The Harmless People*

To stress a close relation between ideas, the writer may coordinate clauses with semicolons, with or without connecting (or conjunctive) adverbs like *however* and *furthermore* or adverbial phrases:

> For us, the cave paintings re-create the hunter's way of life as a glimpse of history; we look through them into the past. But for the hunter, I suggest, they were a peep-hole into the future; he looked ahead.—J. Bronowski, *The Ascent of Man*

> It is natural to come to astronomy straight from mathematics; after all, astronomy was developed first, and became a model for all the other sciences, just because it could be turned into exact numbers.—*The Ascent of Man*

When you *subordinate* you attach to independent clauses phrases and clauses that cannot stand alone. In the Thomas sentence above, the heavily stressed subordinate phrases that conclude the sentence contain specific details that explain the independent clause:

> . . . yet he sat for an hour keeping his patience, putting his hands into the cold blood of the springbok to trace veins to their

source, prefacing all his answers with positive, qualifying remarks.

English sentences often reserve the end of the sentence for the most important idea. This end-focus is evident in the stress given final words in speaking:

My wife's parents live in NEWark.

Even if another word in the sentence is stressed, the final word still receives a degree of stress:

My *WIFE'S* parents live in NEWark (my wife's parents, not my own parents)

This fact has important consequences for building sentences and varying them. It means that the speaker or writer can "load" the end of the sentence, adding ideas and details that cannot easily go at the beginning. You speak or write the following sentence without thinking about its structure:

(1) I know they won't come if they decide to go to Newark.

You would not say or write:

(2) That they won't come if they decide to go to Newark I know.

But you can open the sentence with a shorter complement:

(3) That they're coming I have no doubt.

Notice that the complement [*that*] *they won't come* in (1) is followed by a modifying subordinate clause (*if they decide to go to Newark*) and therefore cannot appear at the beginning of the sentence. The unmodified complement in (3)—*That he is coming*—can appear at the beginning. By contrast, complex modifiers can be added to the end of the sentence without difficulty:

A school of minnows swam by, each minnow with its small individual shadow, doubling the attendance, so clear and sharp in the sunlight.—E. B. White, "Once More to the Lake"

Compound sentences, which coordinate independent clauses to emphasize their connection, can run on indefinitely:

The height of the ginning season in that part of the country is early October, and in that time the loaded wagons are on the road before the least crack of daylight, the waiting is endless hours, and the gin is still pulsing and beating after dark.—James Agee, "Cotton"

This sentence might continue further. The familiar definition of a sentence as a complete thought is of no use in deciding when to end sentences of this kind. For the completeness of the thought lies in the mind of the speaker or writer, who seeks to emphasize each component idea and who alone knows when everything necessary has been said. At the same time, the emphasis or force diminishes for the reader if the sentence seems to run on or drift monotonously.

Richard P. Feynman

THE AMATEUR SCIENTIST

Richard P. Feynman was professor of Theoretical Physics at the California Institute of Technology, where he taught from 1950 until his death in 1988. Feynman was born in Far Rockaway, New York, in 1918, and studied at the Massachusetts Institute of Technology and Princeton University. From 1943 to 1946 he worked as a nuclear physicist at Los Alamos, New Mexico. In 1965 Feynman received the Nobel Prize in Physics for his contribution to quantum mechanics, which increased understanding of the fundamental forces of nature. *"Surely You're Joking, Mr. Feynman!"* is a collection of personal essays that form a memoir of his life. In the essay reprinted here from this collection, Feynman describes how he began to think and experiment like a scientist.

When I was a kid I had a "lab." It wasn't a laboratory   1
in the sense that I would measure, or do important experiments. Instead, I would play: I'd make a motor, I'd make a gadget that would go off when something passed a photocell, I'd play around with selenium; I was piddling around all the time. I did calculate a little bit for the lamp bank, a series of switches and bulbs I used as resistors to control voltages. But all that was for application. I never did any laboratory kind of experiments.

I also had a microscope and *loved* to watch things un-   2
der the microscope. It took patience: I would get something

under the microscope and I would watch it interminably. I saw many interesting things, like everybody sees—a diatom slowly making its way across the slide, and so on.

One day I was watching a paramecium and I saw some-   3
thing that was not described in the books I got in school—in college, even. These books always simplify things so the world will be more like *they* want it to be: When they're talking about the behavior of animals, they always start out with, "The paramecium is extremely simple; it has a simple behavior. It turns as its slipper shape moves through the water until it hits something, at which time it recoils, turns through an angle, and then starts out again."

It isn't really right. First of all, as everybody knows, the   4
paramecia, from time to time, conjugate with each other—they meet and exchange nuclei. How do they decide when it's time to do that? (Never mind; that's not my observation.)

I watched these paramecia hit something, recoil, turn   5
through an angle, and go again. The idea that it's mechanical, like a computer program—it doesn't look that way. They go different distances, they recoil different distances, they turn through angles that are different in various cases; they don't always turn to the right; they're very irregular. It looks random, because you don't know what they're hitting; you don't know all the chemicals they're smelling, or what.

One of the things I wanted to watch was what happens   6
to the paramecium when the water that it's in dries up. It was claimed that the paramecium can dry up into a sort of hardened seed. I had a drop of water on the slide under my microscope, and in the drop of water was a paramecium and some "grass"—at the scale of the paramecium, it looked like a network of jackstraws. As the drop of water evaporated, over a time of fifteen or twenty minutes, the paramecium got into a tighter and tighter situation: there was more and more of this back-and-forth until it could hardly move. It was stuck between these "sticks," almost jammed.

Then I saw something I had never seen or heard of: the   7
paramecium lost its shape. It could flex itself, like an amoeba. It began to push itself against one of the sticks, and began

dividing into two prongs until the division was about half-way up the paramecium, at which time it decided *that* wasn't a very good idea, and backed away.

So my impression of these animals is that their behavior is much too simplified in the books. It is not so utterly mechanical or one-dimensional as they say. They should describe the behavior of these simple animals correctly. Until we see how many dimensions of behavior even a one-celled animal has, we won't be able to fully understand the behavior of more complicated animals. 8

I also enjoyed watching bugs. I had an insect book when I was about thirteen. It said that dragonflies are not harmful; they don't sting. In our neighborhood it was well known that "darning needles," as we called them, were very dangerous when they'd sting. So if we were outside somewhere playing baseball, or something, and one of these things would fly around, everybody would run for cover, waving their arms, yelling," A darning needle! A darning needle!" 9

So one day I was on the beach, and I'd just read this book that said dragonflies don't sting. A darning needle came along, and everybody was screaming and running around, and I just sat there. "Don't worry!" I said. "Darning needles don't sting!" 10

The thing landed on my foot. Everybody was yelling and it was a big mess, because this darning needle was sitting on my foot. And there I was, this scientific wonder, saying it wasn't going to sting me. 11

You're *sure* this is a story that's going to come out that it stings me—but it didn't. The book was right. But I did sweat a bit. 12

I also had a little hand microscope. It was a toy microscope, and I pulled the magnification piece out of it, and would hold it in my hand like a magnifying glass, even though it was a microscope of forty or fifty power. With care you could hold the focus. So I could go around and look at things right out in the street. 13

When I was in graduate school at Princeton, I once took it out of my pocket to look at some ants that were crawling around on some ivy. I had to exclaim out loud, I was so 14 excited. What I saw was an ant and an aphid, which ants take care of—they carry them from plant to plant if the plant they're on is dying. In return the ants get partially digested aphid juice, called "honeydew." I knew that; my father had told me about it, but I had never seen it.

So here was this aphid and sure enough, an ant came along, and patted it with its feet—all around the aphid, pat, pat, pat, pat, pat. This was terribly exciting! Then the juice came out of the back of the aphid. And because it was magnified, it looked like a big, beautiful, glistening ball, like a balloon, because of the surface tension. Because the microscope wasn't very good, the drop was colored a little bit from chromatic aberration in the lens—it was a gorgeous thing! 15

The ant took this ball in its two front feet, lifted it off the aphid, and *held* it. The world is so different at that scale that you can pick up water and hold it! The ants probably have a fatty or greasy material on their legs that doesn't break the surface tension of the water when they hold it up. Then the ant broke the surface of the drop with its mouth, and the surface tension collapsed the drop right into his gut. It was *very* interesting to see this whole thing happen! 16

In my room at Princeton I had a bay window with a U-shaped windowsill. One day some ants came out on the windowsill and wandered around a little bit. I got curious as to how they found things. I wondered, how do they know where to go? Can they tell each other where food is, like bees can? Do they have any sense of geometry? 17

This is all amateurish; everybody knows the answer, but *I* didn't know the answer, so the first thing I did was to stretch some string across the U of the bay window and hang a piece of folded cardboard with sugar on it from the string. The idea of this was to isolate the sugar from the ants, so they wouldn't find it accidentally. I wanted to have everything under control. 18

Next I made a lot of little strips of paper and put a fold in them, so I could pick up ants and ferry them from one place to another. I put the folded strips of paper in two places: Some were by the sugar (hanging from the string), and the others were near the ants in a particular location. I 19 sat there all afternoon, reading and watching, until an ant happened to walk onto one of my little paper ferries. Then I took him over to the sugar. After a few ants had been ferried over to the sugar, one of them accidentally walked onto one of the ferries nearby, and I carried him back.

I wanted to see how long it would take the other ants to get the message to go to the "ferry terminal." It started slowly, but rapidly increased until I was going mad ferrying the ants back and forth.

But suddenly, when everything was going strong, I began to deliver the ants from the sugar to a *different* spot. The question now was, does the ant learn to go back to where it just came from, or does it go where it went the time before?

After a while there were practically no ants going to the first place (which would take them to the sugar), whereas there were many ants at the second place, milling around, trying to find the sugar. So I figured out so far that they went where they just came from.

In another experiment, I laid out a lot of glass microscope slides, and got the ants to walk on them, back and forth, to some sugar I put on the windowsill. Then, by replacing an old slide with a new one, or by rearranging the slides, I could demonstrate that the ants had no sense of geometry: they couldn't figure out where something was. If they went to the sugar one way, and there was a shorter way back, they would never figure out the short way.

It was also pretty clear from rearranging the glass slides that the ants left some sort of trail. So then came a lot of easy experiments to find out how long it takes a trail to dry up, whether it can be easily wiped off, and so on. I also found out the trail wasn't directional. If I'd pick up an ant on a piece of paper, turn him around and around, and then put him back onto the trail, he wouldn't know that he was going the wrong way until he met another ant. (Later, in Brazil, I noticed some leaf-cutting ants and tried the same experiment on them. They *could* tell, within a few steps, whether they were going toward the food or away from it—presumably from the trail, which might be a series of smells in a pattern: A, B, space, A. B, space, and so on.)

I tried at one point to make the ants go around in a   25
circle, but I didn't have enough patience to set it up. I could
see no reason, other than lack of patience, why it couldn't
be done.

One thing that made experimenting difficult was that   26
breathing on the ants made them scurry. It must be an instinctive thing against some animal that eats them or disturbs them. I don't know if it was the warmth, the moisture,
or the smell of my breath that bothered them, but I always
had to hold my breath and kind of look to one side so as
not to confuse the experiment while I was ferrying the ants.

One question that I wondered about was why the ant   27
trails look so straight and nice. The ants look as if they know
what they're doing, as if they have a good sense of geometry. Yet the experiments that I did to try to demonstrate
their sense of geometry didn't work.

Many years later, when I was at Caltech and lived in a   28
little house on Alameda Street, some ants came out around
the bathtub. I thought, "This is a great opportunity." I put
some sugar on the other end of the bathtub, and sat there
the whole afternoon until an ant finally found the sugar. It's
only a question of patience.

The moment the ant found the sugar, I picked up a   29
colored pencil that I had ready (I had previously done experiments indicating that the ants don't give a damn about
pencil marks—they walk right over them—so I knew I wasn't
disturbing anything), and behind where the ant went I drew
a line so I could tell where his trail was. The ant wandered
a little bit wrong to get back to the hole, so the line was
quite wiggly, unlike a typical ant trail.

When the next ant to find the sugar began to go back,   30
I marked his trail with another color. (By the way, he followed the first ant's return trail back, rather than his own
incoming trail. My theory is that when an ant has found
some food, he leaves a much stronger trail than when he's
just wandering around.)

This second ant was in a great hurry and followed, pretty   31
much, the original trail. But because he was going so fast he
would go straight out, as if he were coasting, when the trail

was wiggly. Often, as the ant was "coasting," he would find the trail again. Already it was apparent that the second ant's return was slightly straighter. With successive ants the same "improvement" of the trail by hurriedly and carelessly "following" it occurred.

I followed eight or ten ants with my pencil until their trails became a neat line right along the bathtub. It's something like sketching: You draw a lousy line at first; then you go over it a few times and it makes a nice line after a while. 32

I remember that when I was a kid my father would tell me how wonderful ants are, and how they cooperate. I would watch very carefully three or four ants carrying a little piece of chocolate back to their nest. At first glance it looks like efficient, marvelous, brilliant cooperation. But if you look at it carefully, you'll see that it's nothing of the kind: They're all behaving as if the chocolate is held up by something else. They pull at it one way or the other way. An ant may crawl over it while it's being pulled at by the others. It wobbles, it wiggles, the directions are all confused. The chocolate doesn't move in a nice way toward the nest. 33

The Brazilian leaf-cutting ants, which are otherwise so marvelous, have a very interesting stupidity associated with them that I'm surprised hasn't evolved out. It takes considerable work for the ant to cut the circular arc in order to get a piece of leaf. When the cutting is done, there's a fifty-fifty chance that the ant will pull on the wrong side, letting the piece he just cut fall to the ground. Half the time, the ant will yank and pull and yank and pull on the wrong part of the leaf, until it gives up and starts to cut another piece. There is no attempt to pick up a piece that it, or any other ant, has already cut. So it's quite obvious, if you watch very carefully, that it's not a brilliant business of cutting leaves and carrying them away; they go to a leaf, cut an arc, and pick the wrong side half the time while the right piece falls down. 34

In Princeton the ants found my larder, where I had jelly and bread and stuff, which was quite a distance from the window. A long line of ants marched along the floor across the living room. It was during the time I was doing these 35 experiments on the ants, so I thought to myself, "What can I do to stop them from coming to my larder without killing any ants? No poison; you gotta be humane to the ants!"

What I did was this: In preparation, I put a bit of sugar   36
about six or eight inches from their entry point into the room, that they didn't know about. Then I made those ferry things again, and whenever an ant returning with food walked onto my little ferry, I'd carry him over and put him on the sugar. Any ant coming toward the larder that walked onto a ferry I also carried over to the sugar. Eventually the ants found their way from the sugar to their hole, so this new trail was being doubly reinforced, while the old trail was being used less and less. I knew that after half an hour or so the old trail would dry up, and in an hour they were out of my larder. I didn't wash the floor; I didn't do anything but ferry ants.

Comment

Feynman's essay seems like a long answer to a question he might have been asked while conversing with a friend; his sentences are colloquial in structure—a series of details or short explanatory phrases and clauses often are added to a base sentence; some clauses are compounded in a series, sometimes without conjunctions:

> Instead I would play: I'd make a motor, I'd make a gadget that would go off when something passed a photocell, I'd play around with selenium; I was piddling around all the time.

Feynman is making a point through the details of the experiments he describes. Through these details the reader makes discoveries about Feynman.

Questions for Study and Discussion

1. What features make the sentences in paragraphs 32 and 33 colloquial—that is, suggestive of spoken English?
2. What implicit point is Feynman making about each of his various experiments? Is he making the same point in each instance?
3. Which of the author's personal qualities emerge in his narra-

tive of these experiments? Are the experiments the central focus of the essay, or is Feynman the experimenter the focus? How do you know?

4. Does Feynman leave you with the sense that he has more to tell about his amateur experiments and has merely broken off the narrative? Or does he conclude the essay informally or formally?

5. If you were writing a formal essay on experiments you performed as an adolescent, how different would your essay be in structure from Feynman's? What features in general makes an essay formal?

Sentence Study

1. All but the first sentence in paragraph 1 consist of main clauses. Construct additional complex sentences by subordinating some of these main clauses. What change in emphasis occurs in your revision? Does the revision change Feynman's meaning?

2. Feynman coordinates a series of main clauses in the following sentences. Recast each sentence, combining these clauses or subordinating one or more. What change in emphasis occurs in your revision?

   a. "It took patience: I would get something under the microscope and I would watch it interminably." (paragraph 2)

   b. "I had a drop of water on the slide under my microscope, and in the drop of water was a paramecium and some "grass"—at the scale of the paramecium, it looked like a network of jackstraws." (paragraph 6)

   c. "Then the ant broke the surface of the drop with its mouth, and the surface tension collapsed the drop right into his gut." (paragraph 16)

3. Try to reduce the repetition of words in the following sentence:

   "They go different distances, they recoil different distances, they turn through angles that are different in various cases; they don't always turn to the right; they're very irregular." (paragraph 5)

   What is gained or lost by your revision?

4. The concluding clause in the following sentence adds information about the larder. Speaking the sentence, we would probably raise our voice with *which* to show that it modifies

larder. Revise the sentence so that *which* immediately follows *larder:*

"In Princeton the ants found my larder, where I had jelly and bread and stuff, which was quite a distance from the window." (paragraph 35)

What problems did you meet in revising the sentence? Is your revision an improvement over Feynman's sentence?

Suggestions for Writing

1. Write about a series of related experiences that define your interests. Let the reader draw conclusions from your details. Don't draw these conclusions yourself.
2. Write a characterization of Feynman on the basis of what he tells you about his interests and how he relates them to you.

William Zinsser

JURY DUTY

William Zinsser was born in 1922 in New York City and has written much about life there in numerous articles and books. He attended Princeton University, and later was a feature writer, film critic, and drama editor for the *New York Herald Tribune* and a columnist for *Look* and *Life*. Zinsser taught at Yale University from 1971 to 1979. His books include *Pop Goes America* (1966) and *On Writing Well* (1976).

Jury duty again. I'm sitting in the "central jurors' room" of a courthouse in lower Manhattan, as I do every two years, waiting to be called for a jury, which I almost never am. It's an experience that all of us have known, in one form or another, as long as we can remember: organized solitude.

The chair that I sit in is a little island of apartness. I sit there alone, day after day, and I go out to lunch alone, a stranger in my own city. Strictly, of course, I'm not by myself. Several hundred other men and women sit on every side, as closely as in a movie theater, also waiting to be called for a jury, which they almost never are. Sometimes we break briefly into each other's lives, when we get up to stretch, offering fragments of talk to fill the emptiness. But in the end each of us is alone, withdrawn into our newspapers and our crossword puzzles and our sacred urban privacy.

The room intimidates us. It is a dreary place, done in   3
thirties Bureaucratic, too dull to sustain more than a few minutes of mental effort. On the subconscious level, how-ever, it exerts a strong and uncanny hold. It is the universal waiting room. It is the induction center and the clinic; it is the assembly hall and the office where forms are filled out. Thoughts come unbidden there, sneaking back from all the other moments—in the army, at camp, on the first day of school—when we were part of a crowd and therefore lonely.

The mere taking of roll call by a jury clerk will summon   4
back the countless times when we have waited for our name to be yelled out—loud and just a little wrong. Like every person whose job is to read names aloud, the jury clerk can't read names aloud. Their shapes mystify him. They are odd and implausible names, as diverse as the countries that they came from, but surely the clerk has met them all before. *Hasn't* he? Isn't that what democracy—and the jury sys-tem—is all about? Evidently not.

We are shy enough, as we wait for our name, without   5
the extra burden of wondering what form it will take. By now we know most of the variants that have been imposed on it by other clerks in other rooms like this, and we are ready to answer to any of them, or to some still different version. Actually we don't want to hear our name called at all in this vast public chamber. It is so private, so vulnerable. And yet we don't want to *not* hear it, for only then are we reassured of our identity, really certain that we are known, wanted, and in the right place. Dawn over Camp Upton, 1943: Weinberg, Wyzanski, Yanopoulos, Zapata, Zeccola, Zinsser . . .

I don't begin my jury day in such a retrospective state.   6
I start with high purpose and only gradually slide into men-tal disarray. I am punctual, even early, and so is everybody

else. We are a conscientious lot—partly because we are so surrounded by the trappings of justice, but mainly because that is what we are there to be. I've never seen such conscientious-looking people. Observing them, I'm glad that American law rests on being judged by our peers. In fact, I'd almost rather be judged by my peers than judged by a judge.

Most of us start the day by reading. Jury duty is America's gift to her citizens of a chance to catch up on "good" books, and I always bring *War and Peace*. I remember to bring it every morning and I keep it handy on my lap. The only thing I don't do is read it. There's something about the room . . . the air is heavy with imminent roll calls, too heavy for tackling a novel that will require strict attention. Besides, it's important to read the newspaper first: sharpen up the old noggin on issues of the day. I'm just settling into my paper when the clerk comes in, around ten-twenty-five, and calls the roll ("Zissner?" "Here!"). Suddenly it is 1944 and I am at an army base near Algiers, hammering tin to make a hot shower for Colonel McCloskey. That sort of thing can shoot the whole morning.

If it doesn't, the newspaper will. Only a waiting juror knows how infinite the crannies of journalism can be. I read "Arrival of Buyers," though I don't know what they want to buy and have nothing to sell. I read "Soybean Futures," though I wouldn't know a soybean even in the present. I read classified ads for jobs that I didn't know were jobs, like "key-punch operators." What keys do they punch? I mentally buy 4bdrm 1½bth splt lvl homes w/fpl overlooking Long Island Sound and dream of taking ½ bath there. I read dog news and horoscopes ("bucking others could prove dangerous today") and medical columns on diseases I've never heard of, but whose symptoms I instantly feel.

It's an exhausting trip, and I emerge with eyes blurry and mind blank. I look around at my fellow jurors. Some of them are trying to work—to keep pace, pitifully, with the jobs that they left in order to come here and do nothing. They spread queer documents on their knees, full of graphs

7

8

9

and figures, and they scribble on yellow pads. But the papers don't seem quite real to them, or quite right, removed from the tidy world of filing cabinets and secretaries, and after a while the workers put the work away again.

Around twelve-forty-five the clerk comes in to make an announcement. We stir to attention: we are needed! "Go to lunch," he says. "Be back at two." We straggle out. By now the faces of all my fellow jurors are familiar (we've been here eight days), and I keep seeing them as we poke around the narrow streets of Chinatown looking for a restaurant that isn't the one where we ate yesterday. I smile tentatively, as New Yorkers do, and they smile tentatively back, and we go our separate ways. By one-fifty-five we are seated in the jurors' room again, drowsy with Chinese food and American boredom—too drowsy, certainly, to start *War and Peace*. Luckily, we all bought the afternoon paper while we were out. Talk about remote crannies of journalism!

Perhaps we are too hesitant to talk to each other, to invite ourselves into lives that would refresh us by being different from our own. We are scrupulous about privacy—it is one of the better gifts that the city can bestow, and we don't want to spoil it for somebody else. Yet within almost every New Yorker who thinks he wants to be left alone is a person desperate for human contact. Thus we may be as guilty as the jury system of not putting our time to good use.

What we want to do most, of course, is serve on a jury. We believe in the system. Besides, was there ever so outstanding a group of jurors as we, so intelligent and fairminded? The clerks have told us all the reasons why jurors are called in such wasteful numbers: court schedules are unpredictable; trials end unexpectedly; cases are settled at the very moment when a jury is called; prisoners plead guilty to a lesser charge rather than wait years for a trial that might prove them innocent. All this we know, and in theory it makes sense.

In practice, however, somebody's arithmetic is wrong, and one of America's richest assets is being dribbled away.

There must be a better way to get through the long and tragic list of cases awaiting a solution—and, incidentally, to get through *War and Peace.*

Comment

Zinsser's opening paragraph illustrates important kinds of sentence emphasis. A brief phrase, *Jury duty again,* serves as the opening topic sentence, contrasting with the longer sentences that follow. The first of these adds qualifying clauses and a qualifying phrase to the opening main clause:

> I'm sitting in the "central jurors' room" of a courthouse in lower Manhattan, as I do every two years, waiting to be called for a jury, which I almost never am.

The second sentence—the concluding sentence of the paragraph—uses basically the same structure, but with an important difference:

> It's an experience that all of us have known, in one form or another, as long as we can remember: organized solitude.

A complement to the opening main clause of the sentence, the concluding phrase, *organized solitude,* gains emphasis at the end of the sentence. In many of his sentences Zinsser takes advantage of terminal emphasis. But he uses this effect sparingly. His sentences have the ring of spoken sentences, depending on coordination and occasionally italics to convey vocal inflection:

> They are odd and implausible names, as diverse as the countries that they came from, but surely the clerk has met them all before. *Hasn't* he? Isn't that what democracy—and the jury system—is all about?

Questions for Study and Discussion

1. Which sentences in paragraph 5 are coordinate only? How many sentences consist of one introductory main clause, and one or more subordinate clauses? Do any of the sentences join subordinate to coordinate clauses?
2. Paragraph 6 contains a series of short emphatic opening sen-

tences. Does Zinsser maintain this kind of emphasis in the rest of the paragraph?

3. How different is paragraph 7 from paragraph 6 in sentence construction? What use does Zinsser make of ellipsis? How much emphasis (through pitch and volume) should the parenthetical statements be given?

4. How much subordination do you find in paragraph 8? How many sentences are built through modification?

5. How does Zinsser establish a point of view and a dominant tone? Or do you find changes in tone throughout the essay?

6. Why would Zinsser "almost rather be judged by [his] peers than judged by a judge"?

Vocabulary Study

Write a sentence using each of the following pairs of words, and explain the difference between them. The first word in each pair is Zinsser's:

a. *fragments* (paragraph 2), *parts*
b. *intimidates* (paragraph 3), *threatens*
c. *bureaucratic* (paragraph 3), *governmental*
d. *uncanny* (paragraph 3), *strange*
e. *implausible* (paragraph 4), *unconvincing*
f. *vulnerable* (paragraph 5), *weak*
g. *scrupulous* (paragraph 11), *careful*
h. *bestow* (paragraph 11), *give*

Suggestions for Writing

1. Describe a waiting room and your feelings in it. Make your details specific, and use your description to make a comment about your general situation. Develop several of your sentences with modification, as Zinsser does. Where you can, combine coordinate clauses with subordinate phrases and clauses.

2. Analyze two of the final paragraphs of Zinsser's essay, showing how coordination and subordination are used to give emphasis to particular ideas.

Michael J. Arlen

"RING AROUND THE COLLAR!"

A television critic and essayist, Michael J. Arlen wrote for *Life* magazine
from 1952 to 1956. He began writing a column about television for *The
New Yorker* magazine in 1957. Arlen's books include *The Living Room
War* (1969), *Exiles* (1970), *Passage to Ararat* (1975), *The View from
Highway 1* (1976), and *Say Goodbye to Sam* (1984). In 1976 he
received the National Book Award for Contemporary Affairs. The essay
reprinted here is typical of the keen observation and humor that mark
his writing.

This half-minute commercial for a laundry detergent   1
called Wisk appears fairly frequently on daytime and evening television. In a recent version, a young woman and a
young man are shown being led down the corridor of a hotel by a bellman who is carrying suitcases. The hotel seems
to be an attractive one—not very elegant but definitely not
an ordinary motel. Similarly, the young man and woman are
attractive, but with nothing either glamorous or working-
class about their appearance. Perhaps he is a junior executive. And she is probably his wife, though there is nothing
so far that says that the two people are married. Since the
framework of the drama is a commercial, the assumption is
that they *are* married. On the other hand, against the familiar framework of similar modern movie scenes, there is no
such assumption; possibly it is the beginning of an adventure. Then, suddenly, the bellman drops one of the suitcases
in the corridor; some of the contents of the suitcase spill
out; the bellman crouches down on the corridor carpet to
put the items back in. He notices one of the man's shirts
and holds it up. "Ring around the collar!" he says accus-
ingly; these words are then taken up in the kind of sing-
song chant that has become a feature of these ads. The man
looks puzzled and let down. The woman examines the of-
fending shirt and looks mortified and aghast. By now, whatever slight elegance or intimations of adventure may have

existed at the beginning of the scene have totally disinte-
grated, and, indeed, have quickly reformed themselves into
the classic hubby-and-housewife focus of most television
commercials. The wife admits her mistake—to the bellman
and her husband—of having used an inadequate detergent,
and the scene changes to what is apparently the laundry area
of her house, where the wife (now back in her regular
"wifely" clothes) discusses the merits of using Wisk when
doing the family wash.

In a number of ways, this is the most noticeably irritat- 2
ing of the housewife commercials. There is a nagging, whiny
quality to the "Ring around the collar!" chant which is almost a caricature of the nagging, whiny voices of earlier
Hollywood and TV-commercial housewives but which deliberately stops before the point of caricature is reached. In
the manner of certain other ads—especially those for aspirin
and "cold remedies"—it is a commercial that expressly announces its own irritatingness. We are going to repeat and
repeat and repeat, these commercials say, and we are going
to grate on your nerves—and you are going to remember us.
At times, this sales approach has been given various fine
sounding methodological names by advertisers, but essentially it is the voice of the small boy who wants something:
I want, I want, I want, I want—and finally you give it to
him. In this case, the small boy wants you to buy his detergent, and who is to tell him no?

On the level of anti-female condescension, the "Ring 3
around the collar!" ad seems to go even beyond irritation.
In most housewife commercials, the housewife is portrayed
as little more than a simpering, brainless jelly, almost pathologically obsessed with the world of kitchen floors or laundry, or of the celebrated "bathroom bowl." But in the Wisk
commercials the standard trivializing portrait is accompanied by quite unusual brutality. As if in a reverse Cinderella
process, the young prince and his companion not only are
stopped in their tracks by the hazard of the Dirty Shirt (and
the curse cry of "Ring around the collar!") but, instantly, as
if under a magic spell, are snatched from the hotel-palace

and returned to their previous existence—she to profess folk-happiness among the laundry tubs, and he, presumably, to his northern New England sales route. Sex is back to what it used to be: the identityless woman in the traveling suit is replaced by the beaming housewife in housewifely attire. And it is all the result of *her* failure in not having properly attended to her husband's needs—in having exposed him to the scorn of the bellman who guarded the erotic corridor. The fable does not end in tragedy—for though Cinderella is back among the laundry tubs, she now has good magic on her side. But it has been a sobering experience.

Comment

As in Zinsser, in Arlen we hear someone talking to us. The sentences are close to the rhythms of spoken English, with emphasis indicated by italics to suggest the spoken idiom:

> Since the framework of the drama is a commercial, the assumption is that they *are* married.

Arlen might have written the following:

> Perhaps he is a junior executive, and she is probably his wife, though there is nothing so far that says that the two people are married.

In fact, he breaks the sentence to give particular emphasis to the second main clause:

> Perhaps he is a junior executive. And she is probably his wife. . . .

Arlen uses other means to gain emphasis. The colon in the following sentence focuses our attention on the series that follows. The concluding dash marks an emphatic break in idea and shows its importance:

> At times, this sales approach has been given various fine-sounding methodological names by advertisers, but essentially it is the voice of the small boy who wants something: I want, I want, I want, I want—and finally you give it to him.

Notice how careful Arlen is to give enough details of the advertisement so that the reader who has not seen it will understand his point. The presentation is economical and clearly focused.

Questions for Study and Discussion

1. What examples do you find in paragraph 3 of the kinds of emphasis just discussed?
2. How many formal transitions are there in paragraph 1? What transitional ideas do these express?
3. How soon in the essay do you discover the purpose of the description? Would you consider the essay more effective if Arlen had stated his purpose at the start?
4. What attitudes toward women and marriage is Arlen criticizing? Does he state all of these attitudes directly?
5. Do you agree with his interpretation of the commercial?

Vocabulary Study

Give the dictionary meaning of the following words and be ready to explain how each is used in the essay: *assumption, mortified, aghast, elegance, classic* (paragraph 1); *caricature, methodological* (paragraph 2); *condescension, pathologically, obsessed, trivializing, attire, erotic* (paragraph 3).

Sentence Study

1. Recast the following sentences to give terminal emphasis to the italicized words. Change the phrasing and punctuation as necessary:
   a. "*The hotel seems to be an attractive one*—not very elegant but definitely not an ordinary motel."
   b. "In the manner of certain other ads—*especially those for aspirin and "cold remedies"*—it is a commercial that expressly announces its own irritatingness."
   c. "*On the level of anti-female condescension,* the 'Ring around the collar' ad seems to go even beyond irritation."
   d. "*Sex is back to what it used to be:* the identityless woman

in the traveling suit is replaced by the beaming housewife in housewifely attire."

2. The following simple sentences are adapted from the originals in George Orwell's *The Road to Wigan Pier*. Combine each group into a single sentence, subordinating where possible, and using semicolons or colons only when necessary:

   a. Miners are changed from one shift to another. Their families have to make adjustments to these changes. These adjustments are tiresome in the extreme.

   b. If he is on the night shift he gets home in time for breakfast. He gets home in the middle of the afternoon on the morning shift. On the afternoon shift he gets home in the middle of the night. In each case, of course, he wants his principal meal of the day as soon as he returns.

   c. The rate of accidents among miners is high. It is high compared with that in other trades. Accidents are so high that they are taken for granted almost as they would be in a minor war.

   d. The most obviously understandable cause of accidents is explosions of gas. This cause is always more or less present in the atmosphere of the pit.

   e. The gas may be touched off by a spark during blasting operations. It may be touched off by a pick striking a spark from a stone. It may be touched off by a defective lamp. And it may be touched off by "gob fires." These are spontaneously generated fires which smolder in the coal dust and are very hard to put out.

Suggestions for Writing

1. Discuss what attitudes toward women you find in other commercials for a detergent or another product. You may discover a variety of attitudes—even conflicting ones. Distinguish them, illustrating one or two of them through a careful choice of detail, and draw a conclusion from your analysis.

2. Analyze an ad or commercial for the image it conveys of men or children. Support your analysis through a careful choice of detail, and draw a conclusion from it.

3. Arlen suggests that the *Wisk* commercial appeals to a sense of guilt or shame in the housewife. Analyze the appeals you find in other detergent commercials or those of another product.

Parallelism

Words, phrases, and clauses that are similar in structure and perform the same function in a sentence are said to be *parallel:*

> I have never seen a *maladroit, clumsy,* or *blundering* cat [parallel words].—Lewis Thomas, "To Err Is Human"

> Everyone says, stay away from ants. They have no lessons for us; they are crazy little instruments, *inhuman, incapable of controlling themselves, lacking manners, lacking souls* [parallel words and phrases].—Lewis Thomas, "The Tucson Zoo"

Sentences in a paragraph may be parallel in structure—in whole or in part:

> Science is undeniably hard. *Often, it can seem* quite boring. *It is unfortunately too often presented* as laws to be memorized instead of mysteries to be explored. *It is too often kept a secret* that science, like art, takes a well developed esthetic sense. —K. C. Cole, "Women and Physics"

Parallelism makes the reader aware of the similarity in ideas. If the ideas are not similar, the parallelism may seem awkward. Writers in the past sometimes made parts of sentences exactly parallel, using almost the same number of words in phrases and clauses. This kind of sentence sometimes occurs today in formal speeches, or addresses, like the following:

> Do not let us speak of darker days; let us rather speak of sterner days. These are not dark days: these are great days—the greatest days our country has ever lived. . . .—Winston S. Churchill, an address delivered on October 29, 1941

Modern writers favor a looser parallelism and may vary the length of parallel elements and vary the wording, to avoid a formal effect:

> He watched Martin slip the lens into his pocket, he sighed, he struggled for something else to say, and silently he lumbered into his bedroom.—Sinclair Lewis, *Arrowsmith*

> But if you cleaned the East River you could have ponds all over town, up and down the East Side of Manhattan anyway. If you lifted out the Empire State Building and the high structures nearby, you would have, instantly, an inland sea. A few holes bored in the right places would let water into the subways, and you'd have lovely underground canals all across the Hudson, uptown to the Harlem River, downtown to the Battery, a Venice underground, without pigeons.—Lewis Thomas, "Ponds"

Rachel Carson

SUMMER'S END

Rachel Carson (1907–1964) is one of the great writers on nature. In her books *Under the Sea-Wind* (1941), *The Sea Around Us,* which received the National Book Award in 1951, and *The Edge of the Sea* (1955), she drew upon her experiences as an aquatic biologist at the Marine Biological Laboratory at Woods Hole, Massachusetts and, from 1936 to 1952, with the United States Fish and Wildlife Service. She is perhaps best known for her book *Silent Spring* (1962), which warned of the dangers of pesticides to the environment. The National Council of Women in the United States gave Carson its first "Woman of Conscience" citation in 1963. The section reprinted here from *Under the Sea-Wind* describes an island on the southeastern coast of the United States. Carson tells us that Ship's Shoal is a "point of land . . . where the sea had broken through the barrier island to the sound years before." Mullet Pond is "half encircled by marsh, between the eastern end of the dunes and the inlet beach."

It was September before the sanderlings, now in whitening plumage, ran again on the island beach or hunted Hippa crabs in the ebbing tide at the point of land called Ship's Shoal. Their flight from the northern tundras had been   1

broken by many feeding stops on the wide mud flats of
Hudson Bay and James Bay and on the ocean beaches from
New England southward. In their fall migration the birds
were unhurried, the racial urge that drove them northward
in the spring having been satisfied. As the winds and the sun
dictated, they drifted southward, their flocks now growing
as more birds from the north joined them, now dwindling
as more and more of the migrants found their customary
winter home and dropped behind. Only the fringe of the
great southward wave of shore birds would push on and on
to the southernmost part of South America.

As the cries of the returning shore birds rose once more   2
from the frothy edge of the surf and the whistle of the cur-
lews sounded again in the salt marshes, there were other
signs of the summer's end. By September the eels of the sound
country had begun to drop downstream to the sea. The eels
came down from the hills and the upland grasslands. They
came from cypress swamps where black-watered rivers had
their beginnings; they moved across the tidal plain that
dropped in six giant steps to the sea. In the river estuaries
and in the sounds they joined their mates-to-be. Soon, in
silvery wedding dress, they would follow the ebbing tides to
the sea, to find—and lose—themselves in the black abysses
of mid-ocean.

By September, the young shad, come from the eggs shed   3
in river and stream by the spawning runs of spring, were
moving with the river water to the sea. At first they moved
slowly in the vaster currents as the sluggish rivers broadened
toward their estuaries. Soon, however, the speed of the little
fish, no longer than a man's finger, would quicken, when
the fall rains came and the wind changed, chilling the water
and driving the fish to the warmer sea.

By September the last of the season's hatch of young   4
shrimp were coming into the sounds through the inlets from
the open sea. The coming of the young was symbolic of another journey which no man had seen and no man could
describe—a journey taken weeks before by the elder generation of shrimp. All through the spring and summer more
and more of the grown shrimp, come to maturity at the age

of a year, had been slipping away from the coastal waters, journeying out across the continental shelf, descending the blue slopes of undersea valleys. From this journey they never returned, but their young, after several weeks of ocean life, were brought by the sea into the protected inside waters. All through the summer and fall the baby shrimp were brought into the sounds and river mouths—seeking warm shallows where brackish water lay over muddy bottoms. Here they fed eagerly on the abundant food and found shelter from hungry fish in the carpeting eel grass. And as they grew rapidly, the young turned once more to the sea, seeking its bitter waters and its deeper rhythms. Even as the youngest shrimp from the last spawning of the season came through the inlets on each flood tide of September, the larger young were moving out through the sounds to the sea.

By September the panicles of the sea oats in the dunes ⁵ had turned a golden brown. As the marshes lay under the sun, they glowed with the soft greens and browns of the salt meadow grass, the warm purples of the rushes, and the scarlet of the marsh samphire. Already the gum trees were like red flares set in the swamps of the river banks. The tang of autumn was in the night air, and as it rolled over the warmer marshes it turned to mist, hiding the herons who stood among the grasses at dawn; hiding from the eyes of the hawks the meadow mice who ran along the paths they had made through the marshes by the patient felling of thousands of marsh-grass stems; hiding the schools of silversides in the sound from the terns who fluttered above the rolling white sea, and caught no fish until the sun had cleared away the mists.

The chill night air brought a restlessness to many fish ⁶ scattered widely throughout the sound. They were steely gray fish with large scales and a low, four-spined fin set on the back like a spread sail. The fish were mullet who had lived throughout the summer in the sound and estuary, roving solitary among the eel grass and widgeon grass, feeding on the litter of animal and vegetable fragments of the bottom mud. But every fall the mullet left the sounds and made a far sea journey, in the course of which they brought forth the next generation. And so the first chill of fall stirred in the fish the feeling of the sea's rhythm and awakened the instinct of migration.

The chilling waters and the tidal cycles of the summer's end brought to many of the young fish of the sound country, also, a summons to return to the sea. Among these were the young pompano and mullet, silversides and killifish, who lived in the pond called Mullet Pond, where the dunes of the barrier island fell away to the flat sands of the Ship's Shoal. These young fish had been spawned in the sea, but had found their way to the pond through a temporary cut earlier that year.

On a day when the full harvest moon sailed like a white balloon in the sky, the tides, which had grown in strength as the moon swelled to roundness, began to wash out a gully across the inlet beach. Only on the highest tides did the torpid pond receive water from the ocean. Now the beat of the waves and the strong backwash that sucked away the loose sand had found the weak place in the beach, where a cut had been made before, and in less time than it took a fishing launch to cross from the mainland docks to the banks a narrow gully or slough had been cut through to the pond. Not more than a dozen feet across, it made a bottleneck into which the surf rolled as the waves broke on the beach. The water surged and seethed as in a mill race, hissing and foaming. Wave after wave poured through the slough and into the pond. They dug out an uneven, corrugated bottom over which the water leaped and tobogganed. They spread out into the marshes that backed the pond, seeping silently and stealthily among the grass stems and the reddening stalks of the marsh samphire. Into the marshes they carried the frothy brown scud thrown off by the waves. The sandy foam filled the spaces between the grass stalks so closely that the marsh looked like a beach thickly grown with short grass; in reality the grass stood a foot in water and only the upper third of the stalks showed above the froth.

Leaping and racing, foaming and swirling, the incoming flood brought release to the myriads of small fishes that had been imprisoned in the pond. Now in thousands they poured out of the pond and out of the marshes. They raced in mad confusion to meet the clean, cold water. In their excitement they let the flood take them, toss them, turn them over and over. Reaching mid-channel of the slough they leaped high in the air again and again, sparkling bits of animate silver, like a swarm of glittering insects that rose and fell, rose again and fell. There the water seized them and held them back in their wild dash to the sea, so that many of them were caught on the slopes of the waves and held, tails uppermost, struggling helplessly against the might of the water. When finally the waves released them they raced down the slough to the ocean, where they knew once more the rolling breakers, the clean sandy bottoms, the cool green waters.

How did the pond and the marshes hold them all? On 10 they came, in school after school, flashing bright among the marsh grasses, leaping and bounding out of the pond. For more than an hour the exodus continued, with scarcely a break in the hurrying schools. Perhaps they had come in, many of them, on the last spring tide when the moon was a pencil stroke of silver in the sky. And now the moon had grown fat and round and another spring tide, a rollicking, roistering, rough-and-ready tide, called them back to the sea again.

On they went, passing through the surf line where the 11 white-capped waves were tumbling. On they went, most of them, past the smoother green swells to the second line of surf, where shoals tripped the waves coming in from the open sea and sent them sprawling in white confusion. But there were terns fishing above the surf, and thousands of the small migrants went no farther than the portals of the sea.

Comment

Carson uses parallelism to highlight similar as well as contrasting actions, as in the following sentence from paragraph 1:

> As the winds and the sun dictated, they drifted southward, their flocks *now growing as more birds from the north joined them,*

> *now dwindling as more and more of the migrants found their*
> *customary winter home and dropped behind.* Only the fringe of
> the great southward wave of shore birds *would push on and on*
> to the southernmost part of South America. [italics added]

The parallel construction of the italicized participial phrases in the
first sentence highlights the contrasting growth of the flocks of
birds and their dwindling. The phrase *would push on and on* in
the second sentence emphasizes the contrast with the birds who
dropped from the migration. The parallelism of the following sentence from paragraph 5 allows Carson to combine a large number
of contrasting actions and descriptive details without confusion or
a loss of focus:

> The tang of autumn was in the night air, and as it rolled over
> the warmer marshes it turned to mist, *hiding the herons who*
> *stood among the grasses at dawn; hiding from the eyes of the*
> *hawks the meadow mice who ran along the paths they had made*
> *through the marshes by the patient felling of thousands of marsh-*
> *grass stems; hiding the schools of silversides in the sound from*
> *the terns who fluttered above the rolling white sea, and caught*
> *no fish until the sun had cleared away the mists.* [italics added]

Occasionally Carson makes these elements similar in length as well
as construction and wording:

> The water surged and seethed as in a mill race, hissing and
> foaming. [paragraph 8]

This balancing of sentence elements helps to convey the rhythms
of nature that Carson wishes the reader to experience.

Questions for Study and Discussion

1. What in the behavior of the sanderlings, eel, shad, and other
   fish marks summer's end?
2. In what way is the coming of the young shrimp "symbolic of
   another journey"?
3. What changes in the weather and in the flora or vegetation of
   the island does Carson describe, and for what purpose?
4. What natural process is Carson describing in paragraphs 8, 9,
   and 10? Is she making a point about this process?

5. What sentences in paragraph 8 are approximately parallel in structure? What sentences in paragraph 9 are parallel? What similar ideas does this parallelism highlight?
6. What use does Carson make of parallelism in the first two sentences of paragraph 11?
7. Carson describes various changes in island life. Is her purpose merely to show these changes, or does she use them to make a general point? If so, does she state the point or idea implicitly through her details?

Vocabulary Study

1. Do the dictionary definitions of *heron, killifish, mullet, sanderling, shad,* and *silverside* add to your understanding of the essay? How much of the information given by the dictionary does Carson provide about each? Need she have provided the same information?
2. Use your dictionary to explain the following: *tundra* (paragraph 1); *sound, estuary* (paragraph 2); *spawning runs* (paragraph 3); *brackish* (paragraph 4); *panicles, samphire* (paragraph 5); *torpid, slough, mill race, scud* (paragraph 8); *roistering* (paragraph 10).

Sentence Study

Identify the parallel elements in the following sentences. What does the parallelism contribute to the clarity or effect of the sentence?

a. As the marshes lay under the sun, they glowed with the soft greens and browns of the salt meadow grass, the warm purples of the rushes, and the scarlet of the marsh samphire. (paragraph 5)
b. The fish were mullet who had lived throughout the summer in the sound and estuary, roving solitary among the eel grass and widgeon grass, feeding on the litter of animal and vegetable fragments of the bottom mud. (paragraph 6)
c. These young fish had been spawned in the sea, but had found their way to the pond through a temporary cut earlier that year. (paragraph 7)
d. On they went, most of them, past the smoother green swells to the second line of surf, where shoals tripped the waves

coming in from the open sea and sent them sprawling in white confusion. (paragraph 11)

Suggestions for Writing

1. Describe a seasonal change in plant life and wild life you have observed in your town or city or a place you have visited. Organize your description to make a point. Let your reader discover the point or idea through the details of your description.
2. Describe changes in everyday life that occur in your neighborhood during a change of weather or change of season. Let your details make a point—perhaps a point about the people of your neighborhood or town.

Sentence Variety

Sentences need to be varied to avoid a sense of monotony. Thus, a series of short simple sentences like the following will soon lose the reader's attention:

> You are watching coal miners at work. You realize momentarily what different universes people inhabit. It is a sort of world apart down there. One can quite easily go through life without ever hearing about that world. Probably a majority of people would even prefer not to hear about it.

Few people think or write in such an disconnected way. Here is the actual version of the sentences above:

> Watching coal miners at work, you realize momentarily what different universes different people inhabit. *Down there* where coal is dug it is a sort of world apart *which* one can quite easily go through life without ever hearing about. Probably a majority of people would even prefer not to hear about it.—George Orwell, *The Road to Wigan Pier* (italics added)

Orwell varied his sentences probably as most writers do—without much conscious attention. The italicized connectives come naturally to us as we speak or write: it is the disconnection in the first version of the passage that is unnatural. Indeed, it takes some effort to write in so fragmented and disjointed a way. The rewritten sentences are not only monotonous but hard to understand because we must continually refocus our attention.

As a rule, the more varied the length and construction of our sentences, the less monotonous they are likely to be, and the more apparent the natural emphasis we wish to give our ideas. Notice the choices open to the writer in combining the following:

> You are watching coal miners at work. You realize momentarily what different universes people inhabit.

326

Orwell might have written the following:

> As you watch coal miners at work, you realize momentarily what
> different universes people inhabit.

> You realize momentarily what different universes people inhabit,
> as you watch coal miners at work.

> Watching coal miners at work makes one realize momentarily
> what different universes people inhabit.

These varied sentences achieve emphasis in different ways. In the
first, the emphasis falls on the idea of different universes; in the
second, on watching the miners at work. The third sentence gives
the same emphasis to both ideas. Which sentence the writer chooses
depends on what is emphasized in the whole paragraph or essay.
As Orwell's paragraph shows, the choice can depend on making
the connection of ideas clear.

Russell Baker

THE BEER CULTURE

Russell Baker was born in 1925 in Loudon County, in northern
Virginia, and was raised in a Blue Ridge mountain community and later
in Newark, New Jersey, and Baltimore, Maryland—very different worlds
described in his autobiography *Growing Up* (1982). Upon graduating
from Johns Hopkins University in 1947, Baker began reporting for the
Baltimore Sun. From 1954 to 1962 he reported on Washington and
national politics for the *New York Times.* Since 1963 he has written a
column for the *Times.* His many columns on national politics and
American life—many of them humorous—have been collected in *This Is
Depravity* (1980) and other books. In 1979 Baker received the Pulitzer
Prize for Distinguished Commentary, and the Pulitzer Prize for
Biography in 1983 for *Growing Up.*

The people of Beer World are named Buck, Mike, Al   1
and Mac. There are no Algernons in Beer World, no Mar-
madukes, no Gaylords. Beer World has hair on its chest.

Yes, there are a few women in Beer World. They are   2
named Gladys, though there is one named Elvira. You have

seen the woman who brings a tray of beer to Buck, Mike, Al and Mac while they are sitting in the beer parlor in their mackinaws being rugged and jolly? Of course you have seen her. That woman is Gladys.

You may also have seen Buck recently having his beer at a distinctly sissified ski lodge in company with a lissome young woman. That woman is Elvira. Buck sometimes takes Elvira to these sissy places in order to experience the perfection of beer without sweating.

Buck often feels guilty after these perspiration-free outings with Elvira, for in Beer World it is man's duty to heave and grunt until his pores open and let the honest body juices cascade freely. Only then does he truly deserve beer. Beer is the reward for manly toil in Beer World.

How often have you seen Buck, Mike, Al and Mac exhausted at the end of an honest day's work on the firing squad, sleeves rolled up, shirt collars opened, perspiration dampening their cheeks as they labor to rid the world of malcontents, looters and sissies—how often have you seen them joyfully throw down their tools as the sun sets, embrace each other merrily and tramp over to Gladys's place for their beer?

Now comes beer time. The beer has been created for Buck, Mike, Al and Mac in recognition of their labor, in recognition of all they do. The beer is for them. Not for Algernon. Not for Marmaduke and Gaylord. Someone will object that we never really see the boys putting in a full day's work on the firing squad, that all we ever see are the final few executions at sunset. But of course; in Beer World, sunset is the only time of day. The sun stands eternally in the setting position. Shortly after Buck, Mike, Al and Mac throw down their rifles, or their scythes or their big tractor-trailers, and receive their beer from Gladys, they tramp out into the sunset again and finish building a skyscraper so they can throw down their rivet guns and march back to Gladys's place for another round of well-earned beer.

Why does Buck occasionally sneak away to sissified places with Elvira to drink his beer in dry clothing? Surely

Buck would rather be with Mike, Al and Mac arriving at Beer World's cottage by the lake in their plaid fishing shirts.

Of course, Buck would. It is much more fun racing to the refrigerator with Mike, Al and Mac and discovering four bottles of chilled beer than it is sitting across a table from Elvira. Is Buck—let us phrase the question as delicately as possible—is Buck soft on women?   8

The question is often raised by Mike, Al and Mac when they are all having dinner together in order to deserve a beer, or jogging twenty miles together just at sunset in order to earn the right really to enjoy a beer. Once they even asked Doc—Beer World's psychiatrist—to put Buck on the couch, give him a bottle of beer and find out if he was really one of the boys.   9

Doc had just finished whipping a massive superego down to size and was headed to Gladys's place for his beer when he conducted the examination. He pronounced Buck a perfectly normal beer guy with a slight woman problem.   10

It seems Buck had a mother, which is very rare in Beer World. In his youth, "Old Moms," as Buck called her, used to send him to the corner saloon to buy her what she called "a bucket of suds." "Old Moms" had since been deported under Beer World's rigid legal code, which denies citizenship to most women, especially if, like "Old Moms," they sit around the house in dresses made from flour sacks drinking beer out of tin buckets.   11

The law was necessary because people like "Old Moms" created a bad image of Beer World, which wanted to be viewed as a sweaty but clean-cut place full of boys whose beer had fewer calories and whose mothers, if they must have mothers, wouldn't be caught dead wearing flour sacks. In short, Buck felt bad about the old lady's deportation; when he took Elvira out for beer, he was really taking out his mother who had learned to dress expensively and to drink her beer out of a glass.   12

Elvira actually despises beer and would much prefer a drink with Amaretto in it, but doesn't dare order it for fear Buck would accuse her of not being one of the boys and   13 walk out of her life forever. The women of Beer World do not have much opportunity to get out for a good time. Elvira has often asked Gladys to go out and have some Amaretto with her, but Gladys is afraid that if the boys learned about it they would call her a sissy.

Comment

Baker satirizes not just the characters and situations in beer ads but also, in the phrase of Walker Gibson, their "tough talk." Gibson characterizes tough talk through its "short sentences, 'crude' repetitions of words, simple grammatical structures with little subordinating." Seeking a "tense intimacy with his assumed reader, another man who has been around," the tough talker favors "colloquial patterns from oral speech and . . . a high frequency of the definite article. He lets his reader make logical and other connections between elements" (*Tough, Sweet, and Stuffy*). Tough talk is marked by the monotony of its sentences—the lack of variety that Baker is imitating.

Questions for Study and Discussion

1. The essay opens with three short simple sentences—all lacking modification. These illustrate one of the characteristics of Gibson's "tough talk." What other paragraphs also contain relatively simple or short sentences, compound or complex sentences?

2. How much " 'crude' repetition of words" do you find throughout the essay?

3. How often does Baker depend on "colloquial patterns from oral speech" and a "high frequency of the definite article"?

4. In imitating the tough talker through the style of the essay, Baker is characterizing the tough-talking advertiser. What does he gain satirically in imitating the speech of this person?

5. What does the essay reveal about Baker's personality, outlook, and sense of humor?

6. What satirical points is Baker making not only about beer ads but also about the "beer culture"? Is the essay closer to social satire than to ethical satire (p. 463)?

7. How effective do you find the satire?

Vocabulary Study

Baker depends on connotation—the associations and emotional auras of words—to convey the tone and attitudes about the beer culture. What do the following words mean? What connotations do they convey?

a. paragraph 3: *lissome*
b. paragraph 4: *cascade*
c. paragraph 5: *malcontents, sissies*
d. paragraph 10: *massive superego, slight woman problem*
e. paragraph 13: *Amaretto*

Suggestions for Writing

1. Compare Baker's treatment of beer ads with Michael J. Arlen's treatment of soap ads. Comment on the language and the tone of each essay and the presentation of a thesis.
2. Write a satirical essay on another series of ads depicting a different kind of world—perhaps the world of soda-drinking teenagers. Let your descriptive details and tone convey your thesis.

Concreteness

To make an idea *concrete* is to make it exist for the reader through the senses. The statement "That car's a beauty!" expresses a general attitude and feeling but nothing more. If we want people to share our experience we must give particulars or details, as in this explanation of what California teenagers mean by the expression "low and slow, mean and clean":

> The car a lowrider drives—almost always a sedan produced by the General Motors Corporation—is also called a lowrider, or a ride. If it has been altered with conspicuous success—a multi-colored lacquer paint job, say, and metal-spoke wheels, and skimpy tires that seem to belong on a Datsun rather than a 1967 Chevrolet Impala, and a welded-chain steering wheel no bigger around than a 45-r.p.m. record—it is called a clean ride, or a bad ride. "Low and slow," lowriders sometimes say. "Mean and clean."—Calvin Trillin and Edward Koren, "Low and Slow, Mean and Clean"

Not all abstract ideas can be expressed through physical details. We can, however, show their application to experience or suggest how we came to the idea; or we can give the details that explain it. In a discussion of the emotional makeup of human beings, Desmond Morris says that people enjoy exploring their emotions. Man, he says, "is constantly pushing things to their limit, trying to startle himself, to shock himself without getting hurt, and then signaling his relief with peals of infectious laughter." The abstract idea is here made specific; for we are told what people *do*. But Morris makes the idea even more concrete through the behavior of teenagers when their idols perform on stage. "As an audience, they enjoy themselves, not by screaming with laughter, but screaming with screams. They not only scream, they also grip their own and one another's bodies, they writhe, they moan, they cover their faces and they pull at their hair." From these details he draws a conclusion:

> These are all the classic signs of intense pain or fear, but they have become deliberately stylized. . . . They are no longer cries for help, but signals to one another in the audience that they are capable of feeling an emotional response to the sexual idols which is so powerful that, like all stimuli of unbearably high intensity, they pass into the realm of pure pain.—*The Naked Ape*

The idea has been made concrete. At the same time, we must be careful not to give more details than we need to make the idea clear. Writing can be so colorful—so crowded with details and descriptive words—that the reader is distracted from the main idea.

William G. Wing

CHRISTMAS COMES FIRST ON THE BANKS

William G. Wing was a veteran correspondent of the *New York Herald Tribune.* He is a specialist on natural resources and conservation, writing for *Audubon Magazine,* the *New York Times,* and other periodicals. This evocative essay shows how a popular subject can be written about freshly from a new and unusual point of view.

The Christmas sun rises first, in America, on trawler-men fishing the undersea meadows of Georges Bank.   1

At the moment before sunrise a hundred miles east of Cape Cod, the scene aboard a trawler is so unchanging it can be imagined. The net has been hauled and streamed again. The skipper is alone in the pilot house, surrounded by the radio-telephone's racket and the green and amber eyes of electronic instruments, instruments that are supposed to tell him not only where he is but where the fish are, too. But this is only hope, not science. Despite the instruments, despite the boat's resemblance to a plow horse, methodically criss-crossing the meadow, her men are not engineers or farmers, but hunters who seek their prey in the wilderness   2 of the sea. The trawlermen are, in fact, the last tribe of nomadic huntsmen left in the East.

The skipper is alone, then, with a huntsman's anxieties: 3 the whereabouts of the prey, the uncertainties of the weather, the chances of hitting a good market. On deck before him the men are processing the catch just brought aboard. They sit in a circle of brilliance, the deck lights reflecting from their yellow and Daybrite-orange oilskins and from the brown curve of the riding sail above. They sit on the edges of the pens, holding the big white and silver fish between their knees, ripping with knives and tearing with hands, heaving the disemboweled bodies into a central basket. Nothing is visible beyond the cone of light but the occasional flash of a whitecap or comber. There is much noise, though—wind and water and seabirds that have gathered in mobs for the feast of haulback.

There is an appropriateness to Christmas in this scene, 4 east of the sleeping mainland, so marked that it seems quaint. The names of the trawlers themselves—*Holy Family, Immaculate Conception, St. Mary, St. Joseph*—give the flavor. On the engine room bulkhead of a trawler *Holy Cross*, beyond the ugga-chugging Atlas diesel, is a painting of Christ at Gethsemane. There is an appropriateness, too, among the men. They share alike—equal shares of profit, equal shares of danger. To work together in such small quarters and stern conditions requires a graciousness of spirit that is the essence of Christmas.

The sun is up and the pens are empty. As the deck is 5 hosed down and the trash fish pitchforked overboard, the noise from the birds rises hysterically—barnyard sounds, shrieks, whistles, klaxon horns. Now the birds can be seen flying in a circle around the boat. Each can hold position for only a few moments beside the point where the remains of fish are washing over. Then it falls astern and has to come up to windward on the other side of the boat, cross ahead and fall backward to the critical point. The birds pumping up the windward side look like six-day bicycle riders, earnest and slightly ridiculous, but when they reach the critical point there is a miraculous moment of aerobatics as the birds brake, wheel and drop in the broken air.

Gulls snatch, gannets plunge, but the little kittiwakes 6
balance delicately, their tails spread like carved ivory fans.
There is a column of descending, shrieking birds, a scintil-
lating feathered mass. The birds revolving about the boat
have made themselves not only guests at the feast but have
formed the wreath as well.

Christmas Day has begun, but for the men it is time to 7
sleep. They hose each other off and then disappear through
the whaleback for a mug-up below. Boots and oilskins off,
they will have a minute or two for a James Bond novel or a
crossword puzzle in the bunks, braced against the elevator
motions of the hull, not hearing the sounds of Niagara outside. Then the instant unconsciousness that seamen and children know. The skipper alone remains awake, watching
Christmas come.

Christmas came first to men on lonely meadows. It will 8
come first again to the men on the lonely meadows offshore,
fishing the Bank in boats wreathed by seabirds.

Comment

Wing tells us that he will seek to make the moment before the sun
rises concrete: he will find images that convey the mood and experience of the moment. He does so in the details of the boat, the
trawlermen, their relations—"equal shares of profits, equal shares
of danger." The seabirds have an unexpected appropriateness, for
they wreathe the boats in their circlings. Through careful selection
of details, Wing succeeds in his purpose; through his description,
he is able to make a point without stating it directly.

Questions for Study and Discussion

1. What point is Wing making through his description? Is it important to him where the Christmas sun first rises in America?
2. Is the order of details governed by space (moving from one
   part of the scene to another) or by time, or possibly both?
3. What details make the idea of Christmas in the essay
   concrete?

4. Is Wing saying that the life aboard the trawler and the relations between the men are different during the Christmas season or on Christmas day?
5. How does Wing make transitions throughout the essay?
6. What is the point of the concluding comparison?

Vocabulary Study

For each of the following words, list at least two synonyms that suggest a more specific meaning or use. For example, *forecast* is more specific than *foretell* when referring to a weather prediction.

a. *large*
b. *small*
c. *dirty*
d. *clean*
e. *law*
f. *run*

Suggestions for Writing

1. Describe a scene at a particular moment—for example, the moment of impact in an automobile accident. Select details that contribute to a central impression, but do not state the impression directly.
2. Describe a day of work, showing how the season of the year affects you and your fellow workers. Use your description to develop a thesis.
3. Describe an unusual day in your life—one that perhaps was spent in an unusual setting, away from home. Stress those feelings and details that made the day unusual and memorable.

Carol Bly

GREAT SNOWS

Carol Bly lives in her native Minnesota. She has been a visiting writer and lecturer at various schools in Minnesota, and has written short

stories and poetry for *The New Yorker* and other magazines. Her essay
on Minnesota winters appears in her collection of essays originally
written for a newspaper in Madison, Minnesota—*Letters from the
Country.*

> How strange to think of giving up all ambition!
> Suddenly I see with such clear eyes
> The white flake of snow
> That has just fallen in the horse's mane.
> —"Watering the Horse," by Robert Bly, *Silence
> in the Snowy Fields*

It is sometimes mistakenly thought by city people that 1
grown-ups don't love snow. They think only children who
haven't got to shovel it love snow, or only people like the
von Fürstenburgs and their friends who get to go skiing in
exotic places and will never backslope a roadside in all their
lives: that is a mistake. The fact is that most country or
small-town Minnesotans love snow. They relish snow in large
inconvenient storms; they like the excesses of it, they like
the threat of it, the endless work of it, the glamour of it.

Before a storm, Madison is full of people excitedly lay- 2
ing in food stocks for the three-day blow. People lay in rather
celebratory food, too. Organic-food parents get chocolate for
the children; weight watchers lay in macaroni and Sara Lee
Cakes; recently-converted vegetarians backslide to T-bones.
People hang around the large Super-Valu window and keep
a tough squinty-eyed watch on the storm progress with a lot
of gruff, sensible observations (just like Houston Control
talking to the moon, very much on top of it all) like "Ja, we
need this for spring moisture . . ." or "Ja, it doesn't look
like letting up at all . . ." or "Ja, you can see where it's
beginning to drift up behind the VFW." The plain pleasure
of it is scarcely hidden.

That is before the storm. Then the town empties out as 3
the farmers and their families take their food stocks home
before U.S. 75, Minnesota 40, and Lac Qui Parle 19 close
up. During the storm itself heroism is the routine attitude. I
remember once when the phone was out, before all the telephone lines went underground, and the power was off,
our neighbor came lightly in his huge pack boots across the

drift top, high up from our house level, like an upright black ant, delicately choosing his footing over the hard-slung and paralyzed snow waves. He looked as if he were walking across a frozen North Atlantic. He had come over to see if we were O.K. It was before snowmobiles, at − 40 degrees a welcome gesture.

Then right after a storm we all go back uptown because 4 we have to see how the town has filled. The streets are walled ten and eleven feet high. If they had had underground parking ramps in the pyramids this is what they'd have looked like, white-painted, and we crawl between the neatly carved clean walls. The horrible snow buildup is a point of pride. In 1969 a fine thing happened: the county of Lac Qui Parle imported a couple of gigantic snow-removal machines from Yellowstone Park. It cost several thousand dollars to get those monsters here; when they arrived our heavy, many-layered, crusted snow broke the machines—they couldn't handle it. With glittering eyes we sent them back to Yellowstone Park.

Snowdrifts in the bad years, as in 1969, force us to dump 5 garbage and nonburnables ever nearer the house, until finally in March there is a semicircle of refuse nearly at the front door. Even the German shepherd lowers his standards; the snow around the doghouse entrance is unspeakable.

If one has any kind of luck one garners comfort from 6 great weather, but if there is some anxious and unresolved part of one's inner life, snowfall and certainly snowbound-ness can make it worse. During the winter of 1968–69, the three doctors of our town prescribed between two and three times as much tranquilizing medicine as usual. And Robert Frost, despite being one of the best snow poets going, has an odd, recurring fretfulness about snow:

> The woods are lovely, dark and deep,
> But I have promises to keep

What promises? To whom? If we think about it it sounds moralistic and self-denying—a moral showing-off in some way. The nervousness is stronger, though, in "Desert Places":

> Snow falling and night falling fast, oh, fast
> In a field I looked into going past,

And the ground almost covered smooth in snow,
But a few weeds and stubble showing last.

The woods around it have it—it is theirs.
All animals are smothered in their lairs.
I am too absent-spirited to count;
The loneliness includes me unawares.

I am struck by the malaise of the word *absent-spirited*. It
must mean—this joy in snow or fretfulness in snow—that
whatever is providential and coming to each of us from within
is sped the faster by snowfall.

Being out in a blizzard is not lovely. Nature then feels
worse than inimical; it feels simply impersonal. It isn't that,
like some goddess in Homer, she wants to grab and freeze
your body in her drifts; it is that you can be taken and still
the wind will keep up its regular blizzard whine and nothing
has made a difference. In February of 1969 the fuel men
couldn't get through for weeks; one midnight my husband
and I had to transfer oil from a drum behind an old shed to
our house tank. We did this in cans, load after load, crawling on all fours and rolling in the ravines between the drifts.
It had some nice moments: every ten minutes or so we'd
meet behind the old shed, when one returned an empty can
and the other was coming away with a full one, and we'd
crouch in the scoured place, leaning over the nasty, rusted,
infuriatingly slow spigot of the oil tank there. Looking at
each other, we saw we had that impersonal aspect of snow-
covered people. It was peculiar to think that anyone behind
those freezing, melting, refreezing eyebrows ever objected to
an act of Congress or ever loved a summer woods or memorized the tenor to anything by Christopher Tye. Back inside, our job done, still cold and rough-spoken, still walking
like bears, we studied the children in their beds.

To us in Minnesota a blizzard in itself is of no practical
good, but it is interesting how useful blizzards can be. Ordinary snowfall, not moved into deep-packed areas by wind,
runs off too quickly in the spring and can't be controlled for
good use. The *Proceedings of the American Society of Civil
Engineers* has essay after essay on uses of Rocky Mountain
snowmelt. Twenty-five hundred years ago, and possibly even

earlier, the Persians used deep-drifted snow for irrigation. They built their *qanats*. Qanats are brick-walled tunnels running from the snowfields of the Elburz and other mountain ranges of Iran to villages fifteen or twenty miles away. At a point in the mountains' water table still higher than the land level of the parched miles and miles to be irrigated, the arched brick tunnels were carefully sloped to keep the water moving. The "mother well" was 200 feet deep and deeper. These 22,000 tunnels (there were 30,000 in 1960 but 8,000 were not in working condition) had airshafts for fresh air and maintenance access every 50 to 60 yards. Darius took the qanat technique to Egypt in the 5th century B.C. Nothing could have been cultivated in three-fourths of the now-irrigated fields of Iran without the ancient qanats. Persia was the originator of melons, cucumbers, and pears.

This is just to give an idea of mankind's long use of heavily drifted snow. Since we don't *use* blizzards in western Minnesota, the question lingers: why the pleasure in great weather? As with children in thunderstorms, I think we all have a secret affair of long standing with the other face of things. Children want the parents and the police and the other irritating powers to have their measure taken; they want a change of justice; but it goes further: they have a secret affection for bad weather. ⁹

Storms, what is more, force us to look at nature closely, ¹⁰ and that is never boring. All meetings of the Business Improvement Association and the Countryside Council and the play rehearsal committees stop in a blizzard. It is a help. Two things make nature lovely to people, I think: enforced, extended leisure in a natural place—which storms give us out here; and second, planning our own lives instead of just following along. The moment, for example, that someone finally decides not to take the promising job offered by Reserve Mining, for example, or the moment someone decides not to pad a travel-expense account at the Ramada is a moment in which ice and snow and bare trunks look better, less happenstance, less pointless. C. S. Lewis goes very far: he claims that the fact that we all agree on what is meant by *good* or *holy* (that is, no one thinks robbery or despoiling the land or depriving the poor is good) indicates that goodness and holiness are actually a normal, planned part of our universe—perfectly natural to the species. He would not be surprised at all to see snow on a horse's mane all the better for having just worked out an ethical decision.

Comment

Carol Bly is expressing her feelings about snow through experiences she finds harder to interpret than to describe. Thus, having shown why "being out in a blizzard is not lovely," she finishes by describing how she and her husband, "still cold and rough-spoken, still walking like bears," watch their children in bed. In her final paragraphs, she explores various attitudes towards blizzards. But these statements seem to fall short of capturing their meaning. She ends the essay with ideas expressed by another writer about the world. His ideas perhaps will bring us a little closer to understanding the workings of the world.

Questions for Study and Discussion

1. What range of personal experiences does Bly present in the essay? And what are her various feelings?
2. Describing the experience of ancient Persians with snow, Bly illustrates "mankind's long use of heavily drifted snow." How does this reference to the long history of mankind help to convey her complex feelings?
3. How does Bly show that the "meaning" of the world is difficult both to describe and to interpret?
4. What is the point of C. S. Lewis's ideas and the statement about the sight of snow on a horse's mane?
5. What is the order of ideas in the essay? Why do you think Bly chose this order?
6. What concrete words and phrases develop the topic sentence of paragraph 2, "Before a storm, Madison is full of people excitedly laying in food stocks for the three-day blow"?
7. Bly often introduces an experience with a general characterization. The blizzard of 1969 "had some nice moments," she tells us in paragraph 7; then she describes these moments. What words and images make her feelings about these moments concrete?

Vocabulary Study

Give the denotative and connotative meanings—explain what things or ideas the words point to or name, and give what feelings or attitudes they suggest:

a. paragraph 2: *squinty-eyed, gruff*
b. paragraph 4: *glittering*
c. paragraph 6: *garners, fretfulness, moralistic, malaise*
d. paragraph 7: *inimical, nice*

Suggestions for Writing

1. Describe your own experiences with a series of snowfalls or some other natural occurrence. Use your description to suggest your own complex feelings and the ideas these experiences generate.

2. Families have their own ways of doing things—of celebrating birthdays and other anniversaries, of arguing and making up—that suggest different personalities. Suggest the personality of your own family through concrete details and experiences. Let the details reveal the qualities and the personality you have in mind. Don't name them directly.

Figurative Language

Much of our language is *figurative*—that is, not literal but metaphorical—sometimes without our realizing it is. Certain figures of speech may once have called a picture to mind but have become stale. Here are a few examples:

> *blaze of glory*   *drunk with power*   *hard as nails*

The first of these is a *metaphor*—figure of speech in which one thing is talked about as if it were something else. The metaphor does not tell us that glory is like a fire: it speaks of glory as if it were. "Drunk with power" is also a metaphor: it specifies that power acts like an intoxicant. "Hard as nails" makes the comparison directly through the word *as,* and we therefore call it a *simile.* Another important figure of speech is *personification,* which gives animate or human qualities to something inanimate or nonhuman:

> The tree *cowered* in the storm.

Figurative language is one way of conveying our feelings about an object or experience.

   In exposition and argument, figurative language can make an idea or attitude concrete and persuasive. It can be unobtrusive, and at other times it can be dramatic, as in this description by a surgeon of one of the tools of his art:

> The scalpel is in two parts, the handle and the blade. Joined, it is six inches from tip to tip. At one end of the handle is a narrow notched prong upon which the blade is slid, then snapped into place. Without the blade, the handle has a blind, decapitated look. It is helpless as a trussed maniac. But slide on the blade, click it home, and the knife springs instantly to life. It is headed now, edgy, leaping to mount the fingers for the gallop to its feast.—Richard Selzer, *Mortal Lessons*

Metaphor, simile, and personification here are combined in a highly effective way; the description conveys the excitement of the surgeon as he holds the scalpel and prepares to use it.

David R. Scott

WHAT IS IT LIKE TO WALK ON THE MOON?

David R. Scott was born in San Antonio, Texas, in 1932, where his father was serving as an Air Force brigadier general. Educated at West Point and MIT, Scott served in the Air Force as a jet pilot, and in 1963 began his training as an astronaut. He was one of the three who piloted the *Endeavour,* in the Apollo 15 mission to the moon, entering lunar orbit on July 29, 1971. Scott explored the lunar surface with James B. Irwin, while Alfred Worden remained in the command ship. The *Endeavour* returned to earth on August 7. The essay reprinted here gives a vivid account of his experiences on the moon, and shows how figurative language can serve in exposition.

Sixty feet above the moon, the blast of our single rocket   1
churns up a gray tumult of lunar dust that seems to engulf us. Blinded, I feel the rest of the way down "on the gauges." With an abrupt jar, our lunar module, or LM, strikes the surface and shudders to rest. We have hit our target squarely—a large amphitheater girded by mountains and a deep canyon, at the eastern edge of a vast plain.

As Jim Irwin and I wait for the dust to settle, I recall   2
the twelve revolutions we have just spent in lunar orbit aboard our Apollo 15 spaceship *Endeavour.* Each two hours found us completing a full circuit of earth's ancient satellite—one hour knifing through lunar night, then sunrise and an hour of daylight. As we orbited, I found a particular fascination in that sector of the darkened moon bathed in earthshine. The light reflected by our planet illuminates the sleeping moon much more brightly than moonlight silvers our own night. The mountains and crater rims are clearly seen.

I will always remember *Endeavour* hurtling through that   3
strange night of space. Before us and above us stars spangled the sky with their distant icy fire; below lay the moon's

far side, an arc of impenetrable blackness that blotted the firmament. Then, as our moment of sunrise approached, barely discernible streamers of light—actually the glowing gases of the solar corona millions of miles away—played above the moon's horizon. Finally the sun exploded into our view like a visual thunderclap. Abruptly, completely, in less than a second, its harsh light flooded into the spaceship and dazzled our eyes.

As we looked into the early lunar morning from *Endeavour,* the moonscape stretched into the distance, everything the color of milk chocolate. Long angular shadows accentuated every hill, every crater. As the sun arched higher, the plains and canyons and mountains brightened to a gunmetal gray, while the shadows shrank. At full lunar noontide, the sun glared down upon a bleached and almost featureless world.

Now we have come to rest on the moon, and the last of the dust settles outside the LM. We throw the switches that convert this hybrid vehicle from spacecraft to dwelling. Thus begin our 67 hours of lunar residence. We are on a still and arid world where each blazing day and each subfreezing night stretch through 355 earth hours. We have landed in the bright morning of a moon day. When we depart, the sun will not have reached zenith.

It is sobering to realize that we are the only living souls on this silent sphere, perhaps the only sentient beings in our solar system not confined to earth. Though we have slipped the bonds of our home planet, we remain earthmen. So we keep our clocks set to Houston time and gear our lives to the 24-hour cycle we have always known.

Opening the top hatch for a preliminary reconnaissance, I peer out at a world seemingly embalmed in the epoch of its creation. Each line, each form blends into the harmonious whole of a single fluid sculpture. Craters left by "recent" meteorites—merely millions of years ago—stand out, startlingly white, like fresh scar tissue against the soft beige of the undulating terrain.

I steal a moment and glance straight up into the black sky where the crystalline sphere of earth—all blue and white, sea and clouds—gleams in the abyss of space. In that cold and boundless emptiness, our planet provides the only glow of color. For 30 minutes my helmeted head pivots above the open hatch as I survey and photograph the wonderland of the lunar surface. The incredible variety of landforms in this restricted area (on the moon, the horizon lies a scant mile and a half from a viewer) fills me with pleasant surprise. To the south an 11,000-foot ridge rises above the bleak plain. To the east stretch the hulking heights of an even higher summit. On the west a winding gorge plunges to depths of more than 1,000 feet. Dominating the northeastern horizon, a great mountain stands in noble splendor almost three miles above us. Ours is the first expedition to land amid lunar mountains. Never quickened by life, never assailed by wind and rain, they loom still and serene, a tableau of forever. Their majesty overwhelms me.

Eight years' training in lunar geology makes me instantly aware of intriguing details. A dark line like a bathtub ring smudges the bases of the mountains. Was it left by the subsiding lake of lava that filled the immense cavity of Palus Putredinis, on the fringes of Mare Imbrium, billions of years ago? Mare Imbrium, on whose edge we have landed, stretches across the face of the moon for some 650 miles. The celestial projectile that excavated it must have been huge— perhaps as much as 50 miles across—and it slammed into the moon with a velocity many times greater than that of a rifle bullet. 9

When we descend the ladder of the LM and step onto the moon's surface, Jim and I feel a gratifying sense of freedom. For five days we have been crammed into the tight confines of the spacecraft that brought us here. Now, all at once, we regain the luxury of movement. But, we quickly discover, locomotion on the moon has its own peculiar restrictions. At one-sixth of earth's gravity, we weigh only a sixth our normal poundage. Our gait quickly evolves into a rhythmic, bounding motion that possesses all the lightness and ease of strolling on a trampoline. 10

At the same time, since the mass of our bodies and personal gear—and hence, our inertia—remains unchanged, starting and stopping require unusual exertion. I learn to get 11 under way by thrusting my body forward, as though I were stepping into a wind. To stop, I dig in my heels and lean backward.

To fall on the moon—and I did several times—is to re-discover childhood. You go down in slow motion, the impact is slight, the risk of injury virtually nil. Forsaking the adult attitude that regards a fall not only as a loss of dignity but also a source of broken bones, the moon walker—like a child—accepts it as yet another diversion. Only the clinging moon dust, the untoward demand on the oxygen supply occasioned by the exertion of getting up, pall the pleasure of a tumble. Personally I find the one-sixth gravity of the moon more enjoyable than the soothing weightlessness of space. I have the same sense of buoyancy, but the moon provides a reassuringly fixed sense of up and down.

As we unload and begin to assemble our equipment—including the battery-powered four-wheeled Rover that will carry us across the moonscape at a jaunty six or so miles an hour—I gaze around at the plains and mountains that have become our world. My eyes trace a curiously contoured, totally alien wasteland. I scale the lofty mountains and feel a strange, indescribable emotion: No naked eye has ever seen them; no foot has ever trod them. I am an intruder in an eternal wilderness.

The flowing moonscape, unmarred by a single jagged peak, reminds me of earth's uplands covered by a heavy blanket of fresh snow. Indeed, the dark-gray moon dust—its consistency seems to be somewhat between coal dust and talcum powder—mantles virtually every physical feature of the lunar surface. Our boots sink gently into it as we walk; we leave sharply chiseled footprints.

Color undergoes an odd transformation here. Everything underfoot or nearby is gray, yet this hue blends gradually into the uniform golden tan that characterizes distant objects. And this small spectrum moves with the walker. Most of the scattered rocks share the same gray tint as the dust, but we find two that are jet black, two of pastel green, several with sparkling crystals, some coated with glass, and one that is white. As we advance, we are surrounded by stillness.

No wind blows. No sound echoes. Only shadows move. Within the space suit, I hear the reassuring purr of the miniaturized machines that supply vital oxygen and shield me from the blistering 150°F. surface heat of lunar morning.

Any of a thousand malfunctions in a space suit or the   16
LM could condemn an astronaut to swift death. Yet we have a quiet confidence in our own abilities, and boundless faith in the engineers and technicians who have fashioned the ingenious devices that transport and sustain us in space. Often, in the course of my stay on the moon, I recall the words of American poet Edwin Markham: "There is a destiny which makes us brothers; none goes his way alone."

At first we experience a troubling deception with per-   17
spective. Without the familiar measuring sticks of our native planet—trees, telephone poles, clouds, and haze—we cannot determine whether an object stands close at hand or at a considerable distance, or whether it is large or small. Gradually our eyes learn to cope with the craters—mammoth, medium, and minuscule—that dot virtually every inch of the surface. And gradually the moon becomes a friendlier place. A thought occurs to me: Would human beings born on the moon be able to find their way among the trees and clouds of earth?

Each excursion on the lunar surface is planned to last   18
seven hours, almost to the limit of a space suit's life-sustaining capabilities. We dig and drill into the surface, gather rocks and soil, take endless photographs. The photographs, it seems to me, provide us with a testament that transcends time, for we may be photographing the distant past of our own planet. The Rover functions impeccably as we ride from site to site, accumulating fragments of history. We bounce and pitch across omnipresent chuckholelike craters. The motion exactly resembles that of a small boat in a rough sea; so does the physical effect. Incredible as it seems, in the arid environment of the moon, seasickness could become an occupational hazard.

After each of our expeditions, we climb—sapped of en-   19
ergy—back into the LM. With its oxygen and food and water, it is a tiny artificial earth that comforts us in the void. Re-

moving our space suits and attending to our housekeeping chores consumes two hours. For the first twenty minutes we are conscious of a pervasive odor, similar to that of gunpowder, from the moon dust we have tracked in. Our air-purifying system soon dispels the acrid scent, but the fine, adhesive dust clings to everything. Back on earth, no amount of cleaning will convert our space suits from the gray hue acquired on the moon to their once pristine and sparkling white.

The better to sleep, we create the illusion of night. We   20 place opaque shades over the windows of the LM to exclude the harsh sunlight reflected from the moon's surface. Then we go through all the homey activities of sunset on earth, even to snapping on overhead lights. When finally we switch them off, we settle into hammocks. On earth, I have always found hammocks uncomfortable. But here my 30-pound body adapts marvelously to the canvas crescent, and I easily fall into dreamless sleep.

Bounding along in the Rover on our third and final expedition, we begin to feel fully at home in our new habitat.   21 The craters now seem familiar and help us gauge distances. And we venture across the horizon—the first astronauts ever to do so—without anxiety. Should the sophisticated Rover navigation system fail, we have a small cardboard sun compass fashioned by a technician in Houston—a frail instrument much shriveled by the savage lunar sunlight and coated with moon dust—that will give us our bearings. But our newfound confidence stems less from instruments than from the fact that we have come to know and understand our surroundings.

On our return we even dare a shortcut. The Rover   22 bounces between undulations and crater walls that mask our view of the LM for long minutes, but we emerge on target. Arriving at the LM, I experience a sense of impending loss. Soon I will leave the moon, probably forever. And, in a peculiar way, I have come to feel a strange affection for this peaceful, changeless companion of the earth.

As I mount the ladder for the last time, I halt and glance   23 back at the Rover. It seems poised and ready for its next task. And poised in that same eager attitude it could remain for thousands, perhaps millions of years—a driverless vehicle lost in the loneliness of this lifeless realm. Beside it, like staunch sentinels through the long millenniums, will hulk the LM descent stage and the assorted equipment of our mission. The vacuum of space, which knows only negligible decay, will confer upon all of it—even to the footprints we have left in the undrifting dust—a permanence akin to immortality.

The thought haunts us that the end of the Apollo flights may mark man's last visit to the moon for a long time. American manned exploration of deep space is scheduled for an indefinite hiatus. Most scientists have already suggested that, when it resumes, all effort should concentrate upon reaching Mars and beyond. So our lunar artifacts—bypassed in the race to the planets—could remain undisturbed for eternity.   24

Clutching the ladder, I raise my eyes from the nowfamiliar moonscape to earth, glowing in the black heavens—that incredibly vivid sphere, so blue, so beautiful, so beloved. And so bedeviled; by ecological balances gone awry, by scattered starvation, by a shortage of energy that may motivate us to seek sources beyond our earth. Our Apollo crew believes that a technology capable of exploring space can and will help resolve such problems. We feel a sense of pride in the accomplishments of our program, yet we cannot escape a sense of deep concern for the fate of our planet and our species. This concern has led us to add certain items to the equipment we are leaving on the moon. The sum of these articles, we hope, will form a résumé of our era in the continuing story of the human race.   25

In eons to come, should astronauts from the deeps of space—from other solar systems in other galaxies—pass this way, they may find our spoor, our abandoned gear. A plaque of aluminum affixed to the deserted LM descent stage portrays the two hemispheres of our planet; upon it are engraved the name of our spacecraft, the date of our mission and a roster of the crew. From these data, the equipment, and even the dimensions of our footprints, intelligent beings will readily deduce what kind of creatures we were and   26 whence we came. We leave a piece of fauna—a falcon feather—and of flora—a four-leaf clover.

In a little hollow in the moon dust we place a stylized figurine of a man in a space suit and beside it another metal plaque bearing the names of the 14 spacemen—Russians and Americans—who have given their lives so that man may range the cosmos. Finally we deposit a single book: the Bible. 27

Our mission ends in fatigue and elation. Amazing success has rewarded the first extended scientific expedition to the moon. After debriefing and helping in the analyses of our findings, our crew disbands. 28

Now, two years later, I continue to work in the Lyndon B. Johnson Space Center near Houston. Frequently I reflect upon those three most memorable days of my life. Although I can reconstruct them virtually moment by moment, sometimes I can scarcely believe that I have actually walked on the moon. 29

Occasionally, while strolling on a crisp autumn night or driving a straight Texas road, I look up at the moon riding bright and proud over the clouds. My eye picks out the largest circular splotch on the silvery surface: Mare Imbrium. There, at the eastern edge of that splotch, I once descended in a spaceship. Again I feel that I will probably never return, and the thought stirs a pang of nostalgia. For when I look at the moon I do not see a hostile, empty world. I see the radiant body where man has taken his first steps into a frontier that will never end. 30

Comment

To describe an experience entirely new to human beings, Scott must refer to experiences with which we are familiar. Some of his experiences are exactly like those on earth: the movement of the Rover across the lunar surface "exactly resembles that of a small boat in a rough sea; so does the physical effect." To fall on the moon is to feel as we did as children, and Scott gives examples of that kind of feeling. But not every feeling and experience has an exact equivalent on earth. As his frequent resort to simile shows, we depend on figurative language to express new experiences, feelings, and insights. "Beside it, like staunch sentinels through the long millenniums, will hulk the LM descent stage, and the assorted equipment of our mission."

Questions for Study and Discussion

1. To what does Scott implicitly compare the weightlessness experienced on the lunar surface? What other such experiences does he describe through comparisons?
2. What sights not previously experienced by human beings does he describe, and how does he? How does figurative language help him to make these experiences vivid?
3. What aspects of the total experience does he stress the most?
4. Had he been writing to an audience of future astronauts, how might the description and exposition have been different?
5. Does Scott develop a thesis, or instead describe an experience without drawing conclusions?

Vocabulary Study

1. Explain how Scott uses the following words figuratively: *blotted, dazzled* (paragraph 3); *shrank* (paragraph 4); *embalmed* (paragraph 7); *alien* (paragraph 18); *radiant* (paragraph 30).
2. The phrase "the shadows *shrank*" is an example of personification: the inanimate shadows are given animate or human qualities. What other examples of personification do you find in the essay?
3. Metaphors that do not immediately call a picture to mind or strike us as being comparisons are sometimes called "submerged" or "buried" metaphors:

   So we keep our clocks set to Houston time and *gear* our lives to the 24-hour cycle we have always known.

   Find several examples of such metaphors in the essay.
4. Use your dictionary to investigate the etymology of the following words—that is, their origin: "*firmament* (paragraph 3); *reconnaissance* (paragraph 7); *mantles* (paragraph 14); *mammoth* (paragraph 17).

Suggestions for Writing

1. Describe a recent experience in several paragraphs, in as literal a language as possible. Then rewrite one of these paragraphs, substituting metaphorical for literal language where possible.

2. Narrate and describe an experience that would be strange to a particular audience. Assume that this audience knows nothing about the circumstances, equipment, or world of this experience, and therefore needs them explained or described. Focus on those aspects of the experience that you consider most significant or revealing.

Annie Dillard

UNTYING THE KNOT

Annie Dillard was born in 1945 in Pittsburgh; she describes her early life in her autobiography *An American Childhood* (1987). Dillard lived in the Roanoke Valley of Virginia for ten years; she describes her experiences there in *Pilgrim at Tinker Creek* (1974), for which she was awarded the Pulitzer Prize for General Non-Fiction in 1975. She later lived in the Pacific Northwest and now teaches at Wesleyan University in Middletown, Connecticut. She is also the author of *Tickets for a Prayer Wheel* (1974) and *Living by Fiction* (1982).

Yesterday I set out to catch the new season, and instead I found an old snakeskin. I was in the sunny February woods by the quarry; the snakeskin was lying in a heap of leaves right next to an aquarium someone had thrown away. I don't know why that someone hauled the aquarium deep into the woods to get rid of it; it had only one broken glass side. The snake found it handy, I imagine; snakes like to rub against something rigid to help them out of their skins, and the broken aquarium looked like the nearest likely object. Together the snakeskin and the aquarium made an interesting scene on the forest floor. It looked like an exhibit at a trial—circumstantial evidence—of a wild scene, as though a snake had burst through the broken side of the aquarium, burst through his ugly old skin, and disappeared, perhaps straight up in the air, in a rush of freedom and beauty.

The snakeskin had unkeeled scales, so it belonged to a nonpoisonous snake. It was roughly five feet long by the yardstick, but I'm not sure because it was very wrinkled and dry, and every time I tried to stretch it flat it broke. I ended up with seven or eight pieces of it all over the kitchen table in a fine film of forest dust. [2]

The point I want to make about the snakeskin is that, when I found it, it was whole and tied in a knot. Now there have been stories told, even by reputable scientists, of snakes that have deliberately tied themselves in a knot to prevent larger snakes from trying to swallow them—but I couldn't imagine any way that throwing itself into a half hitch would help a snake trying to escape its skin. Still, ever cautious, I figured that one of the neighborhood boys could possibly have tied it in a knot in the fall, for some whimsical boyish reason, and left it there, where it dried and gathered dust. So I carried the skin along thoughtlessly as I walked, snagging it sure enough on a low branch and ripping it in two for the first of many times. I saw that thick ice still lay on the quarry pond and that the skunk cabbage was already out in the clearings, and then I came home and looked at the skin and its knot. [3]

The knot had no beginning. Idly I turned it around in my hand, searching for a place to untie; I came to with a start when I realized I must have turned the thing around fully ten times. Intently, then, I traced the knot's lump around with a finger: it was continuous. I couldn't untie it any more than I could untie a doughnut; it was a loop without beginning or end. These snakes *are* magic, I thought for a second, and then of course I reasoned what must have happened. The skin had been pulled inside-out like a peeled sock for several inches; then an inch or so of the inside-out part—a piece whose length was coincidentally equal to the diameter of the skin—had somehow been turned right-side out again, making a thick lump whose edges were lost in wrinkles, looking exactly like a knot. [4]

So. I have been thinking about the change of seasons. I [5]

don't want to miss spring this year. I want to distinguish the last winter frost from the out-of-season one, the frost of spring. I want to be there on the spot the moment the grass turns green. I always miss this radical revolution; I see it the next day from a window, the yard so suddenly green and lush I could envy Nebuchadnezzar down on all fours eating grass. This year I want to stick a net into time and say "now," as men plant flags on the ice and snow and say, "here." But it occurred to me that I could no more catch spring by the tip of the tail than I could untie the apparent knot in the snakeskin; there are no edges to grasp. Both are continuous loops.

I wonder how long it would take you to notice the reg- 6 ular recurrence of the seasons if you were the first man on earth. What would it be like to live in open-ended time broken only by days and nights? You could say, "it's cold again; it was cold before," but you couldn't make the key connection and say, "it was cold this time last year," because the notion of "year" is precisely the one you lack. Assuming that you hadn't noticed an orderly progression of heavenly bodies, how long would you have to live on earth before you could feel with any assurance that any one particular long period of cold would, in fact, end? "While the earth remaineth, seedtime and harvest, and cold and heat, and summer and winter, and day and night shall not cease": God makes this guarantee very early in Genesis to a people whose fears on this point had perhaps not been completely allayed.

It must have been fantastically important, at the real 7 beginning of human culture, to conserve and relay this vital seasonal information, so that the people could anticipate dry or cold seasons, and not huddle on some November rock hoping pathetically that spring was just around the corner. We still very much stress the simple fact of four seasons to school children; even the most modern of modern new teachers, who don't seem to care if their charges can read or write or name two products of Peru, will still muster some seasonal chitchat and set the kids to making paper pumpkins, or tulips, for the walls. "The people," wrote Van Gogh in a letter, "are very sensitive to the changing seasons." That we are "very sensitive to the changing seasons" is, incidentally, one of the few good reasons to shun travel. If I stay at home I preserve the illusion that what is happening on Tinker Creek is the very newest thing, that I'm at the very vanguard and cutting edge of each new season. I don't want the same season twice in a row; I don't want to know I'm getting last week's weather, used weather, weather broadcast up and down the coast, old-hat weather.

But there's always unseasonable weather. What we think 8 of the weather and behavior of life on the planet at any given season is really all a matter of statistical probabilities; at any given point, anything might happen. There is a bit of every season in each season. Green plants—deciduous green leaves—grow everywhere, all winter long, and small shoots come up pale and new in every season. Leaves die on the tree in May, turn brown, and fall into the creek. The calendar, the weather, and the behavior of wild creatures have the slimmest of connections. Everything overlaps smoothly for only a few weeks each season, and then it all tangles up again. The temperature, of course, lags far behind the calendar seasons, since the earth absorbs and releases heat slowly, like a leviathan breathing. Migrating birds head south in what appears to be dire panic, leaving mild weather and fields full of insects and seeds; they reappear as if in all eagerness in January, and poke about morosely in the snow. Several years ago our October woods would have made a dismal colored photograph for a sadist's calendar: a killing frost came before the leaves had even begun to brown; they dropped from every tree like crepe, blackened and limp. It's all a chancy, jumbled affair at best, as things seem to be below the stars.

Time is the continuous loop, the snakeskin with scales 9 endlessly overlapping without beginning or end, or time is an ascending spiral if you will, like a child's toy Slinky. Of course we have no idea which arc on the loop is our time, let alone where the loop itself is, so to speak, or down whose lofty flight of stairs the Slinky so uncannily walks.

The power we seek, too, seems to be a continuous loop. 10 I have always been sympathetic with the early notion of a divine power that exists in a particular place, or that travels about over the face of the earth as a man might wander—and when he is "there" he is surely not here. You can shake the hand of a man you meet in the woods; but the spirit seems to roll along like the mythical hoop snake with its tail in its mouth. There are no hands to shake or edges to untie. It rolls along the mountain ridges like a fireball, shooting off a spray of sparks at random, and will not be trapped, slowed, grasped, fetched, peeled, or aimed. "As for the wheels, it was cried unto them in my hearing, O wheel." This is the hoop of flame that shoots the rapids in the creek or spins across the dizzy meadows; this is the arsonist of the sunny woods; catch it if you can.

Comment

Metaphor is particularly appropriate to the ideas of this essay. Dillard uses the knotted snakeskin as a metaphor for existence. She makes her point directly: she can no more "catch spring by the tip of the tail" than she can untie the knot—"there are no edges to grasp. Both are continuous loops." She builds carefully to this statement, her full meaning emerging in the details of her account. The open feeling of spring stands for a larger experience: the sense of "open-ended time." Dillard wants to see the world anew at each moment, though she knows that experiences repeat themselves. That is why she does not want to "catch spring by the tip of the tail." It would fix the experience instead of keeping it open. Having explored these ideas, she can finish her analogy—"Time is the continuous loop"—and she thinks also of a divine power that is everywhere always. It is the oneness and at the same time the variousness of nature that she seeks to express through figurative language.

Questions for Study and Discussion

1. The power of nature, and its openness, are symbolized in many ways in the essay. Through what metaphor is it symbolized at the end?
2. Dillard moves from ordinary experience to the extraordinary. What words and phrases suggest the extraordinary and mys-

terious qualities of life as the essay proceeds? Which of these
words and phrases are figurative?

3. What use does Dillard make of the Bible (Daniel 4:25) in
   paragraph 5?
4. In how many ways is the knotted snakeskin used in the essay?
   That is, how many references do you find to entanglement
   and overlapping?
5. How does the author characterize herself through her response to the snakeskin and the world of Tinker Creek?
6. What use does Dillard make of personification?

Vocabulary Study

Write a paraphrase of the final paragraph, translating similes, metaphors, and other figures of speech into literal language.

Suggestions for Writing

1. Write about your feelings and thoughts concerning a season
   of the year. Focus your discussion on an object you associate
   with this season. You may want to explore the various qualities of the object and what these tell you about the season.
2. Develop one of the ideas of the essay from your point of view
   and personal experience.

Tone

The tone of a statement expresses the attitude or feeling of a speaker or writer. The tone of the following statement is immediately clear:

> Man is, of all quadrupeds, at once the most vain and the most idiotic. A genuine popinjay, whatever that may be, is as a shrinking violet compared to him. He cannot imagine himself save as at the center of situations. He never opens his mouth without talking of himself.—H. L. Mencken, "The Eternal Male"

Mencken's blunt statement expresses his astonishment and exasperation. He says exactly what he means—in contrast to this ironic statement in which the words imply more than they actually say:

> Already architectural designers are toiling to find ways out of the technical trap represented by sealed buildings with immovable glass, ways that might let in some of the naturally cool air outside. Some have lately come up with a remarkable discovery: the openable window. Presumably, that represents progress.—Frank Trippett, "The Great American Cooling Machine"

The designers of sealed buildings, the writer implies, are not very bright if they are making so obvious a discovery as the openable window. The final comment is plainly sarcastic.

Other statements are harder to interpret, particularly in writing. If you heard a person exclaim "What a tragedy!", you would know immediately whether the person is expressing pain, anger, sarcasm, wonder, or bewilderment. If you come upon the exclamation in a piece of writing, however, you would have to examine its context or setting to discover the writer's tone. The following statement by Mark Twain on the novelist James Fenimore Cooper is ambiguous out of context:

> Cooper's gift in the way of invention was not a rich endowment; but such as it was he liked to work it, he was pleased with the effects, and indeed he did some quite sweet things with it.

359

The sentences that follow show that Twain is not praising Cooper. His tone is sarcastic:

> In his little box of stage properties he kept six or eight cunning devices, tricks, artifices, for his savages and woodsmen to deceive and circumvent each other with, and he was never so happy as when he was working these innocent things and seeing them go. A favorite one was to make a moccasined person tread in the tracks of the moccasined enemy, and thus hide his own trail. Cooper wore out barrels and barrels of moccasins in working that trick. . . .

In writing your own essays, you will probably adopt a tone without much consideration. In revising your draft, you might discover shifts in tone that you did not intend, or you might find ambiguous words or statements. Your reader will need help with these shifts and ambiguities. The solution is to clarify your feelings or attitudes, as H. L. Mencken does in the following passage:

> Some time ago I put in a blue afternoon re-reading Joseph Conrad's "Youth." A *blue* afternoon? What nonsense! The touch of the man is like the touch of Schubert. One approaches him in various and unhappy moods: depressed, dubious, despairing; one leaves him in the clear, yellow sunshine that Nietzsche found in Bizet's music.—"Joseph Conrad"

William Aiken

HANGING OUT AND LOOKING GOOD

William Aiken is a poet, essayist, and social critic who teaches poetry at the University of Lowell in Massachusetts. He has published articles in the *Wall Street Journal* and the *Christian Science Monitor,* where his essay reprinted here appeared in 1984. Provincetown and Truro are towns on Cape Cod, Massachusetts.

My son, Matthew, has just turned 15 and arrived at that time when children like to hang out where people are cheerful. As you may know, that is not home.

The days of selling home-picked berries at the beach are   2
gone. (I kept him at that for three years, but he objected to
my taking half the profits.) Now he wants to work with
stainless-steel machines—dishwashers and gas pumps. No
more of this berry-basket stuff.

In the course of my recent belated education I have   3
learned that 15-year-olds will clean up houses as a surprise
for pleasant strangers, but they don't want to clean the house
for me. They go for holistic personalities, which they find at
ice cream parlors or in houses down the street. During this
new age of the public persona the big trick is not to grow
fretful. You want to project a smiley face, pretend you're an
aerobics teacher. It gets hard.

Fifteen is the time when kids are too young to drive,   4
and yet they want to go certain places. You may not want
them to go, but you don't want them to hitchhike, either.
As a result of such dilemmas you begin to perfect various
levels of grumpiness. As Matthew pops out his plans for any
given day I keep thinking there is something he should be
doing around the house, but I can't think what it might be.

I was going over his new summer schedule, scratching   5
my head as my mind drifted back to my own vivid past
raising chickens. After pumping gas for six hours in the
morning he figures the rest of the day is his, so he's off to
town: to dive for quarters off MacMillan Wharf, go water-
skiing in Provincetown Harbor, walk around town pricing
silver bracelets, have a slice of pizza, and join the breakdan-
cers at Union Square.

Listening blankly to his adventures, I feel I'm in some   6
kind of parental limbo of the '80s: almost ready to go out
and have a good time—but not quite. I still find myself waiting by the phone and can't really seem to set out for anywhere. I watch the underlying happiness of my 15-year-old
as he scales the heights of adolescence, and I keep thinking
maybe he'll drop me a rope. But as he wanders farther and
farther from his backyard I become more and more home-
bound. I have begun to take up stamp collecting again. I do
these little garbage things around the house.

One day I decided to slip into a disguise and follow my 7
son up to Provincetown. I have some costumes from the '50s
that I still occasionally wear, and I was going over these in
my closet, confident that in Provincetown no one would notice. The last time I walked down Commercial Street there
was a man dressed as a lobster in front of the Wreck Club
who kept an eye on passers-by through his claws. No one
paid any attention. Besides, I have this underlying certainty
that no young person has looked at me for years.

So I got to town, parked my car, and walked down to 8
the center. Nothing much seemed to be happening, just people moving along in short pants and sequins. As I looked
around through my new reflecting glasses I noticed a ring of
young people in front of the Town Hall playing hackensack—popping this leather thing around on their feet. Suddenly I realized that one of them was my son. Dressed in a
mesh T-shirt, he was playing hackensack in front of the Town
Hall.

There they all were—all his friends—with their smiles 9
and their faces and their stainless-steel presences. And there
I was, all bent over in my tattered overcoat, dreaming of
lobster suits. It suddenly occurred to me that while I was in
disguise, my 15-year-old had decided to go public. Like a
small corporation that had gotten itself together and become
a dazzling new entry on the Exchange, he was "hanging out
and looking good." He saw me and waved. There are certain things a disguise will never cover.

I walked back to my car, which I had left at a foodstore 10
where there's free parking for customers, and a nine-year-
old says, "That'll be $3, mister." "Your store didn't have
any Sure-Gel so I had to go downtown," I say. "That'll
be $3."

I pay up and drive slowly back to Truro. It was almost 11
time for my walk in the marsh.

Comment

Aiken writes informally about his relationship to his fifteen-year-
old son. The tone of his essay is shaped by his attitude toward his

son and also toward his audience—by the relationship that he establishes in his opening paragraph. This audience is a general one, needing some details but not others about Matthew and his world. Aiken's gentle humor arises from the understatement of his feelings, particularly at the end. This understatement is one source of the quiet irony that characterizes the whole essay.

Questions for Study and Discussion

1. Irony is possible when the writer and the audience share certain experiences and facts. What does Aiken assume his audience knows about the towns of Cape Cod, Massachusetts? What other facts and what experiences does he assume his audience possesses? In general, what shared ironies does Aiken develop in the whole essay?
2. How would you define the attitude and feelings of Aiken toward Matthew and his world? What are his feelings at the end of the essay—on the Provincetown street and in the foodstore parking lot?
3. Is Aiken developing a thesis or merely describing personal experiences and feelings?
4. How would you characterize the writer of these experiences? What qualities of personality and outlook emerge in the telling of what happened?

Vocabulary Study

What do the following words, phrases, and sentences contribute to the tone of the essay?

a. paragraph 3: *my recent belated education, a smiley face*
b. paragraph 6: *some kind of parental limbo of the '80s*
c. paragraph 9: *stainless-steel presences, "hanging out and looking good"*

Suggestions for Writing

1. Write about experiences with a younger or older brother or sister or relative that define your relationship. Don't state this relationship directly. Let your details reveal it.

2. Aiken ends his essay with an embarrassing experience. Write about an embarrassment of your own and its consequences. Use the episode to make a point about yourself or people in general.

Hilary DeVries

REAL YUPPIES

Hilary DeVries, a staff writer for the *Christian Science Monitor*, graduated from Ohio Wesleyan University in 1976. She received her M.A. in Creative Writing from Boston University in 1981. In 1983 she was named Magazine Writer of the Year by the New England Women's Press Association. The term *yuppie* became popular in the 1984 presidential election through its association with the primary candidate Senator Gary Hart. DeVries writes humorously about her efforts to join the ranks of yuppies.

Yup. I was proud not to be saddled with an acronym, pleased that I nimbly sidestepped the plethora of life-style manuals—"The Official Preppy Handbook," "Real Women Don't Pump Gas," and the rest of that know-thyself paperback pack. I was poised in the face of Woodstock's 15th anniversary; I had spent the Age of Aquarius trying to ace English in a public high school in Illinois.

Yet, despite my best efforts to avoid being pegged to a generational trait, I find the term "Yuppie" not only unwithered but, like so much gourmet wheat germ, still sprouting, even though Gary Hart, the true Yuppie hero, has come and gone.

If I am to believe what I hear during the waning days of this campaign, I remain a political wooee, an assimilator of food processors, and unbearably upwardly mobile—the latter tips me into yet another socioeconomic category, that of the Yumpie, or "young upwardly mobile professional," in layman's lingo.

Much of this is news to me, not to mention my parents. As far as I can tell, I still write rent-controlled rent checks every month and coddle along a car that is my college grad-uation present.

But in a sociological nutshell, it seems that we baby-boomers have come of age—not by virtue of our achievements, rather by the extent of our style. Make that Style. Brunch has become a rite of passage and an MBA an almost requisite coat of arms.

Apparently we of the Me generation have decided that, if we can't have it all, we can at least have it all First Class—a sort of "I strive, therefore I am." Our goals lie somewhere in the realm of inputtable data: a six-figure salary, live-in help, and the ability to snare the best tables at the city's top restaurants. All of it apparently reflects our insatiable taste for the good life.

As a newly christened Yuppie—an unutterably pert term to my way of thinking—I find my native tongue has under-gone some rehabbing. "Mesquite" and "dhurrie" are all lin-guistically right on, at least for the moment, unlike the already déclassé "Fettuccine Alfredo," "networking," and "cash machine." No one has to tell Yuppies the times, they are a-changing. An appetite for affluence is now the unwritten acme of good taste—a far cry from the creeds of beads and flowers hippies.

Hence, as a true YUP, I will never, according to certain codes of behavior, drink anything instant, cancel reserved tennis court time, or pay cash. I am supposed to be too busy patronizing those restaurants displaying a requisite amount of ferns, brass, and marble, where I never eat macaroni and cheese or tuna on white. I am too busy stoking up on sushi, gravlax, and gourmet chocolates.

And there is more to this way of life style.

I am supposed to do aerobics in the morning, jog at noon, and meet at the health club after work. I am meant to work—better if I can "bill"—60-plus hours a week. But I must never tire and while away the down time in front of the TV. Excuse me, but I think I hear my arugula calling.

If my furniture doesn't float in my loft, if my cookware (and it must be "cookware," not pots and pans) doesn't re-quire copper cleanser or a small loan to finance, if I do not possess multiple vinegars or a particular make of German car, I will be suspected of being out of step. Or, more's the pity, I will miss becoming my own role model.

Yet, in a braver moment, I cannot resist testing the waters. I had successfully brunched in the past, so I picked the yuppiest restaurant I could find and blithely booked a table for four. On the site of a humble eatery where I had previously reveled in plates of meat loaf, mashed potatoes, and brown gravy whenever I felt nostalgic for Mom-type cooking, I picked my way into a stark art deco wonder in order to see if I wore my socioeconomic label well. If I could hold my own with those who knew their way around a wedge of Brie. 12

I was in for trouble the minute I crossed the polished threshold. Getting a meal here turned out to be as intimidating as applying for a bank loan or country club membership. The menu was as elliptical as a French symbolist poem— perfectly designed to make one feel simple-minded should a particular quail item need explication. Maybe I wasn't a true blue Yuppie after all. Not that I trembled in the face of "lightly oiled pasta," but others in the place seemed so at home, as if they had been weaned on warm lamb salad and not Bosco. My quartet stumbled through the ordering process, selecting the most familiar dishes with a relief not felt since getting out of grad school. It looked like a long evening. 13

Ironically, rescue came in the form of our busboy, a pleasant-looking lad who had geometrically shaped hair, wore an earring, and clearly noticed our consternation. As he refilled water glasses and passed out plates of bread and ceramic tubs of pale butter, he murmured without our even asking, "Land o' Lakes served in a ramekin." It was a clear tone of self-mockery totally out of synch with the industrial carpeting and bird-of-paradise flower arrangements. I glanced up. Sure enough, there was a wry twinkle in the busboy's eye not quite obscured by the new-wave coiffure. 14

Comment

Hilary DeVries defines the Yuppie through a series of humorous examples of the codes Yuppies obey, the games they play, the restaurants they patronize, and the food they eat. But being a Yuppie is more than the sum of what Yuppies do. It is a state of mind that DeVries must attain. She tries to convey that state of mind and also her anxiety that she is missing the Yuppie style.

Questions for Study and Discussion

1. The Yuppie is materialistic, DeVries shows. But does the Yuppie want to acquire things for their own sake, or does acquisition satisfy other needs?
2. What other attitudes characterize the Yuppie, and how does DeVries illustrate them?
3. What does DeVries mean by the satirical statement, "I will miss becoming my own role model" (paragraph 11)? What other popular phrases like *role model* does she satirize?
4. What words or phrases suggest Yuppie talk? What is the tone of the presentation of these words and phrases?
5. Is DeVries suggesting at the end that she has succeeded in becoming a Yuppie? Or has she failed? What is the tone of the conclusion? Does her tone change in the course of the essay, or does she maintain the same tone throughout the essay?

Vocabulary Study

1. DeVries depends on the connotations or associations of words to convey the feeling and style that mark the Yuppie. Give the denotative and connotative meaning of the following words— that is, the things the words represent, the feelings and images these words convey. Then discuss what they contribute to the humor or satire of the essay: *brunch, gourmet chocolates, aerobics, arugula, Bosco, cookware, new-wave coiffure.*
2. The phrases *Woodstock's 15th anniversary* and *Age of Aquarius* are references to a rock concert in Woodstock, New York, in 1969, and to a song in the 1960s musical *Hair,* "This is the dawning of the Age of Aquarius." Use the *New York Times Index* and other reference sources to explain these references in the essay.

Suggestions for Writing

1. Describe your own comical efforts to join the ranks of a fashionable group of people. Choose words that give the reader the sense of what you experienced and felt.
2. Define one of the following or a similar slang or faddish word through the connotations or associations the word has for you. Where possible, illustrate the association through images or brief episodes as DeVries does. Use your discussion to make a point about these associations or uses:

   a. funky
   b. jazzy
   c. macho
   d. nerdy

Frank Deford

BEAUTY AND EVERLASTING FAITH— LOCAL LEVEL

The sports writer and novelist Frank Deford attended Princeton University, where he edited *The Daily Princetonian* and the humor magazine *The Tiger*. A senior writer for *Sports Illustrated,* he has written on tennis, basketball, and roller derbies. His books include *Cut 'n' Run* (1973), *The Owner* (1976), and *Alex: The Life of a Child* (1983). In the following section from his book on the Miss America contest, *There She Is* (1971), Deford describes preliminary interviews in the local contest in Wilson, North Carolina, for the state title. The chapter from which this section is taken focuses on Doris Smith and Judi Brewer, who became finalists for first and second place. The veteran judges of the contest have long-standing memories of earlier winners; one of them mentions Jeanne Swanner, Miss North Carolina of 1963, who sometimes helps to conduct local contests.

The judging formally begins with the Saturday luncheon at the Heart of Wilson Motel. Dr. Vincent Thomas, the head of the judges' committee, welcomes all the judges, and is himself thereafter always introduced as "Dr. Vincent," by Jerry Ball, the well-known "dean of beauty-pageant judges." Jerry has sent two state queens on to become Miss America, and judged in states as far away as Alaska. Jerry is joined on the jury by Mrs. Judy Cross, who was Most Photogenic at Miss North Carolina a few years ago, and by Mrs. Marilyn Hull, a former Miss New Jersey. She is married, as so many beauty queens are, to an athlete. Her husband is Bill Hull, a former Kansas City Chief. The other two judges are Jim Church, chairman of the board of the North Carolina Jaycees, and Bob Logan, Charlotte sales manager for Fabergé, the beauty products concern. It is a hot-shot panel for any local Pageant.

2   The eight contestants keep a wary eye out as they sit down to lunch and make sure to reach for the correct implements. The judges, however, show no interest whatsoever in what eating tools are being utilized. They are genial and pleasant; the girls could be dispensing peas with a knife for all they seem to care about such formalities.

3   Doris's hat tumbles off. She does not realize it has gone, which is not surprising, since hats are as foreign to these girls as bustles or U.S. Army fatigues would be. Judi has a hat on for exactly the second time in her life. The first time was when she was in another beauty pageant. There are speeches and everyone in attendance is introduced. Then the room is cleared, and a table set up for the judges at the far end. It is time for the serious interviewing. Officially, the girls in any *Miss America* Pageant are not graded on their interviews. Actually, it is the underside of the iceberg that determines the winner.

4   The girls are directed to another room where, one by one, they will be funneled toward the judges. Following an interview, the contestant will proceed on to another room for a sort of debriefing. The judges arrange themselves and pour coffee. The men must concentrate to do their best, for the South Carolina-Duke basketball game is just starting on TV, and their hearts all lie there. Jerry Ball presides in the middle, like a Chief Justice, a leader among equals, and everyone agrees that there will be no set order to the questioning, just "catch as catch can."

Dr. Thomas sits at the other end of the room with a ₅ stop watch. Jerry says, "All right, Dr. Vincent, bring in the first young lady." The girls have been assigned an order in which they will present their talents in the show; they visit the judges in the same order. Rita Deans is first. Like all the others, she has her little hat on and carries a handbag, and she walks, as she has been taught, in the proper manner. This is an unfamiliar gait for all the girls and makes them resemble the little dogs on the Ed Sullivan Show, who have outfits on, are balanced precariously on their hind feet, and take desperate little steps to keep from pitching forward.

Rita, seated, is straightforward and demure. She assures ₆ the panel that her fourteen-year Sunday School record is not in any danger of being jeopardized by a victory tonight. The judges spring what is considered as a controversial question: what does Rita think of coed college dormitories? Rita thinks awhile. "Well, I haven't formed an opinion about that," she finally says. Mrs. Butner has instructed the girls to answer that way whenever they feel that they are unsure of an answer. The judges nod and agree that Rita would be unwise, indeed, to venture into unknown philosophical territory.

Sharon Shackleford is next. Talkative anyway, she seems ₇ especially garrulous when juxtaposed to Rita. "You've got to pull the plug on her," a judge says upon her departure. Wendy Formo, the third contestant, makes the best approach of all. Over six feet tall, she cannot help walking like a normal person. Also, she shuffles a question about Vice President Agnew beautifully, and the panel is obviously impressed. "It reminds you," Jim Church says. "I always liked that Jeanne Swanner."

Bob Logan asks, "What time is it?" ₈

Jerry answers, "About the end of the first quarter." ₉

Peggy Murphy, recovered from the flu, is next, and for ₁₀ her, the judges reach back for a classic old standard of a question: what kind of person do you think you are yourself? There is one stock answer to this question, which every girl ever in a beauty pageant has always provided. In so many words, it is: that I am naturally a shy, thoughtful person, but I love a good time on occasion. Also, I am nuts about people. Peggy is close enough.

The interviewing is now halfway through, so the judges stand and reach for some coffee. Doris comes in. She is in yellow, with a matching handbag that she sets on the rug by the side of her chair. She banters back the usual polite preliminaries, and then one of the judges asks her if she believes there is a generation gap. "Yes, I definitely believe there is one," Doris replies firmly. All the judges sit up and cock their heads. The regular answer to this question is that there certainly isn't one around my house, where everyone works to understand each other better. Doris proceeds. "Ours is the first generation brought up with the threat of the hydrogen and atom bombs, and the first generation to have grown up with television as a major force in our lives. I really don't even believe it is surprising that there is a gap. Maybe we should only be surprised that there is not more of one."

The judges nod sagely, and to test her further, pull another old chestnut out of the fire. All right, what about coed dorms? Doris backs down here; she comes out with the company line. "It may be fine for other people," she says, "but I can certainly see enough of the opposite sex on dates and other things." Doris has inserted a proper amount of righteous indignation in her voice by the end of her speech. The judges draw a breath, relieved not to have a genuine revolutionary on their hands. They are spent, though, so they ask her if she has any questions for them.

Gay Butner has informed the girls that they may be faced with this request, and to have a question on stand-by. "Yes," Doris says, "I'd like to know why you're still interested in judging. Does it keep you closer to our generation and help close the gap for you?" Yes, the judges agree, yes, it certainly works that way for them.

Time is up; the panel smiles and thanks her; and Doris is hardly out of the door when Jerry slams his hand down. "She came through like 'Gangbusters,'" he exclaims. "She took everything we threw at her and came right back."

"A live cookie," Jim Church says.

Vince Thomas goes to fetch Judi. She comes in, smiling broadly, wearing her aunt's bright orange sleeveless dress. She talks enthusiastically, almost conversationally, from the moment she deposits herself in the chair before the judges.

It is as if she has been doing this all her life. Judi is restrained only by what she keeps reminding herself, to keep her hands anchored in her lap and not to say "you know." She is bright and cheery and carries the judges along with her. "Learn to gain control over the interview," Gay has told all the girls. "Give a brief answer, then lead into another area that you particularly like to talk about."

That advice was like giving Judi a license to steal. She [17] and all the other modern Southern belles are born and bred in this briar patch. In Atlantic City a few months later, Phyllis George, Judi's temperamental and verbal kin, babbled on with such dazzle about her pet crab and her dog that the most serious thing that the judges found time to ask her was whether or not she liked beer—and Phyllis even side-stepped that one, and went rambling right on, absolutely stunning the judges from start to finish of the interview. Judi's footwork is proportionately as good at the Heart of Wilson Motel, but she slows down and twice permits the judges time to reach into the portfolio of controversial questions.

First, they want to know if Judi endorses drugs. Well, [18] she doesn't. Then Marilyn Hull remembers Doris. "Do you think there is a generation gap?" she asks. Judi pauses but for a second, then replies: "I don't think there's any more gap now than there's ever been." The judges nod, and then they want to know if she might have a question for them.

Judi has come loaded for that bear. "What is your idea [19] of a Miss Wilson?" she rips back at them.

A girl with poise, the judges solemnly agree. [20]

"Now, do you have any other question you would like [21] to ask us?" Jerry asks. This is a formality, like drop-over-some-time-and-see-us, but Judi tears into it at face value. "Do you think there is a generation gap?" she asks. Marilyn fields the answer, uneasily, and this time Jerry does not ask Judi if she has another question to ask. "I'm afraid Dr. Vincent is signaling that our time is up," he informs her. Judi thanks everyone and leaves. As soon as she is out of the room, the judges start marveling about her performance. "Imagine," one says, "we asked if she had another question, and she did." There is a first time for everything.

They are still chuckling at Judi's effervescence as Rose [22] Thorne comes in. She expresses a solid opposition to coed dorms, and then Connie Whisenant finishes up by voicing displeasure at those college students who had participated in the Vietnam Moratorium.

Outside the room Doris and Judi are already comparing [23] notes. It is immediately obvious to each that her rival was not disappointed; at the least, neither felt she had done poorly. Judi is stunned to learn, though, that Doris has actually said that there is a generation gap. Was she right? Was that the correct answer that the judges were fishing for? Anyway, it only reinforces Judi's growing opinion. By the time she goes home to put her hair up in curlers, and to affix false eyelashes for the first time in her life, Judi Brewer is absolutely convinced that Doris Smith is the only thing that stands between her and Miss Wilson 1970.

Comment

Deford's attitude toward Miss America is suggested by his opening comment in the book: "Maligned by one segment of America, adored by another, misunderstood by about all of it, Miss America still flows like the Mississippi, drifts like amber waves of grain, sounds like the crack of a bat on a baseball, tastes like Mom's apple pie, and smells like dollar bills." Deford is obviously concerned with the values the contest represents. In the section reprinted here, he is direct about how the contest affects the participants. "Over six feet tall," he says about Wendy Formo, "she cannot help walking like a normal person." And he has similar things to say about how the young women act on the advice of Mrs. Butner, a woman from Rocky Mount who has been tutoring them. Another important indication of tone is the incongruity he stresses. Deford need not comment directly on the young women. His sympathy for them shapes his attitude and therefore his tone; so does his complex attitude toward the contest and the idea of "Miss America." Tone is revealed unmistakably in exaggeration as in understatement—if the author prefers not to state his or her attitude directly. The details selected for emphasis can be equally revealing.

Questions for Study and Discussion

1. How does Deford's choice of details stress the incongruous? How do his comparisons to Army fatigues, bustles, and little dogs make the incongruities vivid to us? What is the tone of these statements and comparisons?
2. Does Deford express or imply the same attitude towards all the girls in the contest? To what extent is his sympathy toward them qualified by his attitude toward the values represented by or implied in the contest?
3. What are those values, and what details best reveal them?
4. How sympathetic is Deford toward the judges? Is it his view that the panel is "hot-shot," or is he giving someone's opinion of it?
5. What does Deford mean by the statement that "it is the underside of the iceberg that determines the winner"? How does he illustrate the statement?
6. Does Deford resort to understatement or irony, or does he depend solely on the details to create tone? Does the essay have an overall tone, or does the tone vary?
7. How does he establish and maintain a consistent point of view in the whole essay?
8. What are your feelings toward the contestants and the judges? How much were they shaped for you by Deford?

Vocabulary Study

Identify words and phrases that you would classify as slang (such as "hot-shot") and determine their use in the essay, in particular their contribution to the overall tone. If this slang is no longer current, suggest how the statements might be reworded to convey the same tone.

Suggestions for Writing

1. Describe a contest in which you participated. Focus on the behavior and attitude of the judges or the participants, and use your discussion to reveal your attitude toward the contest. Choose vivid details that best reveal the values represented by or implied in the contest.

2. Discuss what you think Deford is saying or implying about the contest. Consider his details about the judges as well as about the contestants.

3. Rewrite a part of this essay from the point of view of one of the contestants. Allow her attitude toward the judges and the contest itself to emerge in the details she selects and the feelings she expresses.

Usage

Each of us has a formal and informal vocabulary. We use each vocabulary on different occasions, often without much thought. On formal occasions like weddings, funerals, and job interviews, we use a vocabulary different from that at home or with friends. Though judgments about vocabulary vary from one group of people or one part of the country to another, people do agree on what is extremely formal and informal—the language of insurance policies and that of television comedy and sports writing, for example.

Consider the following formal and informal statements:

> In defying nature, in destroying nature, in building an arrogantly selfish, man-centered, artificial world, I do not see how man can gain peace or freedom or joy. I have faith in man's future, faith in the possibilities latent in the human experiment: but it is faith in man as a part of nature, working with the forces that govern the forests and the seas; faith in man sharing life, not destroying it.—Marston Bates, *The Forest and the Sea*

> He sailed up to me, and then cut to my left for the sidelines, with a little grunt, and I could hear the *shu-shu* of his football trousers as he went by, and the creak of his shoulder pads.—George Plimpton, *Paper Lion*

The vocabulary of the first passage is formal—abstract words and phrases like *faith in the possibilities latent in the human experiment* expressing abstract ideas. In the second passage, the colloquial or everyday conversational phrases like *sailed up* and *cut to my left* contribute to the informality.

Vocabulary and sentence structure work together to make a piece of writing formal or informal. In the first passage the tight parallelism and the opening periodic sentence (a sentence that builds to the core idea) creates a highly formal effect. In the second the loose coordination is characteristic of everyday informal conversation. However, formal English is not limited to ideas, nor is informal English limited to concrete experiences. Formal English often deals with specific concrete ideas and experience and uses a simple vocabulary. Informal English often deals with ideas in concrete language and in sentences containing looser parallelism.

Slang and jargon associated with particular jobs or activities are found in informal speech and writing. Slang consists of colorful, usually short-lived, expressions peculiar to a group of people. Jargon consists of the technical words specific to a trade or profession. Assembly-line workers and telephone and automobile repairmen have their own special language—in particular, special terms and expressions. So have teenagers, jazz musicians, college professors, and baseball fans. This special language is less common in formal speech and writing, mainly because the audience for that writing is usually a general one. Expressions associated with rock music will be understood by a special audience of rock fans, but a general audience will need an explanation.

As in Art Buchwald's following comic series of letters, awareness of usage often begins when a piece of writing creates an unintended impression or effect. Unless you know your audience will be a special one, you will do best to think of it as general—representing many backgrounds and interests. This advice bears especially on diction, for vocabulary gives readers the most trouble—especially inexact, ambiguous words and phrases.

Art Buchwald

JOB HUNTING

Art Buchwald was born in Mount Vernon, New York, in 1925, and was educated at the University of Southern California. During the Second World War he served in the Marine Corps. He has written for many newspapers; his satirical columns have been collected into many books. His chief target has been the Washington scene but he has also written about contemporary social problems.

Vice President of Development
Glucksville Dynamics
Glucksville, California

DEAR SIR,
I am writing in regard to employment with your firm. I have a BS from USC and PhD in physics from the California Institute of Technology.

In my previous position I was in charge of research and development for the Harrington Chemical Company. We did work in thermonuclear energy, laser beam refraction, hydrogen molecule development, and heavy-water computer data.

Several of our research discoveries have been adapted for commercial use, and one particular breakthrough in linear hydraulics is now being used by every oil company in the country.

Because of a cutback in defense orders, the Harrington Company decided to shut down its research and development department. It is for this reason I am available for immediate employment.

Hoping to hear from you in the near future, I remain

> Sincerely yours,
> Edward Kase

Dear Mr. Kase,

We regret to inform you that we have no positions available for someone of your excellent qualifications. The truth of the matter is that we find you are "overqualified" for any position we might offer you in our organization. Thank you for thinking of us, and if anything comes up in the future, we will be getting in touch with you.

> Yours truly,
> Merriman Haselbald
> Administrative Vice-President

Personnel Director
Jessel International Systems
Crewcut, Mich.

Dear Sir,

I am applying for a position with your company in any responsible capacity. I have had a college education and have fiddled around in research and development. Occasionally we have come up with some moneymaking ideas. I would be willing to start off at a minimal salary to prove my value to your firm.

Sincerely yours,
EDWARD KASE

DEAR MR. KASE,
Thank you for your letter of the 15th. Unfortunately we have no positions at the moment for someone with a college education. Frankly it is the feeling of everyone here that you are "overqualified," and your experience indicates you would be much happier with a company that could make full use of your talents.
It was kind of you to think of us.

HARDY LANDSDOWNE
Personnel Dept.

To Whom It May Concern
Geis & Waterman Inc.
Ziegfried, Ill.

DERE SER,
I'd like a job with your outfit. I can do anything you want me to. You name it Kase will do it. I ain't got no education and no experience, but I'm strong and I got moxy an I get along great with people. I'm ready to start any time because I need the bread. Let me know when you want me.

Cheers
EDWARD KASE

DEAR MR. KASE,
You are just the person we have been looking for. We need a truck driver, and your qualifications are perfect for us. You can begin working in our Westminister plant on Monday. Welcome aboard.

CARSON PETERS
Personnel

Comment

Buchwald is not writing in his own person in these letters, but we do hear him indirectly—in the language he has given the correspondents. Buchwald's humor arises in the changes we see in Kase's letters and in the situation itself. Humor must develop out of real problems in the world we know: we will not find humor long in invented qualities and situations. Those problems may be serious—the problem Buchwald deals with is a serious one today. We can laugh with Buchwald because we are laughing not at Kase but at ourselves and at the dilemma of our world.

Questions for Study and Discussion

1. How do Kase's letters change in language? What are the most important changes? What changes do you notice in sentence structure?
2. What situation is the source of Buchwald's humor? Is he satirizing this situation—that is, trying to correct it through ridicule?
3. What do Kase and his correspondents reveal about themselves in the impressions they give of themselves?

Vocabulary Study

Find substitutes for the formal diction in the letters to Kase. Discuss how their substitution would change the humor or point of the letters.

Suggestions for Writing

1. Write three letters of application for the same job. Change your language to give a different impression of yourself. Use these letters to make a satirical point, as Buchwald does.
2. Write an exchange of letters like Buchwald's, satirizing a current social problem through them. Fit the language of each letter to the character and attitude of the writer.

James Thurber

THE PRINCESS AND THE TIN BOX

James Thurber (1894–1961) was born in Columbus, Ohio. He attended Ohio State University for three years, and later worked for the U.S. State Department as a code clerk. From 1920 to 1925 he worked as a journalist on the *Columbus Dispatch* and *Chicago Tribune*. His long association with *The New Yorker* began in 1925, the year it began publication, and most of his stories, sketches, and cartoons appeared in that magazine. Thurber was a humorist and a satirist of many aspects of American life, in particular the relations of the sexes. His many books include *My Life and Hard Times* (1933), *Fables for Our Time* (1943), *The Thurber Carnival* (1945), and *Thurber Country* (1953).

Once upon a time, in a far country, there lived a king whose daughter was the prettiest princess in the world. Her eyes were like the cornflower, her hair was sweeter than the hyacinth, and her throat made the swan look dusty. 1

From the time she was a year old, the princess had been showered with presents. Her nursery looked like Cartier's window. Her toys were all made of gold or platinum or diamonds or emeralds. She was not permitted to have wooden blocks or china dolls or rubber dogs or linen books, because such materials were considered cheap for the daughter of a king. 2

When she was seven, she was allowed to attend the wedding of her brother and throw real pearls at the bride instead of rice. Only the nightingale, with his lyre of gold, was permitted to sing for the princess. The common blackbird, with his boxwood flute, was kept out of the palace grounds. She walked in silver-and-samite slippers to a sapphire-and-topaz bathroom and slept in an ivory bed inlaid with rubies. 3

On the day the princess was eighteen, the king sent a royal ambassador to the courts of five neighboring kingdoms to announce that he would give his daughter's hand in marriage to the prince who brought her the gift she liked the most. 4

The first prince to arrive at the palace rode a swift white ₅ stallion and laid at the feet of the princess an enormous apple made of solid gold which he had taken from a dragon who had guarded it for a thousand years. It was placed on a long ebony table set up to hold the gifts of the princess's suitors. The second prince, who came on a gray charger, brought her a nightingale made of a thousand diamonds, and it was placed beside the golden apple. The third prince, riding on a black horse, carried a great jewel box made of platinum and sapphires, and it was placed next to the diamond nightingale. The fourth prince, astride a fiery yellow horse, gave the princess a gigantic heart made of rubies and pierced by an emerald arrow. It was placed next to the platinum-and-sapphire jewel box.

Now the fifth prince was the strongest and handsomest ₆ of all the five suitors, but he was the son of a poor king whose realm had been overrun by mice and locusts and wizards and mining engineers so that there was nothing much of value left in it. He came plodding up to the palace of the princess on a plow horse and he brought her a small tin box filled with mica and feldspar and hornblende which he had picked up on the way.

The other princes roared with disdainful laughter when ₇ they saw the tawdry gift the fifth prince had brought to the princess. But she examined it with great interest and squealed with delight, for all her life she had been glutted with precious stones and priceless metals, but she had never seen tin before or mica or feldspar or hornblende. The tin box was placed next to the ruby heart pierced with an emerald arrow.

"Now," the king said to his daughter, "you must select ₈ the gift you like best and marry the prince that brought it."

The princess smiled and walked up to the table and ₉ picked up the present she liked the most. It was the platinum-and-sapphire jewel box, the gift of the third prince.

"The way I figure it," she said, "is this. It is a very large ₁₀ and expensive box, and when I am married, I will meet many admirers who will give me precious gems with which to fill it to the top. Therefore, it is the most valuable of all the gifts my suitors have brought me and I like it the best."

The princess married the third prince that very day in 11
the midst of great merriment and high revelry. More than a
hundred thousand pearls were thrown at her and she loved
it.

Moral: All those who thought the princess was going 12
to select the tin box with worthless stones instead of one of
the other gifts will kindly stay after class and write one
hundred times on the blackboard "I would rather have a
hunk of aluminum silicate than a diamond necklace."

Comment

Thurber's humor often arises in his fables and stories from incongruities between what we expect to see in people or expect to
happen to them and what does happen. The humor of "The Princess and the Tin Box" arises from the incongruity of Thurber's
fairy-tale kingdom, which contains wizards and mining engineers.
Another incongruity is found in Thurber's language. Disparities of
this sort are a major source of irony—the sardonic discovery that
life is different from what we expect it to be, that appearances
deceive. Many authors do not comment on what they show; they
allow truths and ironies to emerge from the details of the story—
from the setting, happenings, statements of characters. Thurber
does comment in the moral he attaches to his story. But this moral
by no means expresses all the truths contained in what the princess does and says.

Questions for Study and Discussion

1. How do the details of the first six paragraphs lead us to believe that the princess will choose the fifth prince? Is the order
   of these details important?
2. At what point does the reader discover the real character of
   the princess? What does her manner of speaking or choice of
   words contribute to this discovery?
3. Thurber, in his moral, talks to us in a language different from
   that of the story. What exactly is this difference, and what
   humor arises from it?

4. What human frailties is Thurber satirizing? Is he satirizing the princess or the reader of the essay or possibly both? Do you find other truths in the story?
5. Do you find Thurber's moral pertinent to the world today?

Vocabulary Study

Look up the following words: *parable, fairy tale, fable, allegory.* How closely does "The Princess and the Tin Box" fit the definitions you found?

Suggestions for Writing

1. Write a fairy tale or fable or parable of your own that uses the order of climax.
2. Write a non-satirical essay that examines the values Thurber writes about from your point of view and experience. If you take a different view of them, compare your view with Thurber's.

Sydney J. Harris

THE MAN IN THE MIDDLE

Sydney J. Harris wrote several columns describing "the man in the middle." These columns reflect Harris's interest in language—in particular, the language of the current social and political scene in America. For the details of Harris's life, see p. 200.

I am the man in the middle; for where I stand determines where the middle is.

I am compassionate; those less compassionate than I are "cold," and those more compassionate than I are "sentimental."

I am steadfast; those less steadfast than I are "fickle," and those more steadfast than I are "stubborn."

I am friendly; those less friendly than I are "stand-offish," and those more friendly than I are "pushy."

I am decent; those less decent than I are "disreputable," and those more decent than I are "priggish."

I am civil; those less civil than I are "rude," and those more civil than I are "obsequious."

I am dutiful; those less dutiful than I are "irresponsible," and those more dutiful than I are "subservient."

I am an individualist; those less individualistic than I are "conformists," and those more individualistic than I are "kooks."

I am brave; those less brave than I are "lily-livered," and those more brave than I are "hotheads."

I am a moderate; those less moderate than I are "extremists," and those more moderate than I are "fence-sitters."

I am firm; those less firm than I are "soft-hearted," and those more firm than I are "hard-nosed."

I am competitive; those more competitive than I are "wolves," and those less competitive than I are "worms."

I am normally sexed; those less so are "repressed," and those more so are "promiscuous."

I am prudent; those less prudent are "spendthrifts," and those more prudent are "skinflints."

I am patriotic; those less patriotic are "un-American," and those more patriotic are "jingoists."

I am reasonable; those less reasonable are "too emotional," and those more reasonable are "too logical."

I am a fond parent; those less fond than I are "authoritarian," and those more fond than I are "permissive."

I am a careful driver, those less careful than I are "reckless," and those more careful than I are "slowpokes."

I am the man in the middle, for where I stand determines where the middle is.

Comment

Harris is writing persuasively; he wishes the reader to condemn language that justifies or rationalizes complacent and self-serving attitudes toward other people. The particular means of persuasion Harris chooses is satire—ridicule intended to correct social and moral attitudes and behavior. Thurber and Buchwald use satire for the same purpose although they have different targets in mind. They also use different kinds of ridicule. Satire requires a strategy of some kind. The satirist cannot assume the reader will take the ridicule seriously or recognize its pertinence to an existing social or political situation. A strategy is therefore necessary—a means of forcing readers to face truths about other people and situations and ultimately about themselves. Thurber's deceives the reader; the truth or moral of his story comes unexpectedly and in this way gains the reader's full attention. Harris chooses another strategy in describing himself as the man in the middle.

Questions for Study and Discussion

1. In what way is Harris "the man in the middle?" What does he mean by where he stands "determines where the middle is"?
2. What is the tone of the essay? Is Harris expressing pleasure, amusement, shame, disgust, or some other attitude toward the words he contrasts? Or is he expressing no attitude?
3. Does the word *man* stand for all human beings? Or is Harris describing his own language and outlook?
4. Why does Harris end the essay with the statement that opens it?
5. What strategy does Harris use to force the reader to consider ways of speaking and thinking about oneself and others?

Vocabulary Study

1. Compare the dictionary definitions of the words in quotations in three of the sentences of the essay. To what extent does the dictionary definition convey the particular meaning of the contrasted words in Harris's sentences?
2. Write your own essay using contrasting words in the same way as the man in the middle does.

PART 5

Strategies for Arguing and Persuading

Argument, or proof, is different from exposition, but the two usually occur together in essays. Most arguments require the explanation or illustration that exposition provides, and many explanations seem to be proving an idea.

Arguments seek to establish the truth or falseness of a statement. They often have different purposes and use different kinds of evidence. A lawyer in a court trial may argue the innocence of his client on the basis of eyewitness testimony and supporting circumstantial evidence. A scientist may argue on the basis of repeated experiments that heredity plays a role in some kinds of cancer. A newspaper editorial may argue for equal educational opportunity for the handicapped through an appeal to constitutional precedents.

Arguments are classified as either *inductive* or *deductive* on the basis of the kind of evidence used to prove the conclusion. In the examples above, the lawyer and the scientist are developing inductive arguments that reason from observation, personal experience, and experiment; the editorialist is developing a deductive argument that reasons from given truths or principles. Many writers use both kinds of reasoning to prove various ideas that together form the essay.

An essay that contains argument usually does more than prove or demonstrate the truth of a statement. In developing the argument, the writer usually is trying to change the thinking of people on an issue or is trying to encourage them to take some kind of action. The purpose of the argument in these instances is persuasive. The argument employs strategies intended to capture the reader's or listener's attention and assent to the argument. But not all persuasive writing uses formal argument. Political cartoons are persuasive without being argumentative, for example. So are many satirical essays and poems. In this part of the book, we will discuss argument and persuasion separately, though some of the essays in the two sections illustrate both.

Inductive Argument

When we reason from personal experience, observation, experiments, facts and statistics, and other empirical evidence, we are reasoning inductively. We would be doing so if we predicted that it will rain on the upcoming Fourth of July because it has rained on previous Fourths in the past ten years. A scientist would do so in predicting that vaccines will be effective in fighting new viral diseases because of the success of vaccines in combatting polio, smallpox, and measles. In the essay that follows, Edwin H. Peeples, Jr. uses various kinds of evidence—personal experience, social work, medical observation, testimony, statistical studies— to reach a conclusion concerning hunger and malnutrition in America.

Inductive arguments make predictions about the future on the basis of past and present experience or experimentation. Because it is based on experience, and experience changes, the prediction or conclusion of an inductive argument can only be probable, and it cannot go beyond the particular evidence presented. The probability increases that it will rain this Fourth of July if it did in fact rain on every Fourth of July in the last forty years. But the fact that it has rained does not guarantee that it will do so again; nor can we use the history of the Fourth to predict what will happen on other holidays. The success in treating viral disease suggests that vaccines may be effective in fighting new viral diseases; however, it does not prove that vaccination is the only effective method, or that it will be effective with bacterial and other nonviral diseases.

The writer of an inductive argument must decide how much evidence is needed to draw a well-founded conclusion—to make the "inductive leap." There is, of course, no end to the amount of evidence that can be presented for a conclusion such as Peeples reaches in his essay (p. 393):

> There are those who argue that we do not have enough hard
> data on the human consumption of pet foods. Must we wait for
> incontrovertible data before we seriously seek to solve the prob-
> lems of hunger and malnutrition in America? I submit that we
> have data enough.

As Peeples suggests in this statement, the researcher must make
the decision at some point in conducting an investigation that
enough evidence has been found to warrant a conclusion. The
conclusion must, however, be properly limited or qualified: the
writer or researcher must tell us how broad a conclusion can be
drawn from the evidence available. The phrase "inductive leap"
sometimes means that the writer has drawn a conclusion too soon
on the basis of incomplete evidence.

Probably few writers are satisfied they have found all the evidence needed to make the argument convincing to everyone. Like
Peeples, they find it necessary to draw a conclusion from a limited
amount of evidence because a current situation is growing critical
and must be exposed at once:

> Isn't it sufficient to know that one American child or a single
> elderly person in this bountiful land is reduced to eating the for-
> age of animals or exposed to unknown toxic levels of mercury,
> lead or salmonella to know that something very extraordinary
> must be done?

Peeples admits that his personal experience imposes a limit on his
conclusions; he is careful to state this limitation. If writers have
wide and expert experience in their subject, as Peeples has, their
experience alone may be sufficient to give weight to the conclusion. But the greater the variety of evidence provided for the
conclusion, the more convincing we may find it.

Casual analysis—reasoning about causes and effects—is another kind of inductive argument: identifying the causes that produce an event is the same as drawing a conclusion from particulars
of experience. Michael Nelson is reasoning about causes in arguing that hostility toward government arises sometimes not from
the government worker who applies the law but from necessities
of government that we call bureaucracy:

> The desk, whether physical or metaphorical, is there in every
> encounter between Americans and their government. It turns

unique and deserving citizens into snarling clients, and good-hearted civil servants into sullen automatons. More than anything else, I suspect, it explains why we and our government are at each other's throats—why taxpayers pass Proposition 13s and public employees strike like dock workers.—"The Desk"

Nelson uses a single episode—the encounter of a bureaucrat with a woman in need—to make a judgment about causes. But the episode is not his only evidence; he has talked with other people whose experience he considers representative of this situation—an important consideration in gathering inductive evidence.

The word *cause* has different meanings (see p. 70). Sometimes the word refers to the immediate event that produces an effect—failure of an engine part that leads to a car crash, a drought that leads to widespead starvation. Sometimes the word refers to one or more past events that led to the engine failure or to the drought. The immediate cause of the event may be of less concern to us than the remote cause: we want to know what in the manufacture or maintenance of the engine made it fail, or what changing weather patterns or atmospheric pollution led to the drought. We sometimes use the word *condition* to refer to cause. We may speak of a condition necessary for an event to occur: wheat cannot grow without water. Water is a necessary condition—wheat cannot grow if water is absent. But water is not a sufficient condition: water alone is not enough to produce a strong crop of wheat. Other conditions must be present—fertile soil, proper cultivation, sunlight, to name a few. We would know the sufficient condition if we knew all the conditions needed to assure a strong crop. It is difficult, however, to claim to know all conditions; knowledge of why things happen is seldom complete. The word *condition* is used to avoid making this claim. Statements about causes and effects need to be qualified carefully.

An *analogy* is a point by point comparison used for illustration (see p. 202) or used to prove a thesis. An argument from analogy is inductive because, like causal analysis, it makes an appeal to experience. For example, you might argue that a candidate for the presidency should be elected on the basis of resemblances to an admired former president. Your analogy covers a range of similarities in traits of character, policies, and governmental acts. In an effective argument from analogy, the points of similarity must be pertinent to the issue—here, the qualifications for the presidency. It would be immaterial to the argument if the candidate were shorter than the former president. Important differences would weaken the analogy: it would be a material difference if the candidate had no previous governmental experience. If the similarities noted are genuine and if no significant differences weaken the analogy, it can be argued that the candidate probably would make a good president.

Notice the qualification *probably*. The analogy does not allow us to say with certainty that the candidate will make a good president. Inductive arguments are only probable. As in causal analysis, we can never be certain that we have discovered all the facts—that an exception may not exist to the conclusion drawn from the evidence. In inductive arguments, the major problem is not to claim more in the conclusion than the evidence warrants; the conclusion must be limited properly.

Edward H. Peeples, Jr.

. . . MEANWHILE, HUMANS EAT PET FOOD

Edward H. Peeples, Jr., is associate professor of preventive medicine at Virginia Commonwealth University. Born in 1935 in Richmond, Virginia, Peeples attended Richmond Professional Institute, the University of Pennsylvania, and the University of Kentucky, where he received his Ph.D. in 1972. In the 1960s, he gained knowledge of urban poverty as a social worker in Richmond and South Philadelphia. He has been a leader of the Richmond Human Rights Coalition and Council on Human Relations and has long been concerned with the nutritional problems and medical care of poor people.

The first time I witnessed people eating pet foods was among neighbors and acquaintances during my youth in the South. At that time it was not uncommon or startling to me to see dog-food patties sizzling in a pan on the top of a stove or kerosene space heater in a dilapidated house with no running water, no refrigerator, no heat, no toilet and the unrelenting stench of decaying insects. I simply thought of it as the unfortunate but unavoidable consequence of being poor in the South.

The second time occurred in Cleveland in the summer of 1953. Like many other Southerners, I came to seek my

fortune in one of those pot-at-the-end-of-the-rainbow factories along Euclid Avenue. Turned away from one prospec-
tive job after another ("We don't hire hillbillies," employers
said), I saw my nest egg of $30 dwindle to nothing. As my
funds diminished and my hunger grew, I turned to pilfering
food and small amounts of cash. With the money, I surrep-
titiously purchased, fried and ate canned dog and cat food
as my principal ration for several weeks.

I was, of course, humiliated to be eating something that,   3
in my experience, only "trash" consumed. A merciless pride
in self-sufficiency kept me from seeking out public welfare
or asking my friends or family for help. In fact, I carefully
guarded the secret from everyone, because I feared being
judged a failure. Except for the humiliation I experienced,
eating canned pet food did not at the time seem to be particularly unpleasant. The dog food tasted pretty much like
mealy hamburger, while the cat food was similar to canned
fish that I was able to improve with mayonnaise, mustard
or catsup.

The next time I ate dog food was in 1956 while strug-   4
gling through a summer session in college without income
for food. Again, I was ashamed to admit it, fearing that people would feel sorry for me or that others who had even less
than I would feel compelled to sacrifice for my comfort. I
never again had to eat pet food. Later, while working as a
hospital corpsman at the Great Lakes Illinois Naval Training Center in the late 1950's I had the opportunity to ask
new recruits about their home life and nutrition practices.
While I was not yet a disciplined scientist, I was able to
estimate that about 5 to 8 percent of the thousands of young
men who came to Great Lakes annually consumed pet foods
and other materials not commonly thought to be safe or
desirable for humans. Among these substances were baking
soda, baking powder, laundry starch, tobacco, snuff, clay,
dirt, sand and various wild plants.

My later experience as a public assistance caseworker   5
in Richmond, a street-based community worker in South
Philadelphia, and my subsequent travels and studies as a
medical sociologist throughout the South, turned up in-

stances of people eating pet food because they saw it as cheaper than other protein products. Through the years, similar cases found in the Ozarks, on Indian reservations and in various cities across the nation have also been brought to my attention.

While there do exist scattered scientific reports and commentary on the hazards and problems associated with eating such things as laundry starch and clay, there is little solid epidemiological evidence that shows a specific percentage of American households consume pet food. My experience and research, however, suggest that human consumption of pet food is widespread in the United States. My estimate, one I believe to be conservative, is that pet foods constitute a significant part of the diet of at least 225,000 American households, affecting some one million persons. Who knows how many more millions supplement their diet with pet-food products? One thing that we can assume is that current economic conditions are increasing the practice and that it most seriously affects the unemployed, poor people, and our older citizens.

There are those who argue that we do not have enough hard data on the human consumption of pet foods. Must we wait for incontrovertible data before we seriously seek to solve the problems of hunger and malnutrition in America? I submit that we have data enough. Isn't it sufficient to know that one American child or a single elderly person in this bountiful land is reduced to eating the forage of animals or exposed to unknown toxic levels of mercury, lead or salmonella to know that something very extraordinary must be done?

Questions for Study and Discussion

1. Why do people eat pet food, according to Peeples?
2. What is his purpose in writing, and where does he state it? What makes the essay inductive?
3. To what audience is he writing, and how do you know? Were he writing to public health officials only, would he approach the subject in a different way, or present different evidence?

4. How does Peeples qualify his conclusion that people who eat pet food are affected by it seriously—that is, how does he indicate the degree of probability that this is so?
5. Has Peeples persuaded you that the situation he describes is serious and that something must be done about it? If not, what other evidence would persuade you?

Vocabulary Study

1. Complete the following to show the meaning of the italicized words:
   a. His *disciplined* way of living was shown by
   b. A *conservative* action is one that
   c. An *incontrovertible* proof can never
   d. The *bountiful* harvest
2. Identify the denotative and connotative meanings of the following: paragraph 1: *sizzling, dilapidated, stench;* paragraph 2: *pilfering, surreptitious;* paragraph 3: *"trash";* paragraph 5: *cheaper;* paragraph 7: *extraordinary, forage.*

Suggestions for Writing

1. Write an essay that builds to a thesis through a series of observations and experiences. Qualify your thesis by stating the limitations of your experience and knowledge of the subject.
2. Discuss an experience that resulted when you found yourself short of or without money. Discuss what you did and what you learned about yourself and perhaps about other people.
3. Discuss how your ideas about people changed through experiences in a world different from that you grew up in. Use this experience to persuade a particular audience to change their thinking about these people.

James M. Dubik

AN OFFICER AND A FEMINIST

James M. Dubik, a major in the U.S. Army, was stationed in Savannah, Georgia, at the time he wrote this essay. Dubik describes how his observation of women cadets at West Point and his experiences with his two daughters led him to reject feminine stereotypes. Dubik raises issues similar to those discussed by K. C. Cole in "Women and Physics" (p. 214).

I'm a member of a last bastion of male chauvinism. I'm an infantry officer, and there are no women in the infantry. I'm a Ranger and no women go to Ranger School. I'm a member of America's special-operation forces—and there, although women are involved in intelligence, planning and clerical work, only men can be operators, or "shooters." Women can become paratroopers and jump out of airplanes alongside me—yet not many do. All this is as it should be, according to what I learned while growing up. [1]

Not many women I knew in high school and college in the '60s and early '70s pushed themselves to their physical or mental limits or had serious career dreams of their own. If they did, few talked about them. So I concluded they were exceptions to the rule. Then two things happened. First, I was assigned to West Point, where I became a philosophy instructor. Second, my two daughters grew up. [2]

I arrived at the Academy with a master's degree from Johns Hopkins University in Baltimore and a graduation certificate from the U.S. Army Command and General Staff College at Fort Leavenworth. I was ready to teach, but instead, I was the one who got an education. [3]

The women cadets, in the classroom and out, did not fit my stereotype of female behavior. They took themselves and their futures seriously. They persevered in a very competitive environment. Often they took charge and seized control of a situation. They gave orders; they were punctual and organized. They played sports hard. They survived, even thrived, under real pressure. During field exercises, women cadets were calm and unemotional even when they were dirty, cold, wet, tired and hungry. They didn't fold or give up. [4]

Most important, such conduct seemed natural to them. From my perspective all this was extraordinary; to them it was ordinary. While I had read a good bit of "feminist literature" and, intellectually, accepted many of the arguments [5] against stereotyping, this was the first time my real-life experience supported such ideas. And seeing is believing.

Enter two daughters: Kerith, 12; Katie, 10.   6

Kerith and Katie read a lot, and they write, too—poems,   7
stories, paragraphs and answers to "thought questions" in school. In what they read and in what they write, I can see their adventurousness, their inquisitiveness and their ambition. They discover clues and solve mysteries. They take risks, brave dangers, fight villains—and prevail. Their schoolwork reveals their pride in themselves. Their taste for reading is boundless; they're interested in everything. "Why?" is forever on their lips. Their eyes are set on personal goals that they, as individuals, aspire to achieve: Olympic gold, owning their own business, public office.

Both play sports. I've witnessed a wholesome, aggres-   8
sive, competitive spirit born in Kerith. She played her first basketball season last year, and when she started, she was too polite to bump anyone, too nice to steal anything, especially if some other girl already had the ball. By the end of the season, however, Kerith was taking bumps and dishing them out. She plays softball with the intensity of a Baltimore Oriole. She rides and jumps her horse in competitive shows. Now she "can't imagine" not playing a sport, especially one that didn't have a little rough play and risk.

In Katie's face, I've seen Olympic intensity as she passed   9
a runner in the last 50 yards of a mile relay. Gasping for air, knees shaking, lungs bursting, she dipped into her well of courage and "gutted out" a final kick. Her comment after the race: "I kept thinking I was Mary Decker beating the Russians." For the first time she experienced the thrill of pushing herself to the limit. She rides and jumps, too. And her basketball team was a tournament champion. The joy and excitement and pride that shone in the eyes of each member of the team was equal to that in any NCAA winner's locker room. To each sport Katie brings her dedication to doing her best, her drive to excel and her desire to win.

Both girls are learning lessons that, when my wife and   10
I were their age, were encouraged only in boys. Fame, aggressiveness, achievement, self-confidence—these were territories into which very few women (the exception, not the

rule) dared enter. Kerith and Katie, most of their friends, many of their generation and the generations to come are redefining the social game. Their lives contradict the stereotypes with which I grew up. Many of the characteristics I thought were "male" are, in fact, "human." Given a chance, anyone can, and will, acquire them.

My daughters and the girls of their generation are lucky. 11 They receive a lot of institutional support not available to women of past generations: from women executives, women athletes, women authors, women politicians, women adventurers, women Olympians. Old categories, old stereotypes and old territories don't fit the current generation of young women; and they won't fit the next generation, either. As Kerith said, "I can't even imagine not being allowed to do something or be something just because I am a girl."

All this does not negate what I knew to be true during 12 my own high-school and college years. But what I've learned from both the women cadets at West Point and from my daughters supports a different conclusion about today's women and the women of tomorrow from the beliefs I was raised with. Ultimately we will be compelled to align our social and political institutions with what is already becoming a fact of American life. Or more precisely, whenever biological difference is used to segregate a person from an area of human endeavor, we will be required to demonstrate that biological difference is relevant to the issue at hand.

Comment

Dubik reasons inductively in generalizing about women from his personal experiences and observations. His short essay illustrates one way of writing about a subject without overgeneralizing or making unsupported claims. Dubik gives enough details to let the reader judge whether his experiences justify the conclusions he reaches in his concluding paragraphs. Dubik gives only as much detail as his argument requires. For example, he might have given details on how women cadets behaved in field exercises and in sports; he might have described the reading and writing of his daughters. Dubik instead gives a summary of these activities and gives the most detail on his daughters' sports activities.

Questions for Study and Discussion

1. Why does Dubik give the most details on his daughters' sports activities? Does Dubik suggest that some of his experiences provide more decisive evidence for his thesis, or does he seem to regard his experiences as equally persuasive?
2. Does Dubik state his thesis in the concluding paragraph, or does he state it earlier?
3. Why do his experiences with women cadets and his daughters "not negate what I knew to be true during my own high-school and college years"? Is Dubik suggesting that stereotypes once held of women were in fact accurate?
4. Does Dubik say that men and women have no special characteristics of strength, aptitude, or character? Is he arguing that they have the same characteristics?

Vocabulary Study

Explain the difference between each of the paired words:

a. stereotype, conception
b. persevered, persisted
c. unemotional, passive
d. extraordinary, unusual
e. inquisitiveness, curiosity
f. negate, deny
g. segregate, separate

Suggestions for Writing

1. Discuss whether your own experiences and observations confirm Dubik's conclusions. Give enough details about your experiences to support your ideas. Don't give more details than you need.
2. State a generalization about a class of people that you can support from your own experience and observation. Then present these experiences and observations in enough detail to make your generalization probable. Be careful not to make your generalization broader than your evidence allows.

Richard Moran

MORE CRIME AND LESS PUNISHMENT

Richard Moran teaches criminology at Mount Holyoke College, and he has published a number of articles on crime in America. He is the author of *Knowing Right from Wrong: The Insanity Defense of Daniel McNaughten* (1981). His essay on the problems created by the high crime rate is inductive because his evidence draws upon particulars of experience. Moran makes a number of inferences from available statistical evidence. He also depends upon illustrative analogy—a point by point comparison used to explain an idea—(p. 202) to clarify his argument.

If you are looking for an explanation of why we don't   1
get tough with criminals, you need only look at the numbers. Each year almost a third of the households in America
are victimized by violence or theft. This amounts to more
than 41 million crimes, many more than we have the capacity to punish. There are also too many criminals. The best
estimates suggest that 36 million to 40 million people or 16
to 18 percent of the U.S. population have arrest records for
nontraffic offenses. We already have 2.4 million people under some form of correctional supervision, 412,000 of them
locked away in a prison cell. We don't have room for any
more!

The painful fact is that the more crime there is the less   2
we are able to punish it. This is why the certainty and severity of punishment must go down when the crime rate
goes up. Countries like Saudi Arabia can afford to mete out
harsh punishments precisely because they have so little crime.
But can we afford to cut off the hands of those who committed more than 35 million property crimes each year? Can
we send them to prison? Can we execute more than 22,000
murderers?

We need to think about the relationship between pun-   3
ishment and crime in a new way. A decade of sophisticated
research has failed to provide clear and convincing evidence
that the threat of punishment influences the rate of most

major crimes committed. We assume that punishment deters crime, but it just might be the other way around. It just might be that crime deters punishment: that there is so much crime that it simply cannot be punished.

This is the situation we find ourselves in today. Just as 4 the decline in the number of high-school graduates has made it easier to gain admission to the college of one's choice, the gradual increase in the criminal population has made it more difficult to get into prison. While elite colleges and universities have held the line on standards of admissions, some of the most "exclusive" prisons now require about five prior felony convictions before an inmate is accepted into their correctional program. Our current crop of prisoners is an elite group, on the whole much more serious offenders than those who inhabited Alcatraz during its heyday.

Given the reality of the numbers it makes little sense to 5 blame the police, judges or correctional personnel for being soft on criminals. There is not much else they can do. The police can't find most criminals and those they find are difficult and costly to convict. Those convicted can't all be sent to prison. The social fact is that we cannot afford to do nothing about crime. The practical reality is that there is very little the police, courts or prisons can do about the crime problem. The criminal-justice system must then become as powerless as a parent who has charge of hundreds of teen-age children and who is nonetheless expected to answer the TV message: "It's 10 o'clock! Do you know where your children are?"

A few statistics from the Justice Department's recent 6 "Report to the Nation on Crime and Justice" illustrate my point. Of every 100 felonies committed in America, only 33 are actually reported to the police. Of the 33 reported, about 6 are cleared by arrest. Of the six arrested, only three are prosecuted and convicted. The others are rejected or dismissed due to evidence or witness problems or diverted into a treatment program. Of the three convicted, only one is sent to prison. The other two are placed on probation or some form of supervision. Of the select few sent to prison, more than half receive a maximum sentence of five years. The average inmate, however, graduates into a community-based program in about two years. Most prisoners gain early release not because parole boards are soft on crime, but because it is much cheaper to supervise a criminal in the community. And, of course, prison officials must make room for the new entering class of recruits sent almost daily from the courts.

We could, of course, get tough with the people we already have in prison and keep them locked up for longer periods of time. Yet when measured against the probable reduction in crime, prolonged incarceration is not worth the financial burden it imposes on state and local governments who pay the bulk of criminal-justice costs. Besides, those states that have tried to gain voter approval for bonds to build new prisons often discover that the public is unwilling to pay for prison construction.

And if it were willing to pay, prolonged incarceration may not be effective in reducing crime. In 1981, 124,000 convicts were released from prison. If we had kept them in jail for an additional year, how much crime would have been prevented? While it is not possible to know the true amount of crime committed by people released from prison in any given year, we do know the extent to which those under parole are reconfined for major crime convictions. This number is a surprisingly low 6 percent (after three years it rises to only 11 percent). Even if released prisoners commit an average of two crimes each, this would amount to only 15,000 crimes prevented: a drop in the bucket when measured against the 41 million crimes committed annually.

More time spent in prison is also more expensive. The best estimates are that it costs an average of $13,000 to keep a person in prison for one year. If we had a place to keep the 124,000 released prisoners, it would have cost us $1.6 billion to prevent 15,000 crimes. This works out to more than $100,000 per crime prevented. But there is more. With the average cost of prison construction running around $50,000 per bed, it would cost more than $6 billion to build the necessary cells. The first-year operating cost would be $150,000 per crime prevented, worth it if the victim were you or me, but much too expensive to be feasible as a national policy.

Faced with the reality of the numbers, I will not be so   10
foolish as to suggest a solution to the crime problem. My
contribution to the public debate begins and ends with this
simple observation: getting tough with criminals is not
the answer.

Comment

Tests of strong statistical arguments include the following. The
group surveyed must be sufficiently broad—that is, enough people
must be interviewed in order to support a significant conclusion.
The conclusion must also be warranted by the evidence; in other
words, the conclusion must not go beyond the limits of the evidence. Moran draws a limited conclusion from his evidence: we
must learn to think about crime in a new way. He also notes the
limit of his evidence: he tells us that his estimate of crime in America is approximate, not exact, and he does not use this evidence
to speculate about crime worldwide. Further, the sample must not
be based on unusual circumstances, and all pertinent facts and
circumstances must be taken into account in interpreting the evidence. Moran does not base his argument on crime in a few densely
populated areas with high unemployment, where these special circumstances would call his conclusion into question. His statistical
evidence instead covers the whole United States.

Questions for Study and Discussion

1. Why does Moran not propose a solution to the problems he
    discusses? Why does he consider his analysis useful even though
    he does not propose a solution?
2. Why can't Moran provide exact statistical information on the
    rate of crime in America? What is the value of knowing how
    many parolees are reimprisoned for major crimes?
3. Does Moran say or imply that he would favor harsh punish-
    ments, including capital punishment, if it were practical to ad-
    minister them? Or is he only pointing out a fact?
4. What kind of evidence does Moran present for his conclusion
    that public thinking about punishment is inconsistent? Why
    does Moran emphasize this fact?
5. What use does Moran make of illustrative analogy?

Vocabulary Study

State the differences in the meaning of the words in each group.
Then explain why Moran uses the first of the words in the paragraph cited:

   a. *severity* (paragraph 2), *intensity, harshness*
   b. *sophisticated* (paragraph 3), *intense, serious*
   c. *deters* (paragraph 3), *forbids, stops*
   d. *felonies* (paragraph 6), *crimes, misdemeanors*
   e. *incarceration* (paragraph 7), *punishment, penalty*

Suggestions for Writing

1. Analyze advertisements for similar products—for example,
   cosmetics and toothpaste—to discover what evidence each of
   the advertisers presents for statements about the product. Use
   your analysis to draw a conclusion about the advertising of
   these products. Limit your conclusion carefully.
2. Your college library contains reference books and government
   documents that report crime statistics for particular cities and
   regions of the United States. Locate statistical reports on crime
   in two large American cities—Miami and Los Angeles, for example—and compare the information given about the crimes
   named. Use your comparison to draw a conclusion about the
   nature of crime in these cities.

Page Smith

HUMAN TIME AND THE COLLEGE STUDENT

Page Smith is Professor Emeritus of American History at the University
of California, Santa Cruz. His books include *John Adams* (1962)—
which received the Bancroft Award in American History—*Daughters of
the Promised Land: Women in American History* (1970), *Thomas
Jefferson: A Revealing Biography* (1976), and *Shaping the Nation*
(1980). First published in 1957, his essay on college examinations may
be compared with Edward Rivera's account of a sociology exam
(p. 37).

The tension in the large room is almost palpable. The ¹
air is tainted with the odor of sweat. The faces of the men
and women are drawn and taut. Their bodies are twisted in
postures of agonized thought, of supplication, of despair.
The scene is not that of a torture chamber but of a roomful
of students taking a final examination.

Surely a professor's most disheartening experience is to ²
patrol the classroom during the final examination for his
course. If he has tried to make the course a vital one, if he
has tried to catch the students up in an adventure of learning that has contained some joy and play as well as high
seriousness, he cannot but feel downhearted as he watches
their strained faces, observes their exhaustion and anxiety.
This is certainly a dismal end to an at least theoretically
enlivening experience. Only convention can make it tolera-
ble to the professor and his students. We are bound to ask
ourselves, it seems to me, how well the aims of a particular
course or of education in general are served by this ordeal.
Its avowed purpose is to make sure that the student has accomplished something measurable in mastering a certain body
of material, that he has increased his efficiency or his knowledge. We assure ourselves that the final examination accom-
plishes this, but we have ample testimony that it does not. I
suspect that most of us have little conviction that six years
or six months after the completion of this or that course, its
graduates could pass even a vastly simplified examination
on its content. What we might call the "retention quotient"
is, in most courses, very low indeed. There is much to suggest that because the final examination presents both a
frightening hurdle and an obvious terminus, it actually inhibits retention of the course content. Students at least believe so and often speak cynically of final examinations as a
kind of intellectual purge by which the mind is evacuated of
all the material that has been stored in it during the course.

It should be obvious that the typical examination is not ³
the proper means to ensure the student's carrying away from
the work of a semester an important residue of information
or knowledge. It does give us, however, a conviction that

we are discriminating, that we are forcing the student to comply with certain standards, that we have transferred, even if on a temporary basis, certain information to our passive auditors. What is perhaps most important of all, we have provided a means by which the student's advance toward his ultimate goal—a degree—can be measured. Using it we are able to assign a "mark" which presumably measures the student's accomplishment. And this mark is an integral part of our educational process.

While the final examination is only the concluding trial 4 of the average course, we might take it as a symbol of much that is wrong with our instructional methods on the college level. The fact is that our colleges are, to a considerable degree, neither subject-oriented nor student-oriented but mark-oriented. They are set up, on the undergraduate level, to facilitate the awarding and the recording of marks. Individual courses of instruction are almost invariably organized with an eye on marking procedures. In large courses where the instructor is assisted by graduate students who read and grade the papers, it is especially important to devise examinations that require essentially factual answers. These answers may be in the form of multiple choices, in which case they are often graded by a machine, or they may be in the form of an essay. The essay-type question is an improvement over the true-false or multiple-choice examination since it requires that the student be more or less literate. But in practice this type of examination must still place its emphasis on the factual in order to make possible a uniform system of grading by one or more "readers."

However much, in courses of this kind, the professor 5 may affirm his desire to have the students "think for themselves," the students cannot in fact do so. Ideal answers in these mass-administered and mass-graded tests have to be devised and marks awarded on the basis of the number of essential points included in each answer. Such courses, moreover, are usually taught in conjunction with a textbook, and here the student's impulse, not unnaturally, is to memorize the text at the expense of a thoughtful, critical review of the lecture material. The large lecture courses which use a textbook and in which the grading is done by "readers" or "assistants" are self-defeating. The complex, unfamiliar, and elusive ideas given in lectures cannot compete successfully, in most instances, with the neatly assembled data in the textbook. The student is further discouraged in any speculation by the consciousness that he may have missed or misunderstood the precise point the lecturer was trying to make and may thus render it up in mutilated or unrecognizable form.

Let us assume that the student accepts the invitation to "think for himself." In most cases his thoughts will be confused and banal, a mish-mash of rather unformed ideas that he has picked up in high-school civics courses, at home, from random reading, from movies and television. They will not be worth much in terms of a mark. How is the professor, or his surrogate, the reader, to react? Does he give the student an A for effort, thus encouraging him in the idea that he is a thinker of considerable power and originality? Or does he admonish him gently and give him a C, thus confirming the student's suspicions that the professor never meant what he said anyway? 6

Again the mark is the culprit. The fact is that the mark should be used only as an incentive, as a corrective, as a stimulus. A first-rate student often needs to be most severely marked for sloppy thinking, for intellectual short cuts, for the facile use of academic clichés. As a Cambridge tutor expressed it to me, "The teacher should be free, if the character of the student suggests it is the best course, to tear up his paper before him, denounce his work as careless and inaccurate, berate him soundly, and send him off to do the work of which he is capable." Perhaps the student who suffers most under our marking system is the outstanding individual who, in any comparison with his fellows, must be given an A and thus cannot be treated with the rigor that would eventually make the most of his superior capacities. 7

Since all marks are carefully recorded, added up, weighed and assessed, and stand unalterable upon the student's record, they cannot be used with any real freedom or flex- 8 ibility. Most of us are reluctant to give a mark that will perhaps count against a scholarship, a job, or a cherished academic plum.

I suspect that largely as a result of the grading system a majority of the students regard the professor as, in a sense, the enemy. That is to say, the professor represents an unknown quantity that has the potentiality of damaging the student. As professor he is in a position of almost unlimited power. To counter this the student has a kind of cunning which he has acquired as a by-product of the educational process. He is conditioned to play the game according to the rules. He knows that if, like the psychologist's pigeon, he pecks the right button, he will get a kernel of corn. He has, therefore, very little to gain and much to lose by taking liberties with the system. The prevailing educational conventions combine to make him cagey. He knows that his teachers are at least partly human and that however remote most of them may seem from his real life and interests, they have their crotchets, their small vanities, and their prejudices. At the beginning of a class the student is alert to penetrate these and to discern in what way they can be made to work to his advantage. He knows that despite a pretense of professional objectivity, the instructor has a fairly well-developed set of biases, and the student welcomes evidences of these because they are guideposts to him. Correspondingly, the absence of discernible prejudices is unsettling for the student—it means another anxiety-producing unknown element in the equation that should yield up the desired mark.

The only way that the professor can overcome the student's habit of calculation, which is generally fatal to the learning process, is by lessening some of his apprehensions. The student's attitude is indeed ambivalent, and this is the professor's opportunity. In addition to their feelings of anxiety and hostility, many students genuinely wish to be touched and affected by the professor. The student has had, in his learning experience, a few teachers who have done this and he knows that, while it is unlikely, it can happen. But the professor, in his efforts to create this kind of *rapport*, is at a disadvantage. He is inviting a confidence that he cannot honor. The student may in fact be drawn from his shell and inspired to venture some independent judgment, but the assessment of this hesitant enterprise will not be made by the man who has solicited it but, in many instances, by a third party, the reader.

Even if it were possible to set up a grading procedure   11
by which efforts at original and independent thinking would be encouraged and rewarded, there would still be little incentive for the bright student to make the effort. Being examination-oriented and acutely mark-conscious, he knows that there is always an element of chance in examinations and he has a strong impulse to keep this to a minimum.

He realizes that it is often not so much what he knows   12
as how much mileage he can get out of the information that he has committed to memory. The means of testing now used in most colleges and universities often fall short of measuring the excellence or the capacity of the student. For the most part they record his ability to memorize and record a certain rather narrow range of information, and here technique is of great importance. If, by the painstaking accumulation of facts and approved theories and their careful regurgitation, the student can get the desired mark, he is borrowing trouble to attempt something more ambitious.

The teacher is, of course, as much the victim of our   13
testing conventions as the student is. Examinations play an important part in his conception of himself as teacher and scholar. Not infrequently he comes to view them as weapons in a contest between himself and his students. Unexpected and unorthodox questions affirm his "toughness" and give a comforting spread in marks. Even in the most straightforward examination, some conscientious students will have failed to prepare certain questions adequately since all the significant material in a given course can seldom be mastered with complete thoroughness and an element of chance inevitably enters in. Difficult and obscure questions will scatter the field even further, reducing the number of A's and B's and giving the professor the reassuring feeling that he is a stern marker who is upholding "standards."

It might be said that the whole matter of "distribution" and grading on the "curve" is one of the most patent fallacies in the marking system. It seems to be based on the assumption that the student population in any particular course should be spread out with a certain percentage of A's, B's, C's, and so on, but this assumption, which is treated by many professors with the sanctity of a kind of natural law of education, will not bear close scrutiny. It is certainly conceivable that rigorous and demanding courses can be given to large numbers of students in which no "proper" distribution occurs. When this happens, however, the professor involved often feels under compulsion to revamp his testing techniques to produce a result more in accord with accepted practice lest his colleagues suspect that he is "soft" or perhaps trying to win students by relaxed standards—a kind of academic scab who is willing to accept less than the prevailing scale.

What I have to say about the inadequacies of the marking system applies most directly to freshman and sophomore "survey" courses taken by large numbers of students who, it is hoped, will thereby get a nodding acquaintance with, say, Western Civilization, or Art in World History, or Patterns of Social Development. My strictures apply with somewhat less force to the more advanced courses, but even here, especially in the larger institutions, readers are in evidence, and the more onerous features of the grading system are only slightly ameliorated.

In the first place, by the time they are upperclassmen, the majority of students are thoroughly conditioned to the corruption of marks, and it is correspondingly difficult to break through to the individual, to lure him into any free and uninhibited expression of feeling or opinion. As an advanced student he has found his level—A, B, or C. He knows what kind of effort is required to maintain it in the average course, provided again that the student-intelligence service is functioning effectively.

The student accepts the system because it can be figured out, anticipated, and made, in general, to yield the desired token. The professor often values it for its very impersonality, or "objectivity." Every student, if he is known, presents the teacher with a unique problem. Is the middle-aged schoolteacher from Louisiana, seeking a salary increase by the accumulation of additional course credits, to be judged by the same standards as the brilliant and precocious high school student, or the man with two children who works twenty or thirty hours a week, or the boy who works on a night shift in a railroad yard to help put a younger brother through school, or the housewife who wishes to secure a primary-school teaching credential? Perhaps it can be argued that these are extreme cases, but our existing canons of grading dictate that we treat all individuals the same way.

Now this is not quite as bad if we are giving an essentially professional education to a homogeneous student body with a common cultural background, but if this is no longer our basic task, the only alternative is to attempt to assess each student individually. Of course, such a suggestion alarms the bureaucrats since it involves difficult and dangerous decisions on the part of the professor and smacks of the "progressive" ideas that most of us view with suspicion when we observe them in operation on the secondary-school level. But it might be answered that the failure of the secondary schools is not so much caused by trying to meet the needs of the individual student as it is by watering down and destroying the content of the traditional curriculum in the name of "adjustment" or of "practical" education. If the liberal arts curriculum is maintained and strengthened as the heart of higher education, the effort to adopt a more flexible and more personal approach to the student can only be salutary in its effects. Both the mediocre and the outstanding student will profit from such a change in emphasis, and standards, instead of being lowered, will be raised, since the student who is in a one-to-one relationship to his teacher will more often have his best efforts evoked.

The answer to such proposals will, of course, be that the present ratio of professors to students is not great enough to permit attention to the needs and capacities of individual students. I believe that there is much that can be done within

the existing framework of most college and university cur-
riculums without submerging the professor, but it is probably true that some institutional reforms are needed to reduce
the rigidity of the present system. In any event, a necessary
first step toward breaking the tyranny of the marking and
examination system is the frank admission that these are at
best necessary evils that have about them no savor of sal-
vation, but rather, by their own interior logic, work toward
the increasing formalization of higher education. Perhaps
an uprising against the existing practices should begin with
the destruction of the I.B.M. machines and the dispersion of
those who tend them, followed by the rout of the academic bureaucrats.

Such a revolt would open the way for the establishment   20
of more human and more flexible procedures. One hesitates
to say what these procedures should be. Perhaps it is enough,
at this stage, to insist that time spans must be created for the
student that will relieve him of the continual anxiety of
recurrent tests and examinations. The fragmentation of
the student's learning experience seriously inhibits his intellectual growth and his personal development. Information can be dispensed on a unit basis, but formation and re-
formation require unbroken increments of time. In our present curriculum all marks, all assignments, all chapters are of
equal significance because, as weighed by a mark, all weigh
the same. The trivial takes equal rank with the important
and the student's power of discrimination is soon lost.

A renewed dialogue, the creation of generous time spans,   21
the bold and unabashed reenactment of the historic drama
of the self confronting the cosmos, these are the directions
American higher education must take if it is not to degen-
erate into a fact mill or a colossal trade school.

Comment

Page Smith draws upon his experience as a university professor to
describe the educational establishment of 1957. In doing so, he
assumes that the classrooms and methods of examination in his

own university are typical of those in others. Readers of the essay must therefore test Smith's analysis by comparison with their own university experience. His characterization of students is based upon observation, and here too Smith generalizes about how the marking system affects students. He notes exceptions but suggests that much of his characterization fits all students. The system prevailing in 1957 was dismal enough to injure everyone involved in it, and Smith insists upon this fact strongly.

Questions for Study and Discussion

1. How does Smith suggest what his own experience has been, without giving a detailed account of his teaching career?
2. Why does the marking system discourage independent thought and creativity? Does Smith suggest that other features of university education also discourage students?
3. How would Smith define ideal learning? What are the necessary conditions—the conditions that must be present—if this learning is to take place?
4. Who does Smith blame for the marking system? Or does he blame no one?
5. Does Smith propose abolishing marks or grades? Or can they serve a useful purpose?
6. To what extent does Smith accurately describe the marking system and general attitudes toward learning that prevail in your school? Does your experience suggest that the situation has changed in any way since 1957?
7. Do you agree with Smith's proposals for reform? Would the abolition of grades make you a better student?

Vocabulary Study

Explain the following words and phrases: *palpable, supplication* (paragraph 1); *retention quotient, terminus* (paragraph 2); *residue, integral* (paragraph 3); *oriented, facilitate* (paragraph 4); *speculation* (paragraph 5); *academic clichés* (paragraph 7); *crotchets, prejudices, biases* (paragraph 9); *apprehensions, rapport* (paragraph 10); *regurgitation* (paragraph 12); *academic scab* (paragraph 14); *ameliorated, onerous* (paragraph 15); *uninhibited* (paragraph 16); *canons* (paragraph 17); *bureaucrats, curriculum, mediocre* (paragraph 18); *formalization, dispersion* (paragraph 19); *fragmentation* (paragraph 20); *unabashed, cosmos* (paragraph 21).

Suggestions for Writing

1. Discuss your own conception of the ideal classroom or ideal relationship between student and teacher. Draw on your personal experience in explaining this conception.
2. Discuss the extent to which one of the following statements by Smith reflects your own experience in high school or college. Use your discussion to evaluate one of Smith's proposals for reform of education:
   a. "What we might call the 'retention quotient' is, in most courses, very low indeed."
   b. "There is much to suggest that because the final examination presents both a frightening hurdle and an obvious terminus, it actually inhibits retention of the course content."
   c. "I suspect that largely as a result of the grading system a majority of the students regard the professor as, in a sense, the enemy."
   d. "The only way that the professor can overcome the student's habit of calculation, which is generally fatal to the learning process, is by lessening some of his apprehensions."
   e. "The means of testing now used in most colleges and universities often fall short of measuring the excellence or the capacity of the student."
   f. "The student accepts the system because it can be figured out, anticipated, and made, in general, to yield the desired token."

Ellen Goodman

WAVING GOOD-BYE TO THE COUNTRY

Ellen Goodman wrote for *Newsweek* and the *Detroit Free Press* before joining the staff of the *Boston Globe* in 1967 as feature writer and columnist. She received the Pulitzer Prize for Commentary in 1980. Her columns on a wide range of social and political issues are collected in several books, including *At Large* (1981) and *Keeping in Touch* (1985). Goodman's essay on the issue of "the right to die" appears later in this section (p. 442).

The weekend is over, and we drive down the country road from the cottage to the pier, passing out our last supply of waves. We wave at people walking and wave at people riding. We wave at people we know and wave at people who are strangers.

The island wave is by now a summer habit. It took me time to acquire this salute, but now it feels a natural part of life in Maine. Like year-rounders, we pass back and forth the visual assurance that anyone on our island belongs here, is accepted.

When we arrive at the pier, the boat is already crowded with the end-of-summer exodus. Island emigrants help each other stack cat carriers and lift bags onto the back of the boat. Crossing the water, everyone is patient with each other's dogs and children.

But by the time the three of us have transferred from the ferry to our private car and reached the turnpike, my wave has begun to atrophy. Before we cross the Maine border, my hand has entirely lost its training. As the hundred miles go by, even the tolltakers have turned from smiles to surliness. The jawline of drivers in other cars seems to set as the city skyline rises.

To ease my reentry into workaday life, I decide to walk the last mile home. I am left at a familiar safe city corner and, yes, almost immediately, my accent changes. I begin to "speak" in the city's body language: neutral and wary.

Suddenly conscious of my own adjustments, I notice how few eyes meet on this mile. Women do not look at men. Old people do not look at teenagers. Men do not smile at each other. People don't wave to strangers on these streets. They measure them.

A quarter of a mile from home, inevitably, I pass two young men who give their own obnoxious verbal greeting to every woman who crosses their stoop. By the time I reach my own door, I go over the threshold as if entering a haven.

This small pilgrimage from rural community to city is   8
not unique. But today I am peculiarly aware of how my own
trip seems to mimic American life.

Our whole country has moved from rural communities   9
to cities, from towns where contact was reassuring to cities
where contact may be threatening. In 1900, 60 percent of
us lived in the country; in 1980, 74 percent of us lived in
the city. We have exchanged being known in small communities for being anonymous in huge populations.

It is this easy public space that seems to shrink as the   10
population increases. Millions of us have exchanged a street
life in which we acknowledged each other for a street life in
which we deliberately ignore each other.

I am not glorifying rural life. I know that in small com-   11
munities people have to struggle to maintain their privacy,
their individuality. The same society that supports people
can confine them. The same people who help each other some
days annoy each other on other days.

But in the city, people have to struggle to make a   12
community. We have to recreate a world in which we are
known. We fight against anonymity at the grocer's, the dry-
cleaner's, newsstand, the coffee shop—and are often thwarted
by the supermarket, the discount pharmacy, the fast-food
counter.

The more anonymous we are in public, the more we   13
forget our small towns at work and home, among family
and friends. But our communities are private ones. Indoor
ones.

I'm not sure why it's so hard to maintain some sense of   14
community in the city streets. Perhaps it is just arithmetic.
At a certain point, numbers make strangers.

But I suspect that it is also because we urban people   15
think of ourselves as transients in our communities. Even
the third-generation city people travel light. We don't sink
our roots in neighborhoods as deeply as our grandparents
did. We don't claim the street turf.

Pascal said that, "We do not worry about being re-   16
spected in the towns through which we pass. But if we are

going to remain in one for a certain time, we do worry. How long does this time have to be?"

I don't suppose any visitor cares if he is known in a strange city. But many of us live our whole lives as if we were just passing through.   17

And if we are all tourists, where are the natives to teach us how to wave?   18

Comment

Ellen Goodman uses her experiences of town life in Maine and city life in Boston to draw conclusions about city life in general. Goodman proceeds from particulars of experience to basic truths. In doing so, she makes the "inductive leap" in assuming that her own experience is typical of other city people. Inductive reasoning arrives at generalizations or, in scientific research, hypotheses; but it is the nature of the evidence that defines inductive reasoning, not the nature of the conclusions reached. The deductive argument that Goodman develops in "Whose Life Is It Anyway?" makes generalizations, too. But it does so, not from particulars of experience such as Goodman presents here, but from other generalizations or established truths (see p. 424).

Questions for Study and Discussion

1. Paragraphs 1 through 8 contain an illustrative analogy. What is the analogy, and what idea is Goodman illustrating through it?
2. Does Goodman describe the anonymity of city life? What are the effects of this anonymity?
3. What point is Pascal making in the statement quoted in paragraph 16? Why does Goodman quote the statement?
4. Does she say or imply that city life has any advantages over small-town life? Does she say or imply that she would prefer to live in a small town rather than in a city, or is she merely explaining why city life is different? What is the thesis of her essay?
5. State whether or not you agree with Goodman's characterization of small-town or city life? Why do you agree or disagree?

Vocabulary Study

Explain the difference between the words in each pair. Then explain why Goodman chooses the first:

- a. *exodus* (paragraph 3), *departure*
- b. *emigrants* (paragraph 3), *immigrants*
- c. *atrophy* (paragraph 4), *tire*
- d. *wary* (paragraph 5), *cautious*
- e. *obnoxious* (paragraph 7), *unpleasant*
- f. *pilgrimage* (paragraph 8), *journey*
- g. *anonymity* (paragraph 12), *isolation*
- h. *transients* (paragraph 15), *travellers*
- i. *turf* (paragraph 15), *territory*

Suggestions for Writing

1. Discuss the advantages and disadvantages of small-town or city life as you have experienced them. Draw a conclusion from your discussion, and explain why it does or does not apply to other town or city people.
2. State whether or not you agree with Goodman's explanation for the difference between town and city life, and explain why you do or do not.
3. Describe what you see on a walk down a town or city street or through a college campus. Draw a conclusion about the town, city, or school from the details you present.

Kathy Seelinger

THE HAMLET HANDICAP

Kathy Seelinger writes about small-town life from a much different perspective from Ellen Goodman's (p. 415). Seelinger taught in small-town schools, and she now supervises student teachers at Marshall University, in Huntington, West Virginia. She therefore has had an opportunity to observe young people in the course of making the decisions she describes in her essay.

Kelly Jolley is getting married: I heard it from his own   1
lips last week at our local one-horse town's nine-shop mall.
Kelly was, without question, the single most brilliant individual I ever taught; probably the most gifted person I will
ever know. At the age of 21, he will take a bride and then—
if his plans work out—he will enter a prestigious doctoral
program where, I fear, he may fall victim to "the Hamlet
handicap."

"Hamlet" is the quaint term for a tiny community—   2
Thomas Hardy's "little one-eyed blinking kind o' place"
which C. H. Spurgeon, a 19th-century English preacher,
characterized as "a hive of glass, where nothing unobserved
can pass." By guarding boundaries, we create a highly desirable environment. In the typical small town, the crime rate
is virtually zero save the occasional hit-and-run fender bender
or stereo heist. In the conventional small-town home, children become secure with their niche in the extended family.
And the singular spirit of that community can be easily organized to build teen centers or launch walkathons for the
hungry. All of these attributes are commendable. The warmth
and oneness of the hamlet are rightfully celebrated, and many
of us take pride in and solace from our own provincial ties.

Nonetheless skepticism, founded on years of experience   3
as a small-town inhabitant, tells me that these very same
features often pose a handicap for a hamlet's most talented
citizens. Villagers may proudly praise the champion athlete,
the all-state vocalist and the scholarship winner and advise
them to sally forth and demonstrate their accomplishments
for all who will attend. But in almost the same breath, they
sing a different tune that is barely audible above the surface.
A subliminal, steady beat entreats the adventurous not to
venture too far.

"Come back," the voice calls to the scholar, "and teach   4
at the local high school." "Return," it tells the artist, "and
sing the national anthem in the town square on Founder's
Day." "Stick around," it pleads to the athlete, "and exemplify health and sportsmanship to our children." Such invitations are certainly well meant. One can do far worse than
to remain in the bosom of a cherished hometown, continuing (or instituting) a tradition of sport, art and scholarship.

But like sun-sensitive lenses, the hamlet handicap becomes a filter that distorts vision at the same time that it protects sight.

The brighter the potential prospects for the young and gifted, the harder the hamlet works to shield them from the glare of city lights. Well-intentioned, almost maternal sheltering is understandable, but when we caution against hazards that are present in more cosmopolitan environs—freeways, pollution, the risks of a Type-A lifestyle—we screen out real-world opportunities as well.

Feminists should bemoan the fact that gifted girls graduate from high school believing that freedom means the chance to work behind the register at the local K mart—and then just long enough to earn the trousseau money needed to marry a childhood sweetheart. But the hamlet handicap is more than an issue of feminist perspective. As a teacher in small-town schools, I saw brilliant boys eschew mathematical and verbal skill-building because they knew they would forgo higher education and enter the family business. Talented children of both sexes who do leave hear the Lorelei call and, almost invariably, return. And the town at large will not change its tune, because, in part, its very survival depends upon maintaining the population already present.

Internalized over generations, the small-town song has become so subtle that peers and parents are not even aware they are singing it. So they can lure us with the softly whispered seduction: we appreciate you, we love you; come home and do fine things for us as repayment for the nourishment we have given you. And come back we do, to aspire to those fine things that translate into a partnership with Uncle Paul in the real-estate business or the chairmanship of next year's walkathon or the presidency of the Rotary. All these positions are honorable; they provide most of us with a satisfying and productive role in the grand scheme of things as well as in our immediate community. Yet none of them, very likely, can best capitalize on the gifts of a Kelly Jolley.

And what of Kelly? He's getting married young; that's how we do it here in the hamlet. Having been treated as an equal to all other worthwhile young citizens, he has no sense of his specialness; that, too, is our doing. But since a doctorate in philosophy is also his dream, and there isn't a great demand for one in this tiny, blinking kind of a place, Kelly will have to decide how far he will live from his friends and family. And he will make the decisions shaping his destiny believing wholeheartedly that they are entirely his own with only an offhand nod to the heavy weight of a friendly community's folkways.

I wish Kelly well on his impending nuptials, but I hope 9
he doesn't come home. Coming back to our hive of glass, he would be guaranteed extravagant appreciation but offered a far less potent medium in which to grow. He wouldn't be close to major research centers and foundation grants; to collaborating and cross-pollinating ideas with his intellectual peers. And the chance that this exceptional young man could become the crucial link on the team that solves a social or medical problem would be substantially reduced. I have learned that all blinking hamlets are enriched by the proximity of people like Kelly Jolley. Unfortunately, our enrichment can become his—and humanity's—handicap.

Comment

Kathy Seelinger shows that the decisions of where to live and to work are not simple ones for young people. She does so by exploring the dilemma faced by the young person who must choose between the small town and the city. Both have their handicaps and their attractions. Seelinger's argument is inductive in drawing on personal experience to prove that small town life imposes a handicap on the adventurous. But she also brings personal belief to the argument—a characteristic of deductive arguments, as the following section shows. Seelinger's belief that people should exercise their talents to the fullest underlies her argument that young people with high intellectual ability should enter universities and should later work where they can put their knowledge and skills to best use. Inductive reasoning plays an important role in Seelinger's argument, but the argument is not entirely inductive.

Questions for Study and Discussion

1. What is the advantage in beginning with Kelly Jolley and ending with him?

2. Where does Seelinger first state her thesis? Where in the essay does she restate it?
3. Does Seelinger say or imply that timid, mediocre people prefer to live in small towns and that bright, adventurous people prefer to live in cities? Or is she making more limited generalizations about people and small towns?
4. What statements reveal Seelinger's belief that people should exercise their talents? What other beliefs about people and society does Seelinger hold? Does she state these beliefs or are they implied in the argument?

Vocabulary Study

Explain the difference between the following pairs of words and phrases. Then explain why Seelinger uses the first word of each in the paragraph cited:

a. *hamlet* (paragraph 2), *village*
b. *provincial* (paragraph 2), *parochial*
c. *sally* (paragraph 2), *venture*
d. *subliminal* (paragraph 2), *faintly heard*
e. *cosmopolitan* (paragraph 5), *urban*
f. *eschew* (paragraph 6), *reject*
g. *Lorelei call* (paragraph 6), *summons*
h. *intellectual peers* (paragraph 7), *classmates*
i. *folkways* (paragraph 8), *customs*

Suggestions for Writing

1. Do you agree with Seelinger that Kelly Jolley should not come home? Defend your agreement or disagreement with reference to your own experiences and beliefs.
2. If you grew up in a small town, discuss whether your experiences of small-town life confirm Seelinger's observations. If you grew up in a city, discuss whether your experiences confirm that cities are places of adventure and opportunity.

❦

Deductive Argument

Deductive arguments draw inferences or conclusions from statements that the author of the argument believes to be true. In the essay that follows, "The Confessions of a Miseducated Man," Norman Cousins presents his basic argument as follows:

> In order to be at home anywhere in the world I had to forget the things I had been taught to remember. It turned out that my ability to get along with other peoples depended not so much upon my comprehension of the uniqueness of their way of life as upon my comprehension of the things we had in common.

Cousins restates this argument in subsequent paragraphs:

> Only a few years ago an education in differences fulfilled a specific if limited need. That was at a time when we thought of other places and peoples largely out of curiosity or in terms of exotic vacations. It was the mark of a rounded man to be well traveled and to know about the fabulous variations of human culture and behavior. But it wasn't the type of knowledge you had to live by and build on.
>
> Then overnight came the great compression. Far-flung areas which had been secure in their remoteness suddenly became jammed together in a single arena. And all at once a new type of education became necessary, an education in liberation from tribalism. . . .

Cousins summarizes his argument in the following statement:

> The old emphasis upon superficial differences had to give way to education for mutuality and for citizenship in the human community.

We may restate Cousin's argument informally:

> Since getting along with other people depends on understanding what we have in common, an education that teaches only the differences between people doesn't prepare us to live in a world that has become a single arena.

This argument may be restated in positive terms and arranged as a formal argument or *syllogism:*

> [*Major premise*] An education that prepares us to live in a world that has become a single arena is an adequate one.
>
> [*Minor premise*] An education that teaches what we have in common with other people prepares us to live in a world that has become a single arena.
>
> [*Conclusion*] Such an education is an adequate one.

Such an argument is called deductive because it makes an inference from statements assumed to be true—beliefs held as "self-evident" or axiomatic or truths established by experience, observation, or experimentation. A deductive argument says that *if* the premises of the formal argument are true, the conclusion or inference properly drawn from these statements must also be true. These statements or premises are the evidence for the conclusion. We know that Cousins holds the first two statements to be true because he says so in introducing his basic argument:

> As I write this, I have the feeling that my words fail to give vitality to the idea they seek to express. Indeed, the idea itself is a truism which all peoples readily acknowledge even if they do not act on it.

Writers of arguments know that people will disagree with their premises—with the beliefs, assumptions, or truisms on which they base the argument. For this reason they may defend one or both of the premises by illustrating or explaining them. Cousins does so in describing the contents of the new education. Even if the premises are defended, the argument is deductive as long as the premises themselves provide the evidence for the conclusion. Inferences are drawn from the premises and not from factual evidence like personal experience, observation, or statistical studies—the evidence of inductive arguments (see p. 390).

In arguing, we often omit one of the premises or the conclusion. We do so because we consider the omitted premise or conclusion obvious. Shortened arguments of this sort are called *enthymemes*. Here are some examples:

> Since an education that teaches what we have in common prepares us to live in a world that has become a single arena, such an education is adequate.
> [major premise omitted: *An adequate education prepares us to live in a world that has become a single arena.*]

> Since an adequate education prepares us to live in a world that has become a single arena, an education that teaches what we have in common with other people is an adequate one. [minor premise omitted: *An education that teaches what we have in common with others prepares us to live in a world that has become a single arena.*]

> An adequate education prepares us to live in a world that has become a single arena, and an education that teaches what we have in common with other people prepares us to live in such a world. [conclusion implied: *Such an education is adequate.*]

These examples are typical of arguments we hear everyday—arguments that require us to supply one of the premises or even the conclusion. In other words, we need to consider implied as well as explicit statements in testing the validity of an argument and weighing its soundness.

A deductive argument is considered *sound* if its premises are true and the process of reasoning is proper or *valid*. If the process of reasoning is faulty or invalid or the premises are untrue—if the premises are "glittering generalities" or statements that cannot be defended or do not cover all instances—the argument is considered unsound. Cousins' argument would be judged unsound if an opponent could disprove his assertion that teaching what people have in common is necessary to live in a changing world.

Here is a valid argument:

> Successful farmers are hard-working people.
> My parents are successful farmers.
> My parents are hard-working people.

What is true of all successful farmers, must be true of anyone who belongs to the same class. But note this much different argument:

> Successful farmers are hard-working people.
> My parents are hard-working people.
> My parents are successful farmers.

This argument is invalid because neither premise claims that all hard-working people are successful farmers. Some may be farmers, and some may not be. The tests of validity are complex—the subject of formal logic. Common sense often can detect an error in invalid arguments, but many deceptive arguments require a knowledge of these formal tests. There are many tests; here are two simple ones:

First, no conclusion can be drawn from two negative premises. If one of the premises is negative, so must be the conclusion. The following argument is invalid because it draws a conclusion when none is possible:

> Since no sick people are happy people, and none of us are sick people, we must be happy people.

Secondly, the terms of the argument must not shift in meaning:

> Since sick people are not happy people, and bigots are sick people, bigots are not happy people.

The phrase *sick people* ordinarily refers to the physically ill. If the word *sick* in the minor premise refers to mental aberration, then the term has shifted in meaning in this argument. Bigots may very well be unhappy people, but not for the reason stated.

Norman Cousins

CONFESSIONS OF A MISEDUCATED MAN

Norman Cousins edited the *Saturday Review* from 1940 to 1971, and again from 1971 to 1973. During these years he wrote editorially on a wide range of topics relating to national and international issues. *Present Tense* (1967) contains editorials Cousins wrote between 1940 and 1966; the editorial reprinted here appeared on May 10, 1952. Cousins' other books include *In God We Trust: The Religious Beliefs of the Founding Fathers* (1958), *Doctor Schweitzer of Lambaréné* (1960), *The Celebration of Life* (1975), and *The Human Option* (1981). *Anatomy of an Illness* (1979) describes how he overcame a serious illness. Among his numerous awards are the Benjamin Franklin citation for magazine journalism in 1956, the Eleanor Roosevelt Peace award in 1963, and the United National Peace medal in 1971.

These notes are in the nature of a confession. It is the confession of a miseducated man.   1

I have become most aware of my lack of a proper education whenever I have had the chance to put it to the test. The test is a simple one: am I prepared to live in and comprehend a world in which there are 3 billion people? Not the world as it was in 1850 or 1900, for which my education might have been adequate, but the world today. And the best place to apply that test is outside the country—especially Asia or Africa.   2

Not that my education was a complete failure. It prepared me superbly for a bird's-eye view of the world. It taught me how to recognize easily and instantly the things that differentiate one place or one people from another. Geography had instructed me in differences of terrain, resources, and productivity. Comparative culture had instructed me in the differences of background and group interests. Anthropology had instructed me in the differences of facial bone structure, skin pigmentation, and general physical aspect. In short, my education protected me against surprise. I was not surprised at the fact that some people lived in mud huts and others in bamboo cottages on stilts; or that some used peat for fuel and others dung; or that some enjoyed music with a five-note scale and others with twelve; or that some people were vegetarian by religion and others by preference.   3

In those respects my education had been more than adequate. But what my education failed to do was to teach me that the principal significance of such differences was that they were largely without significance. The differences were all but obliterated by the similarities. My education had by-   4 passed the similarities. It had failed to grasp and define the fact that beyond the differences are realities scarcely comprehended because of their shattering simplicity. And the simplest reality of all was that the human community was one—greater than any of its parts, greater than the separateness imposed by the nations, greater than the divergent faiths and allegiances or the depth and color of varying cultures. This larger unity was the most important central fact of our time—something on which people could build at a time when hope seemed misty, almost unreal.

As I write this, I have the feeling that my words fail to give vitality to the idea they seek to express. Indeed, the idea itself is a truism which all peoples readily acknowledge even if they do not act on it. Let me put it differently, then. In order to be at home anywhere in the world I had to forget the things I had been taught to remember. It turned out that my ability to get along with other peoples depended not so much upon my comprehension of the uniqueness of their way of life as upon my comprehension of the things we had in common. It was important to respect these differences, certainly, but to stop there was like clearing the ground without any idea of what was to be built on it. When you got through comparing notes, you discovered that you were both talking about the same neighborhood, i.e., this planet, and the conditions that made it congenial or hostile to human habitation.

Only a few years ago an education in differences fulfilled a specific if limited need. That was at a time when we thought of other places and peoples largely out of curiosity or in terms of exotic vacations. It was the mark of a rounded man to be well traveled and to know about the fabulous variations of human culture and behavior. But it wasn't the type of knowledge you had to live by and build on.

Then overnight came the great compression. Far-flung areas which had been secure in their remoteness suddenly became jammed together in a single arena. And all at once a new type of education became necessary, an education in liberation from tribalism. For tribalism had persisted from earliest times, though it had taken refined forms. The new education had to teach man the most difficult lesson of all: to look at someone anywhere in the world and be able to recognize the image of himself. It had to be an education in self-recognition. The old emphasis upon superficial differences had to give way to education for mutuality and for citizenship in the human community.

In such an education we begin with the fact that the universe itself does not hold life cheaply. Life is a rare occurrence among the millions of galaxies and solar systems that occupy space. And in this particular solar system life occurs on only one planet. And on that one planet life takes millions of forms. Of all these countless forms of life, only one, the human species, possesses certain faculties in combination that give it supreme advantages over all the others. Among those faculties or gifts is a creative intelligence that enables man to reflect and anticipate, to encompass past experience, and also to visualize future needs. There are endless other wondrous faculties the mechanisms of which are not yet within the understanding of their beneficiaries—the faculties of hope, conscience, appreciation of beauty, kinship, love, faith. 8

Viewed in planetary perspective, what counts is not that the thoughts of men lead them in different directions but that all men possess the capacity to think; not that they pursue different faiths but that they are capable of spiritual belief; not that they write and read different books but that they are capable of creating print and communicating in it across time and space; not that they enjoy different art and music but that something in them enables them to respond deeply to forms and colors and ordered vibrations of sounds. 9

These basic lessons, then, would seek to provide a proper respect for man in the universe. Next in order would be instruction in the unity of man's needs. However friendly the universe may be to man, it has left the conditions of human existence precariously balanced. All men need oxygen, water, land, warmth, food. Remove any one of these and the unity of human needs is attacked and man with it. The next lesson would concern the human situation itself—how to use self-understanding in the cause of human welfare; how to control the engines created by man that threaten 10 to alter the precarious balance on which life depends; how to create a peaceful society of the whole.

With such an education, it is possible that some nation or people may come forward not only with vital understanding but with the vital inspiration that men need no less than food. Leadership on this higher level does not require mountains of gold or thundering propaganda. It is concerned with human destiny; human destiny is the issue; people will respond.   11

Questions

1. Is Cousins saying that an adequate education presents only what people have in common? Or does an adequate education also include the differences between people?
2. Cousins states that "what counts" is the capacity for "spiritual belief" and not the pursuit of different beliefs or faiths. Is he saying that differences in belief or faith are superficial and of no consequence or value?
3. What special view of people does a "planetary perspective" provide of human life? What conclusions does Cousins draw from this view?
4. Why does an adequate education "begin with the fact that the universe itself does not hold life cheaply"? Why should education not begin with the qualities people have in common?
5. Do you agree with Cousins that a person who is aware only of differences between people and cultures is miseducated? What is the basis of your agreement or disagreement with Cousins?

Vocabulary Study

1. Give synonyms for the following words: *comprehend* (paragraph 2); *terrain, productivity* (paragraph 3); *obliterated, allegiances* (paragraph 4); *mutuality* (paragraph 7); *mechanisms* (paragraph 8); *perspective* (paragraph 9); *precarious* (paragraph 10); *propaganda* (paragraph 11).
2. What does the word *tribalism* mean in paragraph 7, and how do you know?
3. Cousins concludes with the statement that "human destiny is the issue." What does he mean by *destiny*?

Suggestions for Writing

1. Discuss one or more ways in which you find your education lacking. Explain why it is lacking—what you should have been taught and what the cost of your miseducation has been.
2. State the qualities that you believe mark the educated person. Then explain why you hold these beliefs. Illustrate these qualities from personal experience or observation.
3. State why you agree or disagree with one of Cousins' statements. Then defend your reasons for agreeing or disagreeing by drawing on personal experience and observation.

Timothy S. Healy

IN DEFENSE OF DISORDER

Timothy S. Healy is president of Georgetown University in Washington, D.C. A specialist in the poetry of John Donne, Healy previously taught English at Fordham University, and he also has served as vice chancellor for academic affairs at the City University of New York and on federal government commissions on education. His essay on student interruption of unpopular university speakers explores this specific issue and then moves on to the broader question of why universities exist.

Over the past weeks, the nation's colleges have taken a beating because of loudmouths who shouted down invited speakers. Eldridge Cleaver at Wisconsin, Ambassador Jeane Kirkpatrick at Berkeley and Sheik Ahmad Zaki Yamani at Kansas were the speakers, and the noise raised in their defense is only slightly less deafening than the shouts that drowned their speeches. No one in the academy approved or condoned the shouting: the clearest defense of the university as an open forum has come from university people themselves through the national associations that represent presidents, faculty members and students.

Whether or not they are aware of it, our critics misread our vulnerability to disruption. They seem to think that universities are orderly places, and if they aren't, presidents and trustees ought to make them so, even by force. Force is, however, our last and least resource, and order in the universities has seldom been more than skin-deep. We order our planning, our upkeep, our payroll and the lawns. But where our most serious work is done, messiness, not to say a kind of anarchy, is part of our nature.

Look first at our teaching. Our job is to put students in touch with beauty or thought and then watch what happens. A young mind seeing for the first time into Virgil, Plato or Burke undergoes an intellectual chain reaction that is uncontrollable. Great works and young minds are "fire and powder which as they kiss consume."

There is an anarchy in the being of our students. The chaos of living in a 20-year-old body translates into the 20-year-old's steady probing at authority. Most students at one time or another tangle with it, not because they want it removed, but because they want to see whether it will stand still long enough for them to measure themselves against it.

At times, the faculty, like parents, cry out in Shakespearean eloquence:

> Let me not live . . . to be the snuff
> Of younger spirits, whose apprehensive senses
> All but new things disdain; whose judgments are
> Mere fathers of their garments; whose constancies
> Expire before their fashions.

But faculty, too, are caught up in our disorderly process. A good class crackles with intensity. The professor knows the long reach of his ideas and the challenge they put not only to his students but to himself. He is also aware of how hard he must crowd and pull to make student growth go as far as it can. The wrestle of mind on mind fills both, and neither faculty member nor student has much time for the dull business of keeping the world, even the world of the university, in good trim. To learn and to teach are beautiful things, but at their intense best, like laughter or pain, they distort.

The faculty knows also the messiness of research. Every scholar who finds himself treading ground no one has trod before feels as though he has been spun off his native planet into a solitary and chaotic orbit of speculation, hypothesis and doubt. Anarchy and loneliness go together. Scholarship in which facts stay in line or ideas in order is either vulgarization or echo.

Our critics take as given the basic tidiness of government, industry and the press, but authority within a university is tentative and dispersed. No one is completely in charge, and no one should be. Academic decisions are made by faculties. Students want a large say in the conduct of their lives on campus. Presidents and deans distribute the seven goods of the university (people, space, money, books, equipment, location and reputation) but are bigger fools than they look if they confuse the ground they walk with the windy heights where the young learn and grow. 7

That growth touches all of us. The faculty offer their experience and knowledge and the students their imagination and energy. The shock between them remakes all our worlds, including our democracy. Alfred North Whitehead's vision of the university as the smithy where a people's ideas and forms are rethought and recast in "the imaginative acquisition of knowledge" is still true. That vision doesn't work where premises or conclusions go untried or where a false neatness is forcibly laid on. 8

Because we are open in our process and open in our places, we are deliberately vulnerable to ill-aimed force, which can at times attack our own freedom. The very being of a university makes it easy to disrupt, and our centuries have taught us that we are weakly defended by policemen. A university's great gift is the grant of room for young and old to speculate, to dream, to rear great buildings of ideas. A second gift is an absolution from consequence should those ideas crash down about our ears. Unless the young learn firsthand how supple and strengthening our freedoms are, they will never learn to defend them. Imposed order is a poor teacher for any free people. 9

Our strong defense, on halcyon as on stormy days, is a discipline as old as man's mind. The worst of our errors are academic and intellectual and we can, given time, correct them. Correction comes not by crowd control, but by reason, by the slow, wearing rub of mind on mind. We live in 10 a glass house that beckons the booby's stone, and none of the numerical barbed wire at the gates of admission can keep out boobies. All of us deal with disrupters, but we try to civilize them, or at least hold them at bay in the strong toils of talk, thought, persuasion. All of us know the acrid shame of failure whenever we must resort to force. We also know that authority alone can never lead a student out of "the prison of his days."

If America's colleges are to be roundly condemned be- 11 cause they feel the best way to handle disruption is to educate disrupters, then something of value to all of us will be lost. Our faculties have at least one large body of allies: the parents of their students. Parents know how hard it is for the young to grow without error, indeed how impossible. They understand why colleges react so often with ambiguous patience. We who teach distrust force because we take the parentage of the mind seriously, because like parents we still at heart love our own.

Comment

Healy's argument is a deductive one. In paragraph 5 he states his conception of the ideal class and the ideal professor: "A good class crackles with intensity. The professor knows the long reach of his ideas and the challenge they put not only to his students but to himself." From this belief and others concerning the purpose and nature of education and the nature of twenty-year-old college students, he makes deductions and uses these to explain the behavior of students who disrupt speakers at college campuses. Healy supports his deductive argument with observations drawn from his experience as a university president; he states that college administrations, trustees, and faculty cannot make universities tidy and well-behaved. He concludes with an appeal to the experience of the reader.

Questions for Study and Discussion

1. What does Healy tell us in paragraphs 3 through 5 about the purpose and nature of education and the nature of college

students? How does he develop his ideas about education in paragraphs 8 and 9?

2. What conclusions does he draw about campus life and, in particular, disruption of speakers from these ideas?

3. Why do college administrators, trustees, and faculty not have the power to control college life? Is Healy saying that anarchy is desirable or necessary? Is he saying that administrators and faculty should not discourage disruption of speakers?

4. What appeal to experience does he make to conclude the essay?

Vocabulary Study

1. What meanings of *order* does Healy explore in paragraphs 2 and 9? What is the meaning of *discipline* in paragraph 10? What kind of order does he believe is possible and desirable on a college campus?

2. In what sense of the word is there "anarchy" in twenty-year-old college students?

3. What images and ideas do the words *wrestle* (paragraph 5), *smithy* (paragraph 8), and *rub* (paragraph 10) convey? How are these metaphors related in idea?

4. What meanings do the words *parent* and *parentage* have in paragraph 11?

Suggestions for Writing

Write an essay stating your views on one of the following issues. In the course of your essay state and answer objections to your position:

a. disrupting speakers on college campuses
b. appointing students to serve as college trustees
c. requiring college students to study a foreign language
d. requiring all students to read some of the classic writings of Western and non-Western cultures

Margaret Mead and Rhoda Metraux

NEIGHBORS VS. NEIGHBORHOODS

Margaret Mead (1901–1978), one of America's most distinguished anthropologists, was a curator of ethnology at the Museum of Natural History in New York City from 1926 to 1969. She also taught at Columbia and other universities, and participated in the work of numerous United States and United Nations agencies. She traveled widely and wrote about many cultures, including her own, in such widely read books as *Growing Up in New Guinea* (1930), *And Keep Your Powder Dry* (1942), and *Male and Female* (1949).

Rhoda Metraux was educated at Vassar, Yale, and Columbia, and has done field work in anthropology in many countries including Haiti, Mexico, Argentina, and New Guinea. She has been on the staff of various government agencies, and has also been a research associate at the Museum of Natural History. She and Margaret Mead worked together for many years, collaborating in the writing of *The Study of Culture at a Distance* (1953) and *Themes in French Culture* (1954).

Most Americans still carry them, like a well-loved picture in a frame, the idea of small-town life—as a way they themselves once lived, or wish they had lived, or hope one day to live. White houses on green lawns set not too far apart, lights in windows at which shades are not pulled down, safety for one's children wherever they wander, everyone known by name and reputation. These are the values remembered by families living in city houses that stand, one just like the other, in bleak and deteriorated or jerry-built rows; in anonymous apartments; and in the vast, unbounded suburbs where the lawns must be kept green but everyone is a stranger. Older people complain and younger people wonder about the disappearance of this neighborly friendliness and trust. In modern American life each family has become, or is fast becoming, a small, self-contained unit in a world of strangers. [1]

One reason that small-town neighborliness has almost vanished is that time and again those who grew up with it found it too confining. "No, son, I wouldn't plan to be a [2] pilot. You Atkinsons always had weak eyes." . . . "You want to be an actress? Now, Mary, take a little advice from someone who knew you *before* you were born. . . ." However well meant, remarks like these could clip the wings of one's ambitions. A world in which the neighbors, which included most of the town, knew one's every act was restricting, limiting, confining. Each child grew up carrying the known and expected characteristics of his grandparents, his parents, his brothers and sisters, and even the marks of his own small failures as a little child. True, the neighbors often were kind, dependable people. But it was good to get away from them, to make a new life where no one knew you and where your aspirations were not treated as pretensions.

Yet, in the new life something is acutely felt to be missing. The frame of neighborly knowledge, which contained both an allowance for weakness and an unwillingness to allow for real ambition, is gone and nothing has taken its place. We have left behind (and may well lament) the familiarity and reassurance of the small, intimate neighborhood, but we have not realized the possibilities inherent in a larger, more complicated setting. In fact, in many instances we have retreated into a way of life even more limiting than the one we left.

In today's housing projects and in suburban developments, conformity—outward adjustment to the opinions and tastes of other people—has been substituted for the old closeness, longed for but also feared. People come to the neighborhood as strangers, from widely different backgrounds and influences. After they arrive, they try to become like the others in the community and hope that the others will be like them. But the difficulty is that making oneself look like other people, and even act like them, is quite different from sharing something with them.

In city neighborhoods and some suburban communities, people have a tendency to keep to themselves—often they know their neighbors only to nod to and keep self-protectively at arm's length—especially if they feel that certain elements of the neighborhood are "bad." Subtly, neighbors are associated with difficulties and times of trouble. They lend you things you have run out of unexpectedly, like butter, or extra things like party glasses and chairs. They keep one child when another is sick. They bring food at a time of death. But these contacts are limited and intermittent, and when things go well there is little give-and-take even with "good" neighbors.

So we are seldom fully aware of our neighbors as people. In fact, many of us today care far less about our neighbors than we do about our neighbor*hoods*. In speaking of "good" neighborhoods or "bad" neighborhoods, we often are not thinking about the neighbors as people at all—witty or dull, happy or sad, kind or indifferent—but as accessories to the neighborhood and their effect on our class position.

In this context, neighbors who spoil the neighborhood are people who put the wrong decorations in their windows, drive the wrong cars, neglect their lawns or come from the wrong racial or religious groups; the wrong neighbors are people whom other people—one's rich or more successful relatives and friends—might see and criticize. The right kind of neighbors are just the opposite; they are people who pull you up rather than drag you down just by living on the same street.

Either way, this is thinking of people as things. If the car stands in front of the house by the neat lawn and no one bangs in and out of the door and the right kind of tree stands in the picture window at Christmas, those who are in search of the "right" neighborhood will be content. When their friends come to visit, they won't mention neighbors at all— just what a pleasant *neighborhood* it is. If, on the other hand, the street is deteriorating, the family will deplore having to live there in the same breath with which they explain the advantages of their own house: "The children can walk to school. It's near Jim's work. We've put so much into fixing it up. But we don't really belong here." All the other people on the block are excluded. So by our particularly American form of social class—in which a class position can be invaded, diluted and lost, in which people are judged not by what they are but by how they dress, where they live and what kinds of cars they drive—the human element that comes through the sheer sharing of the vicissitudes of everyday life is crowded out. People are treated as things, as objects by which one hauls oneself up or is pushed down.

These attitudes need to be re-examined. We have the opportunity to use our new-found freedom, away from the small, familiar worlds that were safe and secure but often stultifying, to develop and diversify our lives. We are not doing this if we regard the neighbors as extensions of ourselves, or as people to be "used" or kept at arm's length, or merely as attractive or unattractive accessories to the community. The child who grows up with such attitudes grows up with a sad lack of what he will need as an American, as a person, as a dweller on this planet. He is robbed of one important dimension of living in the modern world—learning a mutual give-and-take with people of widely different tastes and backgrounds. Just as relatives are, one hopes, people one loves (but may not like) and friends are people one really likes and may come to love, so neighbors can be people whom we may like, or even come to love, or be indifferent to, or not like at all. But we can, at least, come to see them—and ourselves—for what we are as *people*—highly individual people in a very large world.

Comment

Though they focus on neighborhoods and neighborliness, Margaret Mead and Rhoda Metraux deal with some of the aspects of small-town life and city life discussed by Kathy Seelinger (p. 419) and Ellen Goodman (p. 415). And like Seelinger and Goodman, they write from their experience of American small towns and cities. But the idea of neighborliness is not the outcome of factual evidence; Mead and Metraux do not arrive at it inductively. They present it rather as a given truth:

> We have the opportunity to use our new-found freedom, away from the small, familiar worlds that were safe and secure but often stultifying, to develop and diversify our lives. We are not doing this if we regard the neighbors as extensions of ourselves, or as people to be "used" or kept at arm's length, or merely as attractive or unattractive accessories to the community.

Mead and Metraux state this truth several times in the course of the essay. The statement is an extended definition that shapes the whole discussion of neighborliness.

Questions for Study and Discussion

1. Where do Mead and Metraux first state their belief that people are not things? Where do they restate it?
2. What inferences do they make from the truth that people are not things?
3. Is the statement that people are not things the thesis of the essay? If not, what is the thesis? Where does it appear?
4. What explanation and factual support do Mead and Metraux give for their statement that "we are seldom fully aware of our neighbors as people" and that many people care more about their neighborhoods than about their neighbors? Why is their reasoning in paragraph 6 inductive rather than deductive?
5. To what extent do Mead and Metraux agree with Kathy Seelinger that small-town life encourages comformity? To what extent do they agree with Ellen Goodman on the character of city life?
6. Do you agree that city life encourages the attitude that people are things? If you agree, what evidence can you cite that city life has this effect? If you disagree, what evidence shows that it does not?

Vocabulary Study

Explain what the etymology of the following words and phrases contributes to your understanding of the following: *jerry-built*, *neighborly* (paragraph 1); *aspirations, pretensions* (paragraph 2); *intermittent* (paragraph 5); *diluted* (paragraph 8), *vicissitudes* (paragraph 8); *stultifying, dimension* (paragraph 9).

Suggestions for Writing

1. Describe experiences you have had with neighbors in your town or city. Then discuss whether the ideas on neighbors

and neighborliness of Mead and Metraux account for these experiences.

2. State whether you agree or disagree with one of the following statements, and explain why you do:

   a. "In modern American life each family has become, or is fast becoming, a small, self-contained unit in a world of strangers."

   b. "In today's housing projects and in suburban developments, conformity—outward adjustment to the opinions and tastes of other people—has been substituted for the old closeness, longed for, but also feared."

   c. "In speaking of 'good' neighborhoods or 'bad' neighborhoods, we often are not thinking about the neighbors as people at all. . . ."

Ellen Goodman

WHOSE LIFE IS IT ANYWAY?

In her essay on p. 415, Ellen Goodman reasons inductively in drawing upon her experience of small-town and city life. In her essay on Elizabeth Bouvia that follows, Goodman reasons deductively—from truths she holds—about the issue she characterizes as the right to die with the help of doctors. A similar situation exists in Brian Clark's play and later movie, *Whose Life Is It Anyway?*, as a hospitalized quadriplegic is successful in his legal fight to end efforts by his doctor and the hospital staff to maintain his life.

For a time, life has been imitating art in Riverside, California. The courtroom case of a twenty-six-year-old quadriplegic, Elizabeth Bouvia, is every bit as dramatic as the script of the movie, *Whose Life Is It Anyway?*   1

In September 1983, Bouvia admitted herself to the psychiatric ward of Riverside General Hospital with one goal in mind: to starve to death under their roof. She wanted doctors to give her only the medical attention needed to ease pain.   2

Unlike the character in the movie, Bouvia had been paralyzed since birth with cerebral palsy. Her grit was well-   3 recorded in daily life and academic degrees. But after a failed marriage, failed attempts at pregnancy, and deepening depression over her future, her only determination was to die: "I choose no longer to be dependent on others."

Hers is a case that pushes just about all the buttons on our finely engineered ethical panel. The right-to-life and the right-to-die buttons. The one that labels suicide as rational act and the one that labels suicide as a crazy act. The one that opposes medical intervention against a patient's will and the one that supports medical intervention to save lives. 4

It presents us with the dilemma that we've been edging up to slowly, case after case. Ever since Karen Ann Quinlan, we've debated whether a hospital could, should, keep someone "alive" after brain death. Today we discuss the ethics of "heroic" care for the terminally ill as well. 5

Slowly, we have also asserted certain rights to medical care. In 1973, in the case of a woman named Roe, the courts determined that a pregnant woman seeking an abortion had the right to privacy. Recently, in the case of a baby named Doe, the courts determined that parents could deny life-prolonging surgery to a severely handicapped infant. On our own we can refuse therapy, even maintenance therapy like dialysis, and willfully shorten our lives. 6

Meanwhile suicide, at least among the elderly or ill, has gained a certain odd legitimacy. In March 1983, the writer Arthur Koestler, ill with leukemia, committed suicide and his healthy wife, Cynthia, joined him. She was described as "devoted." A Florida couple in their eighties carefully killed themselves as a "solution to the problems of aging." The sheriff commented on how "thoughtful" they were. 7

In this atmosphere, Elizabeth Bouvia's request to be allowed to starve with painkillers and without force feeding seems almost routine. After all, if the parents of Baby Doe have the right to deny treatment, then doesn't the patient herself have the right to refuse it? If Roe has the right to "control her own body," then doesn't Bouvia? Isn't suicide a civil right? 8

The reality is that the Bouvia case has pushed over the established ethical line. We are now entering into a moral arena where words like "rights" begin to lose their meaning. 9

"I'm not asking for anybody to kill me," this woman 10
has said. "I'm asking that the natural process of death take
over." But refusing food is no more a natural process of
death than falling is when you jump off a bridge.

What makes this case different from other "right-to-die" 11
cases is that, however miserable she regards her life, Bouvia
is not suffering a fatal disability. What makes it different is
that she is not just proposing suicide; she is asking for the
help of doctors. Indeed, Bouvia checked into a ward that
specializes in preventing suicide. There are, as Freud said,
no accidents.

The California Superior Court judge made a proper dis- 12
tinction last week when he ruled that, yes, Bouvia had the
right to kill herself—it is her life, anyway—but not "with
the assistance of society." If she did not continue to accept
nourishment, the judge would allow the hospital to force-
feed her. Now, as I write this in December 1983, the young
woman has refused sufficient liquid protein to sustain her
ninety-five-pound body.

No matter how uncomfortable the idea, I think it is 13
appropriate, even imperative, for the hospital to forcibly feed
its despairing patient. Psychiatric wards are not suicide centers where people come for help in terminating their despair.

Deep down, I'm afraid it is too easy for society to "un- 14
derstand" the unhappiness of a quadriplegic instead of alleviating it. It's too easy for us to begin to regard suicides of
the sick or the aged as "thoughtful" solutions.

If we support Elizabeth Bouvia's civil-rights stand, then 15
sooner or later we would passively watch a woman step off
a ledge and a man swallow sleeping pills. As we stood there,
bystanders, would we then remind each other not to inter-
fere? The "right to die" can easily become an excuse for our
own unwillingness to reach out and help.

Comment

People sometimes agree about an ethical principle but disagree about
its definition or its application to a particular situation. Those arguing about abortion usually agree that taking human life is wrong

but many disagree over the definition of *human life*. The point at issue in these arguments is whether a fetus is a human being. Goodman focuses on the issue of whether a person has a right to ask others to assist in the act of suicide. Suicide is not the issue for her. Others may disagree with Goodman, arguing that suicide is the issue, not how it takes place. Goodman bases her argument on truths that she states in explaining why she agrees with the judicial decision to forcibly feed Elizabeth Bouvia. Goodman also asks us to consider the implications of allowing Bouvia to die in the way she requested:

> If we support Elizabeth Bouvia's civil-rights stand, then sooner or later we would passively watch a woman step off a ledge and a man swallow pills. As we stood there, bystanders, would we then remind each other not to interfere?

Questions for Study and Discussion

1. What is "the dilemma that we've been edging up to slowly, case after case"? What is the "established ethical line" that the Bouvia case has made us cross?
2. Does Goodman say that suicide is a right, or does she not state her belief about suicide? Does Goodman say or imply that she agrees with the decisions in the Roe and the Baby Doe cases? Or does she state only that the courts have acknowledged certain rights?
3. What beliefs or truths lead Goodman to concur with the judicial ruling in the Bouvia case? Where in the essay does Goodman state these truths?
4. Why does Goodman note that Elizabeth Bouvia entered a ward specializing in suicide prevention?
5. Do you believe that the judicial ruling was correct? Do you agree with Goodman's reasoning in concurring with the judge? What beliefs guide your reasoning on the issue?

Vocabulary Study

1. What is the difference between a quadriplegic and a paraplegic?
2. Why does Goodman refer to the Bouvia case as a "dilemma"?

3. Goodman states that "suicide, at least among the elderly or ill, has gained a certain odd legitimacy." Does the word *legitimacy* mean *approval?*
4. Goodman quotes the Florida sheriff's comment that the elderly couple who committed suicide were "thoughtful" people, and she returns to this word in paragraph 14. Why is this word significant to her?

Suggestions for Writing

1. Argue your own views on the Bouvia case. State the beliefs that guide your thinking on the issue, and explain why you hold them.
2. State what beliefs guide your thinking on one of the following issues. Then discuss the origin of these beliefs—for example, in your religion, schooling, or upbringing:
   a. private ownership of handguns
   b. establishing the drinking age at 21
   c. drafting young men and women for military service
   d. exempting young women from military service
   e. making voting compulsory

George F. Will

BEARBAITING AND BOXING

George F. Will was educated at Trinity College, Oxford University, and Princeton University. He taught politics at Michigan State University and other universities, and later observed the workings of government as a congressional aide. Since 1972, he has given his full time to journalism, first as editor of the *National Review,* and later as a columnist for the *Washington Post* and *Newsweek,* and as commentator for the American Broadcasting Company. In 1977, Will received the Pulitzer Prize for Commentary. His columns have been collected in a number of books, including *The Pursuit of Virtue, and Other Tory Notions* (1982) and *The Morning After* (1986); his book *Statecraft as Soulcraft: What Government Does* (1983) is a theoretical study of government. His essay on boxing that follows and his essay on New York City in the following section illustrate the range of Will's interests and concerns.

For 150 years people have been savoring Macaulay's judgment that the Puritans hated bearbaiting not because it gave pain to the bear but because it gave pleasure to the spectators. However, there are moments, and this is one, for blurting out the truth: The Puritans were right. The pain to the bear was not a matter of moral indifference, but the pleasure of the spectators was sufficient reason for abolishing that entertainment.

Now another boxer has been beaten to death. The brain injury he suffered was worse than the injury the loser in a boxing match is supposed to suffer. It is hard to calibrate such things—how hard an opponent's brain should be banged against the inside of his cranium—in the heat of battle.

From time immemorial, in immemorial ways, men have been fighting for the entertainment of other men. Perhaps in a serene, temperate society boxing would be banned along with other blood sports—if, in such a society, the question would even arise. But a step toward the extinction of boxing is understanding why that is desirable. One reason is the physical injury done to young men. But a sufficient reason is the quality of the pleasure boxing often gives to spectators.

There is no denying that boxing like other, better sports, can exemplify excellence. Boxing demands bravery and, when done well, is beautiful in the way that any exercise of finely honed physical talents is. Furthermore, many sports are dangerous. But boxing is the sport that has as its object the infliction of pain and injury. Its crowning achievement is the infliction of serious trauma on the brain. The euphemism for boxing is "the art of self-defense." No. A rose is a rose is a rose, and a user fee is a revenue enhancer is a tax increase, and boxing is aggression.

It is probable that there will be a rising rate of spinal cord injuries and deaths in football. The force of defensive players (a function of weight and speed) is increasing even faster than the force of ball carriers and receivers. As a coach once said, football is not a contact sport—dancing is a contact sport—football is a collision sport. The human body, especially the knee and spine, is not suited to that. But football can be made safer by equipment improvements and rules changes such as those proscribing certain kinds of blocks. Boxing is fundamentally impervious to reform.

It will be said that if two consenting adults want to   6
batter each other for the amusement of paying adults, the essential niceties have been satisfied, "consent" being almost the only nicety of a liberal society. But from Plato on, political philosophers have taken entertainments seriously, and have believed the law should, too. They have because a society is judged by the kind of citizens it produces, and some entertainments are coarsening. Good government and the good life depend on good values and passions, and some entertainments are inimical to these.

Such an argument cuts no ice in a society where the   7
decayed public philosophy teaches that the pursuit of happiness is a right sovereign over all other considerations; that "happiness" and "pleasure" are synonyms, and that there is no hierarchy of values against which to measure particular appetites. Besides, some persons will say, with reason, that a society in which the entertainment menu includes topless lady mud wrestlers is a society past worrying about.

Some sports besides boxing attract persons who want   8
their unworthy passions stirred, including a lust for blood. I remember Memorial Day in the Middle West in the 1950s, when all roads led to the Indianapolis Speedway, where too many fans went to drink Falstaff beer and hope for a crash. But boxing is in a class by itself.

Richard Hoffer of the *Los Angeles Times* remembers   9
the death of Johnny Owen, a young 118-pound bantamweight who died before he had fulfilled his modest ambition of buying a hardware store back home in Wales. Hoffer remembers that "Owen was put in a coma by a single punch, carried out of the Olympic (arena) under a hail of beer cups, some of which were filled with urine."

The law can not prudently move far in advance of mass   10
taste, so boxing can not be outlawed. But in a world in which many barbarities are unavoidable, perhaps it is not too much to hope that some of the optional sorts will be outgrown.

Comment

The statement on bearbaiting by the nineteenth-century English historian Thomas B. Macaulay on Oliver Cromwell and the English Puritans, who ruled from 1649 to 1660, is often quoted in the course of ridiculing puritanical views. Will defends the Puritan ethical view as "sufficient reason" for discouraging boxing. He shows that boxing resembles football and automobile racing in different ways, but he focuses on boxing because he considers the sport to be "in a class by itself." His argument is based on what he considers obvious truths about the ideal society. Recognizing that probably few boxing fans would agree with him, he supports his argument with factual evidence. His argument is a deductive one, however, because he makes inferences directly from these truths.

Questions for Study and Discussion

1. What is Will's definition of the ideal society, and where does he present it?
2. What inference does Will draw from this definition about the entertainments of a society?
3. Why does American society fall short of that ideal? What factual evidence does Will present to support this judgment?
4. How does boxing resemble football and automobile racing? Why does Will believe boxing is "in a class by itself"?
5. In paragraph 10, Will states an obvious truth and draws an inference from it. What is that truth and what is the inference?

Vocabulary Study

1. Find information on bear-baiting in a sports dictionary or other reference book. To what extent did bear-baiting in the seventeenth century and other times resemble the sports criticized by Will?
2. Give synonyms for the following: *calibrate* (paragraph 2); *temperate* (paragraph 3); *honed, trauma, euphemism* (paragraph 4); *proscribing, impervious* (paragraph 5); *niceties, inimical* (paragraph 6); *sovereign, hierarchy* (paragraph 7); *prudently* (paragraph 10).

450   Deductive Argument

Suggestions for Writing

1. State whether or not you agree with Will on the issue of boxing. Explain your reasons for your agreement or disagreement.
2. Use the resources of your library to write a research paper on one of the following topics. Limit the topic to a particular period—perhaps a decade in which a large number of fatalities or accidents occurred—or to an aspect on which you find sufficient information to support a significant thesis. Your research paper might be an informative one that provides facts needed to understand an existing situation. Or your paper might be persuasive: you might use your findings to argue for or against a proposal or an existing policy:
   a. professional boxing fatalities and the public response
   b. injuries in stockcar and other automobile races and the public response
   c. injuries in college and professional football
   d. gunshot deaths in the United States and Great Britain
   e. drug-related crime in two American cities
   f. the risks of nuclear power
   g. chemical warfare since 1913
   h. causes of homelessness in America in the 1980s
   i. the increasing cost of hospitalization in the 1980s
   j. standards of welfare eligibility in two American cities

Strategies of Persuasion

Most arguments are directed to a particular audience and organized in light of that audience's knowledge and beliefs; in other words, most arguments are meant to be *persuasive*. We have seen that inductive arguments build particulars of experience and similar kinds of evidence to generalizations or conclusions; deductive arguments, on the other hand, proceed from premises and build to conclusions. But the order of ideas may sometimes be changed to fit particular audiences. Thus the conclusion of the argument may be stated at the beginning, as a way of focusing attention on the point of most concern. Or the essay may start with the least controversial statement (or premise), proceed to the more controversial, and end with the most controversial. The order of ideas does not affect the strength or soundness of the argument itself.

The persuasiveness of the inductive argument depends on the strength of the facts presented. George F. Will, in the inductive argument that follows, immerses his audience in the facts of a notorious episode—one that raises important questions about the situation of poor people in our cities. Will does not ask these questions directly: instead he gives a full account of what happened to a young Harlem mother—stressing those details that dramatize the weakness of welfare systems.

The questions Will raises—in particular, what is a city's responsibility for the lives of the poor—might have been discussed theoretically, as in a sociology textbook. Will does discuss the issues theoretically toward the end of the essay, but he has no solution to offer for the plight of the poor, though he grants that cities must provide "a floor of support" of some kind. It is the intractable problem, for which no solution now exists, that he focuses on in his extended example. The example is indispensable to our understanding—especially so if we believe it is easy to assign blame in crimes of the poor, or that easy solutions are available.

Yet Will does something more: in dramatizing the episode, he allows the reader to imagine the situation of the young woman. This appeal to imagination is his most important persuasive device.

The writer has available numerous strategies of persuasion. Will's essay illustrates dramatization, one of the most important. The satirist uses other means to persuade the audience to change its thinking on an issue or to take action. The satirist usually depends on ridicule and sometimes tries to awaken the conscience of the audience by appealing to shame and guilt. But appeals to conscience may take other forms; for example, writers also appeal to our common humanity. The essays in this section illustrate some of these many appeals.

George F. Will

ON HER OWN IN THE CITY

In his essay on a young woman's tragedy, George F. Will builds his argument to a general statement about the ability of society to care for the poor. The argument is thus different from Will's essay on boxing and other sports in America. In discussing the matter of poverty, Will might have used any one of the thousand daily tragedies that occur in American cities. The fate of the young woman described in the essay raises questions that the reader cannot ignore. For details on Will see p. 446.

When police, responding to her call, arrived at her East Harlem tenement, she was hysterical: "The dog ate my baby." The baby girl had been four days old, twelve hours "home" from the hospital. Home was two rooms and a kitchen on the sixth floor, furnished with a rug, a folding chair, and nothing else, no bed, no crib. 1

"Is the baby dead?" asked an officer. "Yes," the mother said, "I saw the baby's insides." Her dog, a German shepherd, had not been fed for five days. She explained: "I left the baby on the floor with the dog to protect it." She had bought the dog in July for protection from human menaces. 2

She is twenty-four. She went to New York three years 3
ago from a small Ohio community. She wanted to be on her
own. She got that wish.

She was employed intermittently, until the fifth month 4
of her pregnancy, which she says was the result of a rape
she did not report to the police. She wanted the baby. She
bought child-care books, and had seven prenatal checkups
at Bellevue Hospital. Although she rarely called home or asked
for money, she called when the baby was born. Her mother
mailed twenty-five dollars for a crib. It arrived too late.

When labor began she fed the dog with the last food in 5
the apartment and went alone to the hospital. The baby was
born on Wednesday. When she left Bellevue Sunday evening, the hospital office holding her welfare payment was
closed. With six dollars in her pocket and a baby in her
arms, she took a cab home. The meter said four dollars and
the driver demanded a dollar tip. When she asked his assistance in getting upstairs, he drove off.

The hospital had given her enough formula for three 6
feedings for the baby. Rather than spend her remaining dollar that night on food for herself and the dog, she saved it
for the bus ride back to Bellevue to get her welfare money.
Having slept with the baby on a doubled-up rug, she left the
baby and the dog at 7 A.M. It was 53 degrees, too cold she
thought to take the baby. She had no warm baby clothes
and she thought the hospital had said the baby was ailing.
She got back at 8:30 A.M. Then she called the police.

Today the forces of law and order and succor are strug- 7
gling to assign "blame" in order to escape it. Her attorney
and Bellevue are arguing about how she was released, or
expelled, on Sunday evening. Welfare officials are contend-
ing with charges that they are somehow culpable for her
failure to receive a crib before giving birth, and for her living conditions. (She was receiving payment of $270 a month;
her rent was $120.) She has been arraigned on a charge of
negligent homicide, but no one seems anxious to prosecute.
Late in New York's U.S. Senate primary, Daniel P. Moyni-
han, talking like a senator prematurely, said that this case
dramatizes weaknesses of the welfare system, and indicated

that it also dramatizes the need for him in Washington. Perhaps.

But because cities are collections of strangers, they are, inevitably, bad places to be poor. Not that there are good places, but cities, being kingdoms of the strong, are especially hellish for the poor. Cities have their indispensable purposes, and their charms, not the least of which is that you can be alone in a crowd. But that kind of living alone is an acquired taste, and not for the weak or unfortunate. They are apt to learn that no city's institutions can provide protective supports like those of an extended family or real community. No metropolis can provide a floor of support solid enough to prevent the bewildered—like the woman from Ohio—from falling through the cracks.

Through those cracks you get an occasional glimpse of what George Eliot meant: "If we had a keen vision and feeling of all ordinary human life, it would be like hearing the grass grow and the squirrel's heartbeat, and we should die of that roar which lies on the other side of silence."

Questions for Study and Discussion

1. What details of the episode show why it is difficult to assign blame for the death of the child?
2. Is Will suggesting that everyone involved in the death was to blame—the mother, the hospital and welfare officials, the city as a whole—or is he saying that blame is difficult or impossible to define in this case?
3. What is the point of George Eliot's statement, and what is gained by concluding the essay with it? Would the statement be as effective if it introduced the essay?
4. How persuasive do you find the example? Do you have a solution for the plight of the woman? Are there other solutions Will might have presented?

Vocabulary Study

Give the meaning of the following words, in the context of the sentence in which each appears: *intermittently* (paragraph 4); *suc-*

cor, arraigned, negligent homicide (paragraph 7); *apt, extended, metropolis* (paragraph 8).

Suggestions for Writing

1. Will states in paragraph 8: "They are apt to learn that no city's institutions can provide protective supports like those of an extended family or real community." Discuss what the details of the essay tell us about an "extended family" or "real community" by implication.
2. Discuss what you believe a city can and should do for a person like the woman Will describes. You may wish to discuss what responsibility a city has for the lives of poor people in general. State your reasons for the views that you hold.
3. Will states earlier in paragraph 8: "But because cities are collections of strangers, they are, inevitably, bad places to be poor." And he adds in the same paragraph: "Cities have their indispensable purposes, and their charms, not the least of which is that you can be alone in a crowd." Develop one of these ideas from your own experience or observation, or compare his views with those of Robert Coles (p. 233) or Margaret Mead and Rhoda Metraux (p. 437).

The New Yorker

THE ADJECTIVE "UGLY"

The New Yorker publishes fiction, poetry, arts criticism, and social and political commentary. John Hersey's *Hiroshima*, Rachel Carson's *Silent Spring*, and Jonathan Schell's *The Fate of the Earth* first appeared in the magazine. Each issue opens with a section titled "The Talk of the Town"—a collection of short sketches and commentaries written by the staff. E. B. White wrote many of these and so have John Updike and Lillian Ross. This commentary on the homeless in New York City is taken from "The Talk of the Town."

The adjective "ugly" doesn't get around much anymore—it has a restricted range, like the buffalo, which, instead of darkening the plains, is currently crossbred with the occasional cow to create a low-cholesterol steak. Emerson remarked that one man's beauty is another's ugliness, but the years have turned his proverb topsy-turvy, for now all that was ugly is beautiful, or, at least, "interesting." If someone covers the inside of a subway car with his initials, the result is either art or hooliganism to be diligently studied as indicative of social decay; if one comes across a Buick rusting in the woods, it is, you know, stark. What was ugly has become earthy, or industrial, or post-industrial, or "found," and that's fine with us: there *is* some glory in damn near everything—the orange sunsets, say, when the smog is most visible. Anyway, now that the word is not being constantly drained, some force should accumulate behind it, like water building up behind a dam, so that when somebody does put it to use—and shortly we intend to do just that—it will pack some wallop.

There are things we all must do, regardless of race or class or computer literacy: we must eat and sleep and think what we would buy first if we won the lottery. And when our legs get tired we must sit down. In some parts of the world, people have learned to squat, to hunker down, but in America only baseball catchers are really much good at it. Most of us need something to sit on—a chair, perhaps. If you are an average citizen, it is no problem: when you've been shopping a few hours, you can walk into a coffee shop and sit down and order an iced tea and drink it and pay the bill and leave a tip and get up and go home. But imagine for a moment that you have no money at all. Perhaps you are homeless, and what you own you are carrying; it's not so much, but it's more than nothing, because before so very long it will be November and *then* you'll want that parka. You're walking up toward midtown, not because it's midtown but because the daylight lasts fifteen hours this time of year and you have to walk somewhere. You're tired of walking, but you can't go into a restaurant, even a McDonald's, because they'll ask you to leave and then they'll make you leave, and who can blame them? You might go into the Park, but maybe it's on toward evening and you don't want to be hassled. So maybe you head for a ledge in front of a shop or a hotel, or even a church, and when you get there you find they have stuck spikes into the granite or the brick so that you can't sit there. Those spikes—they are *ugly*.

If you try to sit on them, it hurts. We have tried, and if you don't believe us you try. They are meant to hurt; with the exception of a very few places where they are put up to keep people from crashing through windows or falling into cellars, their aim is to deter sitting. Not so much sitting by you or by us. If it was only you and us, the people who put them up wouldn't much mind; if you could design a spike that would afflict the backsides of derelicts and teen-agers but cushion the posteriors of so-called yuppies, you could make some money. The spikes are meant for bums and drunks. It's silly to blame the shopkeepers and the hoteliers for setting up such grotesque barriers; a man who counts the receipts in his register at the end of a day develops some feel for what draws customers in and what keeps them out. If his customers won't come past a smelly fellow snoozing in the sun, or a woman drinking Colt 45 and cadging quarters and singing little made-up songs—well, up go the spikes. What makes spiked ledges so ugly is not that they rob the down-and-out of a place to sit. There is always the sidewalk or, for those with the energy to hop the turnstile, the subway. Anyway, the homeless lack plenty of items dearer than a seat—a roof, a job, a dinner, a family. The ugliness is in the gesture. It would be nice to think that the reason poor people wander the streets is that we've yet to figure out just how to help them. But it isn't like that really. What the spikes say is: Don't wander the streets, or, at least, don't sit yourself down, in my neighborhood, where I shop; go somewhere else.

Comment

There are numerous ways to comment on the despairing world of the homeless. In an article published in 1984, Ellen L. Bassuk gives statistical information on the number of homeless in the United States in 1983 (2.5 million by one estimate) and on unemployment and the shortage of affordable housing; she discusses state and federal policies and programs; she describes the enormous number of retarded and "deinstitutionalized" mentally ill people who are homeless. Her article ends with the following statement:

> The question raised by the increasing number of homeless people is a very basic one: Are Americans willing to consign a broad class of disabled people to a life of degradation, or will they make the commitment to give such people the care they need? In a civilized society the answer should be clear.—"The Homelessness Problem," *Scientific American*, July 1984

Bassuk hopes the facts of homelessness will encourage readers to help solve the problem. *The New Yorker* also seeks to stir the complacent reader, but it does so in a somewhat different way.

Questions for Study and Discussion

1. What information about homelessness does the essay omit? What information does it include? On what aspect of the experience of homelessness does the essay focus?
2. What is gained by focusing on one aspect of the experience instead of providing a broad picture of the New York homeless?
3. Is the tone of the essay unemotional and objective, perhaps even neutral? Or is the tone one of disgust or anger or sarcasm?
4. Why does the essay explore the adjective "ugly" before turning to the homeless?
5. How effective do you find the essay? Does it change your thinking about the homeless or awaken your sympathy for them? How different would the effect be if the essay had given a broad picture of the problem?

Vocabulary Study

1. Does the word *ugly* have the same meaning throughout the essay?
2. *The New Yorker* states: "If someone covers the inside of a subway car with his initials, the result is either art or hooliganism to be diligently studied as indicative of social decay; if

one comes across a Buick rusting in the woods, it is, you know, stark." What point is *The New Yorker* making about the word *stark?*

Suggestions for Writing

1. Describe a sight that seems to you as ugly as the sight described by *The New Yorker*. Explain why you consider it ugly and then discuss what the sight reveals about people or society.
2. Write a persuasive essay on a school policy or a social practice that you consider wrong or obnoxious. Limit your discussion to a consequence or effect that shows best why the policy or practice ought to be changed or abolished. Don't lecture or exhort your reader. Let the details of your discussion do the job of persuasion, or choose another means of persuasion.

E. B. White

THE DECLINE OF SPORT

(A Preposterous Parable)

E. B. White, the distinguished essayist, humorist, and editor, was born in Mount Vernon, New York, in 1899. He was long associated with *The New Yorker* as writer and editor and also wrote for *Harper's Magazine* and other publications. His books include *Charlotte's Web* (1952) and *Stuart Little* (1945), both for children, and *One Man's Meat* (1943), *The Second Tree from the Corner* (1954), and *The Points of My Compass* (1962), collections of his essays. White died in 1985.

In the third decade of the supersonic age, sport gripped the nation in an ever-tightening grip. The horse tracks, the ballparks, the fight rings, the gridirons, all drew crowds in steadily increasing numbers. Every time a game was played, an attendance record was broken. Usually some other sort of record was broken, too—such as the record for the number of consecutive doubles hit by left-handed batters in a

Series game, or some such thing as that. Records fell like ripe apples on a windy day. Customs and manners changed, and the five-day business week was reduced to four days, then to three, to give everyone a better chance to memorize the scores.

Not only did sport proliferate but the demands it made on the spectator became greater. Nobody was content to take in one event at a time, and thanks to the magic of radio and television nobody had to. A Yale alumnus, class of 1962, returning to the Bowl with 197,000 others to see the Yale-Cornell football game would take along his pocket radio and pick up the Yankee Stadium, so that while his eye might be following a fumble on the Cornell twenty-two-yard line, his ear would be following a man going down to second in the top of the fifth, seventy miles away. High in the blue sky above the Bowl, skywriters would be at work writing the scores of other major and minor sporting contests, weaving an interminable record of victory and defeat, and using the new high-visibility pink news-smoke perfected by Pepsi-Cola engineers. And in the frames of the giant video sets, just behind the goalposts, this same alumnus could watch Dejected win the Futurity before a record-breaking crowd of 349,872 at Belmont, each of whom was tuned to the Yale Bowl and following the World Series game in the video and searching the sky for further news of events either under way or just completed. The effect of this vast cyclorama of sport was to divide the spectator's attention, over-subtilize his appreciation, and deaden his passion. As the fourth supersonic decade was ushered in, the picture changed and sport began to wane.

A good many factors contributed to the decline of sport. Substitutions in football had increased to such an extent that there were very few fans in the United States capable of holding the players in mind during play. Each play that was called saw two entirely new elevens lined up, and the players whose names and faces you had familiarized yourself with in the first period were seldom seen or heard of again. The spectacle became as diffuse as the main concourse in Grand Central at the commuting hour.

Express motor highways leading to the parks and stadia   4
had become so wide, so unobstructed, so devoid of all life
except automobiles and trees that sport fans had got into
the habit of travelling enormous distances to attend events.
The normal driving speed had been stepped up to ninety-
five miles an hour, and the distance between cars had been
decreased to fifteen feet. This put an extraordinary strain on
the sport lover's nervous system, and he arrived home from
a Saturday game, after a road trip of three hundred and fifty
miles, glassy-eyed, dazed, and spent. He hadn't really had
any relaxation and he had failed to see Czlika (who had
gone in for Trusky) take the pass from Bkeeo (who had gone
in for Bjallo) in the third period, because at that moment a
youngster named Lavagetto had been put in to pinch-hit for
Art Gurlack in the bottom of the ninth with the tying run
on second, and the skywriter who was attempting to write
"Princeton O—Lafayette 43" had banked the wrong way,
muffed the "3," and distracted everyone's attention from the
fact that Lavagetto had been whiffed.

Cheering, of course, lost its stimulating effect on play-   5
ers, because cheers were no longer associated necessarily with
the immediate scene but might as easily apply to something
that was happening somewhere else. This was enough to infuriate even the steadiest performer. A football star, hearing
the stands break into a roar before the ball was snapped,
would realize that their minds were not on him, and would
become dispirited and grumpy. Two or three of the big
coaches worried so about this that they considered equip-
ping all players with tiny ear sets, so that they, too, could
keep abreast of other sporting events while playing, but the
idea was abandoned as impractical, and the coaches put it
aside in tickler files, to bring up again later.

I think the event that marked the turning point in sport   6
and started it downhill was the Midwest's classic Dust Bowl
game of 1975, when Eastern Reserve's great right end, Ed
Pistachio, was shot by a spectator. This man, the one who
did the shooting, was seated well down in the stands near
the forty-yard line on a bleak October afternoon and was
so saturated with sport and with the disappointments of sport

that he had clearly become deranged. With a minute and fifteen seconds to play and the score tied, the Eastern Reserve quarterback had whipped a long pass over Army's heads into Pistachio's waiting arms. There was no other player anywhere near him, and all Pistachio had to do was catch the ball and run it across the line. He dropped it. At exactly this moment, the spectator—a man named Homer T. Parkinson, of 35 Edgemere Drive, Toledo, O.—suffered at least three other major disappointments in the realm of sport. His horse, Hiccough, on which he had a five-hundred-dollar bet, fell while getting away from the starting gate at Pimlico and broke his leg (clearly visible in the video); his favorite shortstop, Lucky Frimstitch, struck out and let three men die on base in the final game of the Series (to which Parkinson was tuned); and the Governor Dummer soccer team, on which Parkinson's youngest son played goalie, lost to Kent, 4–3, as recorded in the sky overhead. Before anyone could stop him, he drew a gun and drilled Pistachio, before 954,000 persons, the largest crowd that had ever attended a football game and the *second*-largest crowd that had ever assembled for any sporting event in any month except July.

This tragedy, by itself, wouldn't have caused sport to decline, I suppose, but it set in motion a chain of other tragedies, the cumulative effect of which was terrific. Almost as soon as the shot was fired, the news flash was picked up by one of the skywriters directly above the field. He glanced down to see whether he could spot the trouble below, and in doing so failed to see another skywriter approaching. The two planes collided and fell, wings locked, leaving a confusing trail of smoke, which some observers tried to interpret as a late sports score. The planes struck in the middle of the nearby east-bound coast-to-coast Sunlight Parkway, and a motorist driving a convertible coupé stopped so short, to avoid hitting them, that he was bumped from behind. The pileup of cars that ensued involved 1,482 vehicles, a record for eastbound parkways. A total of more than three thousand persons lost their lives in the highway accident, including the two pilots, and when panic broke out in the stadium, it cost another 872 in dead and injured. News of the disaster spread quickly to other sport arenas, and started other panics among the crowds trying to get to the exits, where they could buy a paper and study a list of the dead. All in all, the afternoon of sport cost 20,003 lives, a record. And nobody had much to show for it, except one small Midwestern boy who hung around the smoking wrecks of the planes, captured some aero news-smoke in a milk bottle, and took it home as a souvenir.

From that day on, sport waned. Through long, noncompetitive Saturday afternoons, the stadia slumbered. Even the parkways fell into disuse as motorists rediscovered the charms of old, twisty roads that led through main streets and past barnyards, with their mild congestions and pleasant smells. 8

Comment

Satire is an important kind of persuasive writing. An essay may be entirely satirical, as in E. B. White's satire on the American obsession with sports, or it may be satirical in part. The chief means of persuasion in satire is ridicule: the satirist makes fun of attitudes or behavior or holds them up to shame. The targets of social satire are foolish attitudes or behavior—social snobbery, pretentious talk, sloppy eating, and the like. Though amusing and sometimes even disgusting, these have no very serious consequences for the individual or for society. The targets of ethical satire are vicious attitudes and behavior—for example, racial or religious prejudice, dishonesty, hypocrisy—that do have serious consequences. Social satire is always humorous; ethical satire may be humorous, as in many political cartoons like *Doonesbury,* but it is more often bitter or angry. Many satires like Twain's *Huckleberry Finn* contain elements of both types.

Some satirists are direct in their satire—their statements are angry and biting in their criticism. Others like E. B. White, James Thurber, and Art Buchwald depend on humorous understatement or exaggeration. These are forms of irony. An ironic statement generally implies more through inflection of voice or phrasing than the words actually say; sarcasm is a bitter kind of irony. You are being ironic when you smile or wink while saying something supposedly serious. Your smile or wink may express sarcasm. E. B. White depends on irony in his satire on American sports.

Questions for Study and Discussion

1. What attitudes or habits is White satirizing in the America of late 1947, when this essay first appeared? Are the targets of the satire limited to attitudes and habits relating to sport, or does White have also in mind general attitudes and habits?
2. Is the satire social or ethical? Is White satirizing merely foolish or, instead, vicious attitudes or behavior?
3. To what extent does White depend on exaggeration or overstatement? Does he also use understatement?
4. Names like "Dejected" can be satirical as well as humorous. Do you find other humorous names in the essay, and are they used satirically?
5. White refers to the "high-visibility pink news-smoke perfected by Pepsi-Cola engineers." Why does he refer to "Pepsi-Cola" rather than to "U. S. Steel" or "Dow Chemical"?
6. Do you think the essay describes attitudes toward sport and the behavior of sports fans in the eighties? Do you find the satire persuasive?

Vocabulary Study

1. What is a "parable"? What does the subtitle "A Preposterous Parable" show about White's intention?
2. Write a paraphrase of paragraph 2 or paragraph 6—a sentence-for-sentence rendering in your own words. Be sure to find substitutes for *proliferate, interminable,* and *over-subtilize* (paragraph 2), or *deranged, whipped,* and *drilled* (paragraph 6). Try to retain the tone of White's original paragraph.

Suggestions for Writing

1. Identify the targets of White's satire and explain how you discover them in the course of reading.

2. Discuss the extent to which White's predictions in 1947 have come true. Cite contemporary events and attitudes that support the predictions or that show White to be mistaken.
3. Write a satirical essay of your own on a contemporary social or political issue. You may not discover the best strategy or tone until you have written several paragraphs. Revise your draft to make the strategy and tone consistent throughout.

Charles Osgood

"REAL" MEN AND WOMEN

Charles Osgood was born in New York City in 1933 and graduated from Fordham University in 1954. He worked in radio as a reporter and program director before joining CBS News in 1972. He is seen frequently on the CBS Evening News and other news programs. His essay on man and woman has the concision and sharp focus that we expect of journalism; Osgood combines these qualities with depth and force.

Helene, a young friend of mine, has been assigned a theme in English composition class. She can take her choice: "What is a *real* man?" or, if she wishes, "What is a *real* woman?" Seems the instructor has some strong ideas on these subjects. Helene says she doesn't know which choice to make. "I could go the women's-lib route," she says, "but I don't think he'd like that. I started in on that one once in a class, and it didn't go over too well." So, what is a real man and what is a real woman? 1

"As opposed to what?" I asked. 2

"I don't know, as opposed to unreal men and women, I suppose. Got any ideas?" 3

Yes, it just so happens I do. Let's start with the assumption that reality is that which is, as opposed to that which somebody would like, or something that is imagined or idealized. Let's assume that all human beings who are alive, therefore, are real human beings, who can be divided into two categories: real men and real women. A man who exists 4 is a real man. His reality is in no way lessened by his race, his nationality, political affiliation, financial status, religious persuasion, or personal proclivities. All men are real men. All women are real women.

The first thing you do if you want to destroy somebody   5
is to rob him of his humanity. If you can persuade yourself that someone is a gook and therefore not a real person, you can kill him rather more easily, burn down his home, separate him from his family. If you can persuade yourself that someone is not really a person but a spade, a Wasp, a kike, a wop, a mick, a fag, a dike, and therefore not a real man or woman, you can more easily hate and hurt him.

People who go around making rules, setting standards   6
that other people are supposed to meet in order to qualify as real, are real pains in the neck—and worse, they are real threats to the rest of us. They use their own definitions of real and unreal to filter out unpleasant facts. To them, things like crime, drugs, decay, pollution, slums, et cetera, are not the real America. In the same way, they can look at a man and say he is not a real man because he doesn't give a hang about pro football and would rather chase butterflies than a golf ball; or they can look at a woman and say she is not a real woman because she drives a cab or would rather change the world than change diapers.

To say that someone is not a real man or woman is to   7
say that they are something less than, and therefore not entitled to the same consideration as, real people. Therefore, Helene, contained within the questions "What is a real man?" and "What is a real woman?" are the seeds of discrimination and of murders, big and little. Each of us has his own reality, and nobody has the right to limit or qualify that—not even English composition instructors.

Comment

Where August Heckscher was able to give us an objective definition of *chore*, Osgood cannot give us one of a "real" man or a woman that does the same. He is writing about connotations that some people make but others do not. In opposition to these, he gives the minimum denotative definition. The dictionary does occasionally give us connotations that are widely held or even inherent in a word—objective connotations, as in the definition of *coward*. But these are usually conventional connotations, not personal or subjective ones such as Osgood writes about. Notice, too, that Osgood is using exposition for a persuasive purpose: he wants to change the way people think about men and women. He is attacking a common stereotype.

Questions for Study and Discussion

1. How does Osgood identify the audience he wants most to reach?
2. What formal definition of a "real" man or woman does he give? How does he defend this definition?
3. What other stereotypes does he attack? What do they have in common with the stereotypes of men and women?
4. What meanings does the word "real" gather as the essay builds to the concluding sentence?
5. Do you agree that "masculine" and "feminine" are not descriptive of interests and behavior—that men and women cannot be typed in this way? If not, on what do you base your disagreement?

Vocabulary Study

1. The items in the following synonym group share certain meanings with each other, but each word also has its own meanings. Use your dictionary to distinguish the two kinds of meanings. The first word in each group is used by Osgood:
   a. *idealized* (paragraph 4), *romanticized*
   b. *exists* (paragraph 4), *lives*
   c. *proclivities* (paragraph 4), *preferences*
   d. *discrimination* (paragraph 7), *prejudice, bias*
2. How many of the derogatory words given in paragraph 5 are defined in your college dictionary? What does the etymology of those given tell you about the current meaning of the word, if one is given?
3. The following words are mainly connotative in their meanings. Write definitions for two of them, distinguishing their

objective from their subjective connotations—that is, the general associations that everyone makes from the special associations some people make: *cute, cool, flip, crazy, silly, flaky.*

Suggestions for Writing

Use one of the following statements as the basis for an essay of your own. You may wish to agree with the statement and illustrate it from your own experience. Or you may wish to disagree with it, providing counterexamples or ideas:

a. "People who go around making rules, setting standards that other people are supposed to meet in order to qualify as real, are real pains in the neck—and worse, they are real threats to the rest of us."

b. "They use their own definitions of real and unreal to filter out unpleasant facts."

c. "The first thing you do if you want to destroy somebody is to rob him of his humanity."

d. "Each of us has his own reality, and nobody has the right to limit or qualify that—not even English composition instructors."

Harvey and Nancy Kincaid

A LETTER ON STRIP MINING

Harvey and Nancy Kincaid lived with their seven children in Fayetteville, West Virginia, near Buffalo Creek at the time they wrote the following letter. On February 26, 1972, a dam consisting of slag from the mines and owned by a local coal company burst. The ensuing flood killed 125 people and injured many thousands; most of the victims were coal miners and members of their families. In 1971 Mrs. Kincaid had spoken about strip mining to the Congress Against Strip Mining, in Washington, D.C. Her letter was read before the West Virginia State Legislature and it helped to pass the Anti-Strip-Mining Bill. Mrs. Kincaid told an interviewer:

It used to be that the kids could keep fish, catfish, and minnows in the creeks. Now you can see the rocks in the creek where the acid has run off the mountains, off the limestone rocks. The rocks in the creek are reddish-looking, like they're rusted. There's nothing living in the creek now.

Gentlemen:

I don't believe there could be anyone that would like to see the strip mines stopped any more than my husband and myself. It just seems impossible that something like this could happen to us twice in the past three and one half years of time. We have been married for thirteen years and worked real hard at having a nice home that was ours and paid for, with a nice size lot of one acre. Over the thirteen years, we remodeled this house a little at a time and paid for it as we worked and did the work mostly ourselves. The house was located about a quarter of a mile off the road up Glenco Hollow at Kincaid, Fayette County, West Virginia, where it used to be a nice, clean neighborhood.

Then the strippers came four years ago with their big machinery and TNT. I know that these men need jobs and need to make a living like everyone else, but I believe there could be a better way of getting the coal out of these mountains. Have you ever been on a mountaintop and looked down and seen about five different strips on one mountain in one hollow?

My husband owns a Scout Jeep and he can get to the top of the strip mines with the Scout. I would like to invite you to come and visit us sometime and go for a ride with us. It would make you sick to see the way the mountains are destroyed.

First they send in the loggers to strip all the good timber out and then they come with their bulldozers. If their engineers make a mistake in locating the coal they just keep cutting away until they locate the seam of coal. When the rains come and there isn't anything to stop the drainage, the mountains slide, and the spoil banks fall down to the next spoil bank and so on until the whole mountain slides. There is a small creek in the hollow and when the spring rains come, its banks won't hold the water.

So where does it go?—into people's yards, into their wells, under and into their houses. You have rocks, coal, and a little bit of everything in your yards. When the strip-pers came they started behind our house in the fall sometime before November. There was a hollow behind our house and we asked them not to bank the spoil the way they did, be-cause we knew what would happen when the spring rains came. My father-in-law lived beside us and the property all ran together in a nice green lawn—four acres.

But the rains came in the spring and the spoil bank broke 6 and the water and debris came into our property every time it rained. It would only take a few minutes of rain and this is what we had for three years.

Then the damage comes to your house because of so 7 much dampness. The doors won't close, the foundation sinks and cracks the walls in the house, your tile comes up off your floors, your walls mold, even your clothes in your closets. Then your children stay sick with bronchial trouble, then our daughter takes pneumonia—X-rays are taken, primary T.B. shows up on the X-ray. This is in July of two years ago. About for a year this child laid sick at home. In the meantime we have already filed suit with a lawyer in Oak Hill when the water started coming in on us, but nothing happens. For three years we fight them for our property—$10,000. The lawyer settles out of court for $4,500. By the time his fee comes out and everything else we have to pay, we have under $3,000 to start over with.

So what do we have to do? Doctor's orders, move out 8 for child's sake and health. We sell for a little of nothing—not for cash, but for rent payments, take the $3,000 and buy a lot on the main highway four miles up the road toward Oak Hill.

The $3,000 goes for the lot, digging of a well and a 9 down payment on a new house. Here we are in debt for thirty years on a new home built and complete by the first of September. We moved the first part of September and was in this house *one month* and what happens? The same strip company comes up the road and puts a blast off and damages the new house—$1,400 worth. When they put one blast off that will crack the walls in your house, the foun-dation cracked the carport floor straight across in two places, pull a cement stoop away from the house and pull the grout out of the ceramic tile in the bathroom. This is what they can get by with.

How do they live in their $100,000 homes and have a clear mind, I'll never know. To think of the poor people who have worked hard all their lives and can't start over like we did. They have to stay in these hollows and be scared to death every time it rains. I know by experience the many nights I have stayed up and listened to the water pouring off the mountains and the rocks tumbling off the hills.

I remember one time when the strippers put a blast off up the hollow a couple of years ago and broke into one of the old mines that had been sealed off for 30 years. They put their blast off and left for the evening. Around seven o'clock that evening it started. We happened to look up the hollow, and thick mud—as thick as pudding—was coming down the main road in the hollow and made itself to the creek and stopped the creek up until the creek couldn't even flow.

The water was turned up into the fields where my husband keeps horses and cattle. I called the boss and told him what was happening and the danger we were in and what did he say? "There isn't anything I can do tonight. I'll be down tomorrow." I called the agriculture and they told us, whatever we did, not to go to bed that night because of the water backed up in those mines for miles.

This is just some of the things that happen around a strip mine neighborhood. But they can get by with it, unless they are stopped. Even if they are stopped it will take years for the trees and grass—what little bit they put on them— to grow enough to keep the water back and stop the slides.

Mr. and Mrs. Harvey Kincaid

Comment

The Swiss writer Henri Frédéric Amiel wrote in his journal: "Truth is the secret of eloquence and of virtue, the basis of moral authority." The Kincaid's great letter is an example of eloquence achieved through simple words that state facts plainly and exactly. Instead of reviewing the rights and wrongs of strip mining, Mr. and Mrs. Kincaid describe what happened to them and the land—in enough detail for the reader to imagine the life of people in the hollow. At the end of the letter they state the issue simply and without elaboration: "But they can get by with it, unless they are stopped."

Questions for Study and Discussion

1. The Kincaids state how their life was changed by strip mining. How do they show that their experiences were typical of people in the area?
2. Is the damage caused by strip mining the result of neglect or carelessness, or is it inherent in the process itself—given the details of the letter? Are the Kincaids mainly concerned with this question?
3. What is the central issue for them? Are they arguing against strip mining on moral grounds? Or are they concerned only with the practical consequences? What assumptions about the rights of individuals underlie their argument?
4. Are the Kincaids addressing a general or specific audience? How do you know?
5. What is the tone of the letter, and what in the letter creates it? What do the various questions asked in the letter contribute?

Vocabulary Study

Consult a dictionary of American English or Americanisms on the exact meaning of the following words and phrases and explain their use in the letter: *hollow, strips, spoil banks, grout, pudding.*

Suggestions for Writing

1. Write a letter protesting an activity that has changed your life in some way. Let the details of the change carry the weight of your protest.
2. Look through magazines and newspapers for a defense of strip mining. You will find authors and titles in the *Reader's Guide*

to *Periodical Literature.* Analyze the assumptions and reasoning of the writer. (For a general review of the debate, pro and con, see *Business Week,* November 4, 1972).

Roger Rosenblatt

THE MAN IN THE WATER

Born in 1940 in New York City, Roger Rosenblatt attended New York University and Harvard, where he later taught English. From 1973 to 1975, he was Director of Education for the National Endowment for the Humanities, and from 1975 to 1978 was the literary editor of *New Republic.* Rosenblatt has published essays in numerous periodicals, and is the author of *Black Fiction* (1974). His essay on an airplane crash in Washington, D.C., in the winter of 1982, shows his gift for stating in simple language important truths about contemporary events.

As disasters go, this one was terrible, but not unique, certainly not among the worst on the roster of U.S. air crashes. There was the unusual element of the bridge, of course, and the fact that the plane clipped it at a moment of high traffic, one routine thus intersecting another and disrupting both. Then, too, there was the location of the event. Washington, the city of form and regulations, turned chaotic, deregulated, by a blast of real winter and a single slap of metal on metal. The jets from Washington National Airport that normally swoop around the presidential monuments like famished gulls are, for the moment, emblemized by the one that fell; so there is that detail. And there was the aesthetic clash as well—blue-and-green Air Florida, the name a flying garden, sunk down among gray chunks in a black river. All that was worth noticing, to be sure. Still, there was nothing very special in any of it, except death, which, while always special, does not necessarily bring millions to tears or to attention. Why, then, the shock here? 1

Perhaps because the nation saw in this disaster something more than a mechanical failure. Perhaps because people saw in it no failure at all, but rather something successful 2

about their makeup. Here, after all, were two forms of nature in collision: the elements and human character. Last
Wednesday, the elements, indifferent as ever, brought down
Flight 90. And on that same afternoon, human nature—
groping and flailing in mysteries of its own—rose to the
occasion.

Of the four acknowledged heroes of the event, three are
able to account for their behavior. Donald Usher and Eu-
gene Windsor, a park police helicopter team, risked their
lives every time they dipped the skids into the water to pick
up survivors. On television, side by side in bright blue jump-
suits, they described their courage as all in the line of duty.
Lenny Skutnik, a 28-year-old employee of the Congressional
Budget Office, said: "It's something I never thought I would
do"—referring to his jumping into the water to drag an injured woman to shore. Skutnik added that "somebody had
to go in the water," delivering every hero's line that is no
less admirable for its repetitions. In fact, nobody had to go
into the water. That somebody actually did so is part of the
reason this particular tragedy sticks in the mind.

But the person most responsible for the emotional impact of the disaster is the one known at first simply as "the
man in the water." (Balding, probably in his 50s, an extravagant mustache.) He was seen clinging with five other survivors to the tail section of the airplane. This man was
described by Usher and Windsor as appearing alert and in
control. Every time they lowered a lifeline and flotation ring
to him, he passed it on to another of the passengers. "In a
mass casualty, you'll find people like him," said Windsor.
"But I've never seen one with that commitment." When the
helicopter came back for him, the man had gone under. His
selflessness was one reason the story held national attention;
his anonymity another. The fact that he went unidentified
invested him with a universal character. For a while he was
Everyman, and thus proof (as if one needed it) that no man
is ordinary.

Still, he could never have imagined such a capacity in
himself. Only minutes before his character was tested, he
was sitting in the ordinary plane among the ordinary pas-

sengers, dutifully listening to the stewardess telling him to fasten his seat belt and saying something about the "no smoking sign." So our man relaxed with the others, some of whom would owe their lives to him. Perhaps he started to read, or to doze, or to regret some harsh remark made in the office that morning. Then suddenly he knew that the trip would not be ordinary. Like every other person on that flight, he was desperate to live, which makes his final act so stunning.

For at some moment in the water he must have realized that he would not live if he continued to hand over the rope and ring to others. He *had* to know it, no matter how gradual the effect of the cold. In his judgment he had no choice. When the helicopter took off with what was to be the last survivor, he watched everything in the world move away from him, and he deliberately let it happen. 6

Yet there was something else about our man that kept our thoughts on him, and which keeps our thoughts on him still. He was *there,* in the essential, classic circumstance. Man in nature. The man in the water. For its part, nature cared nothing about the five passengers. Our man, on the other hand, cared totally. So the timeless battle commenced in the Potomac. For as long as that man could last, they went at each other, nature and man; the one making no distinctions of good and evil, acting on no principles, offering no lifelines; the other acting wholly on distinctions, principles and, one supposes, on faith. 7

Since it was he who lost the fight, we ought to come again to the conclusion that people are powerless in the world. In reality, we believe the reverse, and it takes the act of the man in the water to remind us of our true feelings in this matter. It is not to say that everyone would have acted as he did, or as Usher, Windsor and Skutnik. Yet whatever moved these men to challenge death on behalf of their fellows is not peculiar to them. Everyone feels the possibility in himself. That is the abiding wonder of the story. That is why we would not let go of it. If the man in the water gave a lifeline to the people gasping for survival, he was likewise giving a lifeline to those who observed him. 8

The odd thing is that we do not even really believe that   9
the man in the water lost his fight. "Everything in Nature
contains all the powers of Nature," said Emerson. Exactly.
So the man in the water had his own natural powers. He
could not make ice storms, or freeze the water until it froze
the blood. But he could hand life over to a stranger, and
that is a power of nature too. The man in the water pitted
himself against an implacable, impersonal enemy; he fought
it with charity; and he held it to a standoff. He was the best
we can do.

Comment

The Air Florida crash described occurred in Washington, D.C., on
January 14, 1982, during the evening rush hour at a crowded bridge
over the Potomac River. The event received wide coverage because
of these circumstances and the extraordinary acts of heroism performed. Rosenblatt is doing more than describing these events: he
wishes to persuade readers of an important truth. To do so, he
must persuade them that the acts of the man in the water were
indeed heroic, and much of his discussion toward the end of the
essay is given to this point. Notice how appropriate the simple,
direct style is to the subject and ideas of the essay. Rosenblatt
presents the facts without overdramatizing them through colorful
language. All the same, his simplicity of language is eloquent enough
to bring the essay to a fitting emotional pitch:

> So the man in the water had his own natural powers. He could
> not make ice storms, or freeze the water until it froze the blood.
> But he could hand life over to a stranger, and that is a power of
> nature too.

Questions for Study and Discussion

1. Rosenblatt does not give us all the facts of the crash. What
   facts does he present, and what aspects does he emphasize?
2. Is Rosenblatt writing only to those readers familiar with the
   circumstances of the crash, or is he also providing information
   for those unfamiliar with what happened?

3. Rosenblatt builds from the details of the crash to reflections about it. In what order are these details presented? Is Rosenblatt describing the events in the order they occurred?
4. How does he explain the heroism of the man in the water, the helicopter police, and Larry Skutnik?
5. Rosenblatt builds to his thesis, instead of stating it toward the beginning of the essay. What is his thesis, and what is gained by building to it? Do you agree with it?

Vocabulary Study

1. How does the context of the final sentence in paragraph 4 help us to understand the reference to Everyman?
2. In what sense is Rosenblatt using the word *classic* in paragraph 7?
3. Does the word *power* have more than one meaning in paragraph 9?

Suggestions for Writing

1. Explain the following sentence in light of the whole essay: "If the man in the water gave a lifeline to the people gasping for survival, he was likewise giving a lifeline to those who observed him."
2. Explain the statement of Emerson, "Everything in Nature contains all the powers of Nature," in light of the final paragraph. Then illustrate it from your own experience.
3. First state the conception of heroism Rosenblatt presents in the essay. Then discuss the extent to which this conception fits an act of heroism you have observed, or accords with your idea of what makes a person heroic.
4. Discuss a recent event that taught you an important truth about people or life. Describe the event for readers unfamiliar with it, and build to your thesis as Rosenblatt does.

Glossary

allusion: An indirect reference to a presumably well-known literary work or an historical event or figure. The phrase "the Waterloo of his political career" is a reference to Napoleon's disastrous defeat at the Battle of Waterloo in 1815. The allusion implies that the career of the politician under discussion has come to a dramatic end.

analogy: A point-by-point comparison between two unlike things or activities (for example, comparing writing an essay to building a house) for the purpose of illustration or argument. Unlike a comparison (or contrast), in which the things compared are of equal importance, analogy exists for the purpose of illustrating or arguing the nature of one of the compared things, not both.

antithesis: The arrangement of contrasting ideas in grammatically similar phrases and clauses (*The world will little note, nor long remember, what we say here, but it can never forget what they did here*—Lincoln, *Gettysburg Address*). See *parallelism.*

argument: Proving the truth or falseness of a statement. Arguments are traditionally classified as *inductive* or *deductive.* See *deductive argument* and *inductive argument.* Argument can be used for different purposes in writing. See *purpose.*

autobiography: Writing about one's own experiences, often those of growing up and making one's way in the world. The autobiographical writings of Mary E. Mebane and Maya Angelou describe their childhood in the South.

balanced sentence: A sentence containing parallel phrases and clauses of approximately the same length and wording (*You can fool all the people some of the time, and some of the people all the time, but you cannot fool all the people all of the time.*—Lincoln).

cause and effect: Analysis of the conditions that must be present for an event to occur (*cause*) and of the results or consequences of the event (*effect*). An essay may deal with causes or with effects only.

classification and division: *Classification* arranges individual objects into groups or classes (Jonathans, Winesaps, Golden Delicious, and Macintoshes are types of apples). *Division* arranges a broad class into subclasses according to various principles (the broad class *apples* can be divided on the basis of their color, use, variety, or taste). There are as many divisions as principles of division or subclassification.

cliché: A once-colorful expression made stale through overuse (*putting on the dog, mad as a wet hen*).

coherence: The sense, as we read, that the details and ideas of a work connect clearly. A paragraph or essay that does not hold together seems incoherent.

colloquialism: An everyday expression in speech and informal writing. Colloquialisms are not substandard or "illiterate" English. They are common in informal English and occur sometimes in formal English.

comparison and contrast: The analysis of similarities and differences between two or more persons, objects, or events (A and B) for the purpose of a relative estimate. The word *comparison* sometimes refers to the analysis of similarities and differences in both A and B. *Block comparison* presents each thing being compared as a whole (that is, if the comparison is between A and B, then features a, b, c of A are discussed as a block of information, then features a, b, c of B are compared to A in their own block of information). *Alternating comparison* presents the comparable features one by one (a, a, b, b, c, c).

complex sentence: A sentence consisting of one main or independent clause, and one or more subordinate or dependent clauses (*The rain began when she stepped outside*).

compound sentence: A sentence consisting of coordinated independent clauses (*She stepped outside and then the rain began*).

compound-complex sentence: A sentence consisting of two or more main or independent clauses and at least one subordinate or dependent clause (*She stepped outside as the rain began, but she did not return to the house*).

concrete and abstract words: Concrete words refer to particular objects, people, and events (Benedict Arnold, Franklin Delano Roosevelt, the Rocky Mountains); abstract words refer to general shared qualities (treason, courage, beauty). Concrete writing makes abstract ideas perceptible to the senses through details and images.

concreteness: Making an idea exist through the senses. Writing can be concrete at all three levels—informal, general, and formal. See *concrete and abstract words*.

connotation: Feelings, images, and ideas associated with a word. Connotations change from reader to reader, though some words probably have the same associations for everybody.

context: The surrounding words or sentences that suggest the meaning of a word or phrase. Writers may dispense with formal definition if the context clarifies the meaning of a word.

coordinate sentence: A sentence that joins clauses of the same weight and importance through the conjunctions *and, but, for, or, nor,* or *yet,* or through conjunctive adverbs and adverbial phrases (*however, therefore, nevertheless, in fact*).

deductive argument: Reasoning from statements assumed to be true or well-established factually. These statements or assumptions are thought sufficient to guarantee the truth of the inferences or conclusions. In formal arguments they are called premises. A valid argument reasons correctly from the premises to the conclusion. A sound argument is true in its premises and valid in its reasoning. See *enthymeme, syllogism.*

definition: Explaining the current meaning of a word through its etymology or derivation, its denotation, or its connotations. Denotative or "real" definitions single out a word from all other words (or things) like it by giving *genus* and *specific difference.* Connotative definitions give the associations people make to the world. See *connotation.*

description: A picture in words of people, objects, and events. Description often combines with narrative and it may serve exposition and persuasion.

division: See *classification and division.*

enthymeme: A deductive argument that does not state the conclusion or one of the premises directly. The following statement is an enthymeme: *Citizens in a democracy, who refuse to register for the draft, are not acting responsibly.* The implied premise is that the responsible citizen obeys all laws, even repugnant ones.

essay: A carefully organized composition that develops a single idea or impression or develops several related ideas or impressions. The word sometimes describes a beginning or trial attempt which explores the central idea or impression instead of developing it completely.

example: A picture or illustration of an idea, or one of many instances or occurrences that is typical of the rest.

exposition: An explanation or unfolding or setting forth of an idea, usually for the purpose of giving information. Exposition is usually an important part of persuasive writing. Example, process analysis, causal analysis, definition, classification and division, and comparison and contrast are forms of exposition.

expressive writing: Essays, diaries, journals, letters, and other kinds of writing which present personal feelings and beliefs for their own sake. The expressive writer is not primarily concerned with informing or persuading readers.

figure of speech: A word or phrase that departs from its usual meaning. Figures of speech make statements vivid and capture the attention of readers. The most common figures are based on similarity between things. See *metaphor, personification, simile.* Other figures are based on relationship. See *allusion. Metonymy* refers to a thing by one of its qualities (*the Hill* as a reference to the United States Congress). *Synecdoche* refers to a thing by one of its parts (*wheels* as a reference to racing cars). Other figures are based on contrast between statements and realities. See *irony*. Related to irony is *understatement,* or saying less than is appropriate ("Napoleon's career ended unhappily at Waterloo"). *Hyperbole* means deliberate exaggeration ("crazy about ice cream"). *Paradox* states an apparent contradiction ("All great truths begin as blasphemies"—G. B. Shaw). *Oxymoron,* a kind of paradox, joins opposite qualities into a single image (*lake of fire*).

focus: The limitation of subject in an essay. The focus may be broad, as in a panoramic view of the mountains, or it may be narrow, as in a view of a particular peak. For example, a writer may focus broadly on the contribution to scientific thought of scientists from various fields, or focus narrowly on the achievements of astronomers or chemists or medical researchers, or focus even more narrowly on the achievements of Albert Einstein as representative of twentieth century science.

formal English: Spoken and written English, often abstract in content, with sentences tighter than spoken ones, and an abstract and sometimes technical vocabulary. See *general English* and *informal English.*

general English: A written standard that has features of informal and formal English and avoids the extremes of both. See *formal English* and *informal English.*

image: A picture in words of an object, a scene, or a person. Though visual images are common in writing, they are not the only kind. Images can also be auditory, tactile, gustatory, and olfactory. Keats' line "With beaded bubbles winking at the brim" appeals to our hearing and taste as well as to our sight. His phrase "coming musk-rose" appeals to our sense of smell. Images help to make feelings concrete.

implied thesis: The central idea of the essay, suggested by the details and discussion rather than stated directly. See *thesis.*

inductive argument: Inductive arguments reason from particulars of experience to general ideas—from observation, personal experience, and experimental testing to probable conclusions. Inductive arguments make predictions on the basis of past and present experience. An argumentative analogy is a form of inductive argument because it is based on limited observation and experience and therefore can claim probability only. Analysis of causes and effects, like statistical analysis, is inductive when used in argument.

"inductive leap": Making the decision that sufficient inductive evidence (personal experience, observation, experimental testing) exists to draw a conclusion. Sometimes the writer of the argument makes the leap too quickly and bases his conclusions on insufficient evidence.

informal English: Written English, usually concrete in content, tighter than the loose sentences of spoken English, but looser in sentence construction than formal English. The word "informal" refers to the occasion of its use. A letter to a friend is usually informal; a letter of application is usually formal. See *formal English* and *general English.*

irony: A term generally descriptive of statements and events. An ironic statement says the opposite of what the speaker or writer means, or implies that something more is meant than is stated, or says the unexpected (*He has a great future behind him*). An ironic event is unexpected or is so coincidental that it seems impossible (*The firehouse burned to the ground*).

jargon: The technical words of a trade or profession (in computer jargon, the terms *input* and *word processor*). Unclear, clumsy, or repetitive words or phrasing, sometimes the result of misplaced technical words (*He gave his input into the decision process*).

loose sentence: A sentence that introduces the main idea close to the beginning and concludes with a series of modifiers (*The car left the expressway, slowing on the ramp and coming to a stop at the crossroad*). See *periodic sentence*.

metaphor: An implied comparison which attributes the qualities of one thing to another (the word *mainstream* to describe the opinions or activities of most people).

mixed metaphor: The incongruous use of two metaphors in the same context (*The roar of protest was stopped in its tracks*).

narrative: The chronological presentation of events. Narrative often combines with description and it may serve exposition or persuasion.

order of ideas: The presentation of ideas in a paragraph or an essay according to a plan. The order may be *spatial*, perhaps moving from background to foreground, or from top to bottom, or from side to side; or the order may be *temporal* or chronological (in the order of time). The presentation may be in the order of *importance*, or if the details build intensively, in the order of *climax*. The paragraph or essay may move from *problem* to *solution* or from the *specific* to the *general*. Some of these orders may occur together—for example, a chronological presentation of details that build to a climax.

parallelism: Grammatically similar words, phrases, and clauses arranged to highlight similar ideas (*There are neighborhoods of nations . . . There are streets where, on January nights, fires burn on every floor of every house . . . There are meadows and fields*—Mark Helprin). See *antithesis*.

paraphrase: A rendering of a passage in different words that retain the sense, the tone, and the order of ideas.

periodic sentence: A sentence that builds to the main idea (*Building speed as it curved down the ramp, the car sped into the crowded expressway*). See *loose sentence*.

personification: Giving animate or human qualities to something inanimate or inhuman (The sun *smiled* at the earth).

persuasion: The use of argument or satire or some other means to change thinking and feeling about an issue.

point of view: The place or vantage point from which an event is seen and described. The term sometimes refers to the mental attitude of the viewer in narrative. Mark Twain's *Huckleberry Finn* narrates the adventures of a boy in slave-owning Missouri from the point of view of the boy, not from that of an adult.

premise: see *syllogism.*

process: An activity or operation containing steps usually performed in the same order. The process may be mechanical (changing a tire), natural (the circulation of the blood), or historical (the rise and spread of a specific epidemic disease such as bubonic plague at various times in history).

purpose: The aim of the essay as distinguished from the means used to develop it. The purposes or aims of writing are many; they include expressing personal feelings and ideas, giving information, persuading readers to change their thinking about an issue, inspiring readers to take action, giving pleasure. These purposes may be achieved through description, narrative, exposition, or argument. These means may be used alone or in combination, and an essay may realize more than one purpose.

reflection: An essay that explores ideas without necessarily bringing the exploration to completion. The reflective essay can take the form of a loosely organized series of musings or tightly organized arguments.

satire: Ridicule of foolish or vicious behavior or ideas for the purpose of correcting them. *Social satire* concerns foolish but not dangerous behavior and ideas—for example, coarse table manners, pretentious talk, harmless gossip. George Bernard Shaw's "Arms and the Man" is a social satire. *Ethical satire* attacks vicious or dangerous behavior or ideas—religious or racial bigotry, greed, political corruption. Mark Twain's *Huckleberry Finn* is an ethical satire.

simile: A direct comparison between two things (*A growing child is like a young tree*). See *figure of speech, metaphor.*

simple sentence: A sentence consisting of a single main or independent clause and no subordinate or dependent clauses (*The rain started at nightfall*).

slang: Colorful and sometimes short-lived expressions peculiar to a group of people, usually informal in usage and almost always unacceptable in formal usage (*nerd, goof off*).

style: A distinctive manner of speaking or writing. A writing style may be plain in its lack of metaphor and other figures of speech. Another writing style may be highly colorful or ornate.

subordinate clause: A clause that completes a main clause or attaches to it as a modifier (She saw *that the rain had begun; When it rains,* it pours).

syllogism: The formal arrangement of premises and conclusion of a deductive argument. The premises are the general assumptions or truths (*All reptiles are cold-blooded vertebrates, All snakes are reptiles*) from which particular conclusions are drawn (*All snakes are cold-blooded vertebrates*). This formal arrangement helps to test the validity or correctness of the reasoning from premises to conclusion. See *deductive argument.*

symbol: An object that represents an abstract idea. The features of the symbol (the fifty stars and thirteen horizontal stripes of the American flag) suggest characteristics of the object symbolized (the fifty states of the Union, the original confederation of thirteen states). A sign need not have this representative quality: a green light signals "go," and a red light "stop" by conventional agreement.

thesis: The central idea that organizes the many smaller ideas and details of the essay.

tone: The phrasing or words that express the attitude or feeling of the speaker or writer. The tone of a statement ranges from the angry, exasperated, and sarcastic, to the wondering or approving. An ironic tone suggests that the speaker or writer means more than the words actually state.

topic sentence: Usually the main or central idea of the paragraph that organizes details and subordinate ideas. Though it often opens the paragraph, the topic sentence can appear later—in the middle or at the end of the paragraph.

transition: A word or phrase (*however, thus, in fact*) that connects clauses and sentences. Parallel structure is an important means of transition.

unity: The connection of ideas and details to a central controlling idea of the essay. A unified essay deals with one idea at a time.

Copyrights and Acknowledgments

For permission to use the selections reprinted in this book, the author is grateful to the following publishers and copyright holders:

THE AARON PRIEST LITERARY AGENCY   For "Bicycling Toward Wisdom" and "Cheap Thrills" from *Peripheral Visions* by Phyllis Theroux. Copyright © 1982. Reprinted by permission of the author and the author's agent, Molly Friedrich, The Aaron M. Priest Literary Agency, Inc., 122 E. 42 St. Suite 3902, New York, NY 10168

WILLIAM AIKEN   For "Hanging Out and Looking Good" by William Aiken. First published in *Christian Science Monitor*, November 28, 1984. Reprinted by permission of the author.

ATHENEUM PUBLISHERS, INC.   For "Elevators" from *Pieces of My Mind* by Andrew A. Rooney. Copyright © 1984 by Essay Productions, Inc. Reprinted by permission of Atheneum Publishers, an imprint of Macmillan Publishing Company.

GEORGES BORCHARDT, INC.   For "Gossip" by Francine Prose. Originally published in *The New York Times,* May 16, 1985, as "Hers." Copyright © 1985 by Francine Prose. Reprinted by permission of Georges Borchardt, Inc., for Francine Prose.

CAROL BRISSIE   For "Jury Duty" in *The Lunacy Boom* by William Zinsser. Copyright © 1968, 1970 by William K. Zinsser. Reprinted by permission of the author.

MRS. ARTHUR L. CAMPA   For "Anglo vs. Chicano: Why?" by Arthur L. Campa. First published in *Western Review,* Vol. IX (Spring, 1972). Reprinted by permission of Mrs. Arthur L. Campa.

CHRISTIAN SCIENCE MONITOR   For "Doing Chores" by August Heckscher. Copyright © 1978 by The Christian Science Publishing Company. All rights reserved. Reprinted by permission of *Christian Science Monitor.*

MARIE RODELL-FRANCES COLLIN LITERARY AGENCY   For "Summer's End" from *Under the Sea Wind* by Rachel Carson. Copyright © 1941 by Rachel L. Carson. Copyright © renewed 1969 by Roger Christie. Reprinted by permission of Frances Collin, Trustee.

COMMONWEAL   For "Thinking in Packages" by John Garvey. From *Commonweal,* November 6, 1981. Copyright © 1981 by Commonweal Foundation. Reprinted by permission of the publisher.

Index

Abstract words, 284–85, 376
Aiken, William, 360
Analogy, argumentative, 392–93; illustrative, 202, 392
Angelou, Maya, 43
Argument, defined, 389; *see also* Deductive argument, Inductive argument, Persuasive essay
Arlen, Michael J., 312
Audience, 4, 377, 451
Autobiographical writing, 95

Baker, Russell, 327
Balance, in sentences, 323
Berry, Wendell, 266
Bly, Carol, 336
Buchwald, Art, 377

Campa, Arthur L., 192
Carson, Rachel, 318
Cause and effect, in exposition, 70–71; in inductive reasoning, 391–92
Chronological order, 21
Classification, 82
Cliché, 287
Climax, in paragraphs, 22
Coherence, 28–29
Cole, K. C., 214
Coles, Robert, 233
Colloquial English, 283, 286–87, 330, 376
Comparison and contrast, 60–61, 191
Compound sentence, 296–97

Concreteness, 332–33
Condition, in causal analysis, 70, 392
Connotative definition, 77, 466–67
Coordinating words, 295
Coordination, in sentences, 295–97
Cousins, Norman, 424–26, 427
Cox, Don Richard, 184

Deductive argument, 389, 424–27, 451; *see also* Enthymeme, Premises, Syllogism
Definition, 77–78, 156, 466–67; *see also* Connotative definition, Denotative definition, Etymological definition, Stipulative definition
Deford, Frank, 368
Denotative definition, 77–78
Description, 21, 42–43
DeVries, Hilary, 364
Diction, 283–87; *see also* Formal English, General English, Informal English
Dictionaries, kinds of, 249
Didion, Joan, 285–86, 287
Dillard, Annie, 286, 353
Division, 82–83
Dubik, James M., 396
Dunne, John Gregory, 133

Emerson, Gloria, 89, 90
Emphasis, in sentences, 295–97, 314, 327

491

End focus, in sentences, 296
Enthymeme, 426
Essay, 3–4, 117; *see also* Expressive essay, Persuasive essay, Reflective essay
Evidence, in arguments, 389, 390–91, 404, 418, 425
Etymological definition, 77
Example, 48–49, 161, 451
Exposition, 36, 43, 48; defined, 145–46
Expressive essay, 36, 43, 145; defined, 89–90

Feynman, Richard P., 297
Figurative language, 343–44; *see also* Metaphor, Personification, Simile
Flynn, William, 103
Formal English, 283–87, 376–77

Garvey, John, 203
General English, 285–87
Glossary, 478
Goodman, Ellen, 415, 442

Harris, Sydney J., 200, 384
Healy, Timothy S., S. J., 432
Heckscher, August, 78
Hills, L. Rust, 168
Hoagland, Edward, 3–4, 4
Hough, Henry Beetle, 117
Hubbell, Sue, 36–37, 157
Huzicka, Michele, 83

Immediate cause, 392
Implied thesis, 4, 8
Inductive argument, 389, 390–93, 404, 451
Inductive leap, 390–91, 418
Informal English, 283–87, 376–77
Inturrisi, Louis, 152
Irony, 359, 383, 463–64

Jargon, 377

Kincaid, Harvey, 468
Kincaid, Nancy, 468
Klass, Perri, 106
Krents, Harold, 23
Kriegel, Leonard, 112
Kumin, Maxine, 55

Length, in sentences, 326–27
Loose sentence, 283, 376–77

Mead, Margaret, 437
Mebane, Mary E., 96
Metaphor, 343–44
Metraux, Rhoda, 437
Moran, Richard, 401

Narration, 21, 36–37
Necessary condition, in causal analysis, 75, 392
Nelson, Michael, 209, 391–92
New Yorker, 455

Order of ideas, 21–23, 451
Osgood, Charles, 465

Parallelism, in paragraphs and essays, 28–29; in sentences, 317–18, 322–23
Peeples, Edward H., Jr., 390–91, 393
Periodic sentence, 286, 376
Perrin, Noel, 61
Personification, 343–44
Persuasive essay, 36, 43, 145, 451–52; defined, 451
Point of view, in description, 43
Premises, 425–27
Problem and solution, in paragraphs and essays, 22, 26
Process, 54–55
Prose, Francine, 16

Question and answer, in paragraphs and essays, 22

Ramirez, Robert, 42–43, 251
Reflective essay, 117
Remote cause, 392
Rivera, Edward, 37
Rodden, Appletree, 71
Rooney, Andrew A., 129
Rosenblatt, Roger, 473

Safire, William, 247
Samuelson, Robert J., 262
Satire, 386, 463–64
Scott, David R., 286, 344
Seelinger, Kathy, 419
Selzer, Richard, 178
Sentence style, 283–87; *see also* Emphasis, End focus, Parallelism, Variety
Simile, 343–44
Simple sentence, 326
Sissman, L. E., 29
Slang, 377
Smith, Page, 405
Soundness, in deductive argument, 426–27
Spatial order, 21
Specific to general, in paragraphs and essays, 21
Statistical evidence, in inductive reasoning, 404
Stipulative definition, 77
Subordination, in sentences, 295–97

Sufficient cause, 392
Syllogism, 425–26

Theroux, Phyllis, 124
Thesis, 3–4, 7–8
Thomas, Lewis, 145–46, 147
Thurber, James, 381
Tone, 40, 359–60, 373
Topic sentence, 14–16
Toth, Susan Allen, 257
Transitions, 15, 29, 34, 60
Trueblood, Jack, 162

Unity, 7–8, 28–29
Usage, 376–77

Validity, in deductive argument, 426–27
Variety, in sentences, 326–27
Vocabulary, 376–77

Walton, Susan, 9
White, E. B., 459
Wicker, Tom, 49
Will, George F., 446, 451–52, 452
Wing, William G., 333

Yablonsky, Lewis, 220

Zinsser, William, 306

A 8
B 9
C 0
D 1
E 2
F 3
G 4
H 5
I 6
J 7